Realization:

THE FINAL REPORT

OF THE KNAPP

SCHOOL LIBRARIES

PROJECT

Realization:

THE FINAL REPORT

OF THE KNAPP

SCHOOL LIBRARIES

PROJECT

EDITOR: PEGGY SULLIVAN

AMERICAN LIBRARY ASSOCIATION. Knapp School Libraries Project.

CHICAGO

FOREWORD

The successful completion of the Knapp School Libraries Project is a tribute to the professional leadership and dedicated interest of many people throughout the country. Certainly acknowledgments are due to the librarians who had the vision for such a Project; to the public school educators who had schools selected for demonstrations; to the representatives of colleges and universities who worked cooperatively with the demonstrating schools; to the many people who served on local and national advisory committees; and to the visitors who came, observed, questioned, and returned home with new ideas. But above all, acknowledgment must be given to the Director of the Project, Miss Peggy Sullivan.

As in many such endeavors, the Knapp School Libraries Project relied heavily upon the Director. Her responsibilities were many and varied throughout the five years, but always she directed her efforts to the successful implementation of the objectives of the Project. She recognized the problems and needs of the many persons involved in the Project and with sensitive insight sought solutions. She ably represented and spoke for school libraries at a variety of meetings and conferences from coast to coast and frequently contributed to various educational and library publications. Peggy Sullivan as Director of this significant and far-reaching Project gave leadership, status, and dignity to the profession of school librarianship.

The publication of *Realization* brings to a close the five years of concentrated effort of demonstration and development of effective library services for children and young people. Educators, school, college, and public librarians, and library school educators should find this final report informative, useful, and stimulating in their planning for continued vigorous development of school libraries.

Phyllis Hochstettler, *Chairman*
Advisory Committee
Knapp School Libraries Project

KNAPP SCHOOL LIBRARIES PROJECT ADVISORY COMMITTEE

Miss Mary V. Gaver, Chairman, 1962-65
Rutgers—The State University
New Brunswick, New Jersey

Miss Eleanor E. Ahlers, *ex officio,* 1964-66
University of Washington
Seattle, Washington

Miss Cora Paul Bomar, *ex officio,* 1964-66
State Department of Public Instruction
Raleigh, North Carolina

Dr. Richard L. Darling, *ex officio,*
    1965-67 and 1967-
Montgomery County Public Schools
Rockville, Maryland

Miss Sara I. Fenwick, 1962-64
University of Chicago
Chicago, Illinois

Dr. Frances Henne, 1962-
Columbia University
New York, New York

Mrs. Frances Kennon Johnson, 1962-64
University of North Carolina
    at Greensboro
Greensboro, North Carolina

Dr. Jean E. Lowrie, *ex officio,* 1962-64
Western Michigan University
Kalamazoo, Michigan

Miss Phyllis Hochstettler, 1964- , and
    Chairman, 1965-
Portland State College
Portland, Oregon

Miss Dorothy A. McGinniss, *ex officio,*
    1962-66
Syracuse University
Syracuse, New York

Miss Virginia McJenkin, *ex officio,*
    1963-65 and 1965-
Fulton County Board of Education
Atlanta, Georgia

Miss Virginia H. Mathews, 1962-
National Library Week Program
New York, New York

Miss Margaret E. Nicholsen, 1965-
formerly Evanston Township
    High School
Evanston, Illinois

Miss Lu Ouida Vinson, *ex officio,* 1967-
American Association of
    School Librarians
Chicago, Illinois

Miss Carolyn I. Whitenack, *ex officio,*
    1966-
Purdue University
Lafayette, Indiana

PHASE I — *1963-64 and 1964-65 SCHOOL YEARS*

Central Park Road School
Plainview-Old Bethpage Public Schools
Plainview, New York

Teachers College
Columbia University
New York, New York

Marcus Whitman School
Richland, Washington

Eastern Washington State College
Cheney, Washington

PHASE II — *1964-65, 1965-66, and 1966-67 SCHOOL YEARS*

Allisonville School
Metropolitan School District of
  Washington Township
Indianapolis, Indiana

Ball State University
Muncie, Indiana

Mount Royal School
Baltimore, Maryland

Towson State College
Towson, Maryland

Casis School
Austin, Texas

The University of Texas
Austin, Texas

PHASE III — *1965-66 and 1966-67 SCHOOL YEARS*

Roosevelt High School
Portland, Oregon

Portland State College
Portland, Oregon

Farrer Junior High School
Provo, Utah

Brigham Young University
Provo, Utah

Oak Park and River Forest High School
Oak Park, Illinois

University of Illinois
Urbana, Illinois

ACKNOWLEDGMENTS

Mrs. Alice Rusk and Miss M. Bernice Wiese for Mount Royal School and Towson State College

Dr. Janet Nymann for Casis School and The University of Texas

Mr. Don W. James for Roosevelt High School and Portland State College

Mr. G. Gardner Snow for Farrer Junior High School and Brigham Young University

Miss Lura Crawford for Oak Park and River Forest High School and the University of Illinois

All of the photographs appearing in *Realization* were provided by personnel participating in the Knapp School Libraries Project, except for the following, which were provided as indicated:

On pages 10 and 55, by Robley L. Johnson of Richland, Washington

On page 33, by Jeep Hunter of Charlotte, North Carolina

On pages 66, 69, and 74, by David W. Brady of Indianapolis, Indiana

On pages 109, 153, 161, and 164, by the *Baltimore News-American*

On pages 169, 189, and 214, by Page, Southerland, and Page (Architects-Engineers), and Dewey G. Mears

We thank all of these photographers, including those who were in the Project schools, who were so generous with their interest and talent.

After all these reports, photographs, and comments were gathered together, we were still a long way from the realization of *Realization*. Mrs. Edith McCormick of the Project office carried out many responsibilities, including typing of camera-ready copy and proofreading. But it was Edward M. Johnson who, with his tireless urging, insistence on accuracy, ill-concealed good humor, knowledge of book production management, and patience, not only educated and encouraged the Project Director but who made this book as good as it is.

Few books could ever be more truly the product of cooperative efforts than *Realization: the Final Report of the Knapp School Libraries Project*. This is a better book because members of the Advisory Committee generously offered suggestions and encouragements. In each Project school and university or college, several people wrote and edited and refined the final reports, but there was one person or, sometimes, two persons who accepted the final responsibility for answering questions from the Project director, rechecking an elusive figure or a difficult name, and their help is most gratefully recognized. They are:

Dr. William J. Nelligan and Mr. Leonard Kramer for Central Park Road School

Miss D. Marie Grieco and Dr. Paul W. F. Witt for Teachers College, Columbia University

Mrs. Anna M. Beachner for Marcus Whitman School and Eastern Washington State College

Mr. Donald F. Sellmer for Allisonville School and Ball State University

Peggy Sullivan
May, 1968

CONTENTS

OVERVIEW

ANY HISTORY of school library development in the United States will have to recognize the decade of the 1960's as a time of ferment. The Knapp School Libraries Project, spanning the middle five years of that decade, from March 1, 1963, through February 29, 1968, should be recognized as product, contributor, and benefactor of that ferment. The publication of *Standards for School Library Programs* in 1960 was the prime cause of ferment, and the School Library Development Project which followed focused attention on school libraries. All activities and evaluations in school librarianship must be viewed against the background of education and the pressures and policies which shape them.

Financial support of school libraries by federal funds began in a small way with the National Defense Education Act of 1958, which, with its extensions, provided for purchase of some categories of library materials. Beginning in the summer of 1965 with Title XI of that act, support of institutes for school librarians was provided. But the major source of new funds for school libraries has been the Elementary and Secondary Education Act of 1965. For the first time, school libraries were listed as a separate title in Title II of that act, but they benefited also from the titles intended for the encouragement of innovation (Title III), special assistance to the educationally disadvantaged (Title I), and strengthening of state departments of education (Title V). Each of the reports from the Knapp Project schools refers to this legislation, and certainly the availability of federal funds had a great deal to do with the speed with which many of the goals of the Project have been achieved.

The advent of federal funds presented problems in selection and processing of materials, administration, and in the tremendous increase of funds available for specific purposes and to be spent within a specified time. Similarly, the Knapp Project schools had had to contend, on a smaller scale but some time earlier, with the problems created by availability of funds for library collections and increases in staff. When time is the greatest need of all, the task of

selecting, ordering, and organizing a growing collection looms large, and the responsibilities of a considerably increased budget are heavy indeed.

Visitors to Project schools in the first three years of the Project sometimes commented on the delays that had been encountered in adding materials to the collections with the available Project funds, and they frequently voiced surprise at the difficulties reported in recruiting and keeping key staff members. Their reactions were somewhat different when, with ESEA funds available in 1965 and thereafter, they personally encountered some of the problems that were anticipated but could scarcely have been averted by publishers supplying materials, distributors selling equipment, and library science programs providing appropriate personnel—all in unprecedented quantity and with insufficient time to prepare.

Educational ferment often stimulates staff mobility. In several senses, this has been true in the time of the Knapp Project. One of the general difficulties has been the loss of key personnel during the time that schools have been participating in the Project. In the eight teacher education programs which cooperated with the eight Project schools, for example, three of the deans had resigned or changed assignments between the time their colleges or universities applied for the Project and the time their Project participation was concluded. Four of the eight field workers also changed although, fortunately, two of these changes occurred before the college's active participation in the Project had formally begun.

Changes in the administration of Project schools also created problems. Two principals resigned after their schools had been selected for the Project, although, again fortunately, one of these resignations came early in Project participation so that the new principal was able to assert leadership from the beginning of major Project activity. By September, 1967, three more of the principals had moved on to other educational assignments, having completed their commitment to remain while the schools were participating in the Project. Although there were similar changes in assignments of library staff members, the Project benefited from having head librarians who felt a deep responsibility to remain at their schools and to develop further the library programs which had been the major reason for the schools' selection for the Project in the first place. It is probable that schools which are selected for such demonstration projects as the Knapp Project have on their staffs a higher than usual ratio of personnel who have opportunity to advance to positions of greater influence and leadership.

The first brochure distributed from the Knapp Project office in February, 1963, stated that the Project was searching for schools "where the librarians are working with new patterns of curriculum organization, team teaching, flexible scheduling, and the like. . . ." Although this was a reference to secondary schools to participate in Phase III, comments from some readers indicated that they considered this a placement of emphasis on the far out and unusual. Now—just five years later— it sometimes seems to be more difficult to find schools which are not experimenting or working in one or more of these areas, often with the direct cooperation and leadership of the library staff.

Another indication of the general change and improvement of program, especially in elemen-

On a visit to Farrer Junior High School, Miss Peggy Sullivan, Project Director, reviews plans presented by field worker Dr. W. Dwayne Belt while Mrs. Cleone Boshard, librarian, looks on.

tary schools, during this period can be seen in the increase of professional library staff in schools. The 115 schools that applied for Phase I were narrowed down to the forty receiving most serious consideration; the major reason for elimination of some elementary schools applying was that they did not have one librarian on full-time assignment. Some applicants stated frankly that this was the case, but added comments to the effect that they felt sure the Project would be unable to find schools which met this single criterion, so their application was being sent for consideration. By 1967, it was no longer unusual to find entire school districts which have already attained or expect soon to attain the goal of having librarians assigned full-time to each elementary school.

In 1967, there are still educators who refer to school libraries housing all varieties of instructional materials as "new" or "experimental," but their number is decreasing. The philosophy of the school library as a center for all instructional materials was recognized in the standards published in 1945, endorsed by the American Association of School Librarians in 1956, stated in the standards published in 1960, and, in the standards forthcoming in 1968, is expressed as the need for one unified media center in each school building. It has won general acceptance, and a considerable variety of implementations have strengthened it as a concept. Because elementary school libraries are, on the whole, newer than secondary school libraries, it has sometimes been possible for them to move toward this concept more freely, with fewer roles and attitudes to be changed on the parts of teachers, librarians, and students. In 1963, when Phase I applications came to the Project office, few schools noted any relationship between the library and non-print materials, and some stated quite definitely that this concept of the library as a center for instructional materials was regarded with some suspicion. Four years and some months later, it is more common to find the discussion relating more to what term will be applied to this concept, or what steps remain to be taken toward its full implementation.

Technology, too, has set a pace for school library programs. In the four years since 1963, the 8-millimeter single-concept film is only one example of a new material which has won widespread acceptance. When the Project sponsored the 1965 production of *Living School Libraries*, a 35-millimeter sound filmstrip in color, one of the frames showed the principal of the Central Park Road School with a group of youngsters viewing an 8-millimeter film. Even when librarians were the early audiences for the filmstrip, a whisper, "Now what's that?" could frequently be heard. By contrast, queries about the Project schools which were directed to the Project office in 1967 were likely to assume that all the schools had extensive collections of these films, and to relate instead to the extent to which academic games, multi-dimensional materials, science kits, microfilms, and other materials were used. In short, the more precise the statements have been about what constitutes the materials to be included in a center for instructional materials, the more quickly do such statements become dated.

The panorama of educational and social change in the years 1963 to 1968 is only the background for this Project, which was concerned quite specifically with school library development. Its existence was first envisioned by a group of imaginative librarians, including Miss Mary V. Gaver of Rutgers—The State University of New Jersey, Dr. Frances Henne of Columbia University, and Miss Virginia Mathews of the National Library Week Program, all of whom were later members of the Advisory Committee. These leaders in school librarianship were anxious to provide others with the opportunity of observing school library programs which would combine in one place and at one time a variety of the quality elements recommended in the standards, and to add the opportunity to observe classes and individuals really using the library programs as recommended.

The formation of a demonstration project was the conception of the Knapp School Libraries Project, but its birth was attended by a number of handmaidens and months of advance thought and planning. The National Library Week Program provided major assistance. The article, "Is Your Child a Victim of the Book Gap?" which appeared in *This Week* magazine in its National Library Week number in 1961, was one of the first statements of serious lacks in school libraries, especially at the elementary level, and it caught the attention of Mr. C. E. Stouch, the president of the Knapp Foundation, Inc. When he asked the representatives of the American Association of School Librarians to provide a plan of how a demonstration project might help to solve this problem, the interest and good offices of the National Library Week personnel continued to be important assets.

Working at first within a suggested budget of $500,000, the AASL committee—most of them representatives of an earlier advisory committee for the School Library Development Project, which had had $100,000 from the Council on Library Resources, Inc., for an eighteen-month project to implement the 1960 standards—presented a plan which so captured Mr. Stouch's enthusiasm that he asked for a plan that would be based on an unlimited budget. The final proposal, requesting $1,130,000 for a five-year demonstration project to be conducted in five elementary and three secondary schools, and to require the cooperation of a teacher education institution with each of the eight schools, was the result. After months of negotiation and suspense, the American Library Association announced in December, 1962, that the grant of $1,130,000 had been made by the Knapp Foundation, Inc., and that the Project would begin on March 1, 1963.

There were many reasons for the interest of the Knapp Foundation in a project of this kind. Its founder, Joseph Palmer Knapp, had established the Foundation in 1929, and one of its first major grants had been for a model school system in Currituck County, North Carolina. Through two foundations, Mr. Knapp had contributed large sums for hospitals, health and medical research, youth organizations, community funds, and public service agencies. His interests and those of his successors and colleagues who later administered the foundations had always been in favor of groups and individuals who had invested some of their own efforts in an enterprise before seeking foundation funds. The Knapp School Libraries Project, with its aim of selecting schools which had already met some of the standards and which had plans for the further improvement of their libraries, corresponded well with this ideal.

Also, Mr. Knapp had had a long association with the publishing industry. In 1908 he had formed what is now known as the Alco-Gravure Division of Publication Corporation (originally the American Lithographic Company), the largest commercial gravure operation in the United States. In 1906, he had purchased the Crowell Public Publishing Company, whose principal publication was *The Woman's Home Companion;* later purchases included *The American Magazine, Collier's Weekly,* and the book publishing business of P. F. Collier & Son. In 1935 Mr. Knapp founded the United News-papers Magazine Corporation which publishes *This Week* magazine, distributed by 43 leading newspapers throughout the United States, with a circulation of over 13 million copies per week. Thus, his interest in publishing logically extended to libraries.

Mr. Knapp was born in Brooklyn, New York, in 1864 and died in New York City in 1951. The Knapp Foundation includes on its board some of his former friends and associates, so that decisions about foundation grants are usually made in the light of how they think the founder might have reacted to a particular proposal. The deep and sincere personal interest of the officers and board members of the foundation throughout the Knapp Project has contributed to its character and to the freedom with which it has been administered.

Scope of the Project

The second part of the Project proposal, "The Nature of the Proposed Project," stated:

Scope

One of the most important needs in school library development is for demonstration schools which set examples of quality school library services to pupils and teachers. This Project calls for the establishment of school libraries which will serve as living examples of the recommendations in the national standards for school libraries. In order to spread the benefits of these demonstrations, planned programs of teacher training and citizen education would be conducted through cooperative relationships with nearby teacher education institutions, to encourage and assist teachers, administrators, librarians, and citizens in the development and effective use of good school library programs. A national program of information services would be provided for widespread dissemination of information and findings of the Project. A national director would give leadership and coordination to all aspects of the Project.

Four objectives for the Project were then spelled out. It is appropriate in this section of the final report to itemize these and to comment on the extent to which they have been achieved or altered in terms of changed emphasis, more recent information, or other factors. It should be noted that each school and teacher education institution participating in the Project was not expected to adopt these objectives entirely as its own, but rather to set reasonable goals for its own cooperative efforts. These four objectives are the objectives of the Project as a whole, and they provide a framework for the history and evaluation of the Project which follows. They might best be visualized as spreading out (1) from the individual Project schools through demonstration (2) to the cooperating teacher education programs (3) toward community leaders and others with concern for development of school library programs and (4) in a broad, large-scale effort, providing background information not only about the Project schools but also about school library development in general and ways of evaluating and improving individual or local programs.

Demonstration of library programs

The first Project objective is:

To demonstrate the educational value of school library programs, services, and resources which fully meet the national standards for school libraries.

The standards to which this objective refers are, of course, the published *Standards for School Library Programs.* The first search had to be for schools which had made a start in

Picture books and a soft carpet make an attractive combination at Mount Royal School.

achieving standards. The process of selection was repeated in each phase of the Project. A brochure announcing the opportunity of Project participation was distributed to as large a mailing list as could be compiled of school administrators, teacher education personnel, individuals who had written to the Project office, librarians, library educators, and others. Respondents who indicated they represented schools that could meet the criteria, which varied slightly from one phase of the Project to another (see sample brochures and applications in the appendix), were provided with longer applications or questionnaires to determine whether they did indeed meet requirements for Project participation. In some instances, even these did not provide sufficient information, and applicants were asked to clarify their statements in letters, telephone calls, or during visits made by the Project Director to schools considered the most promising of those applying. These applications were usually cooperative efforts in several senses of the term. Representatives of the individual school and of the school district pooled their information for the school's portion of the application, and representatives of the teacher education programs conferred with them before completing their portion of the application, which often was bolstered by references to cooperation with the college or university library or media personnel, research designers, and library education faculty members.

Although parts of the story of selection have been told in articles such as "Underway," "The Knapp School Libraries Project—A Survey of Applicants," both written by the Project Director, and "The Standards Are Minimum," by Mr. John Bradbury (see "Articles about the Knapp School Libraries Project," page 315), some general comments on the process follow.

Actual selection of schools was always determined by vote of the members of the Advisory Committee for the Project. Five members appointed by the president of the American Association of School Librarians and three *ex officio* members with voice and vote comprised this committee. Although the Project Director met with them, prepared for them resumés and evaluations of applications and reports, usually with accompanying photos, of her visits to schools, she was not a member of the committee and did not vote.

In Phase I, the tight time schedule meant that the committee met just about a month after all applications were received. The 115 applications which arrived were many more than had been anticipated, and the corresponding follow-up and preparation for the meeting were accordingly delayed. At the Advisory Committee meeting in May, 1963, the Project Director was asked to visit several more schools and to report in writing to members of the committee. This accomplished, and a meeting of part of the committee having been scheduled, the final decision on selection of two schools was made by mail ballot.

In both Phases II and III, the actual decision on selection of schools was made at the time the committee met. One reason this could be accomplished was that use of preliminary applications in these phases had helped to narrow down the field of applicants even before final applications were distributed. In Phase II, for elementary schools, some 300 preliminary applications were received, which resulted in 100 final applications. Approximately the same number of preliminary applications in Phase III were reduced to 62 final applications. The Advisory Committee which set policy for the Project was reluctant to cut opportunities for applications too drastically, especially after many applicants reported on the stimulus and self-evaluation that preparing the application had given to their library programs. However, it also recognized that the time and effort of the Project Director and committee might be better spent in careful review of a limited number of applications, that it was unfair to encourage schools which did not meet major criteria for selection, and that the time and effort of school and college personnel spent on the application might be better used in more immediate improvement of the school library program.

In every phase, committee members were surprised that the over-all quality of library programs represented by the applications was so low. An extreme example of this was the high school which reported that one of its basic needs was a card catalog because, uncataloged, the books and materials were hard to locate. There is no doubt that, even with use of the preliminary applications, there were applicants who misrepresented their schools' actual situation.

In each meeting of the advisory committee when schools were to be selected, assistance from one or more consultants was sought and used. In May, 1963, a staff member from the National Education Association and one from the Library Services Branch of the United States Office of Education participated. A professor of education served as consultant at the 1964 meeting when the Phase II schools were selected, and, in Phases II and III, when Project funds were allocated for renovation or enlargement of physical facilities, an architect commented on a number of plans for change submitted by applying schools.

It was important to find out what reputation a school or its school district had within its state. It was recognized that support and recognition by the state department of education would be essential if the schools selected were to achieve recognition as centers for demonstration. Objective statements of evaluation were requested in each phase of the Project from the supervisor or consultant for school libraries in the state department of education. Response to these requests was about fifty per-

cent, but the statements received were in most instances quite helpful in providing background for the decisions of the Advisory Committee.

A point often misunderstood by applicants was the emphasis the Project placed on factors affecting demonstration. Many good school library programs were located in areas where travel was difficult or nondiscriminatory accommodations limited. A significant increase was noted during the first three years of the Project in the availability of nondiscriminatory hotel and restaurant accommodations for visitors. Concern about accommodations was not limited to areas of the South, but extended to smaller cities in the North and to some suburban areas where the school representatives commented that they were unaccustomed to having nonwhite visitors in schools. It was for such reasons that visits by the Project Director seemed necessary if schools were to receive serious consideration for selection.

There is no doubt that schools which actively sought opportunity to be demonstration schools were somewhat oriented to the pressures and rewards of demonstration, but it is certainly true that in few instances did the school personnel fully realize what active participation in a demonstration project such as the Knapp Project would entail. Comments in the reports from individual schools bear this out. At Mount Royal School in Baltimore, Maryland, for example, there is reference to the need for increased maintenance staff as the number of visitors to the school increased greatly. In every school, the responsibilities placed on the school principal and other members of the administrative and teaching staff were considerably greater than had been anticipated and provided for in budgeting. It would be wise, in any future demonstration project similar to the Knapp Project, to provide for some portion of clerical and professional salaries of persons who would be caught up in the tasks of corresponding with visitors, making luncheon or travel arrangements, sometimes providing transportation, and, as noted, maintaining physical facilities which receive heavier use because of the influx of visitors. Added responsibilities like these were recognized as being part of the contribution a school was making to the Project without direct financial recompense.

The Project funds allotted to each school ranged from approximately $40,000 to approximately $100,000. In every instance, the budget was increased beyond what the school had originally estimated as sufficient to achieve standards. There were also several instances of indirect financial support from other portions of the Project budget. Publications for individual schools sometimes were subsidized wholly or partially by Project funds, conferences were underwritten by the Project, and, on rare occasions, associations were provided with funds to pay travel expenses for persons identified with the Project who were invited to speak or consult with professional or lay groups.

Administration of funds within the Project schools was left in the hands of the locally designated school or school district representative. These liaison personnel were free to exercise judgment without direct communication with the Project office in overspending one budget line and balancing that overexpenditure with another in the same general category, and, with written approval from the Project Director, to move funds from one category to another. A first priority in all budgets was the implementation of standards. In almost all cases, the schools also received sufficient funds to exceed standards in several categories. The unrecognized aspect of budget which concerns the allocation of time — for example, to recruitment of personnel, processing of materials, and construction or renovation of facilities — was the single greatest deterrent to total meeting of national standards in individual Project schools.

A basic question about a school designated as a demonstration center must be, "But will it really demonstrate?" The question can be further refined with speculation about whether the "right" people will come, whether time and program permit them to observe or to select what is most helpful for their purposes, and whether their visits affect the programs for which they have responsibility and the programs which they have come to observe. In the

Knapp Project, there can be only a positive answer to the question of whether visitors do come.

While sheer volume of visitors was never considered an end in itself, every Project school made great efforts to accommodate as many visitors as possible, sometimes, as noted in the individual school reports, with undesirable effects on the program of the Project school. More than 16,000 visitors came to the eight Project schools during the time of Project participation. It is interesting to note that, while schools like Casis in Austin, Texas, and Oak Park and River Forest in Oak Park, Illinois—which had long traditions of unusual visitor interest—attracted predictably large numbers (6,564 and 2,464 respectively), the number of visitors to individual schools resulted in some surprises. When only two schools were participating in the Project in Phase I, for example, the school in eastern Washington state attracted more visitors than the one on populous Long Island. Farrer Junior High School in Provo, Utah, reported 342 more visitors than Roosevelt High School in Portland, Oregon.

Almost every school noted that the figures submitted for visitors could only be approximate. It was often difficult to have every visitor sign in and frequently hard to judge whether the visitor who had come to observe a science class but who was so strongly attracted to the library that he spent a full class period observing there, should be included in the count of visitors to the library. Similarly, when a class of student teachers arrived from a college or university and some of them came late or had to leave early for the next class on campus, the count of visitors was erratic. Although the figures on visitors submitted by Project schools are approximations, they undoubtedly err on the conservative side.

More details about the visitors, their characteristics, purposes, and reactions will be given later in this chapter (pages 21ff.); but, in reporting here on the schools' work as demonstration centers, some reference to the numbers and kinds of visitors seems essential. The schools were encouraged to group visitors to

Mrs. Elsie Pitts, librarian, holds the attention of a class while visitors observe in the library at the Marcus Whitman School.

the extent possible, first by encouraging team visits rather than individual arrangements, and then by grouping teams so that the schedule of visits could be set for two or three days of the week. In general, the schedules of individual schools for visitors followed the pattern recommended in a handbook prepared at the Project office and distributed to all Project personnel in 1964. This stated:

As far as the schedule for a group visit is concerned, it should be arranged to provide time for:

Orientation to the facility

Groups should assemble in some predesignated area, easily available from the main entrance, for a short welcome, distribution of name tags, brief introductions if necessary, presentation of schedules for the day, and briefing concerning luncheon arrangements, location of rooms to be visited, etc. Some visitors will need a few suggestions of "what to watch" during the observation periods of their day. The early assembly is a good time to alert the visitors to interesting features of the library program they might otherwise miss.

Orientation to the Project

In this same session, groups may be informed of the particular aspects of the school which determined its selection as a Project school library, and may be given a brief overview of the purposes and present status of the Project. Much of this could be accomplished by viewing the filmstrip which is being prepared at the Project office. [This is a reference to *Living School Libraries,*

which was produced early in 1965.] Also, information from Section One [the section of the handbook about origin of the Project] might be useful here.

Visit to the library

Groups should have the largest portion of their visiting time scheduled in the library, to provide opportunity to see a variety of activities—class visits for storytelling, class instruction in use of the library, browsing or selection period, etc., and a chance for the visitors themselves to browse.

Visits to classrooms

With emphasis on library activities, broadly defined, groups should be informed of the classrooms which they may visit, alerted to the times, topics, and purposes of such visits, and permitted to go in smaller groups or as individuals with consideration of their major interest and purpose in making the visit. Typical activities of interest in connection with this Project would be: the preparation period as a class gets ready to visit the library, the presentation of book talks, book reports, or book discussions in the classroom, use of such library materials and/or equipment as overhead projectors, record players, etc. *These suggestions are intended only as examples.* The determining factors in deciding on which classrooms to visit, etc., should be whether the activity being conducted in it is related to the library in the broad sense of the library assistance to the instructional program.

Reassembly of groups

In the case of one-day visits, during the lunch hour, or in the case of two-day visits [which turned out to be quite rare and impractical both for the schedules of visitors and of the Project schools, although visitors often commented later that they would have liked to have had a second day], the group of visitors should reassemble for discussion among themselves, and, if possible, for the opportunity to direct questions to the librarian and/or field worker [from the teacher education program] to clarify information obtained earlier. At this time, some members of the group may wish to observe at greater length an aspect of the program which they had seen; others may request the opportunity to observe what they had missed earlier. When possible, such requests should be honored. This reassembly should also provide for some evaluation of the visit up to that point, and leaders of groups may need to be reminded of the benefit of recording critical comments in order to incorporate them into their reports. This may also be the best time for visitors to examine some of the "giveaways"—pamphlets, bibliographies, etc., which will be provided for them. In order to insure the more effective use of these materials, they should be easily available and tastefully displayed. Attention should be drawn to them at this time, and members of the groups should feel free to browse among them and to select single copies of items of particular interest. (The "Materials List" in Section Five of this Handbook should be kept up to date.)

Final period of time

A final period of time, in which visitors may return to further observe some of the things of particular interest to them, or continue to see something which another visitor has reported on, and which may have particular interest for them, should be provided.

Probably the most controversial part of this schedule was the visiting of classrooms. Although the schools attempted to maintain as free a policy as possible of permitting visitors to enter classrooms at will, there were times when probationary or substitute teachers were reluctant to have visitors, and when visits would probably have had little value; many visitors were reluctant to step into a classroom even when assured they might do so; and many who had come to see the library program felt they could see it best or only in the library. There are references to these problems in the individual schools' reports, and it may be surmised that when there was some hesitancy on the part of school personnel to encourage visits to classrooms, there was corresponding dissatisfaction on the part of visitors. Yet, since the goal of the Project was the demonstration of the impact of the school library on the instructional program, every effort was made to ensure that the instructional program was understood and observed.

Besides demonstrating the educational value of school library programs, the Knapp Project had some responsibility in assessing what that educational value might be. Development of school libraries had always of necessity been tied to the availability of funds and staff, so

programs tended to be strongest where funds and staff for other areas of specialization within the school district were also strong. And, since school libraries have a responsibility for all areas of the curriculum, it had been, and it is, hard to isolate the impact they make. It was recognized in the Project that, as in research in general, there was a choice between doing rather sophisticated research on relatively unimportant topics or doing questionable research on topics with broad implications and deep meaning. It was further recognized that, if the schools participating in the Project were to maintain the support and program which they had attained during the Project, they would have to present to local administrators some proof of progress not only in quantities of library materials, but in quality of instructional program. Appropriately enough, the local community would be interested in the numbers of visitors a Project school had because of the public relations value, but the idea of maintaining a model program for the primary benefit of others to observe and imitate would have little appeal. For this reason, schools were encouraged to adopt criteria for evaluating the library program that would have greatest meaning for them and their communities.

It cannot be stated too often or too strongly that many of the decisions and courses of progress made within the Project resulted from the individuality of the schools which participated. Perhaps the most dissimilar single group were the Phase II schools, including, as they did, an inner-city school in Baltimore, a suburban school near Indianapolis, and a university's demonstration school which was also the public school serving the university community in Austin, Texas. The two schools in Phase I, both of them located in communities and school districts of similar size, had more in common, but the Marcus Whitman School in Richland, Washington, was closely identified with the city of Richland as part of the Tri-cities area, along with Pasco and Kennewick, while the Central Park Road School in Plainview was in a community with a less distinctive identity of its own, as part of the spreading bedroom suburbs of Long Island. Both areas had undergone periods of tremendous growth in population and were reaching the time when population was leveling off and the continued needs for public facilities were encountering stiff competition for the attention and support of the community. The secondary schools in Phase III of the Project ranged from the Oak Park and River Forest High School, Illinois, where a comprehensive program of education constituted an entire school district in one school of 3,500 students, to the 1,800-student senior high school in the blue collar community of St. Johns in Portland, Oregon—the Roosevelt High School. Farrer Junior High School, Provo, Utah, was the only junior high school selected to participate in the Project, and it represented an entire geographic region that had received little recognition for efforts made in school library development.

These individual differences in schools meant that no single test or study of skills could be applied across the board to all schools. Each school had stated the aims of its library program on a long range basis as a part of its Project application; the measure of success or failure would have to be in terms of the extent to which those aims were achieved. One very tangible evidence of the value of participation in the Project would be the decision about whether the Project's provisions of materials, facilities, and personnel would be continued with local support following Project participation. The extent of this kind of support is indicated in the fact that of the six schools in Phases II and III which concluded Project participation in June, 1967, every one began the 1967-68 school year with a staff considerably increased beyond that which was in the school when it began to participate in the Project. One, Oak Park and River Forest, even provided local funds for the employment of one more librarian than had been on the roster when the school was active in the Project.

Each school determined the kind of evaluation instrument that would be most helpful to it, and each used more than one. Testing of students' study skills, questionnaires of teachers' attitudes, and reactionnaires for parents were among these. Some of these tools, or the

results of them, are still in use. Evaluation goes on in the schools. No fewer than three doctoral dissertations and four masters' theses have been studies of Knapp Project schools, and there are references to these in the schools' reports. In addition, in the Project office correspondence with graduate students and others, there are references to several more theses in process or at least in the planning stages.

To a very large extent, the factors that made schools good prospects for demonstration militated against very precise research in evaluation. A thousand "ifs" arose when designers of research looked clinically at the Project schools: "If you had more time for Project participation"; "If you would hold back one class from library activity and let it be a control group for another class which would benefit from the library program"; "If there were not so many visitors"; "If you would eliminate the availability of some materials so that it would be possible to see what happens without them"; "If some elements of the school's instructional program were omitted from library service"—these were a few of the "ifs." But for a demonstration project, the first responsibilities seemed to be to attract and inform the visitors, to serve the whole school, and to provide the broadest range of materials possible. Interestingly enough, in at least one instance when a field worker wished to compare the Project school with others in the area, he was concerned when the control school (which had had a more limited library program) improved its financial support and staffing within the first year. It thus had limited value as a control school; however, the reason for its improvement could be directly attributed to the demonstration impact of the nearby Project school. Whenever pure research impeded the demonstration aspect of the Project, it was *demonstration* that had to be given priority, because that was the Project's first concern. In spite of this, even the limited amount of measurement and evaluation that developed and was publicized while the Project was under way has provided ideas and plans which have been incorporated successfully in the development of other school library programs. These aids included not only those published in *Impact: The School Library and the Instructional Program,* which reported on the Phase I schools, but also questionnaires and other records of progress which were freely loaned or distributed by schools while participating in the Project. Most of these aids are included in the school reports included here.

One of the most serious disadvantages of each school participating in the Project was the inadequate physical facility of the library. In no case was a school able to plan and construct a model physical facility at the time of its entrance into the Project. In the first phase, no Project funds had been budgeted for physical change; it had been hoped that the schools having programs which made them eligible would also have facilities approaching the ideal. This proved not to be true. In the second phase, when the three schools had the longest period of time to prepare to become demonstration centers, a portion of Project funds went for the improvement of physical facilities, but planning time was still quite limited. At the Casis School, for example, where an entirely new library was planned as part of a new wing of the school, the blueprints had already been prepared and it was anticipated that the funds would be available from another foundation and the school district before the school would enter the Knapp Project. When the other foundation grant did not materialize, the Knapp Project provided additional funds, but the delays and difficulties of construction meant that the readiness team (see page **180**) visited before the new facility was occupied.

In Phase III, the general enlargement of library area meant the use of space elsewhere in the school, such as the subject resource centers at Oak Park and River Forest. There were major administrative decisions to be made about staffing and providing materials at several locations. These added considerably to the complexities of preparing the library program to be an excellent one for demonstration. The selection of schools which had less than adequate or barely adequate facilities at the time of selection, and sometimes disappointing facili-

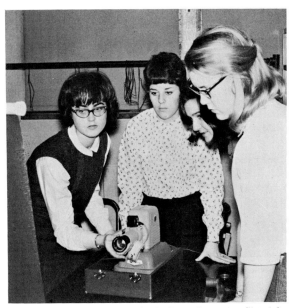

Towson State College students learn to use a filmstrip projector at Mount Royal.

ties even after enlargement, caused some sharp criticism. However, with demonstration of program the major concern, limited facilities offered two advantages. Visitors who were favorably impressed with the library programs they observed frequently commented that they recognized in this way that program did not have to depend on an exceptionally fine facility. They felt a kinship with the Project schools and were more eager to attempt, at least, to incorporate ideas and activities which, in an ideal facility, might have seemed to them impossible of achievement. If the Advisory Committee and Project Director were ever inclined to think wistfully of schools which had applied for the Project while apparently on the threshold of completion of elaborate new facilities, but which had not been selected for a combination of reasons, they could also realize that in several of those schools with which correspondence was maintained, the unexpected construction delays or difficulties with local funding resulted in the new facilities' not being available until long after the demonstration programs at the Project schools were under way.

Demonstration was a heavy responsibility, but in each school there was often the feeling that, without a target date for beginning demonstration, the recruitment of staff, increase of collection, and completion of structural change might have dragged out even longer. The two Phase I schools had the shortest period of time in which to become ready as demonstration centers, and they were the only schools actively demonstrating in the Project for the longest period of time. Notified of their selection for the Project in June, 1963, they began to receive Project-supported visitors soon after the first of the following year. Phase II schools had the longest period of time for readiness. Their selection was announced in April, 1964, and no Project-supported visits were scheduled until the fall of 1965. The schedule was shortened again for the Phase III schools, which were selected in the spring of 1965 and which received their first Project-supported visitors early in 1966. Experience in Phase I pointed up the need for the readiness visit which was used in the two latter phases. The readiness visit provided the Project school personnel with an opportunity to try out their schedule for visitors and to see what typical reactions might be.

Plans for the readiness visit began when members of a team of visitors were selected by local Project school personnel to comprise a fairly typical team, but representing a variety of localities and specialties. Each readiness team included one member of the Project's national Advisory Committee or appropriate alternate, and the rest of the team included teachers, administrators, school board members, faculty members in higher education, and others. With travel expenses paid by the Project, this team was asked to comment in some depth on the good and bad points of the visit, which lasted one school day.

The enthusiastic, first-person publicity given by members of the team was one valued result of this activity. As leaders in their states or professional groups, team members were often responsible for sending other groups to the school, and, in most instances, they maintained a sincere, long range interest in the Project school and its development.

Somewhat similar in purpose was the local advisory committee appointed for each school. The Project handbook recommended:

> A local advisory committee should be designated to assist in disseminating information about the program and to interest citizens of the community in strengthening support for school library programs. For membership on the committee, besides school and school district staff members and the field worker from the teacher education institution, some of the following should be considered: member(s) of the board of education, the state school library supervisor, representatives from the public library, parent or other citizen groups, etc.

The concept of the functions of this committee varied from one Project school to another. Members sometimes served as a "sounding board" rather than a "reacting panel." With a number of high-level persons included on the committee, it was difficult to schedule meetings at times that would be satisfactory to all or even possible for the majority to attend. There was considerable variation in the patterns of the meetings themselves and in their frequency. Several of the schools reported the most satisfactory results when the committee meeting was combined with observation of the library program and of classroom instruction. At the Allisonville School, where each of the four state university teacher education programs was represented on the committee, and where the committee met frequently with considerable opportunity for discussion and criticism, the contributions of the committee were many and obvious. One of the reasons for recommending such a committee in the first place was to provide a way for open channeling of information to the school board by having that group represented officially on the committee. This also usually proved to be an advantage. Where turnover of personnel on the committee was high, there was less continuity and direction, and, in those instances, the committee tended to function less adequately.

Besides receiving reactions from visitors and advisers, personnel in the Project schools were always interested in the work and ideas of their counterparts in the other Project schools. Opportunities for visits by Project school staff to other schools were not provided by the Project, but a number of staff members arranged for these visits independently. Although national professional meetings provided some limited opportunity for Project school personnel to meet, these were usually infrequent and brief encounters. Even though Project school personnel represented different kinds and grade levels of schools and school districts, they had common topics for extended discussion in their Project participation, provisions for visitors, supervision of new staff, and other similar responsibilities.

In the spring of 1965, the Project sponsored a meeting for the field workers, head librarians, and liaison persons (in each case the principal) from the three Phase III schools. This was a two-day meeting at Oak Park and River Forest High School, just a few weeks after the three schools had received word of their selection for the Project. It was hoped that field workers especially might derive from this the stimulus for some cooperative efforts at evaluation and research. To a limited extent, this occurred, since Dr. Jerry L. Walker of the University of Illinois later was able to incorporate responses from Roosevelt High School with some from Oak Park and River Forest where he was working.

Once again, this experience seemed to point up that the differences outweighed the similarities among the Phase III schools. Visitors who saw only one school or others who knew of the Project only at second hand found it hard to believe how individual the schools were. This uniqueness was an asset, but it also meant there never was "a Knapp plan for school library development." There were, instead, eight Knapp Project schools each following its own long range plans.

Working with colleges

The second objective of the Project was:

To promote improved understanding and use of library resources on the part of teachers and administrators, by relating the demonstration situations to teacher education programs in nearby colleges.

In most of the considerable body of articles and talks about the Project, the citation of this

objective is the most underemphasized, and achievement of it is correspondingly most difficult to evaluate. From the start, the institutions of higher education which applied for the Project were expected to play a supporting role. For most of them, this was a novel experience. As one representative of an applying teacher education institution commented to the Project Director: "This is all pretty unusual for us. You're not just asking for token support, are you?" The difficulty and the strength of this idea of having teacher education programs actively engaged in the Project lay in the same place: the college or university was usually sought out by the school to be its co-applicant, and the lion's share of funds and publicity went to the school rather than to the teacher education program. In Phase I especially, several schools reported their inability to get a college to co-apply with them. Others asked the Project office to supply formal statements promising to live up to the agreement outlined briefly in the brochure about Phase I, which stated the Project would want a field worker on half-time assignment from the regular faculty, and that the Project would reimburse the college for these half-time services. Following announcement of the selection of colleges participating in Phase I, there was a notable increase of interest on the part of other teacher education programs in co-applying for future phases. Undoubtedly, this was attributable to the excellent reputations of Eastern Washington State College and of Teachers College, Columbia University, the cooperating institutions in Phase I.

Besides the fairly obvious criteria of accessibility between college and school and the interest of the teacher education program in preparing teachers who would use libraries and library materials effectively, the most important single consideration of a teacher education program was the caliber and background of its proposed field worker. In Phase I, colleges were not required to submit names of the field worker who would be appointed, and the result was a lack of concern in many instances about what his work should be and what his relationship to the Project and Project school would be. Accordingly, in the last two phases of the Project, the application forms included a brief statement about the expected role of the field worker, and each co-applicant was required to submit a name and description. Even with this greater emphasis placed on the importance of the field worker, colleges sometimes indicated that a faculty member would be recruited on a half-time basis for the assignment. In at least two instances, it was proposed that retired professors in their late seventies or eighties would be given the assignment if the college were selected. The design of the Project had been to have the field worker engaged with the Project only half-time, with the other half of his time devoted to faculty responsibilities to ensure feedback to the college of the ideas, reactions, and activities developed in the Project school with which he would be associated.

Of all the persons associated with the Project—head librarians, principals, deans, for example—the field workers were the ones whose roles were newest and most varied as a result of Project participation. They had to be flexible, respected members of their own faculties, and in every case they were also experienced as public school teachers. Their work was carried on with visitors who expected them to be well informed about the Project school but also objective in assessing its strengths and weaknesses; with Project school faculty members

Dr. Walter W. Williamson, field worker, stresses the importance of content on transparencies to be used in instruction by future teachers from Towson.

who were sometimes suspicious of what a college professor might have as an objective in working with them; with their college faculty colleagues who might be unaware of the field worker's new responsibility but who might be asked to assist or advise; with students whom they gathered in groups to observe in the Project school; and with the Project office since their reports, budgets, and outline of plans for evaluation were usually submitted to the Project Director.

In the early days of the Project, a good deal of interest was expressed in Project participation by demonstration schools directly associated with or administered by colleges or universities. In some respects, these offered special advantages to the Project: there would be assurance of cooperation between college and school; the schools were accustomed to visitors; the follow-up of incorporating ideas about the use of library materials into the teacher education program might be expected to be virtually automatic. But the fact that these schools were most often serving a somewhat privileged or quite homogeneous community was a consideration not in their favor. Finally, the Casis School which participated in Phase II was the only participant that was also a demonstration school for a university. At the same time that its participation in the Project was concluded in June, 1967, its close tie with The University of Texas was severed as the result of an agreement made some time ago. This school had always served also as a member school in the Austin Independent School District, and it continues in this role.

Some of the measures used to estimate the potential for positive cooperation between college and school in the Project were the placement of the college's student teachers in the applying school, the co-sponsorship or cooperation in workshops for teachers in service, the similarity of philosophy of education, and the placement of the college's graduates in the school or school district as they accepted their first teaching positions. Most of these factors were given more importance than mere physical proximity. Thus, the University of Illinois was more than one hundred miles away from the Oak Park and River Forest High School with which it cooperated, and Eastern Washington State College almost one hundred miles from Richland, Washington, where the Project school was located. Some colleges or universities agreed to co-apply with more than one school, and, in rarer instances, schools submitted applications with more than one college. In the latter cases, the Project Advisory Committee was most reluctant to consider a school which was unable or unwilling to select the cooperating program with which it could work most effectively. The Committee recognized, however, that a number of reasons might lead to a college's submitting more than one application; for example, sheer lack of colleges in the geographic region, or disinterest on the part of other college programs. In some cases, college personnel indicated that they had felt they could not gracefully refuse to co-apply, but that they definitely felt that the school with which they had co-applied would offer little to the Project. This evidence of concern seemed to speak poorly for long range cooperative effort in a Project with heavy responsibilities for both school and college.

The process of preparing an application cooperatively often provided college and school personnel with their first opportunities to get better acquainted with each other's programs. In at least one instance, a school's cooperative application with a neighboring university led to that university's recognition of the unusually fine instructional program in the district, and eventually, to very full cooperation between the two in summer programs, in-service education, and other cooperative endeavors.

Since the Project field workers were not librarians, their role in the Project schools was less to work directly with the library staff of the school than to work with the teaching staff. The field workers usually worked with teachers first in small groups or in the teachers' own classrooms. It was necessary to assure and reassure teachers that the field worker's responsibility was not to evaluate or to criticize their teaching techniques but to encourage and assist especially in use of library materials in class-room instruction. This part of the role was cause for further confusion when the field worker was, in some instances, later identified as the person responsible for evaluating the Project at the school.

Some of the strengths the field workers brought to the Project were the ability and willingness to write articles, give talks, and conduct workshops. Since they were not librarians, their statements about the needs and potentials of library programs as they observed them frequently carried special value and authority. This status also sometimes made it possible for them to encourage and arrange for visits to the Project school by other teacher education faculty members and students from their own or other institutions. The conviction which each one of them has voiced about the value of school library programs, as a result primarily of experience in the Knapp Project, should prove of long range benefit to school library development.

Among successful and unsuccessful co-applicants, there was sometimes some confusion about the role of the teacher education program and the role of the library science program where the two existed within the same university or in neighboring institutions. In some instances, schools reported that, when they approached deans of education to ask for cooperation in co-applying for the Project, they were referred instead to library science programs. Even when applications came in from schools of education, it was often a faculty member from the library science program rather than the school of education who was named as field worker. The interest and encouragement shown by faculty members in library science was often valuable in opening the way for an application submitted by a teacher education program with a school.

Notably at Brigham Young University in Provo, the continuing interest of the faculty in library science was responsible for excellent cooperation throughout the Project. The summer workshop for faculty members at Farrer Junior High School in Provo, which was conducted in 1965 at the time the school entered the Project, was led by Mrs. Hattie M. Knight of the library science program at Brigham Young University. The Project's financial commitment to this workshop resulted from the fact that on the Project Director's first visit to Farrer, several faculty members had expressed interest in knowing more about how to use materials more effectively, while the school district administration had reluctantly decided it was impossible at that time to budget for a summer workshop. Here was an opportunity for faculty to participate in the actual selection of materials which would be added to the school library with Project funds, while getting first-hand experience in using them. On recommendation of the Project Advisory Committee, provision for this workshop was written into the Project agreement with the junior high school and the university. The work of planning and staffing a workshop with only a few weeks' notice was carried out by Dr. Belt, the field worker at Brigham Young, and with Mrs. Knight's leadership, the workshop served not only to give the Farrer faculty more training but also to stimulate them for the period of demonstration that was to come.

To some extent every Project school went through a period when the library program was providing materials and services which were not immediately recognized or fully utilized by the faculty. This was true even while some teachers were remarking impatiently on the slowness with which materials were being added to the collection. One visitor on a readiness team commented:

> . . . there was little evidence in the classroom of the impact of the library. I visited one classroom in which a film was being shown.

. . . I went into other classrooms and found straight textbook teaching and no evidence that the library was being used in any way in relation to classroom instruction. Other visitors found wonderful instructional materials but not from the library. Probably it just happened that way, but I think we must be able to show how work in the classroom is affected if most administrators and teachers are going to be impressed.

When comments like these reached the schools, it was often the field worker who assumed responsibility for working more closely with teachers, not only in increasing their opportunities for using instructional materials, but for channeling visitors to the segments of classroom instruction during which library materials are used and for increasing the effectiveness with which teachers incorporated materials into their class programs.

Although summer workshops or in-service programs were designed to assist teachers, there were inevitable requests for person-to-person sessions with the field worker. These often resulted in an opportunity for work with a grade level or departmental group of teachers, and the field workers' schedules were kept as flexible as possible to allow for this. It should be noted that, because of the travel time between college campus and school and other demands of the Project, the field workers, like other Project personnel, often worked extra hours without additional financial compensation.

Several special conferences were conducted during the Project. The first of these, held in Richland in February, 1965, was an institute for personnel in teacher education in Washington. The experience of planning and conducting it was valuable not only to the Richland personnel and the Project Director but to representatives at other Project schools who were to plan and lead similar workshops later. Two of the first steps in each of these were estimation of attendance and designation of an audience —by educational specialty, region, size of school district, or the like. Pre-registrations were encouraged so that plans for meals, tours of the buildings, transportation, and group meetings could be based on projected attendance figures. In some instances, as at Richland, the conferences were invitational, but more often, a limit for the number who could be accommodated was set, and announcements were designed and distributed to attract that approximate number in whatever assortment of specialties might be desired, such as librarians, principals, district supervisors, teacher education faculty, and others.

The schools and colleges which sponsored such workshops or conferences have presented fairly thorough accounts of them in their individual reports, but the larger conferences are noted here:

Institute for Teacher Education Personnel at Richland, Washington, February, 1965.

Fall Work-Conference at Austin, Texas, November, 1965.

Children's Literature Conference at Baltimore and Towson, Maryland, April, 1966.

Work Conference at Austin, Texas, June, 1966.

Multi-Media Approach to Learning Conference at Provo, Utah, January, 1967.

The Secondary School Library in Transition Conference at Portland, Oregon, March, 1967.

In each of the above, the field worker assumed major responsibility, and the announcement that the conference had university or college sponsorship was certainly responsible for the conservatively estimated average attendance of three hundred persons at each conference. A series of conferences in conjunction with other programs and grants was scheduled at the Oak Park and River Forest High School in connection with its participation in the Project. These centered on the humanities, use of a variety of media in instruction, the arts, and other academic subjects. Dr. Walker, field worker for the University of Illinois, usually coordinated these programs. The use of telelectures for both students and faculty at Oak Park was a fairly new technique which was supported and extended by the use of Project funds.

Most often, as a part of responsibilities not related to the Project, the field worker supervised student teachers. This usually made

easier his work within the Project school when student teachers were placed there. For example, when Towson's Overview to Elementary Education required a number of class sessions scheduled in the Project school, Mount Royal, the field worker was able to teach the class, which actually is an introduction to education for students before they begin their student teaching. At the same time, the field worker was able to introduce students to an inner-city school and to an exceptionally good library program.

It is possible that the fact that Project schools were associated with a single college or university meant that other colleges and universities in the area felt somewhat left out and less inclined to schedule classes for observation and visits. However, the Project schools and cooperating teacher education programs actively encouraged this kind of visiting. Some evidence of their success can be seen in the fact that almost every school reported visits by classes from at least three or four colleges or universities. In addition, many teacher education and library science faculty members visited the schools, either as members of Project-supported teams, in other groups, or as individuals. The participation of representatives of other teacher education programs on local advisory committees and readiness teams has already been noted. Class groups from colleges participated. Workshops and National Defense Education Act institutes often used Project schools as places to visit. The accessibility of most of the Project schools during the summer months was a special feature much appreciated by these institute leaders who wanted to provide a common experience of observation of school library programs for the participants in their educational media or school library institutes during the summer months.

In the long view, reactions and follow-up activities by college and university faculty members who visited Project schools are probably hardest to evaluate. One college teacher of library science who led a team on a visit to a Project school sent a somewhat cryptic and noncommittal report of the visit to the Project office, but later commented in person to the Project Director that she could see the changes of attitude in the faculty members who had accompanied her on the trip, and that every day these assisted her in her work and goals for better training of future teachers in use of library materials.

There is no question that one of the difficulties—or perhaps a little nest of intertwined difficulties—in assessing the impact of the Project on teacher education results from the fact that there is no general agreement on what teacher education programs should provide in preparing future teachers to use instructional materials effectively. Because present and past opportunities for this kind of preparation have been somewhat limited at the pre-service level, much of the responsibility for teaching teachers to use materials has been assumed by those responsible for in-service programs.

Even when colleges or universities are prepared and able to incorporate demonstration and experience with a wide range of materials into their pre-service courses, there is no general agreement on when, where, and how they best fit into the student's schedule. At a time when there is more external pressure on reducing the number of methods courses and increasing the emphasis on academic subjects, the teacher education program directors may believe that any added courses in materials or library usage are indeed tangential. Those proposing them argue that, if separate courses are not offered, every course taken by the future teacher should provide actual experience with a wide range of materials, well selected and presented by the instructor as vital elements of his teaching. In this way, good use of materials would be an accepted, natural way of life for the teacher throughout his future career. And in response, college representatives note that in many cases their facilities for production and projection of materials are less adequate (or less adequate in proportion to the numbers served) than are those available in the elementary and secondary schools where the students are preparing to teach. The wistful comment that some Project schools had more in the way of equipment, materials, and facilities in which to use them than did their neighboring colleges was made more than once by visiting college

Librarian, principal, and field worker plan together whenever time permits at the Roosevelt High School. Left to right: Mrs. Lois Sayles, Mr. Don W. James, and Dr. Jerome E. Leavitt.

faculty members. All of this serves only to point up the fact that there are no easy answers. As in the Knapp Project, teacher education programs will probably have to employ a combination of techniques at a variety of times to give teachers the choice of varied riches in instructional materials and equipment.

Many teacher education programs have sponsored demonstration or laboratory schools to give their future teachers experience and opportunity to observe in excellent schools. Yet, even in these schools, library programs are not always exemplary, and the select enrollments, special benefits for teachers, and other factors have at times limited the potential impact such schools might have in improving school library development through demonstration.

The large enrollments of the teacher education programs of the colleges and universities participating in the Project meant that anything like a saturation program was impossible. The field worker, on half-time assignment, could talk about the school library program only to a limited number of students in teacher education. Fewer yet could be scheduled for actual visits. Others, however, might hear the Project head librarian or principal as guest speakers in their classes. Materials from the Project were distributed to class groups, and the Project-sponsored films and filmstrips could be part of the program of interesting the students in school library programs. In the colleges as in the Project schools, extra effort to win the attention and support of faculty members might in the long run pay more dividends than exclusive concentration on student response. Field workers and their colleagues put in this extra effort, but the long range results are hard to measure.

One interesting comment, coming with some frequency from almost every one of the participating teacher education programs, was that potential employers of the college's graduates commented on the fact that graduates asked about the school library program and based their interest in teaching positions on the quality of school library support for their teaching. This approach meant that the interviewing administrators' attention was being called to the need for school libraries and that the beginning teachers' pre-service experience and education were making them aware of the value of a school library. It should, of course, be noted that this same phenomenon was probably observable in many other colleges at this time when so much national emphasis was being placed on school libraries and so many schools were having the opportunity to bring to life plans which had been only dreams.

Many students in teacher education programs in the years 1963 through 1967 were the war and post-war babies whose progress through school had been the beginning of an enlarging wedge of student enrollments. For the most part, their own educational backgrounds in elementary and secondary schools had been achieved with minimal library service available within the school. With this in mind, Dr. Donald L. Barnes, the Project field worker from Ball State University, devised a questionnaire which he used as a kind of spot check in one hundred interviews with seniors in the education program. Asked to select which of several aids to instruction they would consider most important to have during their first year of teaching, they overwhelmingly chose a centralized school library and librarian. It is significant that Dr. Barnes, who administered the questionnaire, was not directly associated with the library or the library science pro-

gram at the university, so that students could not consciously have been making choices to please him. Since few of them had had their complete education in schools with school libraries, their decisions must have been based on attitudes developed during their college years.

Difficult though evaluation and future meaning of Knapp Project participation are for teacher education programs, one college received formal recognition of its contributions. The American Association of Colleges of Teacher Education included Towson State College among the teacher education programs cited for excellence at its annual conference in 1967. The text of that citation is included in the report of the college's participation in the Project (see page 129).

Citizen education

The Project's third objective was identified as:

To guide and encourage citizens, from as many communities as possible, in the development of their own library programs through planned activities enabling them to study demonstration situations.

The supporting budget for this objective was based on the calculation of expenses for visiting teams of six persons each, with six teams scheduled to each school during each of two visiting periods each year. In practice, both the schedule and the budget were extended far beyond that allocation.

As noted earlier, when the Project schools had had time to assimilate new staff and materials and to move into new or expanded facilities, brochures announcing opportunities for Project-supported visits were distributed. In each phase, some twenty thousand or more of these brochures were mailed directly to persons likely to be interested. (See brochures in appendix.) Persons on the mailing list included administrators, supervisors, librarians, teachers, and others. To the extent possible, the Project office attempted to direct information about the elementary school programs to persons working at the elementary level, and about the secondary school programs to those at the secondary level.

However, all names added to the Project mailing list as the result of inquiry, correspondence, visits, etc., were included in all general mailings of this kind.

Approximately one-fourth of the applications received for Project-supported visits were approved to receive funds. Aside from stating broad guidelines, such as concern for as broad a geographic coverage of the United States as possible, the Project Advisory Committee did not rule or comment on individual applications for Project travel funds. Supervisors or consultants for state school library programs were invited to comment, however, on the relative merits of teams applying from their states.

In the allocation of funds to these teams, the Project was overcommitted financially with the expectation that changes of personnel, schedule, or other factors would reduce the number of teams finally visiting Project schools. Funds for visitors to each school were not allocated equally. Where demand was greatest, more funds were allocated.

Factors influencing selection of teams for these visits included the thoughtfulness of the statement explaining why a team wished to visit, the varied composition of the team with priority given to those including administrators and

board members or other lay representatives as well as librarians and teachers, and the potential that various teams seemed to offer for actual improvement of school libraries in their communities. One group of librarians who, with their supervisor, applied for Project funds for travel in more than one phase of the Project was not chosen to receive funds, but finally did visit one of the schools at their own or school district expense. Their comment that their visit would have been enhanced had one or more of their school district administrators accompanied them seemed to prove the value of insisting as often as possible on the inclusion of administrators and others in each team.

As noted in the reports of individual Project schools, the comments of visitors were often responsible for innovations in plans for the visitors' schedule of activities and, less frequently, for improvements in the school's library or instructional program. In general these points could be made about visitors' reactions:

1. Visitors writing to the Project schools tended to make rather vague but complimentary remarks both on the school program and on the arrangements for their visit; they were more critical on the reactionnaires submitted to the Project office (of which copies were forwarded to

Interest in the Marcus Whitman School was great enough to bring neighboring administrators to an evening meeting at the library at which Mr. James V. LeClair, the principal, described the school and library program.

the schools), and, in conversation or correspondence with others, they were sometimes more critical still.

2. Visitors who came as Project-supported teams were usually more perceptive and critical than those who came independently.

3. Although the stated purpose of the Project visits was to see school library programs in action, a general cause for disappointment was that district administrators, library supervisors, teacher education faculty members, and school board members were not able to meet with persons holding similar positions in the Project schools, districts, or colleges. Although these kinds of appointments were scheduled to the extent possible, the prospect of a superintendent's being at one of the many schools in his district on a regular basis to meet with visitors was generally quite unrealistic.

4. Visiting librarians were interested in the library program as it could be observed in the library, rather than in classroom visits or discussion; other specialists among the visitors tended to be more responsive to the more varied observations in the classroom.

5. A frequent cause for dissatisfaction was the lack of opportunity for longer visits, or for evening sessions before or after the visits. The persons who made these comments sometimes also noted that they realized the strain this could be for the staff of the Project school, when other visiting teams might have been at the school on the days before and after the same visit.

6. Some visits had to be scheduled many months in advance, and these visitors were the most likely to have to alter or cancel plans for a visit. A period of six weeks' notice appeared to be optimum for assuring that the visitors would be well organized for the visit and less likely to have to make changes of personnel on their teams or changes of dates.

7. There was a significant growth in sophistication of the teams visiting the Project schools in the later years of the Project. The availability of funds, the immediate prospect of enlarged physical facilities, the opportunity of preceding or following the Project school visit with visits to other schools, and the assurance that the

instructional materials center concept was to be implemented in their home communities gave to the later visitors more of a feeling of optimism about incorporating the ideas that they liked or deciding on which practices they would wish to adopt for their own programs.

Reports from the individual schools contain a number of references to reactions of Project visitors. For the most part, there is no distinction between those who came with Project funds and those who came on their own. Groups who were selected to receive Project funds also received, direct from the Project office, information about travel and housing arrangements at the school they would visit, copies of report forms which they would have to submit after their visit, and, in Phases II and III, copies of a sample press release for their use in publicizing their visit. Experience in Phase I had shown that, while team leaders were often willing to send out press releases announcing their team's selection, they lacked the information or time to prepare accurate announcements. The extensive use made of the press releases indicated their value. Copies of more than two hundred published articles about team visits to Project schools were forwarded to the Project office; many more were reported, but copies were unavailable. In many cases, the use of these releases helped to pave the way for reaction to reports of visitors to the Project schools. Team leaders were invited to talk to service clubs, school boards, faculty groups, and others who considered the team's selection in nationwide competition good reason for their views to be promulgated after their visit.

Team leaders were asked to submit a report of their visit before their expenses were reimbursed. In only one instance was a team trip made and reimbursement never requested. It was to be expected that these reports would come in promptly to the Project office. However, another part of the team's agreement was to provide to the Project office a report, approximately one year after the visit, of the action or progress resulting from the visit. The enthusiasm of visitors in general can be measured by the fact that often no reminder of these year-later reports had to be sent from the

Project office. Visitors were eager to report their progress and plans. So that some of these comments could be incorporated into this publication, visitors who had gone to Project schools during the 1966-67 school year were asked to submit their reports early in the 1967-68 school year, regardless of the date of their visit. Approximately two-thirds of the visitors to the Phase II schools and more than one-half of the visitors to the Phase III schools complied before November 1, 1967.

In Phase I, as reported in the section of this publication that is taken from *Impact: the School Library and the Instructional Program,* the change or improvement most often reported by visitors a year after their Project-supported visits was the employment of clerical or paraprofessional assistants for the library program. More frequently mentioned in the later years of the Project was the expansion or implementation of the concept of the library as the center for all instructional materials. Although the forms for year-later reports limited statements to quite cryptic ones, many persons submitted longer letters or statements, plans, and reports of their work in school library development. The availability of funds undoubtedly caused materials to receive greater emphasis at this time. This, too, contributed to a generally more optimistic tone on the part of visitors. Measuring progress, for example, one team from Michigan noted that the number of library personnel serving the eight schools in the district had begun with one teacher and a full-time clerk, had been increased to two professionals, and within the year would have one and perhaps two more professional persons. Another, from Arizona, noted: "The visit allowed us to make some changes in the design of a new library building now on the drawing board. Incorporated in the design of this building will be some of the ideas gleaned from our Knapp Project visit."

Teams that received Project funds for their travel expenses represented every state in the union, but, in number, they represented only about one-third of all the visitors to Project schools. Especially in the second and third phases of the Project, the scheduling of most of the

Participants in the Portland conference take notes on Miss Peggy Sullivan's comments about library facilities.

Project-supported teams in the early months of visitations meant that time was available later as word spread that it would be worthwhile for others to plan trips with funds from other sources. It should be noted that many teams supplemented the limited funds made available by the Project and, in some instances, extended their travel schedules to include other schools in neighboring areas.

In the full reports of each of the Project schools, which are available in the Headquarters Library of the American Library Association, there are lists of visitors by community represented and by category, e.g., librarians, supervisors, principals, and others. Many visitors came "wearing two hats," such as librarians who were also supervisors, curriculum directors who were also students in visiting classes, and principals who were also instructors in administration classes. Of interest, however, is the fact that, although they customarily represented a minority of any group visiting, it was librarians who, as a group, outnumbered any other single category of interest specialty. Students in teacher education and library science, who customarily visited in sizable groups, constituted what was probably the next largest group.

Not only was every state represented among visitors but every continent except Antarctica. Visitors came from Australia, twelve European, nine Asian, seven South American, and five African countries, in addition, of course, to the neighboring North American countries of Canada and Mexico. Sometimes foreign visitors on extensive tours of the United States had an opportunity to visit more than one of the Project schools. A group from Hawaii, representing the state department of education and several educational specialties, received special support from the Project to visit both Roosevelt High School and Farrer Junior High School in the spring of 1966. The original application from Hawaii had been for only one person, but negotiation and correspondence led to selection of a team so that this island state would have more than one person returning with word of the Project schools.

Correspondence relating to the plans for Project-supported visits was necessarily extensive. Although team leaders had signed statements agreeing with terms that dates of visits should not be changed (since team leaders usually were assigned the dates they had requested) and that the personnel of the team should remain as noted on the application, there were many requests for changes. To the extent possible, these were accommodated. Other changes were sometimes necessary because of emergencies either at the Project school or in the visitors' schools or because of hazardous driving or flying weather. To cite one school which was fairly typical: Thirty Project-supported visits were scheduled for the Mount Royal School; there were 32 changes of personnel, twelve changes of dates, and, finally, five cancellations of visits. The number of cancellations of Project-supported visits per Project school ranged from two to six, but, as noted earlier, the funds for team visits had been overallocated in total in the expectation of possible cancellations.

Another way of extending opportunities for educators to visit Project schools was to combine school visits with professional meetings. Arrangements for these were most often made by the Project schools, which were provided by the Project office with listings of national meetings to be held in their geographic areas. The financial investment for the Project ranged from the chartering of buses and reimbursement of transportation expenses to the provision of box lunches or other conveniences. Whenever possible, these visits were coordinated with other tours arranged by the pro-

fessional association sponsoring the conference. For example, during the International Reading Association meeting in Dallas in 1966, a busload of participants was scheduled to visit the Casis School, and the opportunity was announced through the advance program for IRA. Many more persons applied for the trip than could be accommodated, and some of these made the trip independently and joined the group at Casis.

In addition to regional and state library and education associations, such groups as the North Central Association of Colleges and Secondary Schools, the British Columbia Teachers Federation, the Department of Audiovisual Instruction, and the Catholic Library Association arranged visits. Because the visits had to be planned around the associations' conferences, it was sometimes necessary to accommodate these groups after school hours, on days during spring vacation, or on holidays. Sometimes the sheer size of the groups (up to three hundred persons) made it necessary to schedule the visits for times or days when the school library was not in operation. Nevertheless, because observation of ongoing program was the Project's main concern, these unusual schedules were set only as a last resort.

Perhaps it should be noted that the mobility of personnel, which handicapped some of the Project schools in full development of program, also caused changes and may have diluted the effect of visits made to Project schools. Team leaders took positions in other school districts or colleges within the year after their teams

A library secretary at Oak Park and River Forest High School lays out her work in the book processing area.

visited Project schools; occasionally later applications came from districts which had already received Project travel grants, in which it was evident that the members of the team had not fully communicated with other representatives of the school district or teacher education institution. On the other hand, dozens of letters and conversations indicate that when members of a team left one location they carried word of the Project on to the next place where they worked. The experience of visiting a school is a personal one as well as a professional one, and it is the people who visited who will, as individuals, accomplish the goals they have set for themselves as the result of the visit, whether or not the site of this accomplishment is the same school or community from which they set out for their visit.

Telling the story

It was with recognition of the fact that not all of the Project's goals could be achieved simply by demonstration that the fourth and last objective in the Project proposal read:

> To increase interest and support for school library development, among educators and citizens generally, by disseminating information about the demonstration programs and evaluating their effectiveness in reaching the stated goals.

Further itemized as parts of achieving this objective were participation on television and radio programs; production of articles; participation by Project Director, field workers, and staff members of the demonstration schools in conferences of professional and civic groups at national, state, and local levels; production of materials for use by observers, visiting teams, and other interested persons; publication of reports; and production of a film on elementary school library programs. Nowhere is the vision of the group who drew up this proposal more evident than in their enumeration of these activities, and, while evaluation of achievement of these purposes is perhaps necessarily the most long range of any objective, the tangible evidence all points to action and results in each item.

In the early days of the Project, a research consultant commented that opportunities to talk about the Project should be seized and that, while personnel were engaged in developing programs, they were the most enthusiastic speakers and writers. Yet it is hard to draw the line between searching out opportunities for talking about the Project and seeking the limelight for oneself. Furthermore, at the time the Project was getting under way, invitations to talk were more limited, and those that did come in had to compete for time with the demands on staff development of plans for the Project schools. These factors were operative not only for the Project Director, but for personnel at all of the Project schools.

Attendance and talks at state, regional, and national conferences were encouraged to the extent possible. Among the associations to which one or more Project personnel reported were the American Library Association, National Education Association, International Reading Association, Association for Supervision and Curriculum Development, and Department of Elementary School Principals, to mention only a few at the national level. The representation of geographic areas among the audiences gives a truer picture of geographic coverage than does the listing of sites for talks, and this representation was inclusive of every state. As the Project gained recognition, talks by Project personnel, members of the Project Advisory Committee, and others tended to refer to Project materials, Project schools, and opportunities to participate in the Project so that correspondence and visits were the inevitable result, and they in turn often started the cycle of invitations again.

Although no national network television and radio programs were arranged, many local programs featured not only Project personnel but occasionally visitors to Project schools. One Seattle television program, Marty Camp's "What's New in the Schoolhouse?" featured the principal, librarian, and field worker from the Marcus Whitman School. On the recommendation of viewers, a kinescope of this program was edited and distributed by the Project through the Chicago office of Modern Talking Picture Service, Inc., and, again as the result of requests, prints of the kinescopes were sold.

Besides maintaining an extensive mailing list of editors of the educational and library press, the Project office was the origin of many articles, brochures, photographs, and other materials which were distributed on request. Not all of these articles stemmed directly from experience or reports on the Project, but they did relate to school libraries. For example, the January, 1966, issue of *The Bulletin of the National Association of Secondary-School Principals* carried not only an article by the Project Director about the secondary schools which had applied for Phase III, but also an article by the superintendent-principal at Oak Park and River Forest High School; seven of the fourteen other articles in the issue were written by people who served at some time on the Project Advisory Committee. Similarly, the March, 1966, issue of *Education* featured a section on school libraries with one of the Project field workers as guest editor. Of the eight articles included, four were written by persons associated with the Project—the Project Director, the chairman of the Advisory Committee, a Project school librarian, and a field worker.

Articles written especially about the Project, which appeared in national publications, are listed in this publication. In many cases, the articles provide details that have not been repeated in this final report. One of the continuing means of reporting the Project to the membership of the American Association of School Librarians was established at the time the Project was initiated. It was agreed that the Association's official publication, *School Libraries,* at first with Mr. John Rowell and later with Miss Frances Fleming, as editors, would carry an article about the Project in each of its four issues a year. This practice continued throughout the Project, with a shift of authorship from the Project Director to personnel in Project schools as the Project entered its last months of demonstration.

It has been impossible to keep completely informed of the many publications referring to the Project. Many articles in consumer publications and general periodicals included references to the Project or were stimulated by interest in the Project. Such varied sources as yearbooks of the Project schools, daily newspapers in visitors' home communities, and state professional association publications are only a few of the places where the Project was featured. An effort to reach a larger number of papers or periodicals was mounted about midway through the Project, when a contract was let to a public relations firm for placement and clipping service on an article accompanied by photographs to be sent to editors on request. Although the uses of the article and photos spanned several months and led to other queries for materials from the Project office, the article was most heavily used by editors who already had featured the Project prominently.

The articles mentioned above were often reprinted for distribution from the Project office. These reprints served not only as interim reports on the Project but also as replies to requests for specific information and as materials to be distributed to visitors to Project schools, participants at conferences, and other correspondents. Reprints of reprints were often needed for the more popular items. A compilation of articles about the Project which had appeared in *School Libraries* between January, 1963, and May, 1965, for example, was first printed in a quantity of five thousand, but within seven months that supply was exhausted and another ten thousand copies were ordered. The fact that many of these were distributed in single copies and in small numbers from the Project office means that the mailing and handling routines required more time than might otherwise be necessary. However, throughout the Project, an attempt was made to keep a fairly steady flow of materials of general interest directed toward the persons on the Project office mailing list. At first, there were the brochures announcing opportunities to apply for Project participation or to visit Project schools. Then came reprints of articles from *School Library Journal,* the "Guidelines" developed by the Project Advisory Committee, and announcements of the Project's film, filmstrips, and first book, *Impact: The School Library and the Instructional Program.* Following these were proceedings of Project-sponsored conferences, more reprints, and announcement of this publication.

The Project story has been told through more than one medium.

One of the most popular items distributed by the Project was ''Guidelines,'' a statement developed during the special meeting of members and former members of the Project Advisory Committee. This is reprinted in this publication in the appendix. Handicapped by lack of a title for easy reference, the brochure of guidelines has been widely quoted and acclaimed. Some evidence of its popularity can be judged from the fact that from its issuance in July, 1966, through November, 1967, more than 35,000 copies have been distributed. In most instances, Project brochures or reprints were available free for single copies and at prices which covered printing costs for larger quantities. The original Project budget had included funds for publications of this kind, and the reimbursement of some funds through payment for multiple copies simply made possible the production of more materials.

During the years that schools participated in the Project, they were continuously supplied with materials to distribute to visitors. The handbook for Project personnel listed these, and representatives of each school were sent samples of the materials available and were asked to indicate which ones they wished to have for distribution. This was to give them opportunity to feature the materials they found most helpful or most popular for visitors. In practice, however, the individuals responsible for materials in each school tended to ask for replacement of everything at one time, so there seemed to be little indication of relative usefulness. Many of the materials which were supplied had originated with the committees or staff of the American Association of School Librarians or with the School Library Development Project.

As materials became dated or inaccurate, they were removed from the files of materials available. Project schools varied considerably in the amount of materials they requested and used. Undoubtedly their handling of these materials—the attractiveness of the display, the time provided for visitors actually to choose what they wanted, the advance preparation of folders or envelopes in some instances—was the

cause for considerable fluctuation in the amounts and kinds of materials they used.

One of the recommendations made to Project schools at the time they began to participate in the Project was that they plan to produce a brochure or booklet that would help to orient visitors to their school and school district and that would also be useful as a mailing piece for others who might not have opportunity to visit the school. Response to this recommendation varied considerably. The Marcus Whitman School produced two different booklets during its two years of Project participation, and Central Park Road School printed one. The only school in Phase II that produced a booklet was the Allisonville School; this came out early in its first year of Project participation. In Phase III, both Roosevelt High School and Oak Park and River Forest High School prepared booklets during the first year of Project participation. The latter two proved to be especially popular and have been added to many library collections and used for references in school library courses as well as in in-service programs and elsewhere. To some extent, the Project subsidized each of these publications as another means of publicizing the program.

Because colored slides, audio tapes, transparencies, and other audio-visual materials were often incorporated into the orientation sessions or other presentations at each Project school, there were frequent requests from visitors and others for the loan or purchase of these materials. Visitors who brought their own cameras were often disappointed because their pictures did not tell the story they had hoped they would. Yet time and money were involved in providing for extensive duplication and loan of each Project school's materials. Sometimes, too, the principal or field worker at a Project school preferred to change the selection of slides to highlight different activities at different times, or had favorites among the available slides which might not be used as effectively by others. Several of the Project schools made exploratory moves toward developing filmstrips about their own programs, but the time and planning necessary for this were apparently never available. Five filmstrips were planned and their production sponsored by the Project. Each was a sound filmstrip with accompanying record, and each was produced in color by Jack O'Callaghan of Filmwrights in Chicago.

The first of these filmstrips, *Living School Libraries,* appeared as a progress report on the Project early in 1965. It included scenes from the Phase I and Phase II schools, but referred only to the plans for selection of Phase III schools. *Living School Libraries* was planned as a timely report; as such, it became dated within a few months. It was distributed for sale by the Publishing Department of the American Library Association, as were the other four filmstrips; after two printings of five hundred copies each, it was allowed to go out of print within the year.

In July, 1966, *Three for Tomorrow,* a filmstrip about the three schools participating in Phase III of the Project, was produced. In this case, the producer actually visited the schools and included taped comments by school personnel in the narration to accompany the frames, which showed scenes in the schools and neighboring communities. Critical acceptance of this filmstrip and its extensive use in in-service programs and other activities caused it to go into a second printing within six months.

The title, *Focus on Three,* was given to a set of three filmstrips released in July, 1967. Each of these filmstrips, individually titled and available separately for purchase, presented one of the elementary schools participating in Phase II of the Project. The filmstrip titles are: *Allisonville Evaluates, Mount Royal the Inner City,* and *Casis Reading Guidance Program.* Because of the proved need and popularity of the two earlier filmstrips, the first printing of these filmstrips was larger than that of the first two. Following conclusion of the Project in 1968, the last four filmstrips, *Three for Tomorrow* and the three included in *Focus on Three,* will continue to be distributed by the ALA Publishing Department until the American Association of School Librarians decides to withdraw them from the market.

By far the most ambitious single undertaking of the Project in terms of media was sponsored of production of a film on the library program of an elementary school. Plans for this film were going forward during the first year of the Project simultaneously with the selection of the Phase I schools. Because of an agreement with the offices of the American Book Publishers Council, the Project benefited from the consultant assistance of Miss Virginia Mathews, member of the Project Advisory Committee and deputy director of National Library Week. During the spring and summer of 1963, Miss Mathews viewed many documentary and educational films and interviewed a number of film producers. The Advisory Committee delegated major responsibility for decisions about the film to the chairman of the Advisory Committee, the Project Director, and Miss Mathews. On Miss Mathews's recommendation, Guggenheim Productions, Inc.—at that time of St. Louis, Missouri, and later of Washington, D. C. —was selected to produce the film.

Much discussion by the Advisory Committee centered on the concept and intended audience for the film. Consensus was that the intent of the production of the film should be to reach the largest possible audience of the lay public through television and group showings. While the film was widely used by professional groups, classes, and others, this goal of reaching and stimulating groups of adults was also fully achieved.

In the early weeks of the 1963-64 school year, the three representatives of the Advisory Committee visited elementary schools which might serve as sites for the film. Most of the visits followed up earlier correspondence with school librarians, school library supervisors, and superintendents. Because schools did not apply for this selection, as they did for Project participation, the selection had to be based on thorough search and determination of such factors as (1) the library's accommodation of camera equipment, (2) the ability of faculty and students to maintain their usual program in spite of demands of the filming, (3) the racial integration of the student body, and, above all, (4) an effective library program serving the entire school. Elementary schools in eight states were visited and many more

Miss Anna Fehl introduces the television audience to the Mount Royal School library as
Miss M. Bernice Wiese, director of library services, and Mrs. Alice Rusk, library specialist,
await their turns to comment.

were considered before the Sedgefield School in Charlotte, North Carolina, was selected. The interest and support of the school library supervisor, Miss Gertrude Coward, and of the entire administrative staff of the school district proved to be invaluable assets as filming began in April, 1964. To keep the responses of children and teachers as spontaneous as possible and to permit the film crew freedom in selecting scenes for the film, a shooting script was developed, but no dialog was written for the film participants to follow. Also, as part of the effort to keep the film credible and natural, all children and adults shown in it actually were students or teachers at the Sedgefield School. No professional actors or other outsiders were used.

In December, 1963, the three representatives of the Advisory Committee and the executive secretary of the American Association of School Librarians, who was also a member of the committee, met with Charles Guggenheim of Guggenheim Productions and drafted these thirteen basic points to be depicted in the film:

1. The good school library program takes place throughout the school, not in the library quarters alone.

2. The school library program is important in providing individual guidance to pupils.

3. The school library is an instructional materials center and the program employs a full range of materials.

4. The teacher and the librarian work closely together as a team. In the case of the elementary school, this is the classroom teacher.

5. The group and class use of the library for projects, and especially library instruction and use of library materials, are important elements of the school library program.

6. The primary or central function of the school library is to serve all the children in the school in relation to all subject fields.

7. The child is not only a pupil in the school, but a citizen of the community, and there is a relationship between the school and the public library in serving him.

8. The interested adults in the community are responsible for seeing to it that there is good school library service in the school.

9. The program and the materials of the school library serve the curricular needs of the particular school first and foremost, but should enable the child to explore and develop beyond the confines of the curriculum.

10. The school librarian is a faculty member responsible to the principal as are all other members of the faculty in his building. The school librarian takes part with all of the faculty members in common re-

sponsibilities relating to curriculum development and other professional tasks.

11. The centralized school library offers advantages over the self-contained, isolated classroom library units *alone*. In a school with a good centralized library program, there will also be a range of books and other materials in the classroom from the central collection. In other words, the central school library and the availability of books and other materials in each classroom are not mutually exclusive concepts.

12. One of the most important things about the school library program is that it meets the needs of each individual child. It meets each child at the point of his particular need, ability, and interest and enables him to follow more readily his own pattern of learning.

13. The school library has a role in reaching the very youngest child in the primary grades. This is particularly important at a time when so many urban children are from culturally deprived homes and need all the skills of a trained librarian, and all of the materials that can be provided to help them to develop the verbal skills and concepts that will enable them to make the transition into the middle-class learning environment.

It should be noted that these points were really a record of discussion and decisions which gave guidance to the producer. They were not prepared for publication, but are included here as a matter of record and as a basis for determining the extent to which these points were successfully incorporated into the film. One point, which was finally withdrawn, was the plan to show the interrelationships between school and public library. Although representatives of the public library in Charlotte were consulted at the time the Sedgefield School was selected as the film site, the difficulties of production on several sites and the lack of professional staff in the children's room in the neighboring branch library led to the decision to omit actual public library scenes.

The formal premiere of the film was a part of the American Library Association conference in St. Louis, Missouri, Monday evening, June 29, 1964. The title of this twenty-eight-minute 16-millimeter color film is . . . *And Something More*. The title refers to a section of the narration of the film which notes that a school with a library has something more to offer to children and teachers, that the librarian also offers something more in her services and interest, and that there are more varieties of materials than books or printed materials alone to interest, inspire, and inform the child.

On the occasion of the premiere, one commercial film distributor commented that sales of it could optimistically be predicted to reach three hundred prints within three years. No effort was made to recover any portion of production costs. Prints have been sold by Guggenheim Productions, Inc., in cooperation with the Project office, and the suggested goal of three hundred prints within three years was achieved. A program aid or discussion guide for use with the film was prepared and distributed by the fall of 1964 to assist persons planning to use the film in programs.

In September, 1964, the Project entered into an agreement with Modern Talking Picture Service, Inc., to provide for the extensive free loan of the film to groups and individuals. It was recognized that although professional groups of librarians, teachers, and others might schedule the film through the many universities, school districts, and other agencies which had purchased it, there were service clubs, labor unions, school classes, and many other kinds of groups that would be more likely to use the film if it were available through the offices of Modern. Television showings could also be booked in this way. By October 31, 1967, the conservative estimate of television viewers through showings arranged by various Modern offices was of 11,680,100 persons. In addition to television showings arranged by Modern, there were network presentations and wide use on educational and independent stations. More than four thousand showings to audiences totalling more than 200,000 persons had also been arranged by Modern Talking Picture Service during the same period of three years. The agreement for Modern to continue to book the film will be continued through June, 1969, at which time the board of the American Association of School Librarians will decide whether to extend the agreement.

Bookings, purchases, and comments from viewers quickly proved the popularity of the film, but critical acclaim was also welcomed. These are the film's outstanding recognitions:

Blue Ribbon Award from the American Film Festival, May, 1965.

Citation by Landers Associates as one of one hundred excellent films of 1964, received in 1965.

Golden Eagle from the Council on International Nontheatrical Events, Inc. (CINE) as one of the one hundred films from the United States declared eligible and recommended for participation in international festivals and competitions, 1965.

Citation as one of the seventy-five Most Honored Films of 1965, from *Business Screen* magazine.

Certificate of participation in the Edinburgh International Conference on Education, 1965.

Citation for showing in Brussels International Week for Education and Teaching Films, 1966.

Silver Medal and Honor Diploma from the Fifth Festival Internacional de Cinema Infantile de La Argentina, La Plata, 1966.

At the time the Knapp Project was started in 1963, there was a recognized dearth of materials, especially in the non-print forms, about school library programs. By 1967, it was possible, though surely not desirable, for a group to schedule more than two straight hours of viewing the Project-sponsored filmstrips, film, and kinescope. With the discussions these were intended to stimulate, the bulk of a day's program could easily be devoted to the Project materials alone. The reprints, brochures, and other materials emanating from the Project could also provide additional hours of reading time. These means of reaching individuals and groups who might never observe Project schools appeared to be most successful.

For each of the Project schools, a fact sheet was prepared and revised as needed, to provide visitors and others with a single document for quick reference. The last revisions of these fact sheets appear in front of each school's report in this publication, so that the reader can refer to facts and figures as he follows the report on the school.

Conclusion

Although not spelled out as Project objectives, there are two far-reaching results which must be mentioned here. In the past five years, the dramatic increase of interest in demonstration programs in education has some causal relationship to the Knapp Project. Sometimes the instigators of such programs have acknowledged that their plans were modeled on the Knapp Project. Even more frequently, participants in such projects have requested copies of the Project handbook, consultant assistance, or extensive correspondence to answer questions or to solve problems which arise as their plans progress. Some estimate of the extent and number of these projects can be made from the fact that in the 1967-68 school year, twenty-nine states had reserved a portion of their Title II Elementary and Secondary Education Act funds for special-purpose grants, many of which were demonstration programs very similar to the Knapp Project in plan and execution.

A second outcome of the Project results from its success, as recognized by the donor, the Knapp Foundation, Inc., and also from the fact that the Project touched and probed problems beyond its immediate concern. The need for a study of the many kinds of manpower needed in contemporary school librarianship was recognized by the Knapp Foundation, as the result of experiences in the Knapp School Libraries

Cue slate snaps as cameras roll for the Project-sponsored film, . . . And Something More.

Project, and in November, 1967, the Foundation made a grant of $1,163,718 to the American Library Association for a second five-year project. This School Library Manpower Project, according to the American Library Association press release of December 1, 1967, ". . . is designed to attack three aspects of the problem of developing fully and utilizing properly school library manpower—task and job analysis, education for school librarianship and recruitment from specific manpower pools."

The conception, development, and achievement of the main objectives of the Knapp School Libraries Project have been made possible by many people, not least among them the fifteen persons who served on the Project Advisory Committee from 1962 throughout the Project. Leaders named from the membership of the American Association of School Librarians, they carried the responsibilities of demanding full-time positions and many other professional responsibilities in addition to their contributions to the Knapp Project. They received no financial benefit from participation but they were without exception generous not only with ideas, criticism, and time, but also with the freedom which they encouraged the Project Director and other Project personnel to exercise. Committee meetings when Project applications were under consideration were long and exhausting, and there were more demands made when materials in draft form had to be evaluated. The membership of the Advisory Committee included five persons appointed and three who served *ex officio* because of their positions as president, president-elect, and executive secretary of the American Association of School Librarians. Conservatively estimated, these members probably averaged one week each year of work on behalf of the Project. The chairmen and members who took added assignments or responsibilities (e.g., participating on readiness teams, consulting on the film, recruiting the Project Director) probably tripled or quadrupled that amount of time. Some of them had had as their first task the development of the Project proposal; then came selection of the Project Director, establishment of policies for selection of schools,

actual selection of the schools, development of "Guidelines" (page 322), and plans for conclusion of the Project. Although their major concern was policy, their interest and concern spread to many of the details of procedure for the Project, and their insights and experience made those procedures work.

The actual staff of the Project office had been envisioned as small, with a director and secretary as the only full-time persons on the staff of the American Library Association in Chicago. Unanticipated travel demands for the Project Director and other responsibilities led, in 1964, to the appointment of an administrative assistant. Later, there were only two secretaries and the director. It was recognized from the outset that much of the initiative and stimulus for the Project's program would have to come from the schools and colleges participating, and the paid staff at the Project office was intentionally limited. Access to assistance from many other specialists on the staff of the American Library Association made this size of staff feasible, since the services of a Project accountant, part-time clerical assistance, public relations counsel, library service, and other personnel were available. Another feature of the Project was the fact that the concept of demonstration programs was so attractive that the staff of the Project could maintain a high degree of enthusiasm because of the opportunities to participate, often vicariously, in educational programs of purpose and value.

In the fine print of the Project proposal, there is reference to the hope that one of the Project outcomes may be "Heightened professional competence of the Project Director . . ." To work with the highly competent members of the Advisory Committee, to be a member of the ALA staff, to travel not only to conferences and meetings but to individual school libraries and classrooms, to meet not only leaders but able representatives of many phases of education, and to serve in a position which often challenged the Director's capabilities—these have been opportunities which should have heightened that professional competence. They are privileges which this Director has deeply appreciated and can never forget.

Report on *Impact*:
The School Library and the Instructional Program

CENTRAL PARK ROAD SCHOOL
and
TEACHERS COLLEGE, COLUMBIA UNIVERSITY

MARCUS WHITMAN SCHOOL
and
EASTERN WASHINGTON STATE COLLEGE

FACT SHEET—CENTRAL PARK ROAD SCHOOL

Location

Gerhard Road, Plainview, Nassau County, Long Island, New York. Accessible from the Long Island Expressway and from Hicksville station, Long Island R.R.

Personnel

Mrs. Virginia Tozier, Librarian   Dr. Robert F. Savitt, Superintendent, Central School District #4

Mr. Leonard Kramer, Principal   Mrs. Julia Hartmann, Library Supervisor for School District

Enrollment, 1962-1963

592 pupils, grades kindergarten through six. School district total enrollment is 10,119 pupils, in 9 elementary and 2 secondary schools.

Financial Support

Expenditure per elementary pupil, Central School District, 1962-1963: $652.80.

National average expenditure per elementary and secondary pupil: $432.00.

New York State average expenditure per elementary and secondary pupil: $645.00.

Total expenditure for library materials, Central Park Road School 1962-1963: $2,782.00.

Instructional Materials Collection

6,143 books, 48 periodicals, 442 filmstrips, 75 recordings, plus 200 professional books for teachers. A district-wide professional book collection supplements this.

Special Features

Rapport between librarian and faculty.

The library's contributions to closed-circuit television.

Creative use of a classroom-size 800-square-foot library, expanded into nearby rooms in 1963.

Well-selected, curriculum-related collection of library materials.

School district processing center.

Contributions Made by the Knapp Project Grant

Purchase of one additional book per child per year.

Salary of an additional librarian.

Salary of a clerical assistant.

Purchase of additional audio-visual materials and equipment.

Half-time salary and other expenses of half-time field worker appointed by Columbia University.

Contributions for workshops for faculty, student teachers, etc.

PARTICIPATING COLLEGE

Teachers College, Columbia University

Personnel

Dr. Robert J. Schaefer, Dean

Dr. Paul Witt, field worker for this project

Special Features

Library collection of 300,000 volumes in field of education, in addition to 42,000 textbooks, 17,000 courses of study, approximately 700 juvenile books, and programmed instruction aids, filmstrips, recordings, and other instructional materials.

A team of specialists who will work under the direction of the field worker to plan and conduct workshops, visits by teams of administrators and other interested personnel, and other activities in connection with this project.

FACT SHEET—MARCUS WHITMAN SCHOOL

Location

615 Snow Avenue, Richland, Washington, near Hanford Atomic Energy Project. Accessible by air, Pasco Tri-Cities Airport, or via U. S. Routes 410 and 395.

Personnel

Mrs. Elsie Pitts, Librarian

Mr. James LeClair, Principal

Mr. Robert L. Chisholm, Superintendent, Richland School District

Enrollment, 1962-1963

771 pupils, grades kindergarten through six, including 16 students in Special Education. School district total enrollment is 7,565, in 6 elementary and 3 secondary schools.

Financial Support

Expenditure per elementary pupil, Richland School District, 1962-1963: $435.08.

National average expenditure per elementary and secondary pupil: $432.00.

Washington state average expenditure per elementary and secondary pupil: $488.00.

Total expenditure for library materials, Marcus Whitman School 1962-1963: $2,536.51.

Instructional Materials Collection

7,592 books, 10 periodicals, 600 filmstrips, 400 recordings, plus 378 professional books for teachers.

Special Features

Emphasis on development of the instructional materials center.

Projected plan for librarian to serve as curriculum consultant to the faculty.

Well-planned program of library instruction at all grade levels.

Effective use and planned additions to the 1,275-square-foot library.

Contributions Made by the Knapp Grant

Purchase of 600 additional books per year.

Salary of an additional librarian.

Salary of a clerical assistant.

Purchase of additional audio-visual materials and equipment.

Half-time salary and other expenses of half-time field worker appointed by Eastern Washington State College.

Contributions for workshops for faculty, student teachers, etc.

PARTICIPATING COLLEGE

Eastern Washington State College

Personnel

Dr. Roland Lewis, Head, Division of Education, Psychology, Philosophy

Mrs. Anna W. Beachner, field worker for this project

Special Features

A tradition of cooperative workshops, consultant service, institutes, and programs for student teachers with school districts throughout the area, including Richland.

Emphasis on instructional materials in courses for teachers, administrators, and curriculum specialists.

Library collection of 37,000 volumes in the field of education, in addition to audio-visual materials and 5,350 volumes for children and adolescents.

ASSESSMENT AND PLANNING

The two schools which participated in Phase I of the Project were the Central Park Road School in Plainview, New York, and the Marcus Whitman School in Richland, Washington. Their selection was announced at a coast-to-coast press conference in New York City and Richland in June, 1963.

The budget provided to each school by the Project placed major emphasis on personnel, and the schools were strongly encouraged to increase their holdings and use of non-print materials. Because of the limited time before the schools were to function as demonstration centers, the Project budget had allowed no funds for physical enlargement, renovation, or furnishing of the library. At Central Park Road, the classroom-size library which had housed an unusually creative library program was replaced by a larger suite, formerly two kindergarten classrooms. During the summer of 1963, shelving, study carrels, and teachers' work area were installed. The school district had agreed to finance this improvement.

At Marcus Whitman, the physical layout of the library had also been a handicap, but had not limited the sound development of a library program nor the ability to dream and plan for the future. As stated in its application, "Though the present library room is fairly large, it is not supplemented by a good workroom, or conference room, or storage area. Ideally, the present room should be widened from its present twenty feet, and the before-mentioned facilities added. More realistic, however, would be the re-designing of the present area for storage, workroom, and professional library into a workroom. Then a large classroom near the library could be converted into the audio-visual storage and a conference room. There is a classroom now available, and projected enrollment indicates it will not be needed for a regular classroom, so it can be remodeled for library use." These changes were accomplished with funds provided by the school district during the summer of 1963.

Much of the character of both schools is best stated in their applications, in response to quer-ies about the strong and weak points of their present library program, and about their long-range goals if selected for Project participation. The assessment of relative strengths and weaknesses varied as the schools participated in the Project, and some assessments are at variance with other professional viewpoints. In response to the question, "Assess as objectively as you can the strong and weak points of your current library program (See *Standards for School Library Programs*, Chapter 3)," Marcus Whitman School listed:

The strong points

1. Full-time trained librarian
2. Some clerical help
3. Approximately 10 books per pupil
4. Professional library for teachers, including two daily newspapers
5. Good audio-visual aids
   (a) Filmstrip library; 7 projectors
   (b) Record collection in building; record players available in classrooms
   (c) Other aids such as bioscope, overhead projectors, tape recorders
6. Centrally located library, closer to upper elementary grades
7. Library open before and after school for both teachers and students
8. Student assistants
9. Library Club sponsored by librarian

The weak points

1. Only one librarian for over 700 pupils
2. Lack of proportioned furniture
3. Inadequate storage and work area
4. Lack of conference rooms
5. Insufficient clerical help
6. Insufficient recent reference materials
7. Inadequate flat picture and pamphlet files
8. Library room too narrow
9. No display area in or near library

To the same question, Central Park Road School replied:

The strong points

This is an experimental school with a background of modern education which re-

Mrs. Elaine Mazza works with her class in a search for materials on geology at Central Park Road.

quires superior library service, and which in turn provides an excellent chance for the development of new and more effective library services.

For the past year and a half, we have had flexible scheduling in the intermediate grades with two periods each day for all teachers in grades 4, 5, and 6 to sign up for the library, so that they may come with their class to work with the librarian as their class does special reading assignments or research projects. Many of these periods begin with a review of—or instruction in—library skills or the books to be used.

Periods are also set aside for book exchange every day for all pupils in these grades, and six periods a week for individuals to come from these grades for reading and special projects or research. Slow readers come from time to time for special periods to discuss interesting books with the librarian and to select books from among those recommended by the librarian.

The third grade comes once each week to get books and to have a lesson or story read, while the first and second grades come every other week. Kindergarten classes come several times a year. For the most part this has allowed us to teach the use of the library

and of books as children are ready to use them for their class work. Teaching something the children know they need to understand right away makes all the difference, we are convinced.

Since we have a state-supported experiment in team teaching under way, the librarian with the teacher team prepared a large group lesson on "How to Use the *Readers' Guide to Periodical Literature*," which was presented to a group of three sixth grade classes in the assembly hall with complete satisfaction as to the results. We have used our closed circuit TV to give a lesson on "How to Use the Card Catalog" to twelve intermediate classes simultaneously with a follow-up test in the library.

Results seemed to show that it was a more successful lesson than when done in person for individual classes. All grades have had a series of book talks on TV, each one of which produced immediate results in the library circulation. Stories told on TV seem as effective as, if not more effective than, when done in person. For some lessons and book talks a puppet was used on TV, proving highly successful in making the library programs more interesting. The librarian has also conducted a "Book Lovers Club" on TV.

A display case and three bulletin boards outside the library in the hall, and two bulletin boards in the library, are used to feature book covers and special exhibits to promote reading.

Loans are made to classrooms as needed—for as long as needed—and classroom librarians who change every few weeks are selected by the students.

A group of 20 sixth grade library helpers has been organized and trained and greatly assists the librarian. Under the sponsorship of the P.T.A., a special group of books on sex education is circulated to parents for use with their children. Magazines are loaned to teachers on a regular basis each weekend.

The librarian was able to help in improving the curriculum in social studies by providing a large collection of United Nations materials and by influencing the greatly expanded teaching of this subject in every grade. It is now becoming a real part of many other units studied.

Materials are also provided team teachers and those preparing educational TV lessons. In many cases research in the library serves as an excellent follow-up for individuals and classes.

The weak points

Doing all these things takes a great deal of time. It means that the librarian's day is one or two hours longer than the teacher's day, and she has a 20 to 30 minute lunch period and no free time at all during the day.

All ordering of books, preparing of lessons, professional reading, and many other activities must be done at home outside of school hours.

Each experimental library-TV program takes a great deal of time at this stage, since the problems are new and there is no precedent for procedure. All such time, except for conferences and rehearsals, also comes from outside of school hours. Consequently, in order to continue or to expand the number of lessons and TV programs, the library requires additional staffing.

Much more time is needed by the librarian to work with teachers in finding material for the teams, for TV programs, and for regular class work. There are many more activities that are traditionally carried on in the library that might be suitable for TV if time were available to experiment.

Teachers in the experimental programs especially need the librarian to work with them individually and in group situations in order to make the librarian's knowledge of book resources available to them. With the curriculum work presently going on, two or three teacher groups are frequently meeting at the same time making it impossible for one librarian to adequately serve them. Furthermore the librarian is busy in the library during all of the school day when many meetings are held.

To a following question, "What long range outcomes does the school hope to achieve through participation in this program? (Identify desired effects or goals for pupils, teachers, other schools in the system, etc.)," the reply from Marcus Whitman was:

Section 20 [of the application] includes or implies the effects of an extended library program within the Marcus Whitman School. Section 12 notes that Richland's leadership role in southeastern Washington will bring this project to the attention of a number of school districts.

If such a demonstration center were provided in one school, the Richland School District would have some research-in-action to discover whether some of the recommended functions of a library are feasible within our schools. Staff and community readiness could be measured and relative values of certain facets of a total program could be compared. We would hope to test in the Richland schools the following:

1. Will an extension of our present library services bring about an improvement in reading skills and appreciation?
2. Will there also be a growth in over-all educational achievement?
3. If there is sufficient staff, can a librarian act in the capacity of a curriculum coordinator?
4. Does an instructional resources center effectively implement the curriculum within the school?
5. Can an instructional secretary be utilized to implement the use and correlation of audio-visual materials when such personnel prepare materials for teachers?
6. Can children in the elementary school engage in self-directed study through listening and viewing media in a library?
7. Can some supplementary book collections be practically shared among several buildings?

Girls at Marcus Whitman pause in their summer outdoor activities to enjoy a recording in the school library.

8. Will functional research and preview areas promote more staff study and planning?

9. Can parent information and participation be promoted within an instructional resources center?

And from Central Park Road:

Goals for pupils

1. To teach them to use the school library effectively in learning the lessons their teachers present, and to foster their learning beyond the textbook—in many subjects.

2. To encourage independent investigation in new or related areas.

3. To develop the voluntary reading of worthwhile books which are appropriate to the child's growing level of maturity and reading skill.

4. To help each child acquire a rich background of reading experience, and through various methods promote taste in reading and literary appreciation.

5. To promote the habit of using a library frequently—even daily.

Goals for teachers

1. Show them individually and in groups how to use library materials most effectively.

2. Help them to plan for research activities and to find material they can use in preparing class or group lessons.

3. Participate in curriculum meetings to make known available library material.

4. Make them acquainted with the content of some of the many useful and high-quality children's books.

Goals to help other school systems

1. To work out some of the ways the new media can be used to solve old library problems.

2. To develop effective TV lessons and large group lessons, and so free the library room for different and perhaps new patterns of use.

3. To see how a flexible schedule makes possible the use of library books when needed—and not at some arbitrarily set later date.

4. To see if more frequent library use can save duplication of material and so save money and space.

The specific long range goal—toward the attainment of which we seek assistance—is the freeing of a major portion of the curriculum from the narrow boundaries set by textbooks. We are viewing textbooks in many areas as limiting factors in the development of the vital program we deem necessary.

The teacher education institutions which were selected for the Project, Eastern Washington State College at Cheney with Marcus Whitman, and Teachers College of Columbia University with Central Park Road, required some special administrative adjustments in the assignments of the field workers. Because the curriculum coordinator for the Richland Public Schools had been the supervisor of student teachers from Eastern Washington for the past five years, and because the college and the school were some eighty miles apart, the assignment of the curriculum coordinator as field worker was a logical one. During the two years of Project participation, she served as field worker on a half-time basis and as the district's curriculum consultant on a half-time basis. The size of the faculty at Teachers College prompted the request in the application for a team approach to the assignment of the field worker, with one professor or associate professor coordinating the college's work in the Project.

An impromptu puppet play attracts an audience at Central Park Road.

REVIEW OF FIRST YEAR

At the end of the 1963-64 school year, each of the staffs in the Project met with the Project Director to assess progress and to chart plans for the remaining year of Project participation. With the agenda prepared in advance, each person had had an opportunity to cite strengths and weaknesses of the program to date. Of paramount interest at this time was the possibility that some of these suggestions could be of value to the Phase II schools, whose selection had just been announced.

The discussion at Marcus Whitman noted:

The surprising speed with which students had begun to use the new library laboratory (the library's expanded area), especially as a follow-up to televised instruction.

The contributions of the library coordinating council (the group which included one teacher representing each grade level).

Progress in grading the standardized tests which had been administered to students at Marcus Whitman and at a neighboring school where a similar library program had existed, but which had not received the Project assistance that Marcus Whitman did; the plan to study, by item analysis, some test responses which would have special relevance for the library program.

Observation of marked increases in students' development of listening and viewing skills.

Difficulty of isolating effects of the Project and of the increased use of the television program on language arts, both of which had had positive impact on reading interest and appreciation.

Improvement in the orientation which students from Eastern Washington State College received when the field worker provided a full period of orientation prior to their visits to Marcus Whitman.

Plans for the future, including:

(a) Encouragement of more visits from representatives of the State Department of Public Instruction.

(b) More frequent consultation with the Project Director.

(c) Further development of flexible scheduling of library use.

(d) Effort to provide more first-hand information to parents by encouraging

their visits by grade levels during the school day and by devoting two parent-teacher association meetings to the library in the 1964-65 school year.

(e) Selection and purchase of more earphones and more tape recordings (with a wistful note about the corresponding need for more room).

(f) A three-day summer workshop for Marcus Whitman faculty to be conducted by staff from Central Washington State College.

(g) Adjustment of work schedules of library staff, especially to provide the instructional secretary with more time to work on preparation of materials.

(h) Giving student teachers from Eastern Washington State College priority in assignment to Marcus Whitman for their student teaching experience.

(i) Proposal for a teacher education institute, to which representatives of each teacher education institution in the state would be invited.

At the Central Park Road School, discussion centered on:

The interest and support aroused by featuring the library at the parent-teachers association meeting in October, 1963, and follow-up provided by grade-level parents' visits led by the principal.

Presentations about the Project made at state and national meetings of the Association for Supervision and Curriculum Development.

Priority which this Project has received from the district, which had two other major projects under way (a cooperative one on an educational communications center and one on team-teaching).

Needs or problems including:

(a) The need for one librarian to be clearly and consistently designated as head librarian with full authority.

(b) Further flexibility in all of the instructional program.

(c) Recruitment of an assistant librarian to replace the one who had been assigned to the school for the 1963-64 year.

(d) Scheduling of visitors to observe classroom instruction.

Identifying shells is easier when a book and a librarian, Mrs. Virginia Tozier, help a young collector.

(e) Arranging for more group visits by teacher education students during the 1964-65 school year.

(f) Necessity of abandoning the plan for a summer library program in 1964.

(g) Importance of briefing visitors about the plan for the day, etc., which should take priority over first demonstration session in the library if necessary.

(h) Expected improvement in scheduling with change of school-opening hour to 9:15 A.M. in 1964-65, as contrasted with the 8:15 A.M. opening.

(i) Assignment of a representative from Teachers College on a more regular basis to inform Teachers College and other neighboring teacher education institutions about the Project, to work for closer relationship between library and classroom activities, and to direct the work of another Teachers College graduate student who would assume more responsibility for visitors, especially those in teams receiving Project support.

EFFECTS OF PROJECT PARTICIPATION

Final reports from Plainview, New York, and Richland, Washington, were received in the summer of 1965. The report for Marcus Whitman School, prepared by Mrs. Anna M. Beachner, incorporated the report of Eastern Washington State College. The report from the Central Park Road School was prepared by Dr. William J. Nelligan, assistant superintendent, and Mr. Leonard Kramer, principal; that of Teachers College, Columbia University, by Dr. Paul W. F. Witt and Miss D. Marie Grieco.

Each report commented on the school library's development into a better resource center, with additional quantities and kinds of equipment and materials. The Central Park Road report noted: "We are especially pleased with some of the initial responses to our purchase and use of 8mm equipment and continuous loop films. . . . Actual participation helped us to focus upon several of the key needs in developing a resource center and to move more efficiently and quickly toward improved flexible scheduling and the use of non-print materials."

Referring to the attempt to continue staffing at the level made possible by the Project, the Central Park Road report stated that the hope of employing full-time library aides for the school district during 1965-66 had been made impossible by budget considerations, but that "we were able to continue the salary for a full-time aide as provided through the Knapp School Libraries Project for the past two years. Although final determination as to the use has not yet been made, the recommendation is that one [part-time aide] be employed for the entire school year at Central Park Road School; the other [part-time] library aide will be employed at one of our large elementary schools which will have a school librarian who participated for one year in the Project and who is, therefore, well aware of the most productive ways in which to utilize such an aide."

The report did not refer to the position of assistant librarian, which was not retained at the Central Park Road School after Project participation. As at the Marcus Whitman School, school district budget limitations did not allow the position to remain, although both of the librarians who had served in the schools as assistant librarians were re-employed in the district for the 1965-66 school year. A difficult factor here was the problem of justifying to other schools in the district the continued maintenance of one school library's staff at a level considerably above that possible in any other school.

A major goal for pupils at Central Park Road School had been the encouragement of effective independent study. It was reported that "A great deal has been done in this area. Further development will be encouraged in the coming years. . . . Children have become familiar with the procedure of sitting down alone and culling

The library laboratory at Marcus Whitman brings together a variety of instructional materials.

and interpreting information from printed and non-printed sources. This area needs further development and encouragement not only at Central Park Road, but throughout the nation."

Questionnaires were used at Central Park Road to get the reactions of faculty members, students, and parents of students at the conclusion of the Project. Copies of the questionnaires with responses incorporated or summarized follow:

Tabulated responses from faculty questionnaire

1. Has your opinion of the helpfulness of the school library changed since the inception of the Knapp program in October, 1963, in regard to the following? (Please check.)
   Greater Extent 80%
   Remained the Same 6.3%
   Lesser Extent 0%   No Reaction 13.3%

   Usefulness of an instructional materials center to the school curriculum:
   More Frequent 86.3%   Some 0%
   Infrequently 13.3%

   Do you plan units around library materials?
   Frequently 73.3%   Infrequently 13.3%
   Never 0%   No Reaction 13.3%

2. What in your opinion is the value of grade-level meetings with the librarian?
   Very Important 13.3%
   Of Some Value 53.3%
   Not Needed 13.3%   No Reaction 20%

3. In what areas could grade-level meetings be improved? (Check one or many.)
   More Preplanning by Librarians 0%
   More Preplanning and Teacher Suggestions 26.3%
   Satisfactory 46.3%
   Hold More Often 0%
   Discontinue 13.3%
   No Reaction 13.3%

4. What phases of library service have been most helpful to your classes? Please list in order of importance (1-9, No. 1 being most important.)

   1. Independent Study
   2. Books for Pleasure
   3. Encyclopedia Lessons
   4. Book Discussions
   5. Other Reference Lessons
   6. Lessons Using Audio-Visual Aids
   7. Reading Guidance
   8. Biography

9. Poetry

[NOTE.—This is the order in which these were selected, not the order in which they were listed.]

5. Has the instructional program been enhanced effectively with the availability of the school library?
Great Extent 93.3%   No Change 0%
Limited Extent 6.3%

6. Are the children in your class putting to use the study and library skills they have learned in the library?
Great Extent 60%   No Change 0%
No Reaction 33.3%
Limited Extent 6.3%

7. 8mm loop films, projectors can add to the instructional program.
Great Extent 60%   No Change 13.3%
Limited Extent 26.3%

8. Consolidation of printed and non-printed material, records, filmstrips, added to the resources for increased interest on the part of the youngsters.
Great Extent 73.3%   No Change 6.3%
Limited Extent 20%

Faculty comments

1. Independent reading time for primary children of value. Would like dictionary skills and alphabetizing.

2. Would like books available at the moment they are required.

3. "I feel the added services have been of great value to me as a primary teacher; however, I feel the 30 hours (almost one work week) that I have spent in the library listening to stories was not of value."

4. Praise for the availability of outside resource people, authors, educators, etc., made possible by the Knapp program.

5. Availability of multitudes of books for the early primary child has been of great significance to both children and teachers. However, it should be noted that there is room for improvement in deciding what constitutes a book that can be read (or should be read) by 6's and 7's. Little printed matter per page does not necessarily mean that it is material for independent reading. This takes close cooperation between teachers and librarians, or a librarian who has had primary reading background. These books should also be scrutinized for quality.

6. Feel that the teacher should know the lesson to be covered beforehand, so that if a new skill is being taught, the teacher can stay with the class; otherwise she or he need not be in attendance.

7. Under number 4 [in the questionnaire], poetry, biography, and reading guidance can be given in the classroom effectively.

Tabulated responses from student questionnaire

I. What did you like best about the library program?
Books 106
Filmstrips 86
Recordings 39
8mm loop 36
Magazines 20
Pamphlets 9
Pictures 5
Slides 1

Additional comments:

1. Meets all needs (A-V—IMC) Great variety materials.... 28
2. Like research 28
3. Encyclopedia use and lessons 22
4. Daily book exchange....... 19
5. Library open at recreation.. 16
6. The librarians and their help 15
7. All library lessons......... 9
8. Movies 7
9. Visitors 6
10. Storytelling 5
11. Reading for pleasure....... 4
12. New library room and appearance 3
13. Card catalog 3
14. Book fair 2
15. Puppet 2
16. Photographers 2
17. Quiet library 2
18. Well run library.......... 1
19. Chess 1
20. Biography 1
21. Video carrels 1
22. Billy the bookworm........ 1

II. What did you like *least*?
I liked everything (nothing least) 69
Records 23
Magazines 16
Puppets 16
Pamphlets 9
Card catalog lessons not much help, same lesson over....... 8
Transparencies 6
Some of library lessons........ 6
Filmstrips 5
Loop films 5
Group book discussion........ 2

Dictionary work 2
Fiction books 1
Slides of dinosaur............ 1
Tests 1
Noise sometimes 1

III. What materials have you used most frequently?
Books 176
Filmstrips 146
8mm loop films.............. 97
Magazines 58
Pictures 56
Recordings 50
Pamphlets 31
Transparencies 12

IV. Rating:
Excellent 158   Good 26   Fair 8
Poor 0   Terrible 0

Tabulated responses from parent questionnaire

1. Have you noticed that your child has shown interest in reading?
   More 127 Same 47 Less 1

2. Greater variety of reading interests (biography, nonfiction, fiction, mysteries).
   More 88 Same 77 Less 2

3. Shows interest in books and magazines around the house.
   More 101 Same 59 Less 1

4. Seems to enjoy reading.
   More 135 Same 41 Less 0

5. Uses the public library in town.
   More 84 Same 80 Less 7

6. Uses books or materials for homework assignments other than textbooks.
   More 120 Same 46 Less 3

7. Which of the following materials did you realize were contained in the materials resource center of the Central Park Road School library? Please check those that apply.
   Recordings 109
   Filmstrips 123
   Books 163
   Magazines 136
   Transparencies 25
   Pamphlets 99
   Pictures 96
   8mm loop films.............. 53

8. In discussions at home has your child mentioned that he has utilized any of the following in the school library?
   Recordings 85
   Filmstrips 110
   Pictures 85
   8mm loop films 43
   Individual study 97

9. Has your child mentioned the library program at Central Park Road?
   Many times 105 Few times 64 Not at all 5

10. Have you heard your child evaluate, criticize, or praise the library program?
    Many occasions 83 Few occasions 77 Never 20

11. Note any specific remarks you or your child have concerning the program.
    [Samples of comments noted here:
    Praises the library many occasions; his friends from other schools didn't believe him.

    The availability of the above-mentioned facilities and materials seem encouraging. Perhaps interest will grow.

    (This parent checked responses some or less.)

    My child has been pleased with 8mm and film loops. I have heard her mention them with her older brother and sister on a number of occasions.

    I am especially pleased with the way she has learned to handle reference material.]

Students cover "the jolly green carpet" at Marcus Whitman as Mrs. Pitts introduces books.

Although this method of eliciting reactions was recognized as subjective and as possibly of limited value because it was given only at the conclusion of Project participation rather than before and/or during, it had been acknowledged for some time that the demonstration aspect of the Project would be too time-consuming to permit the collection of data through surveys within the schools, or development of a research tool for measurement of impact. Since one intention of the schools' participation was to encourage other schools in the community to further improve their library programs, it was also recognized that comparisons with other schools in the distict would not yield significant returns. And since Project schools represented districts which had made sound, over-all plans for school library development, the other schools were also at a fairly high level of progress at the time Phase I began. Another element hindering objective investigation came from the difficulty in isolating the impact of Project-related activities on students and faculty from the impact of the expanded school library program itself.

At Marcus Whitman, where a similar tool for

Marcus Whitman Library

EVALUATION OF LIBRARY SERVICES - CHECK LIST

Evaluating library services is one step toward meeting our responsibilities to the Knapp School Libraries Project. Please read the statements carefully and use the list of symbols shown below to score each statement. The letter symbols will help us measure degree of frequency, and the numerical symbols will help us measure your judgment concerning the importance of that particular aspect of library service.

Degree of Frequency

A - Very extensively   D - Very little
    (or completely)   F - Not at all
B - Considerably   X - Does not apply
C - Some

Measure of Importance

1 - Of utmost importance
2 - Of considerable
    importance
3 - Of some importance
0 - Of no importance

To what extent does the librarian carry out these services:	High Score High Frequency / Degree of Frequency 1963	1965	Low Score High Importance / Measure of Importance 1963	1965
1. Notify teachers of new books and materials received	68	88	33	27
2. Have frequent informal talks with teachers	79	77	34	37
3. Send teachers lists of interesting magazine articles	30	55	48	46
4. Attend and talk at grade-level meetings	18	69	45	45
5. Ask teachers to suggest new materials to be ordered	77	75	35	29
6. Attend to teachers' requests promptly	89	89	36	27
7. Attend and talk at faculty meetings	70	89	38	36
8. Work with teachers in developing units of work on library services to be included in course of study and to be taught to all pupils	38	73	35	27
9. Become familiar with course of study and assist in developing new courses of study	44	71	43	34
10. Have a faculty reading table in library	28	71	36	30
11. Invite new teachers to library at opening of school year	61	75	24	21
12. Visit classroom at teacher's request for teaching special library skills	34	43	51	40
13. Discuss with teachers what library assignments will be made to the pupils	38	77	50	27

	High Score High Frequency / Degree of Frequency 1963	1965	Low Score High Importance / Measure of Importance 1963	1965
14. Give to teachers names of little-used materials relating to their courses	59	56	37	40
15. Send teachers suggestions for book week activities	47	45	40	49
16. Ask teachers for suggestions for book week activities	36	55	42	42
17. Post on bulletin boards reviews and jackets of new books	88	100	26	42
18. Have library exhibits at faculty meetings	56	57	44	44
19. Have faculty meetings held in the library	90	59	50	50
20. Discuss new library materials and features of library service at faculty meetings	58	99	30	28
21. Give help in selecting and locating suitable audio-visual materials related to class work	82	93	25	30
22. Furnish classrooms with lists of books and materials related to units of study	69	73	23	24
23. Keep in touch with progress of classwork by class observation	18	38	50	30
24. Conferences with teachers	51	62	38	30
25. Make suggestions of suitable stories, films, and records related to units of work in progress in the classroom	71	81	25	30

faculty evaluation of library services had been developed in 1963, it was possible to compare the responses that teachers made in September, 1963, and in June, 1965. This checklist appears on the facing page.

In addition, the analysis of tests of children at the Marcus Whitman School and at the Jason Lee School in the same district had been accomplished. The Marcus Whitman report stated:

Library skills

In fall of 1963 all sixth grade pupils in the demonstration school and in a control school in Richland (of equal size and socio-economic status) were given the W-3 section of the *Iowa Test of Basic Skills* and the *Peabody Test of Library Skills*. In the spring of 1964, the same children were retested with the same tests.

Findings

In the first administration of these tests, the average scores of both schools were above the 99th percentile for this grade level. Item analysis of test items was done with no significant differences noted.

Though it would appear that this testing was of no value, it may be significant that all of these children in both schools had had librarians and library services since kindergarten. It is reassuring to note they had achieved library skills.

Reading

Children in the fourth grade in both the demonstration and the control schools were given the vocabulary and reading sections of the *Iowa Tests of Basic Skills* in the fall of 1963. In May, 1965, at the end of the fifth grade, the same children were retested.

Findings

Again the schools achieved almost identical average scores, so that meaningful comparisons were not possible. Since the average scores in both schools were at the 65th percentile, little information was gleaned from item analysis, e.g., of test items dealing with the organization of information. It is interesting to note, however, that children in both schools who did not achieve high scores on the total reading tests did surprisingly well on these items of organizing ideas.

A comparison of the very high scores on the library tests as compared with the reading scores leads one to consider the nature of the tests. The library skills tests are essentially tests of certain routines taught and reviewed during the seven-year span of the elementary school program in Richland. A more realistic score could have been determined if a performance test had been given on these skills.

As a part of the material on evaluation which had been prepared for the Project schools by the Project office, a list of responsibilities for librarians and clerical assistants was drawn up. The purpose here was to see whether tasks originally performed by the librarian could be assigned to the clerical assistant or to others so that more of the librarian's time would be free for professional work. The Marcus Whitman report that includes the record of this change of assignment appears on pages 50-53.

Younger students adapt quickly to being on their own in the library laboratory.

RESPONSIBILITIES OF SCHOOL LIBRARY OPERATION - Marcus Whitman Elementary School, Richland, Washington

Indicate for the following dates the staff person or other (student, parent, volunteer, etc.) personnel responsible for the duties listed in column one. If more than one person shares the responsibility, check each appropriate column.

CODE: L - Librarian   A - Assistant Librarian   C - Clerk   Other - Specify: Student, Parent, etc.

	June 1963				Dec. 1963				June 1964				Dec. 1964				June 1965			
	L	A	C	Other-Specify	L	A	C	Other-Specify	L	A	C	Other-Specify	L	A	C	Other-Specify	L	A	C	Other-Specify
Select books and other materials for purchase	X			Teacher Principal	X	X		Teacher Principal	X	X		Teacher Principal	X	X		Teacher Principal	X	X		Teacher Principal
Prepare and file orders for materials	X						X				X				X				X	
Inform teachers and principal of materials available and ordered	X				X	X			X	X			X	X			X	X		
Maintains the collection by: Shelving materials	X				X	X			X	X			X	X			X	X		
Mending or refurbishing materials	X				X	X	X		X	X	X		X	X	X		X	X	X	
Revising shelves, etc. for accurate arrangement	X				X	X			X	X			X	X			X	X		
Removing obsolete, outworn materials	X				X				X				X				X			
Prepare bibliographies for teachers	X				X	X	X		X	X	X		X	X	X		X	X	X	
Prepare reading lists for student selection	X				X	X	X		X	X	X		X	X	X		X	X	X	
Advise students on materials for selection	X				X	X			X	X			X	X			X	X		
Give book talks at faculty meetings	X				X	X			X	X			X	X			X	X		
Give book talks to classes and/or other supervisors	X				X	X			X	X			X	X			X	X		
Report on the library to the principal	X				X	X			X	X			X	X			X	X		
Report on the library to the parent groups	X				X	X			X	X			X	X			X	X		
Report on the library to teachers	X				X	X			X	X			X	X			X	X		
Lead discussions of books by students	X				X	X			X	X			X	X			X	X		
Direct research projects of students	X			Teacher	X	X		Teacher	X	X		Teacher	X	X		Teacher	X	X		Teacher
Give instruction to students in: Use of card catalog	X				X	X			X	X			X	X			X	X		

	June 1963				Dec. 1963				June 1964				Dec. 1964				June 1965			
	L	A	C	Other-Specify	L	A	C	Other-Specify	L	A	C	Other-Specify	L	A	C	Other-Specify	L	A	C	Other-Specify
Use of indexes	X			Teacher	X	X		Teacher	X	X		Teacher	X	X		Teacher	X	X		Teacher
Use of reference materials	X			Teacher	X	X		Teacher	X	X		Teacher	X	X		Teacher	X	X		Teacher
Arrangement of materials collection	X				X	X			X	X			X	X			X	X		
Use of non-print materials	X			Teacher	X	X		Teacher	X	X		Teacher	X	X		Teacher	X	X		Teacher
Student instruction-cont'd. Maintenance and use of Audio-visual equipment	X				X	X			X	X			X	X			X	X		
How to take notes	X			Teacher	X	X		Teacher	X	X		Teacher	X	X		Teacher	X	X		Teacher
Use of dictionaries and atlases	X			Teacher	X	X		Teacher	X	X		Teacher	X	X		Teacher	X	X		Teacher
Preparation of bibliography	X			Teacher	X	X	X	Teacher	X	X	X	Teacher	X	X	X	Teacher	X	X	X	Teacher
Evaluation of library materials	X				X	X		Teacher	X	X		Teacher	X	X		Teacher	X	X		Teacher
Use of library	X				X	X			X	X			X	X			X	X		
Confer with teachers on library classes	X				X	X			X	X			X	X			X	X		
Confer with teachers on library-centered projects	X				X	X			X	X			X	X			X	X		
Initiate projects relating to the library	X			Teacher	X	X		Teacher	X	X		Teacher	X	X		Teacher	X	X		Teacher
Orient teachers to use of the library	X				X	X			X	X			X	X			X	X		
Orient teachers to use of library materials	X				X	X			X	X			X	X			X	X		
Attend faculty meetings	X				X	X			X	X			X	X			X	X		
Belongs to and attends P.T.A.	X			Teacher Principal	X	X	X	Teacher Principal	X	X	X	Teacher Principal	X	X	X	Teacher Principal	X	X	X	Teacher Principal
Catalog and classify library materials	X				X	X			X	X			X	X			X	X		
Process (lettering, etc.) library materials	X				X		X	Parents	X		X		X		X		X		X	
Maintain the card catalog by: Filing cards for recent accessions	X			Students	X	X	X	Students	X	X	X	Students	X	X	X	Students	X	X	X	Students

	June 1963				Dec. 1963				June 1964				Dec. 1964				June 1965			
	L	A	C	Other-Specify	L	A	C	Other-Specify	L	A	C	Other-Specify	L	A	C	Other-Specify	L	A	C	Other-Specify
Removing cards for titles withdrawn	X				X	X	X		X	X	X		X	X	X		X	X	X	
Incorporating new information on cards when needed	X				X	X					X				X				X	
Maintain the shelf list	X				X	X	X		X	X	X		X	X	X		X	X	X	
Maintain records of ownership and location of library materials not included in the card catalog and shelf list	X				X	X	X		X	X	X		X	X	X		X	X	X	
Maintain records of ownership and location of library furniture and equipment	X				X	X	X			X	X			X	X			X	X	
Establish bookkeeping records for funds, etc.	X						X				X				X				X	
Train student assistants	X				X				X				X				X			
Supervise student assistants	X				X				X				X				X			
Train clerical assistant	X				X				X				X	X			X	X		
Supervise clerical assistant	X				X				X				X	X			X	X		
Participate in state educational associations	X			Principal	X	X		Principal	X	X		Principal	X	X		Principal	X	X		Principal
Participate in state library associations	X				X	X			X	X		Principal	X	X		Principal	X	X		Principal
Participate in regional educational associations	X			Principal	X	X		Principal	X	X		Principal	X	X		Principal	X	X		Principal
Participate in regional library associations	X				X	X			X	X			X	X			X	X		
Participate in national educational associations	X			Principal	X			Principal	X	X		Principal	X	X		Principal	X	X		Principal
Participate in National Library Associations									X				X				X			
Direct and develop library policies	X			Council Principal	X	X		Council Principal	X	X		Council Principal	X	X		Council Principal	X	X		Council Principal
Schedule use of the library by classes	X				X	X			X	X			X	X			X	X		
Evaluate the library in terms of the school's educational goals	X			Council Principal	X	X		Council Principal	X	X		Council Principal	X	X		Council Principal	X	X		Council Principal

Responsibilities of School Library Operation, Marcus Whitman Elementary School / continued

	June 1963				Dec. 1963				June 1964				Dec. 1964				June 1965			
	L	A	C	Other-Specify	L	A	C	Other-Specify	L	A	C	Other-Specify	L	A	C	Other-Specify	L	A	C	Other-Specify
Establish rules and procedures for circulation of materials to ensure maximum effective use	X				X				X	X			X	X			X	X		
Submit reports to principal on library use	X				X				X				X				X			
Submit reports to state supervisor and other agency as required	X				X	X			X	X			X	X			X	X		
Submit reports to project director								Field Worker				Field Worker				Field Worker				Field Worker
Maintain cooperation and communication with other librarians in the community	X				X	X		Field Worker	X	X		Field Worker	X	X		Field Worker	X	X		Field Worker
Plan for the efficient use of space and equipment in library quarters	X				X	X		Council	X	X		Council	X	X		Council	X	X		Council
Plan for additional equipment and enlarged quarters when needed	X			Principal	X	X		Field Worker Principal	X	X		Field Worker Principal	X	X		Field Worker Principal	X	X		Field Worker Principal
Plan the division of duties among the professional and clerical library staff	X				X	X			X	X			X	X			X	X		
Mounting pictures	X						X				X				X				X	
Re-covering worn books							X				X				X				X	
Preparing instructional materials for teachers							X				X				X				X	
Distribution of audio-visual materials to teachers	X						X				X				X				X	

In addition to information gained from the results of the standardized tests, children's reactions to the library were requested at the Project's conclusion. Of special interest was their reaction to the library laboratory, which was the nearby classroom renovated as an addition to the library facility and intended especially for independent study and for listening and viewing by individuals and small groups. The report states:

> No count of actual users was made because the intent was not to schedule this room but to make it available when classroom teachers and children needed to use it. The librarians estimate an average of 75 children used the area daily. Mr. LeClair, principal at Marcus Whitman, also added that though the room was used independently by children, *without adult supervision*, there was not a single need of disciplinary action.

As part of the final evaluation, children in grades three through six were asked to write on the library services during the last two years. It is interesting to note that only a few children in the third grade made reference to the library laboratory. This was no doubt due in part to the fact that they had been in the first grade when the Project began and had accepted this room as always a part of the library. Also, a study of the use of this room shows that few children of the third grade used the laboratory. An analysis of the comments of these children shows that they all mentioned the number and variety of books, most referred to learning about the card catalog and arrangement of books on the shelves, while over half described the "Jolly Green Carpet," used for storytelling and book talks. (The name of the carpet was selected by the children in a contest at the school.)

Visitors from Oregon and California check their own observations by talking with children at Marcus Whitman.

In the fourth grades slightly less than half of the children mentioned the laboratory by name, while others referred to it by mentioning the materials available there. Most frequently mentioned was the "help" given to them in doing reports on science projects.

Over 75% of the fifth and sixth grade students mentioned the laboratory as an important part of library services. Proximity of these classrooms to this facility and the greater ability of the older students to engage in self-directed activities encouraged teachers of these grade levels to use the laboratory to a greater extent.

Some of these quotations from the children's writing show their enthusiasm for the new study area:

In the library laboratory we are trusted to work without playing. A teacher isn't regularly stationed there, but sometimes a librarian comes to help someone.

When the teacher chooses the people to go to the lab to work, I hope she picks me.

Before the private film viewers were purchased, either a whole class would see a filmstrip or nobody.

What I like most is the freedom of the library laboratory. A person doesn't spend time getting permission to use a machine as long as one is available.

We may go in any time we need to for individual study.

I think the lab is a good way to help improve the ability to work and have fun while working.

Two years ago research was hard to do because you could only work in the main library and other classes were using it. Now that we have the library lab you can work in the morning, noon, after school and during school.

I especially enjoy the listening centers and the recordings we can listen to individually.

Another measure of the Project's impact was cited in the Marcus Whitman report of long range effects:

Though not specifically noted among the objectives, there was no doubt a hope that the demonstration center in Richland would have some good effects on community attitudes and on the total library program in Richland. To promote this, all librarians spent at least a day at Marcus Whitman and lay citizens were encouraged to visit.

1. The library-skills guide for the elementary school was revised and now includes content on the kindergarten and on the team teaching of research skills by teachers and librarians.

2. Visuals for teaching library skills developed at Marcus Whitman have been reproduced for all elementary schools.

3. Recordings for literature and social studies and multi-media kits purchased and evaluated at the demonstration center were purchased for all schools.

4. Book selection sources such as the *Bulletin of the Center for Children's Books*, not previously used, were tried at Marcus Whitman; now other librarians are using these.

5. The practice of listing recordings and filmstrips in the card catalog is being imitated in other schools.

6. One junior high school and two elementary schools already have library laboratories similar to that at Marcus Whitman; another junior high school has requested remodeling for this.

7. Two schools now have library coordinating councils.

8. One principal wrote, "We have changed our entire library program due to the fine influence of the Knapp School Libraries Project. Our program was form-

erly one of rigid scheduling and is now a completely new, flexible operation. Independent study areas are now available to students because of the Knapp program. Many things have taken place in our library during the past year and I give special credit to Mrs. Beachner and the influence that the Project has had on our school, teachers, and students."

9. That more librarians are needed to improve service became evident. If state support for schools had not been so inadequate for 1965-66, Richland schools would have asked for local support to add library staff. Because a large local levy is necessary to maintain the status quo, they have been able to do this only in part—that of adding another half-time librarian to the two full-time ones at the high school.

10. Experience with secretarial help at the demonstration center re-emphasized a known fact: freeing a good librarian from clerical routine makes it possible for her to give more service to teachers and children.

To effect such release the 1965-66 preliminary budget of the Richland schools has doubled the amount allowed for clerical services to librarians. These funds will be used for:

a cooperative central processing center with contiguous school districts
or
commercial processing of books
or
added clerical service in school libraries.

Since the role of "instructional secretary" was not fully realized at Marcus Whitman because of the pressures induced by the demonstration situation, the Richland schools plan to explore this further. These steps will be taken:

(*a*) Study of experiences in other districts using such personnel, e.g., University City, Missouri.

Consultant help on this subject from colleges and/or State Department of Public Instruction personnel.

(*b*) Definition of the role by school staffs under the guidance of principals; identification of evaluative tools.

(*c*) Selection by administration of the school or schools to have an instructional secretary for a trial period.

(*d*) Evaluation, revision of roles, expansion of practice, or termination of experiment.

Visitors have much to watch and note as librarian Mrs. Mildred Boyd works with a class at Central Park Road.

11. No effort was made to log circulation in the library, attendance, and similar details at Marcus Whitman. Dr. Witt of Columbia University suggested that typical days be selected and studied in detail, and this has been the approach. From such evidence it is possible to estimate that:

Approximately 75 pupils per day used the library laboratory.

Circulation is up about one-third, even though the free use of materials in the laboratory cut down on the necessity of personal borrowing. An average day's circulation is about 275, with some peaks (such as the day before the Christmas holidays) at over 700.

The more flexible library schedule encouraged at least 11 extra periods of classroom use to be scheduled at teachers' requests during a week, not counting the period before lunch and at the end of the day when individuals or small groups came from the classrooms.

In addition, four kindergarten classes had regular weekly classes in the library.

All in all, it is estimated that about 800 more students could be accommodated during a single week through the more flexible schedule and the use of the independent study space.

12. Community interest was stimulated through the participation on the local advisory board by the head librarian of the Richland Library, the library specialist from the Hanford atomic energy plant, and a member of the board of directors for the school district.

A survey of certain aspects of the Richland Schools by the League of Women Voters included a study of library services and of the Knapp School Libraries Project. The report of this study noted that Richland libraries compare favorably with others in Washington but fall below national standards in the number of librarians per 300 students. They also commented that the help of a well trained instructional secretary would permit librarians to use their extensive training to better advantage with students and teachers.

13. Dr. Roland Lewis of Eastern Washington State College made these final comments on the value he saw for the college: The Department of Education of East-

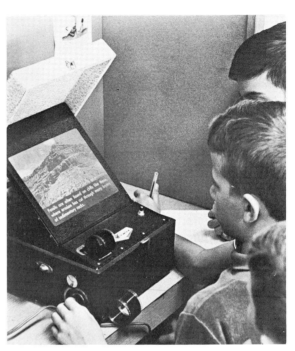

Boys work together at Central Park Road in preparing a report based on a silent filmstrip and other materials.

ern Washington State College has been most pleased to be a part of the Knapp School Libraries Project. We have found it a resource in the following ways:

(a) The regular contact with a public school district is necessary in our teacher education program. The Project provided an ideal vehicle for this.

(b) Each quarter we were able to take a group of students to visit the Project. The discussions before, during, and after the visit in Richland greatly enhanced the understandings that our students have concerning the role a library should play in a good elementary school.

(c) The Project has been the cause of several of the students in the language arts area becoming interested in taking work in the area of school libraries. We are now working on a Master of Education program in Instructional Materials.

(d) Working with the demonstration library project has increased our interest and capacity to develop our campus school library to a demonstration level.

TEACHER EDUCATION IN PHASE I

It was unquestionably much more difficult to assess the impact of the Project on the teacher education institutions which participated than on the schools. Dr. Lewis has stated some of these outcomes above, and the report from Teachers College noted the interest of the faculty there in assisting as consultants on an occasional basis, in permitting students to participate in visits to the school, and in welcoming the consultant for the Project, Miss Grieco, to present and to discuss with classes the Project-sponsored film, . . . *And Something More.*

Because of the insight it provides into the kind of work Miss Grieco did with teachers at Central Park Road School during the second year of its participation in the Project, one section of her report to Dr. Witt, the field worker, is here presented. Referring to her assigned responsibility, "To assist the librarians, faculty, and administrators in the demonstration school in making the most effective use of the library's resources," she notes the need for "a brief overview of concepts," which follows:

First, the working relationship between the librarian and teachers is of paramount importance in the development of full programs of school library services.

Teachers and administrators are so rarely trained to know and use the full resources

Newly arrived books invite a child to browse at Central Park Road.

of either the library collections or the professional librarian that it becomes the responsibility of the librarian to be aware of the ever present opportunities in the classrooms which can lead to more effective use of the library's materials and the librarian's talents which, in turn, can lead to increased and informed demand. The specialized nature of the well trained librarian's contribution to the total school program must be so evident in services to pupils, teachers, and administrators, and so distinct from and yet so complementary to the contributions of a well trained teacher, that more administrators and teachers will be moved to support optimum conditions in elementary school libraries. Optimum conditions can rarely be approached unless the library is sufficiently stocked, staffed, and supported.

All services suggested and performed by the consultant grew out of the particular interests and objectives of individual teachers in specific classroom situations. In a regular school program, sufficient library staff would be necessary to permit the kind of time and flexibility needed to implement such services without interfering with the many other aspects of a full program of library service.

Second, the selection and acquisition of quality multi-media materials are the necessary foundation for a good instructional materials center. However, maximum and optimum use of a cross-media approach to learning often depends on insightful evaluations and analyses of both the medium and the message to furnish clues for both constructive and creative use.

In selecting materials for use in long-term projects with teachers, the consultant emphasized two concepts: (*a*) that each medium must be selected for its unique contribution to the process of communication, and (*b*) that thorough evaluation and analysis of the content and technique uncover questions, concepts, and clues to guide and enhance a variety of learning experiences at different levels and at different times.

An example of point (*a*) is suggested by the use of the film *Neighbors.* No other medium and no other film could have provided the same impact created by this choice at the time and for the purpose. An example of point (*b*) would involve exposure to the complex concept of symbolism. While the trade book *Ferdinand,* the film *Neighbors,* and the film *Hunter in the Forest* were used for varied purposes to promote particular awareness at different times, the symbolic use of a flower in each work provided the opportunity to develop an understanding of the use of symbolism. No unnatural effort or isolated exposure to the idea was necessary. The careful evaluations had provided the questions and clues which guided discussions and led to a spiraling repetition in the interpretation of the concept and greater depth in the appreciation of the works.

Thus, while a well stocked library is a minimum essential, and while the cross-media approach in cataloging and bibliographical services is highly desirable, ease in physical accessibility of materials is not always enough to warrant optimum use. The librarian trained in the art of evaluating both print and non-print materials can provide services to enhance their use in ways that the mere location of them cannot always insure.

Third, while the evaluation of materials is essential to make them intellectually accessible from a large variety of conceptual approaches, the analysis of basic techniques in each medium provides aspects of study which are often appropriate and sometimes essential to the fullest understanding of the materials.

For example, in analyzing the book *Ferdinand* in terms of its setting, plot, characterization, meanings, and values, we determined how the author and the illustrator achieved their desired effects. Thus, we noted that the artist had portrayed the feeling of fear by changing the size of the bull in one illustration; the author had changed the size of the print to achieve the same effect. Even before we verbalized the reasons, we had reacted to the "feeling of smallness," but the analysis heightened our appreciation of both the book and the technique. In the film *Hunter in the Forest,* with neither narration nor dialogue to "tell" the story, we discussed the techniques used by the producer and cameraman to portray their message.

The primary purpose in selecting this book and film was to provide common experiences for discussions designed to promote the teacher's stated objective to develop conceptual understandings basic to writing original stories to be produced in the puppet theater. Many materials and techniques could have achieved this end. The materials and methods used created additional interests and stimulated other explorations in and uses for avenues of inquiry.

In using some 8mm silent film loops, the analysis of film techniques became necessary for adequate interpretation of the concepts. In one of the single session situations, the consultant introduced the use of the 8mm equipment to follow up a classroom experience. A film clip on the metamorphosis of a moth was brought in after the children had actually seen a moth emerge from a cocoon they had in class. Since the entire cycle shown on the film was actually shorter than the one stage the children had witnessed, the obvious questions raised indicated the need to study time-lapse photography. In a short time we were able to find out how to look at the film in order to recognize the various stages of growth. We were also led to discuss the advantages of the film for its unique contribution of motion and detail and the need to use other materials to answer questions raised by close observation, but not answered.

Thus, it is essential to know not only what materials to use for what purposes, but how to study in each medium.

Fourth, it is axiomatic that the librarian should be the liaison between books and readers, between films and viewers, between all kinds of materials and all kinds of learners; that he must know the tools and techniques in the selection and evaluation of print and non-print materials; that he must be abundantly aware of curriculum needs and goals; and that he must be aware of the best approaches to teaching and learning as well as the best materials for teaching and learning. What is not always so obvious is that the librarian is in a natural position to act as a liaison between teachers and pupils, pupils and pupils, and teachers and teachers. The librarian can cross-fertilize many teaching and learning experiences in a "full program of school library services."

For example, when the consultant selected multi-level materials which were appropriately used in different grades for varying purposes, it was possible to compare and contrast reactions and concepts which emerged. It was also possible to demonstrate that optimum use of quality materials often depends on the techniques, attitudes, and awareness inherent in the user and not the limitations inherent in the materials. Thus, the librarian is in a unique position to shatter the sacred status of grade-level materials prepared by publishers with limited appreciation for the real potential of learners and often used with slavish exclu-

Their library visit over, these primary grade students line up with their teacher at Marcus Whitman.

siveness by individual teachers or required as sole or basic fare by administrators.

To achieve these ends the librarian must be prepared to initiate services well beyond those requested. In many instances the consultant selected, located, and delivered materials which would enrich the activities being pursued in a classroom. While a well organized cross-media card catalog and special bibliographies are of fundamental importance, they cannot substitute for individualized service. In most instances when specific materials were highly recommended and locally available, even repeated suggestions did not result in the acquisition and use by individual teachers who expressed the most pronounced interest and enthusiasm. Nor was the situation different in the library.

Thus, to know about materials is not enough; to have materials available may not be enough. The librarian must be the liaison between knowledge about, interest in, and optimum use of materials. Locational tools can be inert without the live and lively librarian.

Until such time as in-service and pre-service programs in schools and colleges prepare teachers knowledgeable "in making the most effective use of the library's resources," and library schools train librarians in the use of non-print as well as printed materials in diverse approaches to teaching and learning programs such as the Knapp School Libraries Project offer magnificent opportunities. The consultant believes that the potential in the participation of Teachers College and the Central Park Road School can be realized in the programs each begins to design in the future.

Report from

ALLISONVILLE SCHOOL
and
BALL STATE UNIVERSITY

FACT SHEET—ALLISONVILLE SCHOOL

The Allisonville School is one of fourteen schools in the Metropolitan School District of Washington Township, Marion County, Indiana. A growing suburban community adjacent to Indianapolis, the school district has established central libraries in each of the fourteen schools. The library program at Allisonville is in its seventh year of operation. Mrs. Audrey Michels, who had formerly been assigned to the Allisonville School as music teacher half-time and as librarian half-time, has been enabled by the Knapp School Libraries Project to expand the library program by serving as a full-time librarian. An additional full-time librarian and a clerical assistant have also been employed with Project funds.

Library services at the school district level include direction from two coordinators of libraries, one for elementary and one for secondary. Centralized ordering, cataloging, and processing have been provided for the ten elementary school libraries and for the four secondary school libraries. The central office now contains the nucleus of a 16-millimeter film library with current holdings of 120 films. The summer library program has been expanded to a seven-week session, with library hours from 8:30 A.M. to 3:30 P.M., Monday through Friday. Summer library personnel is the same as in the winter session.

Ball State University in Muncie, Indiana, has designated Dr. Donald L. Barnes, Associate Professor of Education, as its field worker for this Project with the Allisonville School. Dr. Barnes's experience as field worker for the Midwest Program of Airborne Television Instruction has included the conducting of teacher workshops, seminars, and individual consultations with school faculty members. Ball State has worked in cooperation with the Metropolitan School District of Washington Township in several areas before this Project application. Ball State student teachers have been assigned to schools in this district, and several extended academic curricular offerings have been provided cooperatively.

The curriculum and educational program of the Washington Township schools was surveyed and evaluated by a team from Ohio State University in 1962 and 1963. This and other studies and statements of goals have led to the school district's plan for continuous improvement. The Knapp Project's provision of funds for salaries, materials, equipment, and construction is intended to implement that plan, especially as it relates to the further development of an instructional materials center at the Allisonville School.

STATISTICS

From its Project application, June, 1963
Enrollment: 538 students, grades kindergarten through six.
Materials collection: 4,451 books, 19 periodicals, 309 filmstrips, 38 disc recordings, 1 globe.
Library personnel: One half-time librarian.

As of June, 1967
Enrollment: 867 students, grades kindergarten through six.

Materials collection: 7,656 books, 58 periodicals, 713 filmstrips, 401 disc recordings, 176 tape recordings, 70 transparencies, 136 charts, 12 legal size drawers of vertical file material in 411 subject areas, 50 bioscope slides, 1,156 oversize pictures, 26 models, 87 entries of community resources covering 57 subject areas, 63 slides, 43 reference sets.
Library personnel: Two full-time librarians, one full-time library aide.

PERSONNEL MOST DIRECTLY CONCERNED WITH THE PROJECT

From the Allisonville School

    Mr. Donald F. Sellmer, Principal

    Mrs. Audrey J. Michels, Librarian

    Mrs. Ann Lyn Skene, Assistant Librarian

    Mrs. Marjorie J. Carlson, Library Aide

From the Metropolitan School District of Washington Township

    Dr. J. Everett Light, Superintendent

    Dr. H. Dean Evans, Assistant Superintendent

    Miss Marjorie Dobson, Coordinator of Elementary Libraries

From Ball State University

    Dr. John Dunworth, Dean, Division of Education, Psychology and Special Education

    Dr. Donald L. Barnes, Associate Professor of Education and field worker, Knapp School Libraries Project

PARTICIPATION

Patterns of development and changes of emphasis

From its beginning, the Allisonville School library had developed along the lines recommended in the American Library Association's 1960 *Standards for School Library Programs.* By the time we made application to participate in the Knapp School Libraries Project we felt (1) that we had correctly interpreted the said standards, (2) that their implementation, so far as we had been able to complete it, had given us the kind of program best suited to our needs, and (3) that our most serious lack was fiscal support to provide the additional personnel and materials needed for full implementation of the program. Upon acceptance into the Project, we were able to realize the full implementation of the program as we had envisioned it and to expand our own realization of a utopian situation.

We had never indulged in experimentation simply for the sake of experimentation, and we did not do so now. However, two suggestions from outside sources seemed to have merit, and we attempted to put them into practice. One idea was to key the major units of the curriculum to the library and the community resources. This was to be over and above the regular acquiring and cataloging of materials. Three-by-five cards in a separate section of the card catalog contained as subject headings the major units and their subheadings. Under this appeared all the materials currently available relevant to the development of this unit. This idea was soon abandoned, because of the great amount of time consumed in putting it into a workable state. It was also feared that such spoon-feeding would defeat our purpose of encouraging the child's working independently.

The second suggestion which we considered and which we attempted to put into practice was later altered to meet our needs. The suggestion was that we publish a library report at regular intervals. Included in its pages would be library news, book reviews by children and librarians, and, in each issue, a feature of one teacher's relating some unique library experi-

ence. Again, this proved to be a very time-consuming project, and the paper failed to appear regularly. Substituted was a booklet, *Overview of Library-Related Skills with Suggested Activities.*

During the last year, a monthly calendar of events was forwarded to the members of the "Committee of 21," so that they might be aware of current activities in the Project school. This committee was our local advisory committee and included representatives of our school district, Ball State University and other university faculties, and other agencies related to school library development.

Our program as it has evolved might be divided into services provided to students and services provided to teachers. Our students have an opportunity to become familiar with the workings of the library through weekly scheduled classes. These classes are of a half-hour duration, and approximately half of this time is spent in some library activity that is an integral part of some classroom activity. Here we develop skills that are urgently needed in the classroom at this particular time, or we may schedule book talks or storytelling. The library is open to all potential users at all hours of the day whether or not there is a class in the library. This provides the child with an opportunity to become familiar with materials at his own speed or interest level.

Students have an opportunity to serve their school through our student assistant program. There is no exploitation here. Certainly it takes considerable time to train these children for their role, and, if we did not think they profited by the experience, we could not afford the time required.

Students are given an opportunity to develop poise through giving book talks and telling stories to younger children. We talk to each student about storytelling, help him in the selection of a story, listen to him before he presents his story to the children, and then observe his pleasure as he delights his listeners.

Of help to our teachers is the fact that the library serves as a clearinghouse not only for materials but for ideas. Materials are not zealously hoarded in the classrooms but are gladly shared, as each teacher realizes that he need not fear he will be deprived of material he needs. Because so many teachers and students enter the library each day, because we keep records of the materials charged, and because of frequent classroom visits, the librarians are in a position to know what is going on in each classroom and may well be able to help tie together several projects for the benefit of everyone.

Teachers have the nucleus of a professional collection as part of the Allisonville School library. A much larger collection is available at the district office, and daily delivery service between schools and the office provides for prompt handling of requests for materials.

Teachers have an opportunity to assist in the building and maintaining of the library through participation in the selection of materials. They are provided with book exhibits, filmstrip exhibits, and miscellaneous exhibits of other materials. Upon request, bibliographies are provided and instruction is given in selection aids.

Assembling of materials for classroom use is done in several ways. It may be done by the librarians, or by the teacher, or by joint efforts. At times this assemblage is part of a library lesson, and the material is actually gathered by the children with the teacher and librarian later picking up overlooked items. The task of assembling material is made easier by the fact that the collection is fully cataloged and thus brought to the attention of a potential user. The type of material most recently cataloged is our collec-

tion of pictures too large for the vertical file. These are assigned a Dewey Decimal Classification number and are hung from coat hangers with grip fasteners in shelflist order. As with books, they are fully cataloged, and their cards are interfiled in the card catalog with the cards for all other book and non-book materials.

Librarians make arrangements for the use of films, children's museum exhibits, and community resource persons or places. Librarians also alert teachers to educational radio programs, order the syllabuses coordinated with these programs, and make arrangements for the program to be piped to the classroom at the proper time.

Teachers are acquainted with new materials by displays of such material in the faculty lounge. Request slips are nearby so that material can be automatically forwarded to the teacher desiring it at the end of the display period.

Audio-visual equipment may be scheduled as long as one semester in advance. Also, requests are honored on short notice when equipment is available. Effort is also made to adjust previous scheduling when this can be done without inconvenience to previously scheduled borrowers. Since we insist that every piece of equipment and such auxiliary items as extension cords must be signed for, we have a smoothly running program.

All materials circulate. Reference books may go to the classroom on an hourly basis, and may go out overnight. Models and their guides and audio-visual equipment circulate overnight within the limits of reasonable transportability.

When the enlarged library at Allisonville opened, this view greeted the first comers.

A VARIETY OF VIEWS

This report is a result of great team effort. Some individuals and groups have prepared separate statements which are included here. Others worked in specific areas, for example on the local advisory committee, and those activities are also reported in this section.

A beginning librarian in a demonstration library

Mrs. Ann Lyn Skene, assistant librarian, prepared the following comments:

> The beginning librarian entering a demonstration library directly from library school experiences both advantages and disadvantages that will be reflected in the library program. These fall into four specific areas: (1) adequacy of training; (2) adjustment period; (3) enthusiasm; and (4) her relationship with visitors.
>
> My library school training has proved quite adequate, and a particular advantage was the broadening of my awareness of the kinds of library service. This is especially important for the school librarian who is preparing students to use the many varied resources available in all kinds of libraries.
>
> There were two distinct disadvantages I experienced which were reflected in the total library program. First, as a novice in the profession, I may have required a longer period of time to adjust to my new situation than a more experienced librarian would have needed. A second disadvantage concerned just getting used to teaching and applying all the things I had studied to the practical situation. Preparation for lessons probably takes longer; misjudgement in anticipating the method of presentation that will be most clear to children may occur more frequently.
>
> An advantage which helped me through this period of adjustment was my enthusiasm for my profession. Such enthusiasm and eagerness seemed welcomed; yet, there was enough close supervision that I could not make any colossal mistakes.
>
> A final point to consider is the relationship of the librarian and the library visitor. My inexperience was a disadvantage in persuading visitors that I understood the problems involved in improving library service. It is difficult to illustrate how maintaining an outstanding library program presents problems similar to theirs.

Work of the local advisory committee

The local advisory committee for the Knapp School Libraries Project (Committee of 21) has served as a functional coordinating agency for planning, evaluating, publicizing, and exchanging ideas about the cooperative effort to demonstrate how a library can be best used in the instructional program of an elementary school. The committee brought together for these purposes a group of professional educators including classroom teachers, supervisors, librarians, school administrators, educators of teachers, officers of the State Department of Public Instruction, representatives of professional organizations, school patrons, school board members, resource persons from the Knapp Project, and consultants from other states. Many of these dedicated individuals served on this committee for the duration of the Project, thus providing perspective and continuity in the planning group. Of special note was the interest of faculty members from Indiana University, Indiana State College, and Purdue University who worked on this committee in close cooperation with representatives from Ball State University.

Regular meetings of the local advisory committee provided an opportunity for reporting on progress and problems and for sharing ideas for improvement or modification of the program. Communications between meetings maintained liaison, especially during the final year of Project participation when monthly reports were distributed. Meetings were scheduled in the Allisonville School so that committee members

Four members of the readiness team look over the audio-visual equipment. Left to right: Mrs. David Brown, Mrs. Juen York, Mr. William Morrett, and Mr. Robert Brannock.

would be familiar with the setting for the Project and would have opportunities for classroom visitation and on-the-spot communication with teachers and children. The committee included key personnel who might not otherwise have grasped the significance of what was being attempted in this undertaking and who would, therefore, have been less likely to take advantage of it for purposes of referral, visitation, or citation. Finally, the meetings of the local advisory committee undoubtedly served as another stimulating force for the people directly involved in making this Knapp School Libraries Project center a demonstration program of real merit.

Summer workshops at Allisonville School

The Metropolitan School District of Washington Township, Ball State University, and the Knapp School Libraries Project jointly sponsored special workshops for elementary teachers and librarians in June of 1965 and 1966. The first workshop was a week in duration; the second was extended to two weeks. Both workshops emphasized the several aspects of teacher-librarian cooperation and the imaginative use of library materials and related resources in the classroom. Individuals at the national, state, and local levels assisted in the selection of workshop themes and topics and helped in the development of appropriate procedures which were followed in the conduct of the workhops. Each participant was given an agenda of topics at the outset of each workshop, and ample time was allowed for individual conferences.

Topics scheduled for one or both of the workshops were as follows:

Getting your library started

Patterns of library use in library projects throughout the United States

Services offered by good elementary libraries and materials centers

Developing an awareness and enthusiasm among children in using library materials

Library resources to enrich the social studies

Making effective use of audio-visual materials

Library materials to enrich and extend elementary science activities

Programmed materials and other innovations related to libraries and learning

Measuring children's growth in library skills

Reading disability and the use of library materials

Planning classroom activities around library resources

Patterns of cooperative effort between classroom teachers and librarians

Research findings related to children and books

Choosing the best of children's literature

Helping students understand and appreciate children's literature

Measuring children's ability to interpret aspects of plot, characterization, and setting in children's literature

Considerations in the use of specific types of teaching materials (films, filmstrips, flat pictures, realia, models, printed materials)

Using library materials with gifted children

Creative writing and the use of library materials

In addition to persons associated with the Project at Allisonville, we were able to obtain the leadership of Miss D. Marie Grieco of Teachers College, Columbia University, in 1965, and of Mrs. Maxine Larson of Kalamazoo, Michigan, in 1966. The planning and coordination of both workshops were primarily the responsibility of Dr. Donald Barnes as Project field worker.

Each workshop participant was asked to select an individual project, one that would most benefit his teaching or supervisory work following the workshop. These projects ranged across many school library concerns and activities.

Some proposals related to the planning of new libraries (space allocations, acquisitions, schedules); some concerned the use of library materials with particular groups of children (slow learners, remedial readers, or gifted students); many of the projects focused upon the enrichment of special curricular areas (social studies, science or literature). Each represented a genuine and thoughtful attempt to extend and enrich the participant's own understanding and use of library materials.

Workshop participants came from four states —Kentucky, Illinois, Indiana, and Iowa. Allisonville teachers were well represented at both workshops. Participants could enroll for graduate college credit if they met Ball State University entrance requirements. Approximately one-third of those attending registered for graduate credit. Despite the fact that schedules were rather closely planned and the heat of the summer frequently closed in upon us, the workshops were well received. Participants who completed evaluation forms indicated general satisfaction with the selection of topics, the speakers, and the balance between individual and group activities.

Public relations activities

"The Allisonville Story" has been told in many ways, in many places, by many people. We have had the points of view of a principal, a college professor, library and curriculum coordinators, librarians, and teachers. Types of activities included speeches (some of them en-

The card catalog directs these students to many kinds of instructional materials.

hanced by visual materials), magazine and newspaper articles, dramatic productions, orientation talks, workshops, guided tours of the library, consultant assistance to other libraries, and a number of booklets, pamphlets, questionnaires, and similar material designed to focus attention on important aspects of the library program.

These activities were presented before people who represented every facet of the educational picture. We were also able to reach such individuals as a newspaper publisher interested in helping to develop the schools of his community through positive editorial policy and a school architect who wished to understand a good library situation and then to plan a school around it.

Promotional activities were carried on by local representatives of the Project throughout the state of Indiana and in the states of Illinois, Kentucky, Ohio, Wisconsin, and Oregon. These activities were further extended by the reactions and reports of the many visitors to the school.

Influence of the Project in Washington Township

There is no doubt that the Allisonville Knapp School Libraries Project demonstration has had a marked effect on libraries in the local community. At the onset of this three-year project, there were libraries in the other elementary schools comparable in size and personnel to that at Allisonville. There were long range goals for the future development of all of these elementary libraries. However, the addition of Project funds made possible a rapid expansion of services at Allisonville, and the success of the Project activities there has stimulated more rapid expansion in the other elementary libraries.

Perhaps the single most important phase of development at Allisonville has been the involvement of *all* teachers. This is not easy and is a relatively slow process, since far too many teachers are not really library-oriented. They need assistance in structuring assignments, in classroom organization, etc., to make the most effective use of materials. The concentrated cooperation of librarian, principal, curriculum coordinator, and the university field worker — working together with teachers at all grade levels—has produced the desired outcome: full utilization of a range of resources to make teaching and learning an exciting and vital process.

The additional personnel provided by the Knapp Project at Allisonville ensured the availability of the librarians for consultation with teachers in the matters of resources in curriculum planning. Observation of this has led to recognition of the need for additional personnel in all of the elementary libraries.

Enlarged library facilities have been and are being provided in several existing libraries in the school district. Libraries in new buildings will be larger and more functional than in the past. A great deal of this is a result of observation of space utilization in the enlarged Allisonville library. Listening-viewing study carrels are now standard equipment in all elementary libraries.

The publicity given the Project locally and in national publications has certainly kept the community informed of the progress of the Project. Every effort has been made to inform local librarians and principals about the new ideas and activities being incorporated into the library program at Allisonville. Some of these have been used with success in other local libraries, and

Before viewing this filmstrip, an Allisonville sixth grader checks it for breaks.

others will without a doubt be adapted for use in the other libraries as space and staff permit.

On occasion, local librarians, teachers, and principals have assisted in planning projects. For example, the two coordinators of school libraries in the school district have served for three years as members of the local advisory committee. A teacher from another elementary school in the district participated as a member of the readiness team before Project-sponsored visits began. Most recently, with the cooperation of their instructor, two high school students have put their training in drafting to a practical project. They have completed sketches and blueprints of the library facilities in all phases of its development. The drawing of the present facility is a part of the final report of the Project. (See facing page.)

The influence of the Knapp Project at Allisonville School will certainly not cease with the official closing date. It will doubtless be felt and serve as a guide for development of elementary libraries for many years to come — not only in Washington Township schools, but all over the state of Indiana.

Teacher reaction to the Project

Four Allisonville teachers, working with Mrs. Michels, head librarian at Allisonville, wrote this statement:

Teachers at Allisonville School had been appreciative of the library program in existence at the school long before our participation in the Knapp School Libraries Project. However, they probably were not fully aware of how much a library equipped and staffed according to ALA standards could alter teaching techniques and improve student learning.

This change of techniques did not happen automatically. Guidance was given to the faculty in the form of lectures, discussion groups, professional reading assignments, and in observation and constructive criticism. The Resource Committee (Committee of 21) was most helpful in this respect. The easy accessibility of professional literature in our library also had its effect upon our staff, and hence, upon our students.

Today, students with their sophisticated and creative use of library facilities and materials are adding their own new dimensions to learning.

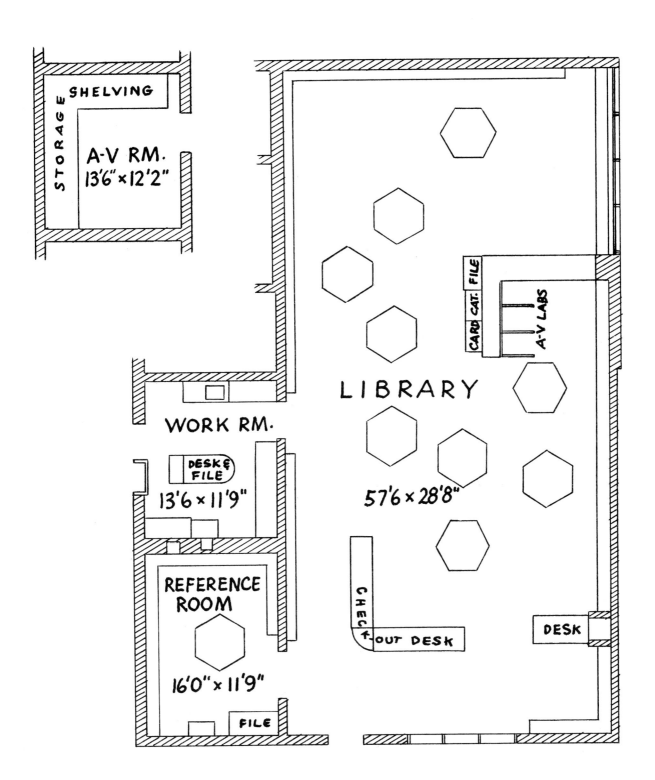

Influence of the Project in Indiana

The publicity, participation of Allisonville staff and the field worker in professional meetings, and visits by educators and community leaders to the school certainly have affected many schools in Indiana. When federal funds became available, elementary library programs received a major share. This is particularly significant in Title I of the Elementary and Secondary Education Act, since over half of the school systems participating in this program felt that the elementary library program had priority in filling the needs of educationally deprived students. Librarians have long contended that a child without a central elementary library program is an educationally deprived child, but it is good to see so many people with ''money in the bank'' thinking along these lines.

In addition to encouraging and influencing the establishment of new elementary library programs, existing programs were improved. This is particularly significant in the development of the instructional materials concept and of more flexibility in program scheduling.

The planning of new elementary library quarters has been influenced by the space provided at Allisonville. Many persons envisioned smaller

Kindergarteners in the library show they have learned how to handle books and enjoy them.

quarters than Allisonville, but, after visiting this project, went home convinced that many more square feet were essential.

Having Allisonville in Indiana has been a recruiting device to encourage teachers to take additional training to qualify for elementary library positions. They could predict the increase in the number of elementary positions in the immediate future. It also has encouraged librarians to participate in in-service training programs, workshops, institutes, etc., to update their training.

VISITATIONS

Initial visitation

Our prime concern at Allisonville School was, and is, that visitors should observe the program and not merely the facilities. We were also concerned to have our visitors see all aspects of program with thoughtful recognition of the ways it has developed and the reasons for that kind of development.

In an effort to meet this challenge, we carefully selected an initial visitation team whose task it was, after spending a day with us, to criticize not only our program, but our presentation of the program. These people from Indiana and neighboring states included a superintendent, principal, curriculum coordinator, teacher, librarian, school board member, school planning committee member, a member of the Knapp School Libraries Project's national advisory

committee and a faculty member from our cooperating teacher education institution, Ball State University.

This visit followed a schedule similar to the one outlined in the Project handbook. (See page 10.) Reactions of these visitors, though generally favorable, suggested some dissatisfaction with the distribution of time allowed in the library and in the classroom, with the regrets divided about equally between a wish for more time in the classroom and a wish for more time in the library. To meet this diversity of interest and opinion, we extended in future visitations the half-hour ''free period'' to an hour and a half. We have continued to follow this procedure for all Knapp Project-sponsored visitors and for other large groups.

Our visitors have come from thirty-five states

and from five foreign countries. We usually attempted to combine small groups with other small groups. This has been most successful. The problems that are aired, the solutions that have taken place, the general exchange of ideas — all contribute to an exciting day.

All correspondence relating to the proposed visits was reviewed by the library staff. We discussed how we could best meet the needs of each group. Sometimes it was decided that an informal day would serve the visitors best. On these occasions, the librarians shared the responsibility of taking the visitors on a tour of the library. Visitors were then permitted to visit classrooms; they returned to the library to ask questions that had arisen during the day. Visitors were also invited to spend some time in the faculty lounge where they had an opportunity to converse with Allisonville teachers, thus gaining another point of view.

Visitors seemed most interested in the following subjects:

(1) How use of audio-visual equipment is scheduled.

(2) How the community resource file works.

(3) Use of the Dewey Decimal Classification in cataloging all books, filmstrips, recordings, pictures, tapes, and models.

(4) How the oversized pictures are housed.

(5) The use of student assistants.

(6) The sophistication students exhibit in their choice of materials.

(7) The high degree of utilization of materials.

Follow-up communications from visitors, return visits by some individuals and groups, and their word-of-mouth recommendations to others indicate that we are meeting the needs of these people with a high degree of success.

Teacher and student reactions to visitors

Teachers and students at Allisonville School have reacted favorably to participation in a demonstration program. First reactions of apprehension at being observed at work in the classroom were quickly replaced by an eagerness to benefit from the enriching experiences of our guests.

There are, perhaps, two reasons for this attitude. First, the school program remained unchanged on the days we had guests, thereby leaving teacher and student in a familiar setting, free to carry on their work as usual. Secondly, the guests, because of their intense interest in quality education, served as stimulants to teachers and students alike.

Guests and students spoke freely to each other both in the library and in the halls, and the faculty lounge served as a place where teachers and guests could have an exchange of ideas.

EVALUATION

A Summary of findings

During 1965, 1966, and 1967, an attempt was made to measure the influence of a well equipped and managed centralized library upon the development of library skills, appreciations, and understandings of the children enrolled in fourth and sixth grade classes at the Allisonville Elementary School, Indianapolis, Indiana. This study was a part of the Knapp School Libraries Project. Testing was carried out in January of each of the three years.

To identify the specific skills, understandings, and appreciations considered important by informed persons in the fields of library science and reading, a broad and unrefined list of many library-related skills, attitudes, and understandings was constructed and sent to library and reading specialists for their judgments. Specialists at the national, state, and local levels were included. Each was asked to rate the items in order of importance. A summary of their ratings begins on page 74. The original list was then refined and shortened, based on the specialists' ranking of items, to serve as a basis for the evaluation of children's library and reading skill development at Allisonville. The list beginning on page 78 and the methods to be used in evaluating were selected.

Tabulation of Responses By Library and Reading Personnel at the Local, State, and National Levels

In tabulating responses a weight of three (3) was given for first choices, a weight of two (2) was given for second choices and a weight of one (1) was given to third choices. With ten respondents the total frequency possible on any item was therefore thirty (30).

He desires to keep materials in
    good order and good repair.23
He respects the integrity of
    others 18
He is obtaining a greater sense
    of moral and spiritual
    values 21
Work and study
He takes pride in his work......24
He asks for help only when
    necessary 20
He does not give up early......16
He plans work before starting..22
He enjoys working on a
    difficult task 13
He follows directions well......26
He uses appropriate materials
    effectively in problem
    solving 23
He works to the best of his
    ability 27
He is gaining in self-direction..15
He is learning to finish work on
    time 17
He is resourceful in finding
    things to do during leisure
    time 20
He is developing an attitude of
    intellectual curiosity 23
He is pursuing persistent
    interests 12
He is developing new interests..20
He is enriching his background
    of knowledge 23
He works creatively with library
    materials 24

Language
He appreciates importance of
    good language 21
He holds to the point in
    discussion 14
He is showing growth in vocabu-
    lary. He uses new words and
    has an interesting vocab-
    ulary 21
He shows interest and progress
    in speaking and thinking
    logically 21
He arranges work on paper
    reasonably well 19
Social studies
He reasons well in solving
    problems 24
He makes interesting reports of
    reference materials read...25
He contributes interesting in-
    formation and materials....21
He shows an alert and question-
    ing attitude 21
Reading
He shows a keen interest in
    reading 26
He reads voluntarily for
    enjoyment 24
He is interested in varied types
    of reading 21
He is able to interpret how
    characters feel about situa-
    tions from reading stories..17
He is forming desirable reading
    habits 22
He is improving in his reading..19
He reads rapidly with good
    comprehension 22
He shows growing interest in
    good literature 24
He reads more widely 23
He reads more high quality
    books 17
He appreciates and respects the
    value of printed materials..17
He becomes intellectually and
    emotionally involved in what
    he reads 13
He establishes purposes in
    reading 17
He is developing the habit of
    appraising critically 21
He is developing an awareness of
    book illustrations 24
He is developing judgment in
    selecting worthwhile books..24
He reads in more interest areas.26
He uses public library more
    frequently 18

Science

A student participates with Mrs. Audrey Michels, librarian, in this library skills lesson.

Mr. Charles Boelke, Allisonville teacher, explains a basketball play with a filmstrip.

The testing and assessment of skills and understandings include an appraisal of children's knowledge of the arrangement and classification of materials within the Allisonville library, their ability to understand the organization and function of the important parts of a book (title page, table of contents, index), and to locate and use basic references, including the catalog cards, unabridged dictionary, encyclopedia, and *National Geographic Index*. Reports of evaluation are listed beginning on page 84. A special reading test was constructed with the help and counsel of reading specialists to measure children's abilities in specific reading study skills, and individual interviews were conducted to assess children's attitudes toward reading, their use of the library, and their ability to express their ideas effectively concerning their readings. Special periods were scheduled for classroom groups to have individual or group data-gathering activities in the library so that observers could make judgments regarding specific aspects of their behavior and performance. Teachers were asked to observe their classes over a month's time and make further judgments about the quality of children's work with library materials. An attempt was made to relate children's performances on these tests to their scores on standardized tests of intelligence and reading. General analysis of performance excluded students who had been enrolled in Allisonville less than six months at the time of testing.

METHODS OF EVALUATION TO BE EMPLOYED IN THE ASSESSMENT OF PUPIL GROWTH IN LIBRARY SKILLS AND ATTITUDES	Standardized Achievement Test	Library Acquaintance Test	Classroom Observation	Library Skills Test	Teacher Evaluation	Librarian Evaluation	Personal Interview	Circulation Records	Special Reading Test
1. The child handles library materials carefully					X	X		X	
2. The student is courteous and orderly			X		X	X	X		
3. The child knows how to check out books						X		X	
4. The pupil knows how to return books						X		X	
5. The child knows how to renew books						X		X	
6. The child knows what and where the title is				X					
7. The student knows what and who the author is				X					
8. The pupil knows what and who the illustrator is				X					
9. The child knows what and who the publisher is				X					
10. The pupil can use the table of contents to determine a book's contents	X			X					
11. The child can use the index to a degree appropriate for his age	X			X					
12. The pupil knows the basic kinds of materials available in the library		X					X		

METHODS OF EVALUATION TO BE EMPLOYED IN THE ASSESSMENT OF PUPIL GROWTH IN LIBRARY SKILLS AND ATTITUDES	Standardized Achievement Test	Library Acquaintance Test	Classroom Observations	Library Skills Test	Teacher Evaluation	Librarian Evaluation	Personal Interview	Circulation Records	Special Reading Test
13. The child knows where to look for fiction books		X							
14. The pupil knows where to look for nonfiction books		X							
15. The child knows where reference materials are located		X							
16. The child can find and use dictionaries	X	X		X					
17. The child can find and use encyclopedias		X		X					
18. The pupil can find and use indexes to library resources		X		X					
19. The child can find and use magazines		X		X					
20. The pupil can find and use maps appropriate for his age group		X				X			
21. The pupil can locate filmstrips appropriate to given topics		X							
22. The child can locate recordings appropriate to particular topics		X							
23. The pupil is familiar with the Dewey Decimal classification system				X					

METHODS OF EVALUATION TO BE EMPLOYED IN THE ASSESSMENT OF PUPIL GROWTH IN LIBRARY SKILLS AND ATTITUDES	Standardized Achievement Test	Library Acquaintance Test	Classroom Observations	Library Skills Test	Teacher Evaluation	Librarian Evaluation	Personal Interview	Circulation Records	Special Reading Test
24. The student knows how to use the card catalog as a means to locating library materials				X					
25. The student is familiar with the differences in the three types of catalog cards				X					
26. The student can locate specific books by using an author card				X					
27. The pupil can locate specific books by using a title card				X					
28. The child can locate specific books by using a subject card				X					
29. The student can identify the author's name on the catalog card				X					
30. The pupil can identify the title on the catalog card				X					
31. The child can identify the name of publisher on the catalog card				X					
32. The pupil can identify the copyright date on the catalog card				X					
33. The student can identify the call number or Dewey Decimal number on the catalog card				X					

METHODS OF EVALUATION TO BE EMPLOYED IN THE ASSESSMENT OF PUPIL GROWTH IN LIBRARY SKILLS AND ATTITUDES	Standardized Achievement Test	Library Acquaintance Test	Classroom Observation	Library Skills Test	Teacher Evaluation	Librarian Evaluation	Personal Interview	Circulation Records	Special Reading Test
34. The child is able to scan for particular information									X
35. The pupil can browse for special books		X			X				
36. The student can outline relevant information from materials appropriate to his grade level									X
37. The student can take notes on particular topics appropriate to his grade level									X
38. The child can read for particular purposes (to organize ideas into sequence, cause and effect or other relationships)	X								X
39. The pupil can choose worthwhile reading materials independently					X	X	X	X	
40. The child can give, take and use suggestions and criticism					X				
41. The child can express ideas effectively in discussing books or other materials			X		X		X		
42. The pupil can distinguish between fact and opinion, the significant and the trivial									X

METHODS OF EVALUATION TO BE EMPLOYED IN THE ASSESSMENT OF PUPIL GROWTH IN LIBRARY SKILLS AND ATTITUDES	Standardized Achievement Test	Library Acquaintance Test	Classroom Observations	Library Skills Test	Teacher Evaluation	Librarian Evaluation	Personal Interview	Circulation Records	Special Reading Test
43. The student can form his own judgment about ideas presented in books or other materials			X						
44. The child is developing standards of taste and appreciation in reading					X		X	X	
45. The child can make and use a bibliography									X
46. The child can retain a normal number of ideas from readings									X
47. The child works well with groups of other children			X		X				
48. The pupil respects the rights and properties of others					X				
49. The student displays good self-control			X		X				
50. The child is normally attentive when others are talking			X		X				
51. The child is developing leadership based upon the knowledge he has acquired					X				
52. The pupil takes pride in his work					X				
53. The child asks for help only when necessary					X	X			

METHODS OF EVALUATION TO BE EMPLOYED IN THE ASSESSMENT OF PUPIL GROWTH IN LIBRARY SKILLS AND ATTITUDES	Standardized Achievement Test	Library Acquaintance Test	Classroom Observations	Library Skills Test	Teacher Evaluation	Librarian Evaluation	Personal Interview	Circulation Records	Special Reading Test
54. The student follows directions well					X				
55. The child uses appropriate materials effectively in problem-solving			X		X				
56. The student is resourceful in finding constructive things to do during leisure periods of time					X				
57. The pupil is developing an attitude of intellectual curiosity			X		X		X		
58. The child is actively extending his knowledge					X				
59. The student works creatively with library materials			X		X				
60. The child shows interest and progress in thinking and speaking logically					X				
61. The student reads voluntarily for enjoyment					X		X		
62. The pupil reads fluently with good comprehension	X								X
63. The child is developing an awareness of book illustrations					X				
64. The child is finding increasing satisfactions in using library materials							X		

In an effort to determine how students with limited library resources would score on these tests, a population of students at fourth and sixth grade levels enrolled in the 25th Street School in Anderson, Indiana, was included. The fourth and sixth graders from the Forest Hills School in Anderson, which had no library services, were also used in this study.

LONG RANGE GOALS FOR SCHOOL LIBRARIES

When the Knapp Project started at Allisonville, we had only a half-time librarian without secretarial help; Project funds increased staff to two full-time librarians and a full-time secretary. We plan to continue in the future with a full-time librarian, a library aide, and a full-time secretary.

The Knapp Project has certainly influenced the remodeling of three libraries in other elementary schools in Washington Township last summer. Much of the equipment and program which had been developed in the Knapp Project has been included. One new elementary school has opened since the Knapp Project began, and this elementary school library was air-conditioned and equipped on a plan similar to that for the Allisonville School library, which was expanded and air-conditioned and which received additional equipment principally because of Knapp Project funds. It seems obvious that the expenditure of the Knapp Project investment has stepped up use of tax money not only in the elementary school library at Allisonville but in all other elementary school libraries in the district as well. It has also stimulated the planning, equipping, and provision of services in all of our nine other elementary libraries (instructional materials centers) and the inservice education of library personnel and all elementary teachers in our system.

We are confident that the level of instruction has been and will be improved in all of our elementary schools because of the Knapp School Libraries Project at Allisonville Elementary School. We are also confident that it has had an equally positive influence on the education of elementary librarians and teachers at Ball State University.

INTERPRETATION OF TABULATED DATA

Until the data presented in the table on pages 86 through 107 are processed through the computer, it is necessary to rely upon very simple comparisons and interpretations. In comparing successive groups of fourth and sixth grade children at Allisonville with similar children in control schools, it appears that the following conclusions are warranted:

Reading Test:
1. Successive fourth grades enrolled at Allisonville School improved on seven phases of the test (forming judgments, distinguishing fact from opinion, building a bibliography, outlining, notetaking, timed comprehension, and distinguishing significant from less important information). They did not improve in skimming and identifying sequence. (See page 86.)
2. Fourth graders during the last year of the testing outscored their counterparts in the control school without a library on seven of the nine subtests. (See page 86.)
3. Successive sixth grades enrolled at Allisonville

School improved on five of the nine subtests (forming judgments, distinguishing fact from opinion, outlining, timed comprehension, and notetaking). They did not improve in skimming, building a bibliography, identifying sequence and distinguishing significant from less important information. (See page 87.)

4. Sixth graders during the last year of the testing outscored their counterparts in the control school without a library on all nine subtests. (See page 87.)

Library Acquaintance Test:

1. Successive fourth grades enrolled at Allisonville equalled or improved their performance on seven of the nine subtests included in the library acquaintance assessment. Very small differences in favor of earlier groups may be noted in locating magazines and recordings. (See page 88.)

2. The students enrolled in successive sixth grades remained the same or improved on all nine subtests included in the library acquaintance assessment. (See page 88.)

Library Skills Test:

1. Students enrolled in successive fourth grades improved on twenty-one of the twenty-three subtests in the library skills assessment. Slight differences favored the earlier groups in finding the title on title pages of books and locating encyclopedias. (See page 89.)

2. Allisonville fourth grades (1967) outperformed their counterparts in the control school without a library on all subtests except finding the table of contents within books (1 percent difference in favor of the control school group). See page 89.)

3. Successive sixth grades remained the same or improved on twenty-two of the twenty-three subtests in the library skills assessment. Scores, however, were generally very high. Greatest improvement was recorded in the identification of catalog cards and publisher and the use of the *National Geographic Index.* (See page 90.)

4. Sixth graders during the last year outperformed their counterparts in the control school without a library except in finding the table of contents, in which all students (1967) scored 100 percent. (See page 90.)

Teacher's Checklist:

The annual turnover of teachers at Allisonville (approximately 20 percent additions or replacements) made this portion of the assessment extremely difficult to administer. There seemed to be no way to standardize judgments. Teachers' expectations vary greatly, and their judgments about children's skills and understandings reflected these differences in expectations. (See page 91.)

Personal Interview:

1. The library ranked first among fourth grade children's choices of activities each year, but there was a slight drop in interest as the excitement which accompanied the opening of the new library facilities diminished. (See pages 96-100.)

2. Fourth grade children at Allisonville read consistently more than children attending the control school without a library.

3. Fourth grade children at Allisonville improved in their ability to express ideas over the three-year period and consistently outstripped their counterparts in the control school without a library.

4. The breadth of reading interests of fourth graders remained much the same over the three-year period. They greatly surpassed their counterparts in the control school without a library.

5. The library ranked first among sixth grade children's choices of activities each year, although there was a slight drop the second year. (See pages 101-107.)

6. A great majority of the sixth grade children read books regularly, but there was a slight drop in this category over the three-year period.

7. Successive sixth grades at Allisonville improved in their ability to express themselves and outstripped their counterparts in the school without a library.

8. Sixth grade children at Allisonville read more widely than sixth graders in the control school without a library.

READING TEST—GRADE 4
(Expressed as Percent Successful)

	Allisonville			Control (No Library)			Control (With Library)		
	1965	1966	1967	1965	1966	1967	1965	1966	1967
Number	80	97	104	28	21	26	26	32	29
1. Forming your own judgment:									
2	39	45	47	41	19	31	46	56	45
1	46	42	41	24	48	42	35	31	34
0	**15**	**13**	**12**	35	33	27	19	13	21
2. Distinguishing fact from opinion:									
5	38	50	39	14	0	38	65	56	45
4	10	7	21	14	19	27	8	16	34
3	30	27	23	34	33	23	23	16	14
2	19	11	10	21	29	12	4	12	7
1	3	4	6	7	19	0	0	0	0
0	0	1	1	10	0	0	0	0	0
3. Skimming:									
6	46	58	46	38	43	35	65	41	35
5	40	29	33	38	43	38	23	28	38
4	9	9	15	24	5	8	12	19	14
3	5	1	5	0	0	15	0	9	10
2	0	3	1	0	5	4	0	3	0
1	0	0	0	0	4	0	0	0	3
4. Building a bibliography:									
6	41	30	44	52	43	46	46	41	42
5	24	31	25	24	28	19	19	25	17
4	18	29	22	18	19	27	19	16	24
3	12	9	6	3	10	8	8	12	7
2	4	1	2	3	0	0	8	6	10
1	1	0	1	0	0	0	0	0	0
5. Outlining:									
Outstanding	17	31	36	24	14	30	11	19	21
Good	59	51	52	62	43	35	54	62	55
Poor	24	18	12	14	43	35	35	19	24
6. Sequence:	61	64	59	59	52	46	69	63	48
7. Notetaking:									
Outstanding	6	12	7	0	4	4	4	3	17
Good	53	58	70	41	48	46	65	56	48
Poor	41	30	23	59	48	50	31	41	35
8. Timed comprehension:									
Exercise 1									
5	38	49	36	48	43	42	50	56	55
4	45	33	47	31	33	42	34	19	21
3	10	12	11	21	14	0	8	16	7
2	7	5	6	0	10	0	8	6	10
1	0	1	0	0	0	12	0	0	7
0	0	0	0	0	0	4	0	3	0
Exercise 2									
5	43	52	49	55	38	50	46	44	45
4	43	28	36	41	33	26	27	31	24
3	11	15	10	4	21	12	19	22	14
2	1	5	4	0	5	0	4	0	14
1	2	0	1	0	0	12	4	3	3
0	0	0	0	0	0	0	0	0	0
9. Distinguishing the significant from the less important:									
6	18	25	19	7	19	12	0	16	24
5	21	40	38	38	10	15	27	19	24
4	28	14	20	14	33	19	11	28	17
3	12	9	11	7	14	23	35	16	17
2	5	7	10	14	10	19	8	12	10
1	5	3	2	10	14	0	8	6	4
0	**11**	**2**	**0**	10	0	12	11	3	4

READING TEST—GRADE 6

(Expressed as Percent Successful)

	Allisonville			Control (No Library)			Control (With Library)		
	1965	1966	1967	1965	1966	1967	1965	1966	1967
Number	77	81	95	35	32	33	31	26	31
1. Forming your own judgment:									
2	31	41	43	23	37	16	48	50	32
1	39	34	46	51	41	42	45	42	39
0	30	25	11	26	22	42	7	8	29
2. Distinguishing fact from opinion:									
4	74	78	82	69	56	58	87	73	81
3	13	12	10	8	22	21	10	12	6
2	11	6	6	20	9	18	0	15	10
1	1	4	2	3	4	3	3	0	3
0	1	0	0	0	9	0	0	0	0
3. Skimming:									
3	51	43	48	23	59	15	42	39	52
2	36	43	40	57	23	40	48	46	35
1	12	14	11	20	15	33	10	15	3
0	1	0	1	0	3	12	0	0	10
4. Choosing books for a bibliography:									
6	59	51	54	49	25	33	48	46	42
5	23	27	34	28	25	37	36	38	36
4	9	19	10	23	41	18	16	12	13
3	5	2	2	0	6	9	0	4	6
2	3	1	0	0	3	0	0	0	3
1	1	0	0	0	0	3	0	0	0
5. Outlining:									
Outstanding	27	16	39	6	16	6	19	31	29
Good	47	64	53	57	53	42	55	54	39
Poor	26	20	8	37	31	52	26	15	32
6. Sequence	79	83	75	71	75	61	77	85	68
7. Notetaking:									
Outstanding	13	13	20	3	12	6	7	12	32
Good	49	70	71	66	66	42	74	61	55
Poor	38	17	9	31	22	52	19	27	13
8. Timed comprehension:									
Exercise 1									
7	23	21	4	14	13	4	29	27	52
6	40	31	52	43	25	12	32	23	16
5	19	28	24	23	34	9	26	35	13
4	7	11	12	11	13	4	10	11	6
3	7	5	3	3	3	3	3	4	10
2	0	4	5	6	6	1	0	0	0
1	4	0	0	0	6	0	0	0	3
0	0	0	0	0	0	1	0	0	0
Exercise 2									
7	4	1	32	0	3	0	0	0	16
6	58	38	38	54	50	33	55	61	55
5	30	24	21	12	19	33	19	15	7
4	7	7	5	14	3	16	13	12	10
3	1	9	3	14	9	6	10	0	6
2	0	2	1	3	13	12	3	12	3
1	0	0	0	3	0	0	0	0	0
0	0	0	0	0	3	0	0	0	3
9. Distinguishing the significant from the less important:									
4	30	11	22	14	9	18	10	19	7
3	19	22	21	14	9	9	13	19	26
2	35	48	49	40	57	46	55	46	42
1	13	10	6	23	22	15	19	12	6
0	3	9	2	9	3	12	3	4	19

LIBRARY ACQUAINTANCE TEST
(Expressed as Percent Successful)

	Allisonville						Control (With Library)					
	Grade 4			Grade 6			Grade 4			Grade 6		
	1965	1966	1967	1965	1966	1967	1965	1966	1967	1965	1966	1967
Number......	79	101	104	79	81	95	26	34	29	26	26	31
1. Fiction books	68	90	89	54	86	95	54	86	79	93	92	81
2. Nonfiction books	74	87	87	91	91	94	46	94	83	93	88	87
3. Dictionary	80	100	99	97	100	100	96	46	79	90	100	74
4. Encyclopedia	100	100	100	100	100	100	73	80	62	90	85	90
5. Index	95	100	98	91	100	100	—	—	—	—	—	—
6. Magazines	99	96	97	99	100	100	—	—	—	—	—	—
7. Maps	65	85	82	87	96	99	—	—	—	—	—	—
8. Filmstrips	98	100	99	91	100	100	77	91	79	93	92	97
9. Recordings	91	96	90	87	100	99	—	—	—	—	—	—

LIBRARY SKILLS TEST—GRADE 4
(Expressed as Percent Successful)

	Allisonville			Control (No Library)			Control (With Library)		
	1965	1966	1967	1965	1966	1967	1965	1966	1967
Number...............	80	102	105	29	21	26	26	35	29
I. Identification: Catalog cards									
Author card	69	75	85	38	24	62	85	80	52
Title card	55	61	82	34	19	58	73	77	66
Subject card	55	55	75	31	10	31	58	77	52
II. Use: catalog cards									
Call number	86	97	96	66	86	92	62	91	97
Author	90	87	95	72	52	81	96	89	90
Title	49	85	96	62	67	92	77	97	86
Publisher	20	18	61	34	29	38	62	43	65
Copyright date	55	77	95	62	81	50	81	86	83
III. Finding book	63	68	84	—	—	65	77	77	86
IV. Finding title page	84	86	97	52	48	62	88	60	86
Title	100	100	99	100	81	96	100	97	100
Author	93	97	99	83	81	88	88	91	97
Illustrator	88	88	93	83	71	65	85	83	93
Publisher	56	66	98	66	48	35	88	57	76
V. Table of contents									
Finding	98	99	99	93	100	100	100	91	97
Using	91	92	93	86	81	85	100	89	83
VI. Index									
Finding	95	93	100	66	71	77	92	100	97
Using	80	78	83	86	62	73	100	89	66
VII. Dictionary									
Word meaning	73	95	91	86	67	85	88	80	86
Word pronunciation	35	59	48	69	43	38	69	54	55
VIII. Encyclopedia	91	81	89	41	52	38	54	80	45
IX. *National Geographic Index*	78	78	95	—	—	—	77	84	98

LIBRARY SKILLS TEST—GRADE 6
(Expressed as Percent Successful)

	Allisonville			Control (No Library)			Control (With Library)		
	1965	1966	1967	1965	1966	1967	1965	1966	1967
Number..................	75	81	95	35	33	33	30	26	31
I. Identification:									
Catalog cards									
Author card	89	95	99	20	39	55	100	85	94
Title card	68	91	89	33	39	49	94	92	87
Subject card	67	88	88	40	27	42	87	88	94
II. Use:									
Catalog cards									
Call number	95	90	99	97	100	100	94	100	100
Author	95	96	100	66	91	88	100	92	100
Title	83	99	93	43	97	88	97	100	97
Publisher	35	77	83	57	58	58	71	69	77
Copyright date	83	95	97	94	94	88	100	100	97
III. Finding book	92	91	95	—	—	76	93	85	100
IV. Finding title page	80	80	97	71	58	76	97	88	94
Title	100	100	100	97	100	97	100	100	100
Author	100	100	98	94	94	97	97	96	97
Illustrator	95	89	97	71	82	91	94	96	94
Publisher	91	95	96	63	79	91	87	81	87
V. Table of contents									
Finding	99	99	100	91	97	100	100	100	94
Using	96	100	99	89	79	91	100	100	90
VI. Index									
Finding	100	100	100	80	91	97	100	100	100
Using	97	98	100	83	76	76	94	96	97
VII. Dictionary									
Word meaning	85	100	99	94	85	94	100	96	94
Word pronunciation	64	75	76	66	55	39	100	85	58
VIII. Encyclopedia	97	96	98	86	85	88	87	85	84
IX. *National Geographic Index*	77	84	98	—	—	—	—	—	—

TEACHER'S CHECKLIST TO BE USED IN ASSESSING PARTICULAR BEHAVIORS

CLASS: Grade 4, Allisonville Number of students: 1965—98; 1966—131; 1967—129	Percent of Children Displaying a Strength in This			Percent of Children Displaying an Inadequacy in This			Percent of Children That Could Not Be Observed		
	1965	1966	1967	1965	1966	1967	1965	1966	1967
1. The child handles library materials carefully.	61	90	83	34	10	12	5	0	5
2. The student is courteous and orderly.	74	78	73	26	12	11	0	10	16
3. The pupil can find and use maps appropriate for his age group.	77	60	66	23	20	15	0	20	19
4. The pupil can browse for special books.	78	66	70	18	21	12	4	13	18
5. The student can choose worthwhile reading materials independently.	77	89	70	23	11	12	0	0	18
6. The child can give, take, and use suggestions and criticisms.	73	60	75	23	14	13	4	26	12
7. The pupil can express ideas effectively in discussing books or other materials.	51	63	42	49	24	15	0	13	43
8. The child is developing standards of taste and appreciation in reading.	72	67	73	28	19	7	0	14	20
9. The child works well with groups of other children.	79	74	81	21	22	11	0	4	8
10. The pupil respects the rights and properties of others.	86	71	81	14	10	5	0	19	14
11. The student displays good self-control.	78	79	91	22	16	6	0	5	3
12. The child is normally attentive when others are talking.	76	62	69	24	18	12	0	20	19
13. The child is developing leadership based upon the knowledge he has acquired.	49	38	44	39	24	24	12	38	32
14. The pupil takes pride in his work.	64	64	82	36	17	11	0	19	7
15. The child asks for help only when necessary.	69	57	55	31	19	24	0	24	21
16. The student follows directions well.	64	65	85	36	33	15	0	2	0
17. The child uses appropriate materials effectively in problem-solving.	40	39	47	27	28	23	33	33	30
18. The student is resourceful in finding constructive things to do during leisure periods of time.	53	69	74	40	28	20	7	3	6

Teacher's Checklist to Be Used in Assessing Particular Behaviors

CLASS: Grade 4, Allisonville Number of students: 1965—98; 1966—131; 1967—129	Percent of Children Displaying a Strength in This			Percent of Children Displaying an Inadequacy in This			Percent of Children That Could Not Be Observed		
	1965	1966	1967	1965	1966	1967	1965	1966	1967
19. The pupil is developing an attitude of intellectual curiosity.	59	56	48	39	14	21	2	30	31
20. The child is actively extending his knowledge.	73	66	81	15	18	13	12	16	6
21. The student works creatively with library materials.	76	61	54	24	20	23	0	19	23
22. The child shows interest and progress in speaking and thinking logically.	84	44	62	16	30	19	0	26	19
23. The student reads voluntarily for enjoyment.	79	84	82	17	11	14	4	5	4
24. The child is developing an awareness of book illustrations.	41	64	74	21	18	7	38	18	19

TEACHER'S CHECKLIST TO BE USED IN ASSESSING PARTICULAR BEHAVIORS

CLASS: Grade 6, Allisonville Number of students: 1965—97; 1966—98; 1967—114	Percent of Children Displaying a Strength in This			Percent of Children Dispaying an Inadequacy in This			Percent of Children That Could Not Be Observed		
	1965	1966	1967	1965	1966	1967	1965	1966	1967
1. The child handles library materials carefully.	89	95	89	10	5	7	1	0	4
2. The student is courteous and orderly.	80	90	81	20	10	16	0	0	3
3. The pupil can find and use maps appropriate for his age group.	57	91	67	10	9	8	33	0	25
4. The pupil can browse for special books.	92	93	94	8	7	6	0	0	0
5. The student can choose worthwhile reading materials independently.	88	89	85	12	11	15	0	0	0
6. The child can give, take, and use suggestions and criticisms.	81	89	83	19	11	16	0	0	1
7. The pupil can express ideas effectively in discussing books or other materials.	76	67	79	24	31	17	0	2	4
8. The child is developing standards of taste and appreciation in reading.	90	96	93	10	4	7	0	0	0
9. The child works well with groups of other children.	86	88	90	13	12	10	1	0	0
10. The pupil respects the rights and properties of others.	93	86	91	7	14	8	0	0	1
11. The student displays good self-control.	88	91	89	11	9	11	1	0	0
12. The child is normally attentive when others are talking.	86	88	86	14	12	14	0	0	0
13. The child is developing leadership based upon the knowledge he has acquired.	75	82	65	25	18	10	0	0	25
14. The pupil takes pride in his work.	87	81	85	13	19	11	0	0	4
15. The child asks for help only when necessary.	77	88	83	23	12	13	0	0	4
16. The student follows directions well.	76	80	84	24	20	16	0	0	0
17. The child uses appropriate materials effectively in problem-solving.	74	52	75	26	15	18	0	33	7

TEACHER'S CHECKLIST TO BE USED IN ASSESSING PARTICULAR BEHAVIORS

CLASS: Grade 6, Allisonville Number of students: 1965—97; 1966—98; 1967—114	Percent of Children Displaying a Strength in This			Percent of Children Displaying an Inadequacy in This			Percent of Children That Could Not Be Observed		
	1965	1966	1967	1965	1966	1967	1965	1966	1967
18. The student is resourceful in finding constructive things to do during leisure periods of time.	76	57	76	24	36	24	0	7	0
19. The pupil is developing an attitude of intellectual curiosity.	75	73	76	25	27	24	0	0	0
20. The child is actively extending his knowledge.	86	87	85	14	13	15	0	0	0
21. The student works creatively with library materials.	78	81	90	22	19	9	0	0	1
22. The child shows interest and progress in speaking and thinking logically.	79	87	82	21	13	18	0	0	0
23. The student reads voluntarily for enjoyment.	92	76	91	8	24	9	0	0	0
24. The child is developing an awareness of book illustrations.	80	92	98	20	8	1	0	0	1

LIBRARIAN'S CHECKLIST

CLASS: Grade 4 Number of students: 1965—99; 1966—126; 1967—129	Percent of Children Displaying a Strength in This			Percent of Children Displaying an Inadequacy in This			Percent of Children That Could Not Be Observed		
	1965	1966	1967	1965	1966	1967	1965	1966	1967
1. The child handles library materials carefully.	73	100	92	2	0	0	25	0	8
2. The student is courteous and orderly.	31	100	92	10	0	0	59	0	8
3. The child knows how to check out books.	100	100	92	0	0	0	0	0	8
4. The pupil knows how to return books.	100	100	92	0	0	0	0	0	8
5. The child knows how to renew books.	100	100	92	0	0	0	0	0	8
6. The pupil can choose worthwhile reading materials independently.	37	97	80	6	0	9	57	3	11
7. The child asks for help only when necessary.	15	99	89	6	0	3	79	1	8

LIBRARIAN'S CHECKLIST

CLASS: Grade 6 Number of students: 1965—97; 1966—93; 1967—114	Percent of Children Displaying a Strength in This			Percent of Children Displaying an Inadequacy in This			Percent of Children That Could Not Be Observed		
	1965	1966	1967	1965	1966	1967	1965	1966	1967
1. The child handles library materials carefully.	100	100	100	0	0	0	0	0	0
2. The student is courteous and orderly.	62	99	100	17	1	0	21	0	0
3. The child knows how to check out books.	100	100	100	0	0	0	0	0	0
4. The pupil knows how to return books.	100	100	100	0	0	0	0	0	0
5. The child knows how to renew books.	100	100	100	0	0	0	0	0	0
6. The pupil can choose worthwhile reading materials independently.	22	92	97	3	4	3	75	4	0
7. The child asks for help only when necessary.	68	99	100	1	0	0	31	1	0

PERSONAL INTERVIEW SHEET—GRADE 4
(Expressed as Frequency)

	Allisonville			Control (No Library)			Control (With Library)		
	1965	1966	1967	1965	1966	1967	1965	1966	1967
Number................	79	101	104	29	21	26	26	34	29
What kinds of materials have you used in the library?									
Magazines	20	14	17	0	0	1	2	0	2
Filmstrips	60	89	86	0	1	0	8	9	0
Recordings	53	57	46	0	0	0	5	0	0
Encyclopedias	53	78	85	2	2	19	3	9	7
Atlases	6	21	30	0	0	0	0	0	5
Nonfiction	46	44	66	9	3	15	22	19	16
Fiction	54	43	70	12	7	13	21	20	19
National Geographic Index (or other index)	17	25	21	1	0	0	0	0	0
Card catalog	46	42	50	2	4	12	18	26	15
Dictionary	10	24	34	1	1	3	6	7	7
Vertical file	7	12	0	0	0	0	0	0	1
Globes	2	0	4	0	0	0	0	0	0
Statesman's Yearbook	3	8	4	0	0	0	0	0	0
Reference room	5	8	1	0	0	0	1	0	0
Viewers	1	0	2	0	0	0	0	0	0
Models	0	2	4	0	0	0	0	0	0
Tapes	0	2	8	0	0	0	0	0	0
Almanac	0	2	0	0	0	0	0	0	0
Never go	0	0	0	0	5	0	0	0	0
Seldom go	0	0	0	0	1	0	0	0	0
Cutting box	0	0	2	0	0	0	0	0	0
Opaque projector	0	0	2	0	0	0	0	0	0
Book of Nations	0	0	2	0	0	0	0	0	0
Geographical dictionary	0	0	2	0	0	0	0	0	0

Note: Fifteen other categories or examples of materials and equipment were mentioned once by Allisonville students and not at all by students in the other schools. These included pamphlets, maps, overhead projector, and planetarium.

PERSONAL INTERVIEW SHEET—GRADE 4

(Expressed as Frequency)

	Allisonville			Control (No Library)			Control (With Library)		
	1965	1966	1967	1965	1966	1967	1965	1966	1967
Number.................	79	101	104	29	21	26	26	34	29
What kind of stories do you enjoy most?									
Mysteries	33	51	56	7	16	6	11	16	11
Biography	26	17	16	4	3	4	5	13	10
Animal	22	13	33	12	5	5	2	3	2
Adventure	16	15	25	5	2	7	3	10	6
Sports	12	12	8	0	2	3	1	4	0
Fiction	12	7	7	0	0	0	0	2	0
Science	7	7	6	3	1	0	1	0	1
War	3	2	1	0	0	1	4	3	0
Humorous	3	15	15	6	3	5	3	7	7
Science fiction	3	1	1	0	1	0	0	2	0
Fairy tales	1	15	5	2	1	0	0	0	3
Airplanes	2	3	1	0	1	0	0	0	0
Space	1	5	3	0	2	0	1	0	0
History	2	4	3	0	0	0	2	1	0
Sea	1	0	3	0	0	1	0	0	0
Pirates	0	1	0	1	0	0	0	0	0
Family	0	2	8	0	0	3	0	3	2
Cars	1	0	1	0	0	0	0	0	0
Western	0	0	1	1	0	0	1	0	0
School	0	0	0	1	0	0	0	0	0
Fish	0	0	0	0	1	0	0	0	0
Dinosaurs	0	0	0	0	0	0	1	0	0
Holidays	0	0	0	0	0	0	0	1	0
FBI	0	0	0	0	0	1	0	0	0
Poetry	0	0	2	0	0	1	0	0	0
Eskimos	0	0	0	0	0	1	0	0	0
Dancing	0	0	0	0	0	1	0	0	0

Note: Seven other kinds of stories (racing, pioneers, railroading, electricity, archeology, icebergs, and mythology) were mentioned once at Allisonville and not at either of the other schools.

PERSONAL INTERVIEW SHEET—GRADE 4

(Expressed as Frequency)

	Allisonville			Control (No Library)			Control (With Library)		
	1965	1966	1967	1965	1966	1967	1965	1966	1967
Number.................	79	101	104	29	21	26	26	34	29
How did you become interested in the last book you read?									
Part of series I enjoy	4	6	4	0	0	2	1	1	1
Supplementary to class studies	6	2	2	1	0	0	1	0	0
Card catalog	7	6	5	0	0	0	1	1	0
Wanted a mystery	1	1	1	0	0	0	0	0	0
Interested in author	3	0	1	0	0	0	0	0	1
Enjoyed author previously	3	6	2	0	0	0	0	0	0
Found on shelf	20	15	35	9	0	11	10	16	11
Book jacket	3	4	2	1	0	0	0	1	0
Read first page	1	1	1	0	0	0	0	1	0
Interested in subject	10	8	7	2	1	11	0	3	3
Was read to me several years ago	1	0	1	0	0	0	0	0	0
Skimmed through	4	5	8	0	1	0	0	0	0
Liked title	9	6	2	0	0	2	0	0	0
Read table of contents and preface	1	1	0	0	0	0	0	0	0
Recommended by a friend	10	13	14	5	5	1	3	6	3
Interested in pictures	2	1	0	0	0	1	0	1	1
Saw movie	1	0	1	0	1	1	0	1	0
A gift	1	0	4	0	5	0	0	0	0
Suggested by teacher	2	6	4	0	0	1	1	1	0
Browsing	0	15	11	10	0	0	6	2	0
Found at home	0	1	0	1	4	2	0	0	0
Saw on television	0	0	0	0	0	0	2	2	1
Wanted it for reference	0	0	0	0	0	0	1	0	0
Recommended by brother	0	1	2	0	0	0	0	0	0
Book club	0	1	1	0	0	0	0	0	0
Heard book report	0	2	0	0	0	0	0	0	0
Subject recommended by mother	0	0	0	0	1	0	0	0	0
Public library shelf	0	0	0	0	1	0	0	0	0
Presented to class by librarian	0	0	1	0	0	1	0	0	12
Librarian's help	0	0	3	0	0	0	0	1	0
Saw subject on TV	0	0	2	0	0	0	0	0	0
Read previously	0	0	1	0	0	1	0	0	0
Classroom book	0	0	0	0	4	0	0	0	0

Note: Nine other reasons for interest were mentioned once at Allisonville but not at either of the other schools. These were: wanted to build something, recommended by sister, recommended by father, principal read to class, recommended list in textbook, class assignment, bought in store, interested in building model, and easy book.

PERSONAL INTERVIEW SHEET—GRADE 4

(Expressed as Frequency)

	Allisonville			Control (No Library)			Control (With Library)		
	1965	1966	1967	1965	1966	1967	1965	1966	1967
Number................	79	101	104	29	21	26	26	34	29
If you had more time in the library, what would you do with that time?									
Look at magazines	4	0	0	0	0	0	0	0	0
Listen to records	19	16	7	0	0	0	0	0	0
Work on classroom assignments	14	3	5	1	0	1	1	0	0
Look at books and read	39	45	36	8	13	24	12	27	19
View filmstrips	31	47	26	0	1	0	3	1	1
Work as library aide	8	5	7	0	0	0	0	6	1
Use of reference room materials	4	1	3	0	1	0	0	0	0
Prepare report	8	13	17	0	0	0	0	0	0
Read about geography	1	1	1	0	0	0	0	0	0
Read a mystery book	1	0	0	0	0	0	0	1	0
Read about science	2	1	3	0	1	0	0	0	0
Look through card file	1	1	0	0	0	0	0	1	0
Look at encyclopedia	0	3	3	0	1	0	0	0	0
Read about animals	1	1	1	0	1	0	0	0	0
Browse	2	2	10	0	1	2	0	0	5
Dictionary	0	0	1	0	1	0	0	0	0
Look at models	0	0	0	0	1	0	0	0	0
Read about sports	0	0	0	0	1	0	0	0	0
Become familiar with library	0	0	0	0	2	0	0	1	1
Read about war stories	0	0	0	0	0	0	0	1	0
Read humorous book	0	0	0	0	0	0	0	1	0
Don't know	0	0	0	0	0	0	0	0	1
Select books	0	0	9	0	0	0	0	0	0
Look at atlas	0	0	2	0	0	0	0	0	0
Listen to tapes	0	0	3	0	0	0	0	0	0

Note: Seven other activities (read about railroading, use vertical file, read short books, rewrite stories in books, read biographies, study, and research) were mentioned once at Allisonville and not at either of the other schools.

PERSONAL INTERVIEW SHEET—GRADE 4
(Expressed as Percent Indicating)

	Allisonville			Control (No Library)			Control (With Library)		
	1965	1966	1967	1965	1966	1967	1965	1966	1967
Number	79	101	104	29	21	26	26	34	29
If you had a free period, would you rather:									
A. Play a table game?	4	7	3	10	10	7	4	3	10
B. Watch a moving picture or slides in the room?	10	9	10	7	10	23	4	9	17
C. Work with art materials?	6	6	14	10	14	31	11	21	14
D. Go to the library?	80	78	73	73	66	39	81	67	59
Do you generally have a book that you are reading for enjoyment? (Yes)	95	91	93	76	62	88	100	91	90

EVALUATOR'S RATING

	Allisonville			Control (No Library)			Control (With Library)		
Does the child express ideas effectively in discussing books and other materials?									
Outstanding	25	31	42	10	14	8	15	29	38
Good	66	51	52	66	48	50	70	65	55
Poor	9	18	6	24	38	42	15	6	7
Does the child's best list of readings indicate that he has fairly wide reading interests (is reading on three or more topics)? (Yes)	78	75	79	31	48	58	92	88	76

PERSONAL INTERVIEW SHEET—GRADE 6

(Expressed as Frequency)

	Allisonville			Control (No Library)			Control (With Library)		
	1965	1966	1967	1965	1966	1967	1965	1966	1967
Number	79	81	95	29	33	33	26	26	31
What kinds of materials have you used in the library?									
Magazines	16	29	39	0	2	3	2	1	1
Filmstrips	45	61	80	0	3	0	10	12	13
Recordings	38	48	54	0	0	0	1	0	0
Encyclopedias	55	78	84	8	5	24	18	15	23
Atlases	9	12	26	1	0	1	1	1	4
Nonfiction	49	44	60	18	15	15	24	9	19
Fiction	41	43	51	22	19	18	23	12	16
National Geographic Index	15	32	64	2	1	0	0	2	0
Card catalog	29	35	34	9	7	15	21	21	20
Reference books	8	0	7	0	0	0	1	0	0
Almanac	13	9	5	0	0	0	0	0	2
Vertical file	20	31	64	0	0	1	1	10	1
Dictionary	17	46	27	3	2	5	13	10	18
Lincoln Library	1	2	0	0	0	0	0	0	0
Science dictionary	3	10	2	0	0	0	0	0	0
Junior Book of Authors	3	0	3	0	0	0	0	0	0
Maps	2	4	1	0	0	0	0	0	0
Globes	1	7	5	0	1	1	1	0	0
Forms and models	1	10	7	0	1	0	0	0	0
Biography references	1	6	2	0	0	0	2	1	0
Tapes	0	8	23	0	0	0	0	0	0
Who's Who in America	0	2	5	0	0	0	0	0	0
Famous First Facts	0	4	5	0	0	0	0	0	0
Thesaurus	0	5	2	0	0	0	0	0	1
Newspaper	0	1	2	0	0	0	0	0	0
Never go	0	0	0	0	3	0	0	0	0
Seldom go	0	0	0	0	1	0	0	0	0
Statesman's Yearbook	0	0	28	0	0	0	0	0	0
Natural science books	0	0	2	0	0	0	0	0	0
Bartlett's Familiar Quotations	0	0	3	0	0	0	0	0	0
Readers' Guide to Periodical Literature	0	0	4	0	0	0	0	0	0
Oversized pictures	0	0	3	0	0	0	0	0	0
Music dictionary	0	0	2	0	0	0	0	0	0
Music encyclopedia	0	0	2	0	0	0	0	0	0
Geographical dictionary	0	0	3	0	0	0	0	0	0

Note: Twenty-three other categories or examples of materials and equipment were mentioned once by Allisonville students and not at all by students in the other schools. Most of these were in the social studies and science areas, such as books on World War II, North American wild flowers, and biographical dictionary.

PERSONAL INTERVIEW SHEET—GRADE 6

(Expressed as Frequency)

	Allisonville			Control (No Library)			Control (With Library)		
	1965	1966	1967	1965	1966	1967	1965	1966	1967
Number...............	79	81	95	29	33	33	26	26	31
What kind of stories do you enjoy most?									
Mystery	25	38	42	18	24	12	18	17	18
Biography	19	21	22	7	3	3	4	8	6
Fiction	18	6	3	0	0	0	2	5	3
Adventure	15	18	18	0	6	1	4	6	3
Sports	11	9	9	3	6	4	5	7	4
Animals	7	13	21	6	6	13	4	7	4
Science	6	6	4	7	0	1	1	2	0
Science fiction	4	5	3	1	4	2	1	0	1
Nonfiction	4	0	0	0	1	0	1	0	1
History	5	7	1	3	0	2	2	0	0
War	3	3	6	1	1	0	5	0	3
Humorous	3	8	11	0	3	4	2	2	7
Pioneer	2	0	0	0	0	0	0	0	0
Doctors	2	0	0	0	0	0	0	0	0
Medicine	2	0	0	0	0	0	0	0	0
Teen-age stories	1	2	2	0	0	0	0	0	1
Nature	1	0	0	0	0	1	0	0	0
Radio-electronics	1	1	0	0	0	0	0	0	0
Myths	0	2	1	0	0	0	0	0	0
Family	0	3	4	0	1	1	1	1	2
Spy	0	1	1	0	0	0	0	0	1
Fairy tales	0	0	2	2	1	0	0	0	1
Space	0	0	3	1	2	1	0	0	1
Jungle	0	0	0	1	0	0	0	0	0
Classics	0	0	0	0	1	0	0	0	0
Other countries	0	0	2	0	0	0	1	0	0
Automobiles	0	0	1	0	0	2	0	1	0
Dinosaurs	0	0	0	0	0	0	1	0	0
Airplanes	0	0	1	0	0	1	0	1	1
Submarines	0	0	0	0	0	0	0	0	1
Monster	0	0	0	0	0	0	0	0	1
Mechanics	0	0	0	0	0	1	0	0	0

Note: Ten other kinds of stories (planets, boys, travel, pirate, Air Force, ancient, poetry, sea, historical fiction, and geography) were mentioned once at Allisonville and not at either of the other schools.

PERSONAL INTERVIEW SHEET—GRADE 6

(Expressed as Frequency)

	Allisonville			Control (No Library)			Control (With Library)		
	1965	1966	1967	1965	1966	1967	1965	1966	1967
Number..............	79	81	95	29	33	33	26	26	31
How did you become interested in the last book you read?									
Found on shelf	10	15	23	0	0	13	10	8	6
Browsing	10	15	9	0	0	1	2	2	5
Title looked interesting	8	9	7	1	1	2	1	1	0
Introduced to class by teacher	0	0	3	0	0	0	0	0	0
Book jacket	4	1	4	0	0	1	1	0	0
Card catalog	2	4	7	0	1	0	0	1	0
Recommended by teacher	3	5	1	3	1	1	2	0	0
Interested in subject	11	8	13	5	7	10	6	1	2
Recommended by friend	20	13	23	8	4	1	12	4	3
Read previously	1	2	1	0	0	1	0	0	0
Saw movie	0	2	1	3	1	1	0	0	1
Liked author	2	2	5	0	0	0	0	0	1
Recommended by librarian	2	2	1	0	0	1	2	5	7
Librarian's book talk	0	0	0	0	0	0	1	0	5
Liked series	1	1	3	0	0	2	1	2	2
Book fair	0	0	2	0	0	0	0	0	0
Table of contents	0	0	1	0	0	0	1	0	0
Recommended by sister	1	2	0	0	1	0	0	0	0
Gift	1	1	0	0	6	0	0	1	0
Read first few pages	2	2	0	0	0	0	0	1	0
Read book summary	2	1	0	0	0	0	0	1	0
Recommended by brother	1	0	0	0	1	0	0	0	0
Book club book	1	0	0	1	3	0	0	0	0
Liked chapter titles	3	0	0	0	0	0	0	0	0
Pictures	0	0	0	0	2	0	1	0	1
Story in reader	0	0	0	0	0	1	0	0	0
At home	0	0	0	1	1	1	0	0	0
Found in store	0	0	0	0	1	0	0	0	0
Church library	0	0	0	0	1	0	0	0	0
Classroom library	0	0	0	9	0	0	0	0	0
Read about in magazine	0	0	0	1	0	0	0	0	0
Heard book report	0	0	0	1	0	0	0	0	0

Note: Four other reasons (read introduction, found it as a library aide, recommended by mother, and suggested by adult) were mentioned once at Allisonville and not at either of the other schools.

Personal Interview Sheet—Grade 6

(Expressed as Frequency)

	Allisonville			Control (No Library)			Control (With Library)		
	1965	1966	1967	1965	1966	1967	1965	1966	1967
Number...............	79	81	95	29	33	33	26	26	31
If you had more time in the library, what would you do with that time?									
Do reference work	1	1	0	3	0	0	3	0	0
View filmstrips	12	13	16	0	1	0	4	0	2
Work on research	1	0	1	1	0	0	0	0	0
Listen to recordings	14	6	16	0	0	0	0	0	0
Work as library aide	8	1	4	8	0	3	0	2	3
Read (find book)	30	46	44	16	20	23	25	16	22
Read science books	4	2	0	0	2	0	0	0	0
Read about animals	2	0	0	0	0	2	0	2	0
Listen to tapes	1	0	8	0	0	0	0	0	0
Browse	9	1	8	9	3	4	7	3	5
Read about geography	2	1	3	0	2	0	0	0	0
Read biographies	1	0	1	0	0	0	0	0	0
Read sports books	2	1	0	0	0	0	0	1	1
Use library materials for classroom assignments	8	6	4	6	1	2	0	1	0
Look through reference material	5	0	2	0	0	0	0	0	0
Look at magazines	3	0	2	0	1	0	0	0	0
Read mystery book	2	0	0	0	1	1	0	3	0
Look through vertical files	1	0	0	0	0	0	0	1	0
Nothing	0	0	0	2	0	1	0	0	0
Prepare reports	0	16	12	0	2	1	1	1	2
Dictionary	0	3	0	0	0	0	0	0	1
Science project	0	4	0	0	0	0	0	0	0
Encyclopedia	0	1	0	0	1	0	0	0	1
Study models	0	1	1	0	0	0	0	0	0
Don't know	0	0	0	0	1	1	0	0	0
Humorous books	0	0	0	0	1	0	0	0	0
Preview movies	0	0	0	0	0	1	0	0	0

Note: Twelve other activities were mentioned once at Allisonville and not at either of the other schools. These were: read books on display, read ancient history, read fiction books, read about doctors, look for experiment to perform, check card catalog, look at *National Geographics*, read informational books, read about art, find information on airplanes, look at travel books, and research.

PERSONAL INTERVIEW SHEET—GRADE 6
(Expressed as Percent Indicating)

	Allisonville			Control (No Library)			Control (With Library)		
	1965	1966	1967	1965	1966	1967	1965	1966	1967
Number	73	81	95	35	32	33	31	26	31
If you had a free period, would you rather:									
A. Play a table game?	3	7	6	9	0	9	6	15	7
B. Watch a moving picture or slides in the room?	8	10	11	14	9	13	23	12	16
C. Work with art materials?	26	35	21	11	19	39	19	23	19
D. Go to the library?	63	48	62	66	72	39	52	50	58
Do you generally have a book that you are reading for enjoyment? (Yes)	90	85	81	77	59	91	90	81	94

EVALUATOR'S RATING

	Allisonville			Control (No Library)			Control (With Library)		
Does the child express ideas effectively in discussing books and other materials?									
Outstanding	30	31	54	17	25	15	19	31	48
Good	58	62	42	60	53	61	68	54	48
Poor	12	7	4	23	22	24	13	15	4
Does the child's best list of readings indicate that he has fairly wide reading interests (is reading on three or more topics)? (Yes)	73	85	75	77	56	61	87	62	84

PERSONAL INTERVIEW SHEET

(Expressed as Frequency)

	Allisonville						Control (With Library)					
	Grade 4			Grade 6			Grade 4			Grade 6		
	1965	1966	1967	1965	1966	1967	1965	1966	1967	1965	1966	1967
Number	79	101	104	79	81	95	26	34	29	26	26	31
What would you like to see added to the library that isn't there now?												
Want no additions	40	66	71	33	51	55	12	6	13	3	5	9
Recordings	3	0	0	1	0	0	0	0	0	0	0	0
Biographies	2	0	0	10	0	1	0	0	1	3	1	0
Reference books	0	0	0	2	0	0	2	7	0	2	0	0
Science books	2	2	0	4	0	0	0	0	0	0	0	0
Animal books	1	0	1	3	0	1	0	1	0	0	0	1
Mysteries	7	7	1	7	11	2	5	8	0	4	4	2
Books about other countries	0	1	0	1	0	1	0	0	0	0	0	0
Fiction	0	0	0	4	0	1	0	0	0	0	1	0
Maps	0	0	0	2	0	0	1	0	1	0	0	0
Science fiction	1	0	0	2	0	0	3	1	0	0	0	0
Books	8	13	8	4	1	6	7	5	9	11	10	9
Vertical file information	0	0	0	1	0	0	0	0	0	0	1	0
History	0	0	0	2	1	1	0	0	1	0	0	0
Filmstrip viewers	6	2	1	2	0	1	0	0	0	0	0	1
Books on sports rules	0	0	0	2	0	0	0	0	0	0	0	0
War stories	2	0	0	2	0	0	0	1	0	0	0	1
Books on medicine	0	0	0	1	1	0	0	0	0	0	0	0
Books on health	0	0	0	2	1	0	0	0	0	0	0	0
More time in library	0	0	0	0	1	0	0	0	1	0	0	0
Magazines about cars and racing	2	0	0	1	0	0	0	0	0	0	0	1
Sports stories	0	0	0	1	3	0	0	0	0	1	1	2
More room	0	0	0	0	0	2	0	0	3	10	5	4
Film projector	4	2	2	0	0	0	0	0	0	1	0	0
More series books	0	0	5	0	1	2	0	0	0	2	0	0
Books on aviation	0	0	0	0	0	1	0	0	0	1	0	0
Nonfiction	0	0	0	0	0	0	0	0	0	1	0	0
Filmstrips	4	1	1	0	0	1	0	0	1	1	0	0
Electrical books	1	0	0	0	1	0	0	0	0	0	0	0
Larger reference room	0	0	2	0	1	3	0	0	0	0	0	0
Science books (fossils, geology, fish, rocks)	0	0	1	0	1	0	0	0	0	0	0	0
Adventure books	2	0	0	0	3	0	0	6	0	0	1	1
More room in booths for committee work	0	0	0	0	1	0	0	5	0	0	0	0
TV	1	0	1	0	1	4	0	0	0	0	0	0
Films	0	0	0	0	1	0	0	0	0	0	0	1
Visual aids room	1	0	2	0	0	0	0	0	0	0	0	1

Personal Interview Sheet
(Expressed as Frequency)

	Allisonville						Control (With Library)					
	Grade 4			Grade 6			Grade 4			Grade 6		
	1965	1966	1967	1965	1966	1967	1965	1966	1967	1965	1966	1967
Number.......	79	101	104	79	81	95	26	34	29	26	26	31
Carpeting	3	2	0	0	0	0	0	0	0	0	0	0
Sports (football)	2	0	0	0	0	0	0	0	0	0	0	0
Encyclopedias	1	0	2	0	0	0	0	1	1	0	0	0
Record player	2	0	0	0	0	1	0	0	0	0	0	0
Earphones	2	2	0	0	0	0	0	0	0	0	0	0
Humorous books	1	0	0	0	0	0	0	1	0	0	0	1
Flag	0	0	0	0	0	0	1	0	0	0	0	0
Books on art	0	0	0	0	0	0	1	0	1	0	0	0
Drinking fountain	0	1	0	0	0	1	0	0	0	0	0	0
Dictionary	0	0	0	0	0	0	0	1	0	0	0	1
Shelves	0	0	0	0	0	0	0	1	1	0	0	0
Movie star books	0	0	0	0	0	0	0	1	0	0	0	0
Another desk	0	0	1	0	0	0	0	1	0	0	0	0
Charlotte's Web (more)	0	0	1	0	0	0	0	0	0	0	0	0
More horse books	0	0	2	0	0	3	0	0	0	0	0	0
Large screen	0	0	2	0	0	0	0	0	0	0	0	0
More tables	0	0	0	0	0	3	0	0	0	0	0	0

Note: Students at Allisonville made one request for forty other items not mentioned at either of the other schools. Models of various kinds, baseball magazines, books about mental retardation, and exhibits of rare plants were among these items.

Report from

MOUNT ROYAL SCHOOL
and
TOWSON STATE COLLEGE

FACT SHEET—MOUNT ROYAL SCHOOL

The Mount Royal School, an inner-city school in Baltimore, Maryland, was established at 121 McMechen Street in February, 1959. The faculty of the school includes a number of young persons who have had experience in schools in other sections of the city and who are now eagerly working with young children in an inner-city neighborhood.

Mrs. Idella Nichols has served as librarian at the school since September, 1959. Her full-time assignment there is one indication of the emphasis placed on serving the special needs of this school's community. Another is the Early Admissions program for three- and four-year-old children to give them experience which the kindergarten can build upon when they enter the class at the age of five. This program is jointly financed by the Baltimore City Public Schools and the Ford Foundation.

System-wide library services in the 203 Baltimore City public schools include supervising and consultant services, centralized processing and cataloging, professional library services, access to a sample collection of 4,000 titles recommended for purchase, and access to the services of a central instructional materials center for the school system. Mrs. Alice Rusk, School Library Specialist, was released from other responsibilities to work more closely with the Mount Royal School library program and to further its development as an instructional materials center for the school.

Towson State College has named Dr. Walter W. Williamson the field worker for the Project. Dr. Williamson is Professor of Education at Towson State College. He has been an elementary classroom teacher and has had extensive experience as an instructor in elementary education. He has worked in the Sequential Tests of Educational Progress (STEP) and School and College Ability Tests (SCAT) testing programs for the Educational Testing Service. He is a member of the World Tapes for Education Association and is chairman of the Teaching Methods and Materials section of that group. The college and the school system see in the selection of the Mount Royal School as a demonstration center the opportunity for further cooperative projects and conferences.

STATISTICS

From its Project application, June, 1963

Enrollment: 716 students, grades kindergarten through six, plus Primary and Intermediate Opportunity classes and Early Admissions classes.

Materials collection: 3,500 books, 12 periodicals, 48 filmstrips, 133 recordings.

Library personnel: One full-time librarian.

As of June, 1967

Enrollment: 675 students, grades kindergarten through six, plus Primary and Intermediate Opportunity classes and Early Admissions classes.

Materials collection: 8,075 books, 46 periodicals, 1,048 silent filmstrips, 235 tape recordings, 161 disc recordings, 40 exhibits, 141 picture sets, 25 sound filmstrips.

Library personnel: Two full-time librarians, one half-time librarian, one full-time clerk.

PERSONNEL MOST DIRECTLY CONCERNED WITH THE PROJECT

From the Mount Royal School

Mr. LeRoy Hardesty, Principal
Mrs. Nancy Bloom, Librarian
Mrs. Idella Nichols, Librarian
Mrs. Devorah Freeman, Librarian (half-time)

From the Baltimore City Public Schools

Dr. Laurence G. Paquin, Superintendent
Dr. Vernon S. Vavrina, Associate Superintendent, Curriculum and Instruction
Mrs. Edith V. Walker, Assistant Superintendent, Elementary Education
Miss M. Bernice Wiese, Director of School Library Services
Mrs. Alice Rusk, Specialist in School Library Services

From Towson State College

Dr. Carl Schroeder, Director of Teacher Education and
Chairman of the Elementary Department
Dr. Walter W. Williamson, Professor of Education and field worker,
Knapp School Libraries Project

PARTICIPATION

City school in the Project

Baltimore, sprawling and venerable industrial center, U.S.A., is a city in transition. Urban renewal replaces inner-city slums as burgeoning suburbs describe new metropolitan boundaries. The economy, revolutionized by automation and revitalized by port development, seeks to provide for a mobile population of diverse cultural and ethnic patterns. This is the Baltimore whose children challenge its schools.

Early in April, 1964, the Mount Royal Elementary School of the Baltimore City Public Schools was chosen as one of the three demonstration centers to participate in Phase II of the Knapp School Libraries Project. The only inner-city school in the Project, it serves a unique community which cuts diagonally across socio-economic strata and is in the throes of demolition, rebuilding, and rehabilitation. Contributing factors to its selection were the present status of the school library program and evidence of plans for its improvement.

One of the terms of Project participation was that there must be a cooperating teacher education institution. Towson State College, the co-participant, received a grant of $25,000, and Mount Royal received $74,265 from the Project for a two-year period.

The library quarters were expanded and remodeled to meet recommended national standards. Air conditioning, carpeting, and draperies provided an attractive atmosphere and comfort during summer use. The book collection was increased to 8,000 volumes to average ten books per pupil. A sizable collection of tapes, disc recordings, filmstrips, pictures, realia, etc., was developed. Additional library equipment such as overhead projectors, photocopier, transparency maker, 8mm loop projector, and carrels were acquired. Additional staff included a second librarian, a half-time third librarian, and a clerk.

Co-participant. The field worker, a faculty member of Towson State College, spent half of his time in the Knapp Project at the Mount Royal School. He scheduled and conducted the demonstration program for visitors to the Project and coordinated the activities of Towson State College with the Project. In addition to his close involvement with other aspects of this experiment, he directed groups of students from Towson in their experience with the Project and worked closely with teachers at Mount Royal and Towson, to encourage and increase their understanding of the concept of the library as a learning source center.

Multi-media service. A full program of multi-media library service was inaugurated. The regular library program — a balance of reading stimulation, skill instruction, and supplementary reference activities — was explored in greater depth and breadth, reinforced by use of a wide variety of non-book media, as well as a greatly increased and expanded book collection. Longer hours and an eleven-month program were advantages gained because of more professional staff and greater resources. Classes and individuals were able to come to the library more often and receive professional guidance. Emphasis on the instructional materials concept of library service had positive implications in this inner-city school where many pupils had low reading levels and lacked facility in communication skills. Highlights of the program included greater teacher-librarian teamwork, more visits of librarians to classrooms, increased creation of teaching materials by teachers, greater use of community resources, invitation of persons with special talents to enrich library and classroom programs, and the sponsoring of a creative writing club.

The impact. Evaluation and reactions by pupils, teachers, student teachers, librarians, administrators, parents, and visitors endorsed this kind of library program as being valuable and necessary. The overwhelming feeling was that a good school library does make a difference.

Knapp Project funds

In addition to the grant of $74,265 to the school, the Bureau of Research of the Baltimore City Public Schools received a direct grant of $2,640 from the Knapp School Libraries Project. This money was to cover expenses for personnel and materials related to research activities for

Project Budget 1964-1967

	1964-65	1965-66	1966-67	Total
MATERIALS				
3,700 books @ $3.00 per book (purchases spread over two-year period)...........	$ 5,500.00	$ 5,500.00	—	$11,000.00
Processing of 3,700 books................	2,312.50	2,312.50	—	4,625.00
Audio-visual materials (purchases spread over two-year period)..................	2,500.00	2,500.00	—	5,000.00
Professional materials for teachers........	500.00	500.00	—	1,000.00
PERSONNEL				
Regular term salaries:				
—Second librarian, full-time..............	6,250.00	6,500.00	$ 6,750.00	19,500.00
—Third librarian, part-time..............	—	3,000.00	3,170.00	6,170.00
—Clerical assistant	3,492.00	3,660.00	3,828.00	10,980.00
Summer term salaries:				
—Librarian, one month..................	855.00	855.00	855.00	2,565.00
—Second librarian, one month............	625.00	650.00	650.00	1,925.00
QUARTERS				
—Renovation and equipment, including audio-visual equipment	6,800.00	—	—	6,800.00
—Air conditioning	4,700.00	—	—	4,700.00
TOTALS	$33,534.50	$25,477.50	$15,253.00	$74,265.00

Mrs. Idella Nichols, librarian, helps select holiday stories in the fall of 1964.

certain aspects of the demonstration project at the Mount Royal Elementary School.

An additional grant of $25,000 was awarded Towson State College, the participating teacher training institution, to pay half the salary of the field worker, transportation of students to and from the demonstration center, and other expenses incurred by the Project.

Project expenditure of funds

Elasticity was allowed by the Knapp School Libraries Project in the expenditure of grant funds. Any saving effected in one category of the budget could be used for additional purchases in another category. The following table explains the use of grant funds at the Mount Royal Elementary School demonstration center:

Item	Allotment	Expenditure
MATERIALS		
Books and magazines	$11,000.00	$13,100.00
Audio-visual materials	5,000.00	7,240.00
Other materials (cataloging supplies, etc., and some magazines for teachers)	1,650.00	2,195.00
PERSONNEL		
Salaries	45,115.00	34,975.00*
QUARTERS		
Remodeling	3,200.00	2,390.00
Audio-visual equipment including some shelving, etc.	3,600.00	5,084.00
Air conditioning	4,700.00	5,429.00
Carpeting and cleaning equipment	—	3,239.00
Draperies	—	613.00
GRAND TOTAL	$74,265.00	$74,265.00

*Salary expenditures were less than the Project allotment for several reasons:

(1) Two additional professional librarians were employed at salaries lower than estimated in the budget request.

(2) The clerical position was unfilled for six months. (A substitute library aide was employed without cost to the Project.)

(3) Salary increments anticipated in 1966 were delayed for four months.

Enlarging the library

To accommodate a multi-media program, the adjacent classroom was annexed to the library, a doorway being cut through the wall. The additional room produced a total of 102 feet in length and 28 feet in width, or 2,856 square feet in the entire library area. Additional shelving was arranged in the annex to create two areas. Draperies were installed, including room-darkening ones in the annex.

Wall-to-wall carpeting provided by Knapp Project funds was an acoustical advantage, and also made on-the-spot browsing in any corner of the library easier.

The readiness visit

Guidelines of the Knapp School Libraries Project suggested one year as a realistic period of preparation for operation as a demonstration center. When the Project school was ready, it held a "dry run" of a typical visit. These visitors came by invitation and consisted of persons who could react to the visit from various points of view, criticize procedures in terms of strengths and weaknesses, and make suggestions for modification and improvement. Such a group visited Mount Royal Elementary School on May 7, 1965 and consisted of:

Miss Mary V. Gaver
Professor of Library Science
Rutgers—The State University
New Brunswick, New Jersey
Miss Mae Graham
Supervisor of School Libraries
Maryland State Department of Education
Baltimore, Maryland
Dr. Robert Schockley
Assistant Superintendent
Board of Education of Allegheny County
Cumberland, Maryland
Mrs. Helen Stull, Chairman
Secondary School Library Services Committee
Baltimore City Council of Parent-Teacher Associations
Baltimore, Maryland
Mrs. Fred Bull
Baltimore, Maryland

At the end of its visit, this group discussed their findings and selected Miss Gaver as chairman to communicate with the school. Following

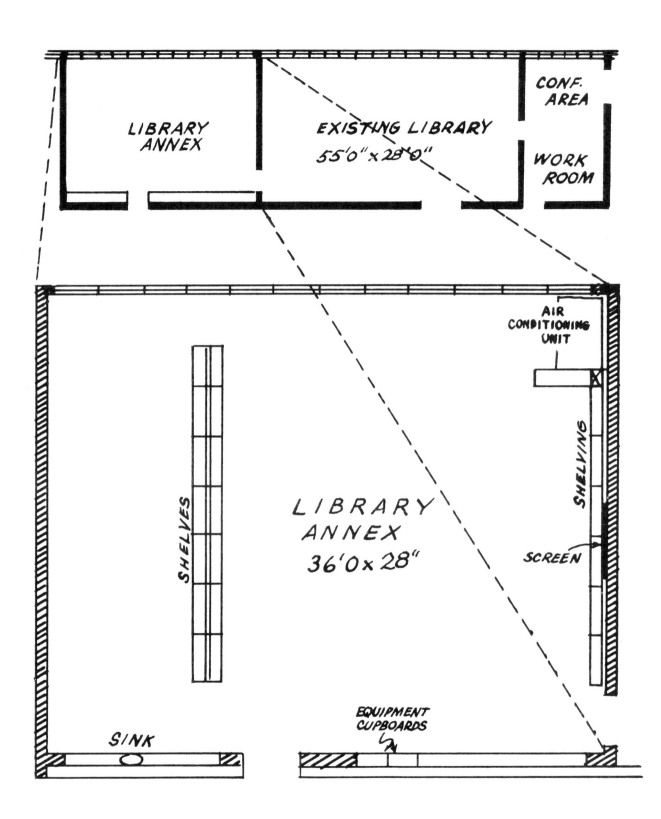

LIBRARY
ANNEX

EXISTING LIBRARY
55'0" x 28'0"

CONF.
AREA

WORK
ROOM

AIR
CONDITIONING
UNIT

SHELVING

LIBRARY
ANNEX
36'0 x 28"

SHELVES

SCREEN

SINK

EQUIPMENT
CUPBOARDS

are excerpts from her letter received by the principal, Mr. Hardesty:

> The Committee asked me to take the responsibility for writing a report back on our most interesting visit with you and the members of the Knapp Project staff last Friday. . . . Although we thought there was some tightening-up which could be effected in the time schedule, I particularly liked the general layout of the schedule.
>
> [We] liked . . . the way in which [Dr. Williamson, the field worker] has already built the teacher education program at Towson into the project. . . . We would have liked to have emphasized from the start the relationship of the library to the instructional program. . . . You could well emphasize those characteristics of your school program and especially of the library program which are particularly geared to the community needs. These would include:
>
> *the early admissions program—* . . . The lack of attention to primary grades in *some* elementary library programs would lead me to want particular emphasis on this in the discussion if not always in observation.
>
> *the opportunity class*
> *selection of materials—* . . . in what way her [Mrs. Nichols's] selection is skewed to meet special needs . . .
>
> We hope that visitors will have opportunities to talk with children and to teachers and the librarian, as well as to yourself and Dr. Williamson.
>
> I particularly liked—and other committee members commented on — the evidence we saw of use of materials in the classrooms and the effective use of non-print as well as book materials. . . . I was particularly encouraged at the answer Mrs. Rusk gave as to the probable future for maintaining this standard in yours and other schools in the system. I am most gratified that we were able to select an inner-city school to receive one of the grants. . . .

PROGRESS

Supported by the advantages of increased materials, staff, and quarters, the library of the Mount Royal School was prepared to explore in breadth and depth the basic philosophy of school library services in the Baltimore Public Schools and to experiment in a new dimension of its program—the school library as a multi-media learning resource center. A balanced core of reading stimulation, skill, and reference activities was undergirded and enriched by the advantages accrued by the Knapp School Libraries Project. How, then, did the library serve the school?

Service to teachers

One important function of the school library is service to pupils through service to teachers. More librarians meant more opportunities to plan cooperatively with teachers, both in and out of the library, for close coordination of library materials and activities with classroom programs and pupil needs. In some instances, the librarian, as an experienced teacher working with a beginning teacher, was able to give guidance in planning, over and above the involvement of the library, which resulted in more effective instruction of boys and girls.

Many more materials were available to make teaching meaningful and effective and, with more staff, it was possible to keep teachers abreast of the new and to encourage experimentation with them in the teaching-learning process. Clerical assistance facilitated the production of lists and bibliographies and the preparation of classroom collections of print and non-print resources.

Development of the school library as a multi-media learning center was supported by acquisition of a rich collection of book and non-book resources. A knowledgeable library staff introduced new materials and equipment to the faculty, giving instruction in the use of the unfamiliar. Assistance was always available, both for preparation of instructional materials and operation of audio-visual apparatus.

Increased opportunities for conferences, formal and informal, enabled teachers and librarians to probe the depths of their needs for meaningful teaching. Such fruitful discussions contributed to improved selection of books and other instructional media which produced a library collection tailored to the needs of the children of this school.

Close involvement of teachers and librarians developed quite naturally into team teaching. Teacher and librarian, or librarians, worked simultaneously and cooperatively with the same class, either in the library or in the classroom. Their procedures with the various groups within the class were based upon the solid foundation of mutual preplanning.

Service to pupils

A strengthened library staff had more time to work with boys and girls. More librarians meant opportunities to work more frequently with groups within classes and also to have more direct and personal contact with individual children.

An example of this was the work with small reading groups from several classes. Children were chosen by the teacher according to abilities and needs to come to the library as a group. The librarian talked with them, guided their book selection, read with them, and listened as they read aloud or discussed their books. These frequent sessions helped boys and girls develop a feeling for finishing a book.

Increased staff made it possible for two classes to have periods in the library simultaneously. At the same time, the third librarian was available to give reference or reading guidance to boys and girls who came to the library for individual, unscheduled use.

Longer hours, one of the benefits of more staff, provided more service to pupils. No longer was it necessary to close the library during the school lunch hour. The after-school hours were lengthened to 4:30 P.M. in the winter months and to 5:00 P.M. in spring and fall.

Summer programs during July of two successive years operated in two different ways. In 1965, the library was open daily from 8:30 A.M. to 3:30 P.M. for the children of the Mount Royal Elementary School, two nearby public schools, and one neighboring parochial school, as well as for other children in the community who wished to participate. The weekly program was planned around activities to create interest in coming to the library—story hours, poetry time, movies, the secret guest, etc.

The summer program of 1966 had a dual role

—to support an Elementary and Secondary Education Act Title I project for improving reading and to provide library service for children in the community similar to the previous summer. All summer school classes came to the library. Flexible scheduling was used. Emphasis was on reading stimulation related to interest themes of classes and schoolwide activities.

Creativity was stimulated through two clubs sponsored by the library. The Writers Club drew membership from boys and girls in grades three to six and met weekly after school. In the process of writing stories and using a variety of media to illustrate and bind them, they learned some of the procedures of publishing. The help of the art resource teacher with the binding of the books demonstrated another type of teamwork. Sixth graders in the Story-tellers League selected stories to learn and tell to younger children. In preparation for their visits to these classes, they developed a variety of illustrations to make their stories more appealing.

Addition of a significant number of paperbacks to the library collection sparked the idea of a Paperback Club. A member of the club could read four paperbacks in one category (fiction, poetry, science, or folklore), discuss them with one of the librarians, and earn a paperback in that category which he could keep for his own. Besides stimulating more reading, this introduced some printed material into homes with few books or none and may have provided the incentive for developing a home library.

At full strength, the Mount Royal library staff meets with Mrs. Alice Rusk, second from right. The others, left to right: Mrs. Idella Nichols, Mrs. Nancy Bloom, and Mrs. Devorah Freeman.

The Knapp Project grant made it possible to improve both quality and quantity of library service to pupils. The individualizing of instruction, a benefit of more staff and wide resources, was particularly meaningful in this inner-city school where the spectrum of student abilities was wide and the need for compensatory activities great.

The concept of the library as a multi-media learning resource center had many implications for the pupils. For the academically able, nonbook materials widened and reinforced concepts formed by reading. Intellectual curiosity, once aroused, stimulated individual reading and reference activities for personal interests. For the slow learner, who might have reading difficulty, materials other than books afforded successful and satisfying learning experiences pending the development of greater facility in reading.

Service to visitors

More than three thousand visitors came to the Mount Royal Elementary School from 1964 to 1967 to see the Knapp School Libraries Project demonstration center. Their visits were scheduled and conducted by the field worker from the cooperating teacher training institution, Towson State College, and some of the visits were financed by the Knapp Project. Although the terms of the grant described a "radius of 500 miles" as the boundary for Project-supported visitors, other groups came from as far away as Australia and South Africa, and many of those receiving Project support for travel supplemented the funds to make longer trips possible.

And what did they come to see? From the reactionnaires of the visitors, it was apparent that they came with definite purposes in mind and achieved not only these, but also learned many additional facts about a school library and its role in the elementary school program.

As expected, the visitors came from school systems representing many stages in the development of good library services and often were able to make worthwhile suggestions for the improvement of the program in the Mount Royal Elementary School. A majority of them, however, seemed satisfied with the visitation program that had been planned for them and offered only minor suggestions for its improvement. From the reactions, evidently, the visitation program was successful in meeting their needs.

Service to student teachers

During the second half of the 1964-65 school year, an extensive program of visits of Towson State College classes to the Mount Royal School was initiated. Within two years, twenty-five classes visited the Mount Royal School, observing and participating in the library program. As an orientation on the campus before the visit, the classes were shown the award-winning Knapp Project film, . . . And Something More. Following this, the field worker gave an illustrated talk on the Mount Royal School and described the Knapp School Libraries Project.

In the school, students observed in library and classrooms and were taken on a conducted tour of the library facilities. In connection with the visitation program, the librarians demonstrated all equipment and materials and explained how each item was utilized by the teachers and students.

The most intensive work by college students at the school, however, was in the Overview to Elementary Education course. Each semester, one day a week for six weeks, a section of approximately sixteen juniors came to Mount Royal School for extended experiences. After they had observed in the library and classrooms, a series of workshops was conducted for them, utilizing a variety of library materials and equipment. Following each workshop session, every student planned for the succeeding week at least one lesson involving a variety of library materials and equipment and then taught it to a class of children. Additional assistance in selection of material was given by the librarians and classroom teachers.

Each semester, three or more student teachers were assigned to work with cooperating teachers at the Mount Royal School. Several were students who had been in the school during the Overview course and had volunteered to return. Of course, the students were familiar with library procedure and were able to make full use of all facilities with little assistance. The librarians continued to give any needed aid.

Report from Towson State College

The Knapp Project application had spelled out the work and had implied the qualifications of the field worker to be named by the college in these words:

> A field worker would be appointed by the cooperating teacher education institution to devote at least half of his work load to the Project. The field worker would be responsible for coordinating the program of teacher-training and citizen education, working in cooperation with the staff of the demonstration school. He would serve in a consultant capacity to the staff — librarians, teachers, and administrators — of the demonstration school.

In accordance with this specification, Dr. Walter W. Williamson, Professor of Education, was appointed as the college representative and he immediately began to apply the following methods and procedures to achieve the specific goals:

1. Planned observations of the demonstration school library by the students and faculty of the cooperating teacher education institution and other nearby teacher colleges.
2. Use of the demonstration library by the school faculty and by student teachers.
3. Team visits to the demonstration school by educators and citizens from as many communities as possible. Each team would consist of a school administrator, school board member, citizen, teacher, and librarian.
4. Individual observations and visits to the demonstration school by interested persons in the community or region.
5. Workshops and conferences in the demonstration school sponsored by the school and the cooperating teacher education institution.

An extensive tape library was organized, using as a basis for the collection taped programs from the University of Michigan, the University of Minnesota, and the Oregon State Department of Education tape libraries. At a later date, these libraries gave permission to distribute the tapes to other schools through World Tapes for Education. The Mount Royal School became a member of this organization.

Audio-visual equipment of many kinds was added to the library collection. Workshops were held for the teachers on the use of the equipment, followed by small-group and individual instruction. Frequently, the field worker also gave assistance to teachers in the classroom until they acquired the skill to operate all the equipment independently.

Two workshops for cooperating teachers who worked with Towson student teachers in other schools were planned and conducted. A full day's program for twenty-five Early Childhood Education cooperating teachers and college staff included several demonstrations, both in the library and in the classroom, illustrating the type of materials that could be used effectively with young children. The second workshop, for approximately one hundred elementary education cooperating teachers and college supervisors, was for a half a day and included a tape-slide orientation to the Knapp Project, a reception given by the college staff, and demonstrations in the library. The program concluded with a general discussion of the library activities observed.

An open house for all faculty members of Towson State College was held during the Maryland State Teachers Convention in October, 1965. During the year, the president of the college and the director of teacher education also visited the Mount Royal School to observe the project. Other visits were made by members of the psychology, geography, drama, and education departments and of the campus laboratory school. The director of the college audio-visual education program assisted in two series of workshops for Overview students on the use of audio-visual equipment, and the chairman of the drama department spoke to the Mount Royal faculty on the topic, ''Creative Dramatics.'' Another member of this department worked with nine teachers who were interested in developing creative dramatics with their children.

During the first two years of the Project, the event that attracted the largest audiences was a children's literature festival planned to publicize the role of literature in an enriched library program. On the program for this two-day affair held in the spring of 1966 were Madeleine L'Engle, the Newbery Award author; Richard Chase, the Appalachian folklorist and author; John Langstaff, author-singer; Annis Duff,

A teacher introduces a small group to the string family in music.

author and editor; Edwin Tunis, author and illustrator; Ruth Hill Viguers, editor; Peggy Sullivan, author and Director of the Knapp School Libraries Project; and Elizabeth Nesbitt, author and lecturer. Events were held on the Towson campus, in the Mount Royal School, and in a local high school. Included on the program were presentations for children and adults by Richard Chase and John Langstaff, a talk by Madeleine L'Engle, and a panel discussion by the authors and editors. Several thousand children, college students, and adults, including a group from Canada, attended the events.

For teacher education, participation in the Knapp School Libraries Project has several implications. Although the library may be the center of learning in a school, unless the teachers understand its function and utilize its resources, it will not fulfill its role adequately. As an instructional materials center with a wide variety of materials of all types, both print and non-print, the library can assist the teacher in providing information for each child on his own level of learning, regardless of cultural background. The teacher training institution has a responsibility to prepare teachers who understand this role of the library and who will make use of all its resources. This challenge is one that few such institutions meet at the present time.

Perhaps one of the most important implications of the work with the college students, especially the Overview students, is that a team approach to teaching, utilizing the services of classroom teachers, librarians, and college instructors, and emphasizing a multi-media approach to learning, constitutes a worthwhile introduction to the elementary school program for college students who are prospective teachers. This approach gives the students a balance between theory and practice.

An attempt has been made to provide continuous evaluation of the Knapp Project by the Mount Royal staff, the college students, and the visitors. Several surveys have been made concerning the involvement and reaction of the Mount Royal faculty. One of the first of these showed a considerable increase in the use of audio-visual equipment and materials since the beginning of the Project. The Faculty Evaluation Questionnaire used in that survey begins on page 122. Another survey, done by a Towson graduate student as a thesis requirement, showed conclusively that the teachers had positive attitudes toward the Project and felt that it had helped them improve the quality of instruction. This survey is described in more detail on pages 166-67.

KNAPP SCHOOL LIBRARIES PROJECT
MT. ROYAL SCHOOL
BALTIMORE, MARYLAND

FACULTY EVALUATION QUESTIONNAIRE

Since the first year of the Knapp Project is nearing an end, we want to evaluate some phases of the program. In order to do this we should like you to evaluate the use of audio-visual equipment and material. Would you please complete this evaluation questionnaire and return it to Dr. Williamson before the end of the school year?

1. In the classroom prior to the present school year I have used the following equipment: (check the correct responses)

Equipment	Never	A few times	Occasionally	Frequently
Filmstrip projector				
Movie projector				
Overhead projector				
Record player				
Tape recorder				

2. In the classroom prior to the present school year I have used the following materials:

Materials	Never	A few times	Occasionally	Frequently
Filmstrips				
Movies				
Records (teaching)				
Slides				
Tapes (blank)				
Pre-recorded tapes (programs already recorded on them)				
Transparencies Original (made by teacher or children)				
Duplicated (copied from other material)				

3. In the classroom since September I have used the following
   equipment:

Equipment	Never	A few times	Occasionally	Frequently
Filmstrip projector				
Movie projector				
Overhead projector				
Record player				
Tape recorder				

4. In the classroom since September I have used the following
   materials:

Materials	Never	A few times	Occasionally	Frequently
Filmstrips				
Movies				
Records (teaching)				
Slides				
Tapes (blank)				
Pre-recorded tapes				
Transparencies--				
Original				
Duplicated				

5. In an elementary school the following audio-visual equipment
   has these values for my grade level:

Equipment	No Value	Questionable Value	Some Value	Considerable Value
Filmstrip projector				
Movie projector				
Overhead projector				
Record player				
Tape recorder				

6. In an elementary school the following <u>materials</u> have these
    values for my grade level:

Materials	No Value	Questionable Value	Some Value	Considerable Value
Filmstrips				
Movies				
Records (teaching)				
Slides				
Tapes (blank)				
Pre-recorded tapes				
Transparencies--				
Original				
Duplicated				

7. Additional equipment is needed for the Mt. Royal School,
    as follows:

Equipment	Sufficient number now available	One more needed	Several more	Many more
Filmstrip projectors--				
Individual				
Small group				
Standard size				
Movie projectors				
Overhead projectors				
Record players				
Tape recorders				

8. The following <u>material</u> is needed for the Mt. Royal School:

Materials	No more	A few	Some	Many
Filmstrips				
Pictures				
Records (teaching)				
Slides				
Tapes (blank)				
Pre-recorded tapes				
Transparencies				
Vertical file material				

9. More auditory and visual <u>material</u> is needed in the library in these areas:

Material	Auditory	Visual
Literature--		
Stories - primary level		
Stories - intermediate level		
Biographies		
Poetry		
Science		
Social Studies		
Music		
Arithmetic		

10. My reactions to the new audio-visual materials in the library are--

11. My children's reactions to the new audio-visual materials in the library are--

12. Probably the most worthwhile addition to the classroom program from the library this year has been--

13. In addition to the equipment and materials listed in this survey, are there any services you would like the Knapp Project to provide for the next school year?

14. Additional comments concerning the value of all phases of the Knapp Project from a classroom teacher's viewpoint follow:

For determining attitudes of the college students toward the importance of the library and librarian, a rating scale was devised by the field worker and administered to three groups of Overview students. The scale, entitled "The Role of the Librarian in the Elementary School," is included in this report beginning on page 129. The scale was given to each group when the students came to the Mount Royal School for the first time and before the orientation to the Project was made and then six weeks later when the students had completed their work at the school. A comparison of the results taken from both scales showed that all groups had a statistically significant gain in attitude toward the importance of the library in an elementary school. The students made written evaluations also concerning their understanding of teaching culturally disadvantaged children primarily through the use of a wide variety of material.

The Knapp Project has been successful at Towson State College in acquainting students and faculty with an enriched library program in an inner-city school and demonstrating that, given a wide variety of learning materials, so-called culturally disadvantaged children can and do learn. The importance of a good library in an elementary school is shown in a graphic manner. Evidence shows that faculty and students at Towson State College have developed an increased interest in school libraries as a result of the Knapp School Libraries Project.

In February, 1967, the American Association of Colleges for Teacher Education cited Towson State College for its program of excellence in helping to provide enriched library services on the elementary school level as its responsibility in the Knapp School Libraries Project. The citation reads: "To develop an enriched library program in an inner-city elementary school and to demonstrate its value, a three-year project was cooperatively planned by Towson State College and the Mt. Royal Elementary School in Baltimore, Maryland. The project was supported by a grant from the Knapp School Libraries Project. Through extensive use of demonstrations, observations, workshops, discussions, illustrated talks, motion pictures, and a children's literature festival, teachers, administrators, cooperating

Children read about good breakfasts on a silent film-strip.

teachers, students, and interested citizens were educated regarding the function of a library as an instructional materials center and in the utilization of all library materials. National and international interest was focused on this project."

Facts and figures

The tables on the next few pages show progress achieved at Mount Royal Elementary School during the Knapp School Libraries Project years as contrasted with a comparable prior period. Figures are given to show increases in the library collection, circulation, classroom borrowing of audio-visual equipment, and library attendance and changes in class scheduling.

THE ROLE OF THE LIBRARIAN IN THE ELEMENTARY SCHOOL

It is the purpose of this inventory to determine what you think the duties of a librarian should be in an elementary school. Please give your own opinion for each item, regardless of what you may have read on the topic.

After each statement draw a circle around the answer that corresponds closest to your opinion.

> SA = strongly agree with statement
>
> A = agree with statement
>
> U = uncertain
>
> D = disagree
>
> SD = strongly disagree with statement

1. The librarian should be familiar with all areas of the elementary school curriculum . . . . .SA A U D SD

2. The main function of the elementary school library is to dispense books . . . . .SA A U D SD

3. The librarian should be aware of recent developments in all subject areas of the elementary school program . . . SA A U D SD

4. The elementary school library is considered as the center of learning in the school . . . . SA A U D SD

5. A leadership role in curriculum planning and revision should be attained by the librarian . . . . SA A U D SD

6. The librarian should be thoroughly familiar with all audio-visual equipment . . . . .SA A U D SD

7. The field of children's literature should be the main concern of the librarian . . . . .SA A U D SD

8. The librarian should keep the elementary school faculty aware of current research in education . . . . .SA A U D SD

9. Any instruction by the librarian should be confined to teaching children the use of reference skills in the library . . . . .SA A U D SD

10. A wide variety of learning materials of all types, including visual and auditory, should be used in the library . . . . .SA A U D SD

11. Provision for facilities for pupils to work in small groups should be included in the library floor plan . . . .SA A U D SD

12. The improvement of reading skills should be the major aim of the librarian . . . . SA A U D SD

13. The librarian should have available for teachers the latest teaching material, including books, filmstrips, recordings, charts, posters, pamphlets, films, pictures and kits . . . . SA A U D SD

14. For the most part the library should be a place in which children may work quietly on assignments . . . . SA A U D SD

15. Despite the complexities of the library program, the librarian should make provision for individual difference in pupils . . . . .SA A U D SD

16. The librarian should conduct workshops for teachers in the use of audio-visual equipment . . . . .SA A U D SD

17. The improvement of instruction in the school should be a concern of the librarian . . . . SA A U D SD

18. In the elementary school the library is used mainly for studying . . . . SA A U D SD

19. The librarian should understand causes of behavior, seek and use information about individual pupils for guidance purposes .SA A U D SD

20. The librarian guides children in developing attitudes of mutual helpfulness and concern for others . . . . SA A U D SD

21. Techniques, such as used in book talks, storytelling, choral reading and speaking, recordings, role playing and creative dramatics, should be used frequently by the librarian . . . . SA A U D SD

22. The librarian identifies and interacts with pupils in a variety of learning situations . . . . SA A U D SD

23. An analysis of the needs of each class using the library is made by the librarian and a plan formulated for each one . . . . SA A U D SD

24. Daily unit and semester plans should be developed cooperatively by the librarian and the classroom teacher for each class to visit the library . . . . .SA A U D SD

25. The librarian should be acquainted with the total school program and also extend personal and professional interest in pupils in classroom situations . .SA A U D SD

26. Active pupil participation during the teaching of library reference skills should be discouraged by the librarian . . . . .SA A U D SD

27. The librarian should seek to discover th unique problems, culture patterns, and interests of the school community and make use of community resources in working with children . . . . .SA A U D SD

28. The librarian should participate in parent-teacher conferences . . . . .SA A U D SD

29. Opportunities for teachers to preview visual materials should be provided by the librarian . . . . . . .SA A U D SD

30. For the most part the duties of the elementary school librarian are clerical in nature . . . . SA A U D SD

Library Collection

	Prior Years			Knapp Project Years		
	1961-62	1962-63	1963-64	1964-65	1965-66	1966-67
Books, total	2,829	3,097	4,000	5,710	6,734	8,075
(Average per pupil)	(3.7)	(4.0)	(5.0)	(7.5)	(9.0)	(10.5)
Exhibits	0	0	0	0	37	40
Filmstrips—silent	0	0	48	600	834	1,048
—sound	0	0	0	0	18	25
Magazines (subscriptions)	13	12	12	18	36	46
Maps	0	0	0	0	90	120
Pamphlets	8	13	18	93	193	493
Picture sets	0	0	0	0	135	141
Recordings—disc	0	0	0	70	106	161
—tape	0	0	0	180	208	235
Slides	0	0	0	200	200	292
Transparencies	0	0	0	0	55	110
Grand Total	2,850	3,122	4,078	6,871	8,646	10,786

Circulation

	Prior Years			Knapp Project Years		
	1961-62	1962-63	1963-64	1964-65	1965-66	1966-67
Books, magazines, and pamphlets Regular term	14,680	14,900	14,700	18,300	20,800	25,400
Summer term	—	—	—	1,339	3,586	N.A.
(Average per day, regular term)	(81)	(83)	(81)	(101)	(116)	(141)
(Average per pupil, regular term)	(18)	(20)	(18)	(24)	(29)	(36)
Exhibits	—	—	—	—	60	70
Filmstrips—silent	—	—	300	337	1,800	1,900
—sound	—	—	—	—	50	60
Picture sets	—	—	—	73	156	210
Recordings—disc	—	—	—	88	140	154
—tape........	—	—	—	153	900	900
Summer A-V total	—	—	—	—	418	N.A.
Total Book Circulation..	14,680	14,900	14,700	19,639	24,386	25,400
Total A-V Circulation...	—	—	300	651	3,524	3,294
Grand Total Circulation.	14,680	14,900	15,000	20,290	27,910	28,694

Total circulation, prior years.......... 44,580

Total circulation, Knapp years......... 76,894

Total increase, circulation 32,314

% of increase, circulation............. 72.4%

N.A.—Not available.

CLASSROOM BORROWING OF AUDIO-VISUAL EQUIPMENT

Equipment	1964-65	1965-66	1966-67	Total
Sound filmstrip projector....	382	665	710	1,757
Motion picture projector.....	202	244	269	715
Tape recorder	227	367	311	905
Overhead projector	30	76	169	275
Listening post	54	113	134	301
Opaque projector	12	24	82	118
TOTAL	907	1,489	1,675	4,071

Note: Some equipment was available prior to 1964 and was borrowed from a central storeroom, but no records were kept of use. Since 1964, more equipment has been provided, is housed in a central storeroom, and records of use are kept. Most classrooms have a phonograph and many have a filmstrip projector as permanent equipment. The record above refers only to the number of days equipment was borrowed from the instructional materials center.

LIBRARY ATTENDANCE

	Prior Years			Knapp Project Years		
	1961-62	1962-63	1963-64	1964-65	1965-66	1966-67
Total regular term........	22,679	23,000	22,540	23,900	26,385	37,950
(Average per day)........	(126)	(127)	(125)	(132)	(147)	(210)
Total summer term.......	—	—	—	1,339	3,586	N.A.
(Average per day)........	—	—	—	(44)	(119)	N.A.
GRAND TOTAL	22,679	23,000	22,540	25,239	29,971	37,950+

Note: Total attendance during the three years of the Knapp Project, 1964-67, shows an increase of 37% over the three previous years, 1961-64.

PROGRAM

	Prior Years			Knapp Project Years		
	1961-62	1962-63	1963-64	1964-65	1965-66	1966-67
CLASS SCHEDULING						
Skill instruction	160	140	120	200	340	400
Supplementary reference	95	90	80	200	510	604
Reading stimulation and recreational reading ...	627	625	670	500	510	560
GRAND TOTAL	882	855	870	900	1,360	1,564

Note: Increases in class use of library, 1964-67 (Knapp Project years):
   47% increase, total class periods.
   124% increase, total class periods for instruction in library skills.
   400% increase, total class periods for supplementary reference.
   18% decrease, total class periods for reading stimulation.

Visitors and their response

As a help in evaluating the effectiveness of the program for visitors to the Knapp School Libraries Project at the Mount Royal Elementary School, a reactionnaire was formulated and distributed to most of the persons who came to see the Project in action. Five hundred fifty forms were returned, representing a fair sample of all the visitors. A tabulation of the response follows:

VISITORS' REACTIONNAIRE TO OBSERVATION OF MOUNT ROYAL SCHOOL
(550 Responses)

Question 1. What was the main purpose of your visit?

Responses—843

	Number	Percent
I. Instructional Materials Center:		
IMC in action	240	
Use of audio-visual materials	41	
Cataloging of audio-visual materials	15	
Total	296	35
II. Library role:		
Library as center of learning	43	
Library as a functional unit in the curriculum	72	
Enriched library	13	
Ideal library and perfect program	31	
Total	159	19
III. Personal improvement:		
Improvement of own program	58	
Gaining new ideas	92	
Total	150	19
IV. Materials:		
Organization in library	31	
Utilization in library and in classroom	72	
Total	103	12
V. Communication:		
Teacher-librarian interaction	40	
Classroom-librarian relationship	51	
Teacher participation in library	8	
Total	99	12

	Number	Percent
VI. General purposes:		
Effect of adequate staff	22	
Needs of culturally disadvantaged	11	
Daily library schedule	3	
Total	36	3

Question 2. What was most helpful in your visit to the Mount Royal School?

Responses—653

	Number	Percent
I. Instructional Materials Center:		
Audio-visual materials usage	108	
Cataloging of audio-visual materials	34	
Storage of audio-visual materials	13	
Total	155	24
II. Observations:		
In the library	88	
In the classroom	25	
Total	113	17
III. Communication:		
Cooperation of teachers and librarians	51	
Interaction of library and classrooms	59	
Total	110	17
IV. Visitation schedule:		
Orientation—slides and talk	33	
Discussion period	32	
Well-planned visitation schedule	26	
Tour of library	17	
Total	108	17
V. Library activities:		
Diversity of activities	59	
After-school activities	3	
Total	62	9
VI. General comments:		
Enthusiasm and sincerity of staff	43	
Organization of library	31	
Quality of learning	20	
Contacts with children	11	
Total	105	

Question 3. Which experiences would you have changed or eliminated?

Responses—520	Number	Percent
I. No response or no suggestion made	396	71
II. Classroom observations:		
Shorten	30	
Eliminate	16	
Increase	11	
Total	57	10
III. Library observations:		
Increase	26	
Lessen repetition of activities	10	
Lessen structure by librarians	5	
Total	41	7
IV. Criticism of lessons observed	16	3
V. Special activity observations:		
Paperback book club	1	
Writers' club	1	
Story hour	7	
Eliminate story hour	4	
Total	13	3
VI. Tour of school:		
Eliminate some parts	5	
Eliminate	4	
Total	9	2
VII. General comments:		
More discussions	11	
Observe classroom-library interaction	7	
Greater use of audio-visual materials including listening center	5	
Longer tour of library	4	
More background on children	2	
Total	29	4

Question 4. Which experiences would you suggest that we add to our program?

Responses—588	Number	Percent
I. No response or nothing to suggest	290	49
II. Library observations:		
More independent work by groups and individuals	35	

II. Library observations (cont'd)	Number	Percent
More emphasis on student selection of books, materials, etc.	30	
More teaching of library skills	24	
More creative use of materials	18	
More emphasis on teacher-librarian planning—possible observation	16	
More informal reference periods	13	
Total	136	23
III. Communications—visitors:		
More discussions with teachers	20	
More discussions with librarians	15	
More discussions with children	11	
Total	46	8
IV. Classroom observations:		
More classroom observations	22	
Observe classroom-library interaction	7	
Observe low ability children	5	
Observe early admissions class	5	
Observe gifted child	2	
Total	41	7
V. Materials:		
More information concerning purchase of materials	13	
More information concerning central processing and cataloging	9	
More information concerning preparation of materials	7	
More information concerning budget	2	
Total	31	5
VI. Audio-visual materials:		
More general use	15	3
VII. General comments:		
Set-up of staff	3	
Floor plan of building	2	
Organization of library	1	
Total	6	1

	Number	Percent
VIII. General suggestions for improving library program:		
More staff	5	
More flexible scheduling	3	
More pupil participation in circulation of material	3	
More audio-visual equipment	2	
More films geared to "locale"	2	
Larger reference department	2	
Newspapers and more periodicals	2	
More space	1	
Centralized ordering of all materials for school	1	
Listening center	1	
Equipment repairs	1	
Total	23	4

An analysis of the visitors' responses to the reactionnaire shows that the largest percentage of persons represented in the survey came to observe a library functioning as an instructional materials center. For the most part, this relatively new role of the library in the elementary school was directly related to its function as an IMC and many school personnel had not seen this in operation prior to their visit. By gaining new ideas, they hoped to improve library services in their own communities.

Visitors and students watch Mrs. Sandra Ullman, fourth grade teacher, use the controlled reader.

In reply to the second question, concerning the most helpful phase of the visit, the largest percentage of replies stressed the instructional materials center. The percentage stating this was eleven percent less than the number listing the IMC as the most important reason for visiting the project. This difference could be misleading, however, because of the large percentage who chose the observations as most helpful. In the observations, both in the classroom and the library, the visitors saw in action a fully operating instructional materials center. The close communications between teachers and librarians and also the carefully planned program for visitors rated high on the list of responses.

A second survey was made of visitors a year after their visits to determine the nature and extent of changes in the school library programs which they represented. Sixty responses were received; since they reflected the same kinds of interest and activity that were reported in year-later reports from Project-supported teams received at the Project office, they are not reported separately here.

Study Of Knapp School Libraries Project

In the fall of 1964, the Bureau of Research of the Baltimore City Public Schools was asked to design a research study for the Knapp School Libraries Project at the Mount Royal School—for the school years 1964-65, 1965-66, and 1966-67. Mount Royal Elementary School had already been selected as the Project (experimental) school. The choice of a control school still had to be made. It was decided that children in grades three and four during the 1964-65 school year would be observed, as they would remain within the elementary schools for the three years of the experiment.

At several meetings of the committee including personnel from the Bureau of Research and the Bureau of Library Services the choice of a control school or schools was discussed. Several were considered. In early January, 1965, the control school (another public elementary school in Baltimore) was selected.

Preliminary records observed. Analysis charts of the Division of Educational Testing were used to obtain data on the experimental and control children who would be included in the experiment. Pupils were divided into three ability groupings—(1) pupils in the low-average group (IQ 85-94); (2) pupils in the mid-average group (IQ 95-104); and (3) pupils in the high-average group (IQ 105-114). To secure a sufficient number of pupils for meaningful statistical analysis, all of the pupils at these intelligence levels for whom records were available were used. Thus, the control group had 121 pupils and the experimental group had 105 pupils. Tables 1 and 2 reveal that the attrition rate at the end of the two and a half years of the experiment approached 50 percent.

After the sample had been selected on this basis, each pupil's third grade reading achievement score was then recorded. All pupils were given the "library" tests, whether or not they had taken a reading test. Several children had entered the fourth grade from other school systems which accounted in part for their not having taken a reading test or having their reading score recorded if they had.

First year: questionnaires. Three questionnaires were devised:

1. The first, called "K-01," was a detailed estimate by teacher and librarian of what they considered each pupil knew about using the school library. This is included on page 138.

2. The second, "K-02," answered by the pupils, had eight questions. Six questions were multiple-choice questions and had to do with how much use the pupil made of the school library, how much he liked various aspects of the library, and the extent to which he made use of the public library in his school or home neighborhood. Questions 7 and 8 were write-in requests for each pupil's opinions on library service and usage. This questionnaire appears on page 141.

3. The third, "K-03," was addressed to the parent and consisted of five questions designed to elicit information as to the child's *present* habits in reading, bringing home books, talking of books, and use of a public library, as compared with his *former* habits in these re-

Mrs. Freeman meets with members of the Paperback Club.

gards, prior to the initiation of the Knapp Project at Mount Royal. (Page 143.)

These questionnaire data were collected through the use of all three of these questionnaires as of February 1965, May 1966, and February 1967.

First year: selection of a test. In March, 1965, the chairman of the committee on evaluation and a member of the committee from the Bureau of Research met with the director of educational testing services to discuss the matter of selecting a useful library skills test. For children of the ages to be using the test, the Iowa Test W-3 ("Knowledge and Use of Reference Materials") was selected as the test which would most nearly fill the requirements of a library skills test, though it had not been designed primarily for this purpose.

First year: pilot studies. The Iowa Test, Part W-3, was administered to the third and fourth grades of a third Baltimore public school (neither the experimental nor the control school) in May, 1965. Toward the end of the first year of Project participation—before the administration of the June, 1965, tests — a copy of *Effectiveness of Centralized Library Service in Elementary Schools*, by Miss Mary Gaver of Rutgers — The State University, which contained the author's "Library Skills

K-01

Teacher_____   School
                        No._____ Grade_____   Pupil's
                                                Name_____   Code
                                                                                No._____

Instructions: Please rate each child on each item listed, in accordance with your
(To teacher   judgment, as follows:
and librarian)

    A. If the pupil knows the material or can do the
        activity described: Rate 1

    B. If the pupil is fairly well versed in the item
        described: Rate 2

    C. If the pupil indicates only slight knowledge: Rate 3

    D. If there is no indication that the pupil under-
        stands what is involved: Rate 4

I LIBRARY REGULATIONS AND PRACTICE

    Rate the pupil's knowledge of:

    A. Library Regulations

        a____When he may visit the library

        b____How to check out books

        c____How to return books

        d____How to renew books

    B. General Organization of the Library

        a____Definition of terms in common usage in a library

        b____Shelving of books (library arrangement--fiction, history, biography,
             science, etc.)

        c____The vertical file

        d____Special references such as World Almanac, Junior Book of Authors,
             atlases, etc.

        e____Encyclopedia

        f____Subject Index to Children's Magazines

        g____Filmstrips, recordings, etc.

h____The card catalog

i____Magazines, newspapers, pamphlets

j____Listings of community resources

k____The parts of a book (title, author, preface, index, appendix, etc.)

II BEHAVIOR OF PUPIL

Rate the student for the following characteristics:

A. Behavior Which Reflects Attitudes Toward Library Use

a____The child is courteous and orderly.

b____Handles books carefully.

c____Accepts responsibility for materials borrowed.

d____Is careful not to disturb others.

e____Is attentive when others are talking.

f____Works well with groups.

g____Does not needlessly interrupt.

h____Shares interesting experiences with the group.

B. Behavior Towards Library Work and Study

a____The child asks for help only when necessary.

b____Is not easily discouraged.

c____Takes pride in his work.

d____Follows directions well.

e____Enjoys tackling a difficult task.

f____Is gaining in self-direction.

g____Plans work before starting.

h____Is learning to finish work on time.

i____Is developing new interests.

j____Perseveres in his interests.

k____Is working effectively with library materials.

III SKILLS IN RELATED AREAS WHICH ARE IN EVIDENCE AND WHICH MAY REASONABLY BE
CONSIDERED TO RESULT FROM THE PUPIL'S LIBRARY EXPERIENCES

Rate the student's progress in the following areas:

A. Language Improvement

a____The pupil seems to appreciate the importance of proper use of
language.

b____Is showing growth in vocabulary.

c____Shows progress in speaking and thinking logically.

d____Is developing good listening habits.

B. General Growth in Skills

a____The child is able to scan for particular information.

b____To browse for special books.

c____To select pertinent material in answering questions.

d____To make and use a bibliography.

e____To make a simple book report.

f____To distinguish between fact and opinion.

g____To distinguish between the significant and the trivial.

h____To outline relevant information.

i____To form own judgment about ideas presented.

C. Evidence of Intellectual Development

a____The child shows interest in voluntary reading for enjoyment.

b____Is interested in varied types of reading.

c____Shows growing interest in good literature.

d____Is developing a habit of appraising critically.

e____Is learning to withhold decisions until he has evidence from several
available sources.

f____Is learning to respect differences of opinion.

g____Is learning to challenge sources of information.

K-02

Dear Boys and Girls:

We want to know how you feel about books and reading. Please check ONE answer to each of the questions below:

1. I go to the school library before school, after school, or at lunch time:

    a. Many times_____

    b. Sometimes_____

    c. Not at all_____

2. I like to go to the school library with my class:

    a. Very much_____

    b. A little, but not very much_____

    c. I do not like it at all_____

3. I like to learn about how books are divided into parts, such as title page, table of contents, index, etc.:

    a. Very much_____

    b. A little, but not very much_____

    c. I do not like it at all_____

4. I like to look in the card catalog and then find my own book:

    a. Very much_____

    b. A little, but not very much_____

    c. I do not like it at all_____

    d. I do not know how to use it_____

5. I think what I am being taught in the use of the school library is:

    a. Hard_____

    b. Easy_____

    c. About right_____

6. I get books from the public library in my neighborhood:

    a. Many times_____

    b. Sometimes_____

    c. Not at all_____

7. What do you like most about going to the school library? (Write your answer)

8. What would you like to see changed in your school library? (Write your answer)

K-03

Teacher_____   School No._____ Grade_____   Pupil's Name_____   Code No._____

Dear Parents:

   We are trying to find out some things which will help our children to learn better. Please fill in the form so that we can know how you feel about these things. In the questions below, please let us know how you feel about your child's work last year and your child's work this year.

PERSONAL OPINION   (Check ONE answer to each question.)

1. Have you seen a change in how your child feels about studying this year—at home and in school:

   a. Child likes to study better than in past_____

   b. Likes to study less than in past_____

   c. About the same as in past_____

   d. Don't know_____

2. Books from School Library. Please answer whether you have noticed a change in your child's unassigned reading this year:

   a. Child brings home more books to read_____

   b. Child brings home fewer books to read_____

   c. Number of books about the same_____

3. Books from Enoch Pratt Free Library. Please answer whether you have seen any change in your child's use of the public library:

   a. Child visits public library more_____

   b. Child visits library less_____

   c. About the same number of visits_____

   d. Child does not get books from public library_____

4. My child talks about BOOKS, READING, THE LIBRARY (either public or school library):

   a. Much_____   b. Little_____   c. Never_____   d. Don't know_____

5. My child talks about school movies, listening to tapes, and other school machines:

   a. Much_____   b. Little_____   c. Never_____   d. Don't know_____

Test," was received. This test was discussed with the director of the testing division who suggested that it would be best to try the test on pupils who were not at the Knapp Project school or at the control school. Therefore, the same school used in May was used to try out the Gaver test. Quoted in part is the memorandum from the director of testing to the Bureau of Research after results on this pilot project had been analyzed:

> After scoring the test papers for the pilot school's third and fourth grade students, I have the following results to report: In the fourth grade class, the median score was 35 with a range from 21 to 51, and at the third grade, the median was 21 with a range from 8 to 33. This means that the average number correct at the fourth grade was 44 percent of the total number of questions and for the third grade it was 26 percent. This suggests that the test was very difficult for both grade levels and especially so for the third grade.
>
> All things considered, I would recommend that another test be used; this one seems far too difficult for students at this age. The only test available seems to be the one we had discussed [appropriate sections of the Iowa Test of Basic Skills]. Time factors probably permit no other course of action since the research project is already past the middle of its first year.

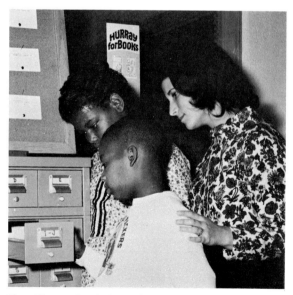

Mrs. Bloom stands by to help children using the card catalog.

In June, 1965, the Iowa Test was administered to the experimental and control pupils at Mount Royal School and at the control school. For testing the status of knowledge and use of reference materials in experimental and control groups, results of this first year's Iowa Test (June, 1965) were at first subjected to quite simple tests. Non-parametric methods were employed to test the significance of the differences between the achievement of the experimental group and of the control group. When results showed no significant differences, it was suggested that a more sophisticated test be applied.

First year: method employed. Two analyses were first matched on intelligence, grade, and sex with control pupils; secondly, experimental and control pupils were matched on third grade reading achievement, grade, and sex. In each case, a critical ratio was computed. The critical ratio formula used was:

$$\frac{M_1 - M_2}{\text{Standard deviation of the difference between the means}}$$

Four comparisons (two for each grade) were made.

In 1966, the same testing process was repeated: Questionnaires K-01, K-02, K-03 were again distributed (in May); the Iowa tests were administered in June. However, in this year, there was an additional test administered, which was called "The Supplementary Test of Library Skills." It was designed by Baltimore Public School personnel, including the director of library services, the library specialist coordinating the Project locally, and staff from the Bureau of Research and Bureau of Testing.

Second year: supplementary test. The "Supplementary Test of Library Skills" consisted of 25 questions which were added to the 141 questions of the Iowa Test. The "Supplementary Test of Library Skills" was pilot-tested in the same school that had been used for the Iowa test. Seventy-five pupils were used, 25 each from Grades four, five, and six. The supplementary test begins on page 145.

Supplementary Test of Library Skills

Knapp School Libraries Project

Baltimore City Schools

Directions: This is a test of library skills. Read each question very carefully, then mark your answers to the questions on the answer sheet.

----

142. You will find BIOGRAPHY books about one person put on the shelves:

    a. Alphabetically, by the name of the person written about.

    b. Alphabetically, by the author's last name.

    c. By the dates the person lived.

    d. By the place where the person lived.

143. Books of fiction are put on the shelves:

    a. Alphabetically, by title.

    b. Alphabetically, by the author's last name.

    c. By what the story is about.

    d. By whether a book would be more interesting to boys or girls.

144. Which one of these books would not need an index?

    a. An arithemetic book

    b. A story book (fiction)

    c. A history book

    d. A poetry book

145. If you want to know the author, title, and publisher of a book, all at one time, you will look in the book's:

    a. Table of contents

    b. Preface

    c. Index

    d. Title page

146. If you want to find a book and do not know the call number of the book, you will look it up:

    a. In the card catalog in the library.

    b. On the edge of the shelves in the library

    c. In the index of another book.

    d. In the encyclopedia.

```
+--------------------------------------------------+
|                        TIME                      |
|    529        Bell, Thelma                       |
|      B          Riddle of time.                  |
|               Viking, 1963                       |
|                                                  |
|                 1 TIME I title 4                 |
+--------------------------------------------------+
```

147. This card is:

    a. A cross-reference card

    b. A title card

    c. A subject card

    d. An author card

148. The book was published in:

    a. 1963

    b. 1942

    c. 529

    d. None of these

149. The book was published by:

    a. Thelma Bell

    b. TIME Magazine

    c. Viking

    d. Riddle

150. The call number of a book tells:

   a. When the book is due.

   b. Where to find the book on the shelves.

   c. The date the book was written.

   d. What the book is called.

151. The card catalog shows 910 to be the call number for "George
   Washington's World". The letter "F" under the number tells you:

   a. That the book is fiction.

   b. The first letter of the author's last name.

   c. That book is in the history section.

   d. That this book is for fast readers.

152. There is one place in your library that will tell you all of the
   books the library own. This is:

   a. The encyclopedia

   b. The shelves

   c. The card catalog

   d. The dictionary

153. Sometimes new words in a book are put in a list with their meanings.
   This list is called:

   a. A glossary

   b. An index

   c. A catalog

   d. A bibliography

154. Pictures in a book are called:

      a. References

      b. Table of Contents

      c. Illustrations

      d. Captions

155. The best place to look to find out about the life of a famous person in the news is:

      a. The picture collection

      b. CURRENT BIOGRAPHY

      c. A book about newspapers

      d. A dictionary

156. Books have bibliographies:

      a. So that you will not have to use the index of the book.

      b. So that you can tell what the book is about.

      c. So that you can find other books about the same subject.

      d. To tell something about the company which published the book.

157. When you go to the library to find facts about birds, the best thing to do is:

      a. To look among the fiction books for stories about birds.

      b. To look up "BIRDS" in the card catalog.

      c. To look through magazines.

      d. To look in the National Geographic Magazine Index.

These are some sections of the library and their numbers:

a. Language 400

b. Science 500

c. Literature 800

d. History and Travel 900

158. Where will you find a book about a real boy who is living in Japan?

    a. 400
    b. 500
    c. 800
    d. 900

159. Where will you find a book about snakes?

    a. 400
    b. 500
    c. 800
    d. 900

160. Where will you find a dictionary?

    a. 400
    b. 500
    c. 800
    d. 900

161. "See also" cards are in the card catalog:

    a. To guide us to other books on a subject.
    b. To warn us to read a card carefully.
    c. To guide us to books about eyes.
    d. To tell us other books an author has written.

162. A pseudonym is:

    a. A word that sounds like another word.

    b. A word that has the same meaning as another word.

    c. The name of a publisher of a book that has won a prize.

    d. A name that a writer uses which is not his own.

This is a section label in a library:

---

550 - 589

---

163. You will find a book with the call number $\frac{590}{F}$:

    a. In this section

    b. Before this section

    c. After this section

    d. In the Fiction section

164. You will find a book with the call number $\frac{551}{F}$:

    a. In this section

    b. Before this section

    c. After this section

    d. In the Fiction section

165. You will find a book with the call number $\frac{572}{F}$:

    a. In this section

    b. Before this section

    c. After this section

    d. In the Fiction section

166. You will find a book with the call number $\frac{523}{F}$:

    a. In this section

    b. Before this section

    c. After this section

    d. In the Fiction section

Third year: Testing in 1967, the third year of the experiment, was conducted very early in the second semester. Questionnaires K-01, K-02, K-03 were administered during the first week of February, 1967.

Third year: analysis. As will be seen from Tables 1 and 2, in the twenty comparisons that were made in the two-and-a-half-year experiment, matching boys *vs.* boys and girls *vs.* girls on intelligence quotient first, and then on reading level, there was only one instance in the twenty in which comparisons reached a significant difference at the five percent level. This was when the original third grade's Iowa scores were compared in February, 1967.

It must be pointed out, however, that the real import of the finding of equal effectiveness is subject to the following qualifications:

1. No comparison to third and fourth grades of previous years was available. It may have been true that previous third and fourth graders at the two schools had always reached this level of skills by the middle of sixth grade.

2. Other uncontrolled factors at the Mount Royal School, such as teacher and class-size differences, may have been the important influences rather than library services *per se.*

3. The attrition rate was very high in both schools and there may have been some differential bias. Those who left could not be tested at the end of the study. The number of matched pairs remaining in the universe in later years was small.

Mrs. Bloom helps students in the reference area.

(Name: Last   First)   (Code No.)

School No.   Grade   Code   Date of Birth

IQ_____ Reading_____ (3d gr.)

		'65	'66	'67	'68

Library Test 1_____   K-01 _____ _____ _____ _____

Library Test 2_____ _____   K-02 _____ _____ _____ _____

Library Test 3_____ _____   K-03 _____ _____ _____ _____

2/1/65

Record Cards for Testing Program. A note in the upper right corner indicated whether the subject was at the Control or Experimental school.

TABLE 1

Critical Ratio—Iowa Test of Basic Skills, Part W-3
(Experimental Pupils, Control Pupils, Original Grades 3 and 4*)

Year	Base of Comparison	Original Grade	Mean$_1$ Experimental School	Mean$_2$ Control School	Test (z)**	Number of Pairs
First	Reading	3	48.4	43.9	1.55	35
(1964-65)	Intelligence	3	50.8	44.1	1.77	42
(June)	Reading	4	54.7	55.3	—0.22	39
	Intelligence	4	58.0	56.6	0.42	41
Second	Reading	3	59.8	63.6	—1.17	24
(1965-66)	Intelligence	3	64.2	63.6	0.16	25
(June)	Reading	4	75.0	72.9	0.54	27
	Intelligence	4	73.1	73.4	—0.07	31
Third	Reading	3	70.6	72.2	—0.30	17
(1966-67)	Intelligence	3	77.6	66.1	2.46	24
(February)	Reading	4	88.8	85.7	0.83	22
	Intelligence	4	89.5	87.4	0.56	25

*Original Grade 3 became: Grade 3 — 1964-65   *Original Grade 4 became: Grade 4 — 1964-65
                          Grade 4 — 1965-66   Grade 5 — 1965-66
                          Grade 5 — 1966-67   Grade 6 — 1966-67

**z is the difference divided by the standard error of the difference.
z of 1.96 indicates a difference significant at the 5% level.
z of 2.33 indicates a difference significant at the 2% level.
z of 2.58 indicates a difference significant at the 1% level.

TABLE 2

Critical Ratio—Supplementary Test of Library Skills
(Experimental Pupils, Control Pupils, Original Grades 3 and 4*)

Year	Base of Comparison	Original Grade	Mean$_1$ Experimental School	Mean$_2$ Control School	Test (z)**	Number of Pairs
First (1964-65) (June)	Reading	3	—	—	—	—
	Intelligence	3	—	—	—	—
	Reading	4	—	—	—	—
	Intelligence	4	—	—	—	—
Second (1965-66) (June)	Reading	3	11.6	11.3	0.03	25
	Intelligence	3	12.8	11.6	1.23	25
	Reading	4	13.6	14.5	—0.89	25
	Intelligence	4	13.7	15.4	—1.64	27
Third (1966-67) (February)	Reading	3	13.0	13.7	—0.48	17
	Intelligence	3	14.4	12.0	1.94	24
	Reading	4	16.4	14.9	1.42	22
	Intelligence	4	16.7	16.2	0.56	25

*Original Grade 3 became: Grade 3 — 1964-65   *Original Grade 4 became: Grade 4 — 1964-65
                        Grade 4 — 1965-66   Grade 5 — 1965-66
                        Grade 5 — 1966-67   Grade 6 — 1966-67

**z is the difference divided by the standard error of the difference.
z of 1.96 indicates a difference significant at the 5% level.
z of 2.33 indicates a difference significant at the 2% level.
z of 2.58 indicates a difference significant at the 1% level.

Comparison of experimental and control schools

	Mount Royal School (Experimental School)	Control School
FACILITIES		
Classrooms	24	27
Kindergarten rooms	2	2
Early Admissions room	1	0
Administrative suite	1	1
Auditorium	1	1
Art resource room	1	1
Cafeteria	1	0
Gymnasium	1	1
Health suite	1	1
Library	1 (2,856 sq. ft.)	1 (1,830 sq. ft.)
Meeting room, small	1	1
Multi-purpose room	1	1
Teachers' room	2	1
Book rooms	1	1
Playground, large	1	1
Playground, small	1	1
Recreational Center suite	1	0
Supply rooms	More than one	More than one
STAFF		
Principal	1	1
Vice principal	1	1
Counselor	1	1
Librarians	2½	1
Reading Center teacher		1
Supplemental teaching service teacher	1	
Classroom teachers	21	29
Tenure status:		
Elected	16	11
Probationary	0	4
Provisional	5	13
Per diem substitute	0	1
Sex of classroom teachers		
Male	3	6
Female	18	23
Race of classroom teachers		
White	13	22
Negro	8	7

	Mount Royal School (Experimental School)	Control School
Resource persons, part time:		
Physical education teacher	Alternate weeks	Alternate weeks
Art teacher	2 days per week	2 days per week
Vocal music teacher	0	2 days per week
Instrumental music teacher	½ day per week	½ day per week
Speech therapist	½ day per week	½ day per week
Social worker	0	2 days per week
Nurse	2 days per week	2 days per week
Doctor	1 day, alternate weeks	1 afternoon per month
Lip reading teacher	0	½ day per week
Dentist	2 days per week for 3 neighboring elementary public school and 1 parochial school	
Additional personnel:		
Full-time secretary	1	1
Clerical aides	0	No. varies
Dentist's assistant	1	
Custodians	4 (2 at night)**	2
Janitresses	1½	2½
PUPIL POPULATION	657*	1,000
Turnover—1965-66:		
Withdrawals	80	103
Transferred out	251	169
New pupils	182	228
Transferred in	198	177
Socio-economic background range:		
Upper (about 5%)	Middle class, parents professionals	Children of students and professors at Johns Hopkins University
Lower	Families on welfare; children in foster homes (majority of pupils are in this category)	Families on welfare; children in foster homes

*Enrollment at Mount Royal has dropped below 700 pupils during the past year because houses have been torn down around the school, as part of an urban renewal project, and pupils have moved out of the neighborhood.

**Extra custodial help was necessary to care for the needs of 3,000 visitors during the three-year period of the Knapp Project.

Comparison of experimental and control schools (continued)

	Mount Royal School (Experimental School)	Control School
*Ethnic background:		
White	20%	53%
Negro	80%	47%
Other (a few Orientals and/or East Indians)	Yes	Yes
NEIGHBORHOOD		
Near business community?	Yes	Yes
Housing	Row houses, good and bad; high-rise apartments, luxury and other; urban renewal construction and rehabilitation (very little rebuilding done at time of report)	Row houses, good and bad; apartments, mostly converted single-family houses
RECREATION AND CULTURAL FACILITIES IN VICINITY OF SCHOOL		
Recreation center	Yes	Yes
YMCA or YWCA	Yes	Yes
Public library	No	Yes
Park	Yes	Yes
Art museum or art gallery	Yes	Yes
Theatre	Yes	Yes (motion picture)
Other	None	Stadium
SPECIAL SCHOOL PROGRAMS		
Intern teaching program	No	Yes
Student teaching	Yes	Yes
Special reading programs:		
SRA	No	Yes
Special reading series (experimental)	No	Yes
Phono-visual	No	Yes
Team teaching	No	Yes
Summer remedial reading program	1966	1966

*At the beginning of the project, the racial balance at the Mount Royal School was 50 percent white and 50 percent Negro. The bussing of 200 children from other inner-city schools, for the last year, has caused the change in racial balance, because all bussed-in children were Negro.

Report on achievement

Twenty-six goals were implicit in the responses given to Questions No. 27 and No. 28 of the Project application by the staff representing the Mount Royal school. To what degree were these goals achieved at the end of the three-year period? Following is a restatement of these two questions, coded to indicate how much each aim was attained.

KEY

* Received special emphasis

** Achieved

† Improved or expanded

‡ Some improvement or tried out to a limited degree

QUESTION No. 27

How would you extend and/or improve your present school library program if you receive the grant? Is there any one type of service or activity which you would like to emphasize?

**1. Develop a library program in greater depth.

**2. Promote the use of the library as a learning center—an instructional materials center—with viewing and listening activities in addition to reading activities and with servicing of audio-visual materials in addition to printed materials.

*†3. Explore ways and means to extend reading enrichment programs for disadvantaged students.

†4. Promote more intensive teamwork with all teachers, especially new teachers.

‡5. Participate more actively with the teachers and pupils in the Early Admissions project.

*‡6. Develop a program for parents to stimulate their active cooperation in encouraging their children to read at home and to form a strong library habit.

**7. Share promising practices with librarians and teachers through demonstration lessons, bibliographies of useful materials, etc.

**8. Extend library hours—after school and during the summer.

**9. Develop a program in cooperation with Towson State College to acquaint student teachers and beginning teachers with the values of library services for the elementary classroom and with suggestions for expanding the use of library resources. Demonstrate to potential teachers the rewards and challenges that can be gained from using school libraries in teaching disadvantaged boys and girls.

QUESTION No. 28

What long-range outcomes does the school hope to achieve through participation in this project? (Identify desired effects or goals for pupils, teachers, other schools in the system, etc.)

For pupils:

‡1. Improve academic achievement of pupils and assist in raising reading levels.

‡2. Raise the cultural level of the children and possibly some parents by exposing them to a variety of books and good literature.

†3. Assist in developing good reading habits and growing interest in books.

†4. Assist in stimulating more creative and critical thinking.

†5. Establish the lifetime library habit in some students.

†6. Help more students to achieve a background in use of library resources so they may have a better foundation for learning in the junior high school.

For teachers:

**1. Provide more resource materials for classroom instruction, especially in variety and duplication of printed materials, pamphlets, pictures, and in audio-visual materials within the school building, making all resources available in one place.

**2. Expand present library services and initiate additional services to assist the teacher.

**3. Make professional books and materials readily accessible to teachers.

**4. Promote more individual work with teachers.

†5. Improve methods of using teaching tools with more printed and audio-visual materials being made available.

Other schools:

1. Develop guidelines for planning and implementing effective library programs for other schools with disadvantaged students. (Plans in progress.)

‡2. Develop bibliographies of good titles, filmstrips, recordings, etc., for disadvantaged children, which can be shared with other librarians and teachers.

**3. Arrange demonstration lessons to show librarians and teachers some good library practices in working with classes of disadvantaged students, some effective techniques for using audio-visual materials in the library program, and the educational benefits that can be derived from having library collections, library facilities, and library staff that meet the national standards.

Others:

**1. Demonstrate to supervisors, administrators, and parents how adequate library resources, staff, and quarters serve all teachers and students to a greater degree and how these factors assist in providing quality education.

‡2. Demonstrate to administrators the values of this type of school library program, so they, in turn, will provide greatly increased library budgets to achieve the same quality of library service for all schools.

‡3. Develop an awareness in parents of the advantages of helping children to acquire interest in reading to the extent that they make a definite effort to promote this interest in a favorable climate.

SUMMARY

Achieved	11
Improved or expanded	7
Some improvement or tried out to a limited degree	7
Plans in progress	1
GRAND TOTAL	26

Budgeting for an IMC library

Many administrators want to know, "How much does it cost to carry on a program like the Knapp School Libraries Project at the

	First Year	Second Year	Third Year	Fourth Year	Fifth Year	Total
MATERIALS						
3,700 books @ $3 net purchased over 5-yr. period.......	$ 2,220	$ 2,220	$ 2,220	$ 2,220	$ 2,220	$11,100
Processing books @ $1.25	925	925	925	925	925	4,625
Audio-visual materials, including cataloging ...	2,000	2,000	1,000	1,000	1,000	7,000
Professional materials, teachers' materials	500	500	200	200	200	1,600
Equipment, audio-visual shelving, card catalogs, etc.	2,000	1,000	1,000	500	500	5,000
PERSONNEL						
Regular term:						
2nd librarian	7,500	7,750	8,000	8,000	8,000	39,250
Clerk	3,000	3,100	3,200	3,300	3,400	16,000
QUARTERS						
Renovation	1,500	—	—	—	—	1,500
TOTAL	$19,645	$17,495	$16,545	$16,145	$16,245	$86,075

Note: Costs will vary according to local salary schedule, etc.

Mount Royal Elementary School?" The table on the facing page shows an approximation of the cost of initiating such a program, pro-rated over five years and based on the following assumptions for a school of 750 to 800 pupils:

1. That the school has a central library equivalent at least to a standard classroom, approximately 750 square feet, with an additional area equal to 375 square feet as work space for the librarian.

2. That an adjacent classroom, approximately 750 square feet, can be converted to library use.

3. That there is one full-time librarian serving the school five days a week.

4. That there is a basic collection in the library of 4,000 books and that these books have been cataloged and processed.

5. That there are *no* non-book materials—filmstrips, recordings, etc.—or audio-visual equipment in the library.

REACTION AND EVALUATION

Mr. Le Roy Hardesty, who has served as principal at the Mount Royal School throughout the Project, comments:

> The library facilities and library staff in our school have helped develop in our pupils concepts and understandings with greater clarity, greater depth, and through many more channels than ever before. The teaching of skills which we want children to acquire in all areas of the curriculum now becomes much easier to present and develop because of the excellent and wide variety of material and assistance which the Knapp Project has made available to us.
>
> The process of learning new ideas and enlarging upon old ones can start and be developed in both the classroom and the library. Through conferences, work sheets, and planning together, our librarians and teachers know what each is doing in units of work and in interest areas. Each reinforces the efforts of the other in helping children to learn. As children move back and forth between the classroom and the library in groups and as individuals, their learning becomes a continuous thing, with enrichment and depth far beyond what could be obtained in the classroom alone.
>
> The library and library personnel have encouraged and helped classroom teachers develop new curricula and give new meaning and an expansion of understandings of existing curricula. Our children, teachers, parents, and community are benefiting greatly from the excellent library situation which the Knapp Foundation grant made possible in the Mount Royal School.

The three librarians of the Mount Royal School share their views:

> Added library staff gives added opportunities . . . to guide boys and girls in book selection, read with them, and listen as they read aloud or discuss their books.

> The three years of the Knapp School Libraries Project have given us at the Mount Royal Elementary School a widening vision of what a school library should encompass.

> We feel that we have gained strength in our approaches to various areas of the curriculum through more frequent conferences with teachers and more opportunities to plan cooperatively.

> In many areas of the curriculum we now can use the broad range of instructional materials, as well as books and vertical file materials, to help children gather information, make generalizations, and understand concepts.

> Having more librarians and greater flexibility in scheduling has meant that we have been able to incorporate many of the radio and TV offerings of the Department of Education into our library plans.

> It is gratifying to see that many of our boys and girls, by the time they reach the sixth grade, are able to locate items for themselves, set up the needed equipment, and use the materials with purpose.

> The three years have been both stimulating and challenging. . . . We see greater interaction between the library and the total life of the school.

> We feel that we are making greater impact upon the teachers and children through

the greatly expanded collection of our library and through breadth and depth of more services from more librarians.

Teachers at Mount Royal voice individual opinions and evaluations of the library program:

The science kits were wonderful in helping me get concrete materials for the children to see, touch, and work with.

The wonderful picture sets, transparencies, and filmstrips have made unknown concepts accessible where actual trips to see such things would have been impossible.

Being a new faculty member I was able to get an abundance of material for my units that I wouldn't have otherwise known existed.

I have been given many new and creative ideas by the school librarians who are always willing to plan and work with me and my pupils.

Bright pupils are able to work at a faster pace due to this program because they can engage in various independent activities, both in the library and in the classroom.

The Knapp School Libraries Project has helped me to reach my children through extended grouping. I can almost be in two places at once through the use of teacher-made tapes and other material which can be prepared ahead of time and used by pupils independently.

For both slow and bright pupils, a secondary, but very important, outcome was observed. This was an improved self-image and a gain in self-confidence.

By hearing dramatizations of historical events, or biographical incidents, children could become a part of history as they studied it.

When I used scientific models which were available in our library, difficult concepts became clear.

I learned how to individualize my program with the help of the library staff and

the resources of the library. I learned how to prepare my own teaching tapes and transparencies.

The library staff . . . worked closely with me so that during class library periods they could follow up what I was doing in the classroom.

As a supervising teacher, I was able to train student teachers in the use of a wide variety of machines, materials, and techniques . . . to carry on a better program.

Student teachers assigned to Mount Royal made these comments:

The library experiences were extremely helpful because I did not know before the importance of a library in the elementary school.

Learning to use audio-visual aids was a very useful experience. The realization of how these aids may be integrated into the curriculum and of the help that informed librarians can offer the classroom teacher was also helpful.

The use of audio-visual aids for teaching, the relaxed atmosphere of the school, the progressive library program, and the cordial attitudes of the librarians coupled with their willingness to help the teacher present an effective and purposeful lesson — all of this impressed me.

Both the teacher and the library workshop programs were extremely helpful to me. My teacher was willing, thoughtful, and flexible. The library and the audio-visual workshop provided materials, experiences, and knowledge that proved to be not only helpful, but fundamental.

The only thing I believe should be added is time. I would have liked to explore the library more and closer. However, I am glad to have had the time I did.

You have a fantastic library here that far surpasses most schools, and I did enjoy using the equipment in the classroom. I wish I could have had a course in the operation of the equipment only.

Pupils

The principal of Mount Royal wrote, "It has been somewhat difficult to get an objective evaluation of the library and effects of the total library program on pupils and classroom programs. Reasons are many—lack of appropriate published test material—large turnover of pupils —bussing in pupils and necessary class reorganization. . . . However, we devised some simple questionnaires for the Mount Royal boys and girls to show to some degree how they feel about the library, how they use it, and ways in which it has helped them."

Parents

For purposes of assaying the impact upon the community of the Knapp School Libraries Project at Mount Royal Elementary School, 190

STUDENT PREFERENCES IN LIBRARY

| | Unselected Group (170 Students) | | | | Experimental Group* (35 Students) | |
	List the things you like about the library	List the things you like about the library	List the *one* thing you like best about the library	List the *one* thing you like best about the library	List the things you like about the library	List the *one* thing you like best about the library
Grades	1-3	4-6	1-3	4-6	4-6	4-6
Books	117	122	38	58	34	16
Tapes	51	103	3	6	31	4
Records	35	46	2	1	9	—
Earphones	4	46	—	6	7	—
Individual viewers	—	13	—	1	—	—
Reference books	—	20	—	—	4	—
Hearing stories	46	13	8	2	4	2
Librarians	29	37	1	2	20	2
Air conditioning	—	26	—	—	12	1
Filmstrips	89	90	7	4	30	8
Making transparencies ..	16	7	5	1	4	—
Library clubs	—	2	—	—	4	2
Carpet	19	32	1	4	12	—
Overhead projector	—	9	—	—	2	—
Card catalog	—	30	—	—	9	—
Furniture	2	16	—	—	1	—
Clerk	—	1	—	—	1	—
Demonstration	1	11	—	—	—	—
Television	6	—	—	—	—	—

* This group, originally composed of 100 students, included students who were in the school three years and who were identified by the Bureau of Research to take tests on library skills and to be paired with comparable students in a control school. No primary grade students are included in this group.

questionnaires were distributed to a random sampling of pupils in March, 1967. All socioeconomic and achievement levels were included in the sampling. Represented were children new to the school as of September, 1966, and pupils in the school prior to September, 1966. Pupils took the questionnaires home to their parents to be filled in. Of the questionnaires distributed, 128, or 68 percent, were completed and returned. Thirty-five included comments.

A sample of the questionnaire, with summary of responses, is shown here:

QUESTIONNAIRE

Dear Parents:

We want to find out how you feel about our School Library. The answers to these questions will help us very much.

The School Librarians   Mount Royal Elementary School

I. DIRECTIONS: Check (x) your best answer for each question.

1. Do you know that we have a library in our school?
   Yes 127   No 1

2. Do you know that our school library was given a grant of money from the Knapp Foundation to make our library better?

   Yes 63   No 65

3. If you did know, how did you find out?

   30 A. Your child told you.
   21 B. You read it in the newspaper.
   19 C. You saw a program on television.
    4 D. Other source — P.T.A., friend.

4. Does your child bring library books home more often than before?

   Yes 99   No 27   2 did not answer

5. Is your child reading more at home this year?

   Yes 108   No. 17   3 did not answer

6. Have you seen your child bring home a paperback book from the school library this year?

   Yes 56   No 69   3 did not answer

7. Has your child stayed after school to visit the library this year?

   Some 49   Often 13   Not at all 65   1 did not answer

8. Did you know our school library was open one month last summer?

   Yes 78   No 50

9. Did your child use the school library last summer?

   Some 27   Often 29   Not at all 72

10. Have you ever visited our school library?

    Yes 47   No 81

II. If you care to say anything about the school library, please do so on the back of this paper.

    35 made comments   93 did not make comments

Comments included references to reactions of individual children, to hopes for the library's being kept open in the summer, and to the attractive physical facility. Most comments reflected the attitude of one parent who wrote: "If every school . . . could enjoy the same kind of library facility, I feel both teachers and the children would be able to do a much better job in the classroom."

Statement of the director of school libraries, Miss M. Bernice Wiese:

> The demonstration of the Knapp School Libraries Project at the Mount Royal Elementary School has had a significant influence on the system-wide development of library services. When the American Library Association standards were published in 1960, librarians, teachers, principals, and administrators considered the quantitative requirements exaggerated and unobtainable. Few understood fully the concept of the school library as an instructional materials center. During the three years of the project, opportunities have been provided for Baltimore City teachers, librarians, principals, supervisors, and other administrators to observe that a good school library with a multimedia collection and sufficient library staff does make a difference. The Knapp Project has helped to support the recommendations for expanding school libraries. It has shown how space is used for listening, viewing, and reading, and how much space is needed for the many types and quantities of printed and non-printed materials. More important, it has demonstrated the function of the library as a learning resource center.

> Personnel from the Baltimore City schools have been impressed with the enriched literature program for every child afforded by the increased collection of books, by the close teamwork of teachers and librarians made possible by a larger library staff, by the expanded use of audio-visual materials in the library and in the classroom, by the availability of the library for use by individuals, small groups, and classes throughout the school day. The easy access to all types of supplementary materials in one place combined with "instant" service has had a special appeal to teachers and has promoted a familiarity with these materials among students.

> Seeing is believing, but more important, it is stimulating, too, when believing leads to action in other schools to centralize audio-visual materials in the school library. Though space, staff, and funds are limited, in many schools principals and librarians who have visited the Mount Royal School have obtained ideas and been encouraged to draw up plans to enlarge and remodel their library quarters for expanded services. Seeing librarians as members of the teaching team, as materials specialists, and as resource people has demonstrated the role of the librarian in the instructional program and has prompted requests for increased library staffs by principals in other elementary and secondary schools.

> From the point of view of the library administrator, the most rewarding aspect of the Knapp Project has been the impact on the students in the school. The library experiences of these boys and girls during the school day and after school hours have provided variety and depth for their self development. One sees extensive individual reading guidance and development of good library habits to assist the student in acquiring basic knowledge for his continuing education. Special activities sponsored by the library such as reading clubs, writing clubs, visits of authors and special guests add to their cultural background. The increased opportunities for librarians to arouse the individual child's curiosity in a new field of interest and to encourage a student to pursue a new topic is most important for children in this community. When a variety of media — filmstrips, recordings, pictures, books — are available, the chances are greater for appealing to the interest and needs of more individuals. At the Mount Royal Elementary School, it is a familiar sight to see a child enjoying a story by listening to a recording of a story which he might not be ready to read for himself, another child viewing a filmstrip to obtain information on a topic, another making a transparency for his report. All of these are as common to them as books. The school library is contributing to their learning and enriching their background by opening many doors to knowledge.

> To the director of school libraries, the statistics in class use of the library are significant and rewarding. Increases in circulation and attendance indicate that more people borrowed more materials. The statistics do not reveal the use made of the materials, or if they were used at all. Class use reflects activity and interaction. Over a three-year period, the greatest gains were

Listening, reading, touching, observing — these students acquire many skills.

in class visits to the library by students and teachers to find information to supplement and enrich classroom instruction — a 400 percent increase over 1961-63. Class use devoted to developing skills and helping students to learn how to use libraries and library resources independently increased 124 percent. Though there was a decrease of 18 percent in class use for recreational reading, the increase in circulation, the paperback reading club, and individual reading guidance activities reassure one that reading for pleasure and reading appreciation have expanded, too.

Year-round school libraries have been talked about for many years, and some of our libraries have been opened during the summer with the help of volunteers. Having the Knapp Project school operating on a year-round basis provided opportunities for trying out the most successful enrichment programs for children in the community. Though summer plans included programs for parents, too, few parents participated. The need for parent involvement in helping children to learn in this community is recognized and continuing efforts will be made to try out other devices to appeal to the parents.

The Knapp School Libraries Project has made significant contributions to the development of school library service in the Baltimore City schools. It has helped to make many librarians, teachers, and administrators more knowledgeable about the programs and services of learning resource centers. It has supplied guidelines for plans for pilot libraries on both the elementary and secondary level. It has demonstrated full library programs to support the instructional pro-

grams in inner-city schools. It has provided opportunities to learn the effectiveness and practical uses of many types of equipment, and suggested ways to improve planning of library facilities in new schools and in remodeling existing libraries. All new schools include libraries planned as instructional materials centers. The project coordinator has prepared a list of basic audio-visual equipment for school libraries, including buying information, which was based on needs and use at the Project school.

With the help of funds from the Elementary and Secondary Education Act and in cooperation with the system-wide instructional materials center, it has been possible to put some plans into action [in Baltimore schools]. Materials and equipment have been placed in the libraries of a number of schools. One federal grant of $10,000 was received to build up a collection of filmstrips, recordings, and other instructional materials to help an elementary school develop a center and serve as a demonstration school next year. Some Title II funds were used to begin collections of filmstrips and recordings in fifteen schools.

Comments by the Project coordinator, Mrs. Alice Rusk:

One of the rewards of coordinating the Knapp School Libraries Project at the Mount Royal Elementary School has been the close association with this experiment and opportunities to watch it blossom. The impact of the project has been felt in diverse ways, but the coordinator, who works as a library specialist of the Baltimore Public Schools, has been affected most by the evidence of staff growth and the many opportunities offered for sharing with others.

The professional growth of the Project librarians has been impressive. The staff members had been well trained in the precepts of book-oriented library services. The philosophy of the Knapp Project opened up new vistas to them for developing a multimedia program, and they were quick to adapt. While maintaining and practicing that books are basic, they saw and utilized fully opportunities to extend and reinforce book experiences with carefully planned use of non-book media. Their enthusiasm was shared outside the project through their teamwork with other city schools, Towson State College, and the Bureau of Library Services in communicating the know-how they developed through their involvement with this library program.

Sharing has been the keynote of many activities. The librarians have shared their knowledge of the operation of a learning resource center with other librarians and teachers in the system. They have shared their expertise in the use of audio-visual equipment and the incorporation of these aids into the instructional program.

Another shared experience has been the cataloging of the non-book media. The Mount Royal scheme, which employs color-banded cards, has stimulated many to do something similar in their own schools to make more accessible the materials they already have. As an outgrowth of this, a color code has been developed for the spectrum of materials in a multi-media collection, as well as specific directions for processing and cataloging filmstrips and disc recordings. Both the code and the directions, now standard for Baltimore City school libraries, are patterned on Mount Royal.

The coordinator, herself, has been stimulated to be more creative through planning program with the librarians in the Project. A new dimension has been added to her thinking in relation to effective library activities and the interaction of the school library with the classroom. As she has worked with other librarians outside of the Project school, she has been able to share her enthusiasm and growing background of knowledge about a multi-media library program.

Statement of the Project field worker, Dr. Walter W. Williamson:

From the viewpoint of the field worker, perhaps the most important outcome of the Knapp School Libraries Project at the college has been the development of a philosophy of education emphasizing a library-centered, multi-media approach to learning. Through realistic demonstrations and experiences the college students and staff have seen the value of using a wide variety of materials, print and non-print, in meeting the needs of all children; the range of abilities in Mount Royal classrooms is often unbelievably wide. Because of their involvement in the Mount Royal program, the college students understand that rigid grade norms and standards are educationally unfeasible, since each individual, regardless of imposed expectations, progresses according to his own pattern and at his own rate. When the students who have participated in the program begin to teach, they will have basically sound educational principles to guide them in working with children.

The variety of services offered by a teacher training institution, both in personnel and materials, has been another factor in the total development of the Project. The involvement of the college staff and students has brought about close communication with the Mount Royal School administration and faculty to the mutual benefit of each institution. This has demonstrated conclusively the advantages of a close relationship between a teacher training institution and a large city elementary school in providing services that neither could have alone.

The visitation program has been especially forceful in stressing the need for educators on all levels to be aware of recent developments and constantly to appraise the curriculum, materials, and methods used to achieve worthwhile objectives. Technological advances made within recent years, and the ones planned for the future, will challenge education especially in a way that it has never been challenged before. The schools must be ready for this and projects such as the Knapp School Libraries Project help in bringing about the needed changes.

Statement of the assistant superintendent—elementary education, Edith V. Walker:

I have been impressed . . . with the wealth of fine material which has been provided for this community, with the fine manner in which the entire faculty has entered into the Project and cooperated in carrying on its work, by the interest and involvement of the principal and vice-principals of the school, and by the feeling of belonging which the children show in their free use of the library in all of its aspects and services. It is very evident that children have gained independence in the use of the materials in the Project, that they have learned to look to the instructional materials center for solutions to many of their learning problems and as a good place to be in leisure moments.

My only reservation is a concern that many of the children who have not been "sold" on reading as a means of obtaining pleasure and information will turn to films, recordings, and other types of audio-visual media to satisfy their needs rather than pursuing reading to the point where their skill is sufficient to gain satisfaction from the printed page. It is my feeling that any future work which is done in connection with this or similar projects should be very conscious of the need to develop reading skills to the full extent of each child's potential.

Area director Vivian I. Cord views Mount Royal School as one of many for which she has administrative responsibility:

I am convinced that pupils and teachers who have the opportunity to work in a school where the library functions as the hub of the curriculum developments experience a depth in their teaching and learning that is not possible under the traditional concepts of a school library. The multi-media approach, combined with teacher and librarian teams planning with and for pupils, results in a quality of interaction that can have the one result desired most by all educators — better instruction and increased learning. I heartily endorse and will work for the growth of elementary school libraries along the instructional materials center concept. There is no doubt that it will be money well spent.

Mrs. Anne Z. Schilling, a candidate at Towson State College for the degree of Master of Science in Education, chose as her thesis study, *An Evaluation of Teacher Participation in and Use of the Mount Royal School Library Program.* Following are excerpts from her conclusions, as a result of this study:

It can be concluded that the instructional program of the Mount Royal Elementary School was favorably affected by its improved school library. Through the use of instructional materials from the library collection, through the resource assistance of the librarians, and through the use of the library facilities, teachers were able to present to children a learning program that was appropriate, functional, and meaningful. Teachers were enabled to meet more of the needs and abilities of students at varying levels within their classrooms. Teachers considered that their teaching had improved because they were better able to meet teaching situations by drawing from the library's program and services. The more academic areas of the curriculum were the studies most immediately affected by the school library and its instructional materials, particularly social studies and reading.

Teachers did make extensive use of the library's professional collection and its instructional materials and equipment. There was some teacher evaluation of the library program and the materials collection. Some of the teachers made suggestions to the library staff concerning the acquisition of new materials. Teachers encouraged student use of the library and sent children in groups and individually to the library for independent study and for recreational reading, although few teachers sought extra library periods for their entire class.

It cannot be said that teachers were involved in the over-all development of the library program and library policies to any great degree, although they were kept informed about the Project and they were invited to make suggestions. System-wide policies for Baltimore City school libraries and the pressures of bringing the Mount Royal library to a state of readiness for participation in the Knapp Project very possibly required the librarian to make decisions when, at another time, she might have consulted with the faculty on some of them. It should also be considered that while many of the teachers had had experience with the Mount Royal School library, they were still not completely familiar with a full program of library service and were thus not prepared or able to make suggestions. Teachers' responses did indicate, however, that teachers have begun to identify a good library program as a necessary part of the instructional program in order to meet the needs and abilities of children. They have begun to evaluate resources and to see areas for improvement in the existing collection and services.

Faculty attitudes as a whole will ultimately determine the success or failure of the library program. The Mount Royal teachers felt that their school library was an asset to the instructional program. They indorsed the

idea that the library should function as an instructional materials center and they believed that the use of instructional materials was important to successful, meaningful teaching. Teachers judged their teaching to have improved and to be more creative and effective in meeting the needs of children with the use of library personnel and they commented repeatedly about the assistance and cooperation given them by the library staff. They felt that the library offered many opportunities and provided many experiences which a large majority of the student population needed and lacked. Further, teachers considered themselves to have certain responsibilities toward the library program, particularly in their use of the library as an instructional materials center.

It was concluded from this investigation that the Mount Royal teachers generally made effective use of the school library and that it had become an essential part of their instructional program.

Toward a wider audience

Opportunities to talk and write about the Knapp Project at Mount Royal were used to good advantage. In addition to presentations to Baltimore area groups, Miss Cord, the area director, Mrs. Rusk, and Dr. Williamson appeared on several professional programs throughout the country, and articles on different facets of the Project appeared in a variety of journals. (See pages 315ff.)

On Sunday, September 18, 1966, a half-hour program about the Knapp School Libraries Project was televised over WBAL-TV in Baltimore. This program, presented at 4:40 P.M. on a Sunday afternoon, is estimated to have reached 20,000 viewers. In addition to the head librarian and pupils from the school, participants included the director of libraries, principal, coordinator, field worker, a member of the local project advisory committee, a teacher, and a student teacher. The moderator and commentator was a member of the Radio and Television Division of the Baltimore City Public Schools.

And the future?

And what of the future? The foundations for superior library services have been established — adequate staff, materials, equipment, and space. The second librarian and the clerk will be continued with the assistance of federal funds. The system-wide school library budget has doubled since 1964, and budget proposals for 1967-68 indicate further increases, which will make it possible to maintain the rich collection of materials at the Mount Royal Elementary School and also to implement the first phase of long-range plans to develop libraries as instructional materials centers in a selected group of elementary and secondary schools.

Techniques for effective teacher-librarian teamwork and library programs based on the multi-media concept have been successfully demonstrated. Maintaining the high level of service achieved by the Mount Royal Elementary School library at the conclusion of the Knapp Project will strengthen and expand learning opportunities for students not only in that school, but indirectly in other schools in the system. To support the continuation of the program, the Project goals and outcomes have been reviewed and evaluated and used as guides for planning the future growth and development of the library program in the Mount Royal Elementary School. When demonstrations and visitors no longer absorb portions of the librarians' time, greater effort will be directed toward expanding individual help to students, resource help to teachers, and more experimentation with techniques related to library needs of inner-city children. The librarians will continue to share suggestions for resource help and lists of materials with other librarians.

In 1967-68, the Mount Royal Elementary School library will function in a dual role in the in-service training program of the Bureau of Library Services. The position of the second librarian will serve as a means for providing trained librarians with a one-year experience in a learning resource center. At the end of the year, the librarian can be assigned to another library to promote its development as an instructional materials center. Demonstration programs and observation visits will be scheduled for new as well as experienced librarians, teachers, and workshop groups to show them a learning resource center in action.

Report from
CASIS SCHOOL
and
THE UNIVERSITY OF TEXAS

FACT SHEET—CASIS SCHOOL

The Casis School, as one of sixty-three schools in the Austin Independent School District, Austin, Texas, has, from its beginning more than fifteen years ago, served also as an active cooperative research and demonstration center for the University of Texas and the school district. Dr. Alice Brooks McGuire, librarian, has served at the school since its opening, and has been a leader in the school's growth as a center for curriculum development and demonstration. Mr. John Glenn, principal, actively supports the library program, and is committed to its playing an integral role in the total curriculum.

The Knapp School Libraries Project has raised the library to quantitative standards by providing funds for additional staff for the library program, for materials to replace outworn materials in the collection and to enlarge the non-print materials collection, and for equipment and furnishings for the new library quarters which opened in September, 1965. This makes possible the achievement of a richer and more extensive program of service and provides an opportunity for further demonstration of the value of a good library at the elementary level. Library services at the school district level for the schools of the Austin Independent School District include assistance from two library supervisors and provision for centralized purchasing of materials.

Dr. Janet R. Nymann, Assistant Professor of Curriculum and Instruction at The University of Texas, has been named field worker for the Project with the Casis School. Dr. Nymann brings to the Project a background of study, experience, and research in the several fields of language arts, elementary school guidance, and elementary curriculum.

The Casis School, as a laboratory-demonstration school, has been owned and operated jointly by the Austin Public Schools and The University of Texas. This cooperative interest provides an exceptionally favorable climate for the cooperative commitment of university and school district to the Knapp School Libraries Project.

STATISTICS

From its Project application, June, 1963

Enrollment: 748 students, grades kindergarten through six, including 46 students in special education.

Materials collection: 10,415 books, 17 periodicals, 488 filmstrips, 9 films (16mm), 570 disc recordings, 20 transparencies, 85 tape recordings.

Library personnel: One full-time librarian, one half-time assistant librarian.

As of June, 1967

Enrollment: 739 students, grades kindergarten through six, including 58 students in special education.

Materials collection: 13,531 books, 26 periodicals, 594 filmstrips, 12 films (16mm), 660 disc recordings, more than 400 transparencies, 155 tape recordings, 14 loop films (8mm).

Library personnel: Three full-time librarians, one secretary.

PERSONNEL MOST DIRECTLY CONCERNED WITH THE PROJECT

From the Casis School

Mr. John Glenn, Principal
Dr. Alice Brooks McGuire, Librarian
Mrs. Helen Keel, Assistant Librarian
Miss Judy Moltz, Assistant Librarian
Mrs. Sally Lacy, Secretary

From the Austin Independent School District

Mr. Irby B. Carruth, Superintendent
Miss Ruth Junkin, Supervisor of Libraries

From The University of Texas

Dr. Wayne Holtzman, Dean, College of Education
Dr. Janet R. Nymann, Assistant Professor of Curriculum and Instruction and field worker, Knapp School Libraries Project
Mrs. Helen M. Brown, Assistant to the field worker

REPORT OF PARTICIPATION

In the spring of 1964, when Casis Elementary School, Austin, Texas, was selected as one of three Phase II schools of the Knapp School Libraries Project, those who had worked so hopefully on the application received the news first with an exhilarating flash of delight—pure joy at receiving this recognition of a program of elementary school library services which was felt to be exemplary. At the same time, these people felt keenly the magnitude of responsibility which was inherent in the selection, a responsibility to contribute fully to the intent of the Knapp School Libraries Project so that its mission would truly be served.

The individuals who would assume key roles in the Project were well suited to the positions they would hold. Dr. M. G. Bowden, principal of Casis, had received national recognition for his administrative ability. School people over the state of Texas associated his name with the idea of excellence in education. Dr. Alice Brooks McGuire, head librarian, was a past president of the American Association of School Librarians, and her achievements in the provision and promotion of excellent library services for children were well known both regionally and nationally. Dr. Alma Freeland of The University of Texas, who had been designated field worker, was well respected as a leader in the fields of reading instruction and children's literature.

The Casis Elementary School was well suited to demonstration functions. At the time of its opening in January, 1951, the school was designated to serve not only as one of the public schools of Austin, but by contractual agreement, to serve as an experimental demonstration school for The University of Texas. Thus for some thirteen years, the school had "grown up" with demonstrations. Both Dr. Bowden and Dr. McGuire had held their positions in the school since its beginning. Because of their total commitment to the importance of excellent library services for elementary school children, the curriculum which developed in this school was built around what the library could offer in terms of resources for learning and also in terms of

services to promote children's ability to do independent study.

As suggested by the Director of the Knapp School Libraries Project, outstanding leaders in the community were invited to serve as an advisory committee to help guide the Project at the local level. This committee consisted of the following members:

Dr. Irby B. Carruth, Superintendent of Schools, Austin Public Schools

Dr. Henry J. Otto, Chairman, Department of School Administration, The University of Texas

Dr. Thomas D. Horn, Chairman, Department of Curriculum and Instruction, College of Education, The University of Texas

Dr. T. P. Baker, Director of Instruction, Austin Public Schools

Mrs. Garrie Bray, Secretary, Board of Education, Austin Public Schools

Mr. Homer E. Scace, President, Casis Parent-Teacher Association, and member of the staff, Texas Research League

Miss Ruth Junkin, Supervisor of Libraries, Austin Public Schools

Miss Mary Rice, Librarian, Austin Public Library

Mrs. Mary Boyvey, Supervisor of Libraries, Texas Education Agency

Dr. M. G. Bowden, Principal, Casis-Dill Schools

Dr. Alma M. Freeland, Project Officer, College of Education, The University of Texas

Dr. Alice Brooks McGuire, Project Librarian, Casis School

The members of the committee were invited to participate actively in the implementation of the Knapp School Libraries Project at Casis School through keeping informed of the progress of the Project, taking note of and reacting to plans for the operation of the Project.

The agenda of the first meeting of the advisory committee held in June, 1964, consisted of an historical account of the Knapp School Libraries Project and an explanation of financial arrangements provided in the grant. The committee was also oriented to plans for moving the program into action. Moreover, plans which had already been made for a new library addition to Casis School were presented to the committee.

Since one of the benefits the school would receive from the Knapp School Libraries Project was financial support to increase the library staff up to ALA standards, this meant that several new staff members had to be recruited. Recruitment proved to be no problem. Miss Judy Moltz, who had previously served as a half-time librarian at Casis, was appointed to full-time status; Mrs. Helen Keel, an experienced teacher who had become an elementary librarian in the Austin Public Schools, and who had done her library practice work at Casis, was also appointed to full-time status. Miss Moltz, Mrs. Keel, and Dr. McGuire were already acquainted with one another and were in agreement regarding the philosophy of what an elementary school library program should be. The fourth library staff member to be appointed was a secretary-clerk, Mrs. Sally Lacy, who had been the school secretary. Her knowledge of the inner workings of the school, her acquaintance with the children, and her secretarial skill constituted just the qualities needed for that fourth position.

The program which developed because of the additional resources and staff provided by the Knapp School Libraries Project amounted to a sizable extension in both depth and breadth of the services offered by the library to children and teachers. The faculty and principal were already library-minded and agreed that the library program should be a flexible one, reflecting and serving all facets of the school program.

The library had always been a materials center, a learning laboratory, and a reading and guidance center. Scheduling of library use had been kept to a minimum, for it was felt that the library should be used whenever the need or the desire was felt by children, and that they should be free to come to the library at any time even if a scheduled activity was in progress. The only periods scheduled were those during which classes of children were to come for a literature-sharing time taught by the librarian. These lessons were designed to help children enjoy the world of literature, to increase their

knowledge, to stimulate their perception of literary quality, and to promote their understanding of the human values portrayed in good literature. As classroom lessons aroused the need for independent and small-group study, periods would be scheduled during which the librarian would orient children to the various resources which offered information pertinent to those topics receiving attention in the classroom. In the days which followed the orientation, however, children were still free to come and go, using the library as needed in their pursuit of the topic.

This flexibility in scheduling allowed the librarian to serve the total school at all times, acting as a resource person in areas of materials, study skills, literature, and reading. In order to further facilitate her serving in these capacities, self-service was encouraged in every way possible. Children were taught how to use the card catalog, how to find materials, and how to check their materials in and out. Moreover, a parents' committee had assisted with certain duties so that the librarian would be relatively free of the burden of routine and clerical activities—so necessary, but so time-consuming and limiting to a librarian who wishes to work directly with the school program.

Dr. McGuire had always worked very closely with teachers of all grade levels, so that she was constantly aware of units of study being carried on in classrooms, making certain, at the same time, that each teacher knew just what resources were available in the library to support and extend classroom learning. Dr. McGuire also kept in close contact with teachers concerning the needs and achievement of individual children, for she saw this possibility for guidance as an extremely important facet of library service. Certain individuals or small groups of children could be given attention through personal conferences with her or in specially formed classes, so that the richness of various resources could be made evident to children and their zest for learning would be increased. The services offered by this library, then, might be described as dedicated to bringing teachers and pupils in contact with the many possible resources for learning, and to promoting the assimilation and integration of information, ideas, and human values, which together result in an educated person. It should be evident from the foregoing that a program of exemplary library service was already begun. The funds which would be received from the Project would allow further development of the comprehensiveness of this program.

In determining particular responsibilities of the enlarged staff, it was decided that all should have equal participation in the library program. However, it was important to take advantage of the particular strengths and background of each member. For example, while Mrs. Keel's teaching experience had been in the lower grades, Miss Moltz had worked with older children. Consequently, it happened quite naturally that Mrs. Keel would work more with children in kindergarten through second grade, Dr. McGuire with third and fourth grades, and Miss Moltz with children in fifth and sixth grades. This did not mean that any of the librarians worked exclusively with these grade levels. All

librarians would be concerned with all children. But in planning lessons and selecting materials, the experience and interest of each librarian would be drawn upon in order to achieve a truly well-rounded program of service. Book and multi-media selection was to be a cooperative affair; cataloging of printed materials was to be a duty of Mrs. Keel and Miss Moltz, while Dr. McGuire was to have charge of cataloging the non-book media. The planning and setting up of exhibits in the library was to be a cooperative venture, too. (The job-analysis chart— page 176 — provides an overview of staff commitments.) The compatibility of the several staff members made for a very congenial, flexible team who pooled their talents in the interest of providing the best service possible for the children of Casis. (See library schedule, page 177.)

It had been expected that construction of the new library quarters would start in the spring of 1964 so that it would be available for use some time the following fall. Anticipation of the move into the new library was particularly

Librarian Miss Judy Moltz and her storytelling made children forget the crowded conditions of Casis's old library.

JOB ANALYSIS AND STAFF ASSIGNMENTS

STAFF

Professional

Alice Brooks McGuire (ABM), Knapp Project librarian

Judy Moltz (JM), Casis School librarian

Helen Keel (HK), Casis School librarian

Non-professional

Sally Lacy, secretary-clerk

Helen Brown, volunteer storyteller

PTA library committee (20+ members)

ACTIVITIES AND ASSIGNMENTS

Library instruction—6-10 lessons

1. Grade level large-group instruction

   Grade 1 (in small groups) JM, HK (spring term)

   Grade 2 (3 sections) ABM, HK (September)

   Grade 3 (3 sections) ABM (Sept.-Oct.)

   Grade 4 (5 sections) HK (Sept.-Nov.)

   Grade 5 (5 sections) JM (Oct.-Nov.)

   Grade 6 (5 sections) ABM (Nov.-Dec.)

2. Integrated lessons—As any class needs special instruction or orientation in connection with a new unit or particular library tools or techniques, the teacher arranges a class period in the library. This is taught by a professional staff member and the classroom teacher.

Reading guidance—Designed to instill love of good books, enthusiasm for reading, as well as breadth and depth in reading in children.

1. Literary appreciation periods (grades 3-6)—Each class receives one literature sharing period per week in the library, conducted by professional staff and storyteller.

2. Storytelling (kindergarten-grade 2)—One period per week. Volunteer storyteller and professional staff members.

3. Small group projects—On invitation of teachers, professional staff will conduct literature projects with selected members of any class. Examples: poetry, folk literature, projects with able readers, reluctant readers.

4. Individual guidance — Book choice, reading lists, etc. Professional staff.

Daily service program

1. Reference and research—Direction of individual and small group work of children in class projects. Professional staff.

2. Bibliographic services—Collection of instructional material for classroom needs; compilation and continuous revision of extensive lists of learning materials for all units and depth studies. Professional staff and secretary-clerk.

3. Circulation of science and arithmetic instructional materials. Secretary-clerk.

4. Fulfilling miscellaneous faculty and student needs. Staff.

Team teaching

1. Grade-level planning sessions — Wednesday, 2-5 o'clock. Professional staff participates on invitation or at their own request.

2. Participation in class activities — On invitation of any class or grade level particularly in area of literature, biography, reading, book reports and reviews, writing style, study techniques, "Great Images," librarians become resource people. Professional staff.

School committees—Members of the professional staff are members or chairmen of many committees.

Organizational work

1. Materials—Books, pamphlets, periodicals, pictures, audio-visual materials.

   a. Selection—staff assisted by faculty and principal

   b. Order work—secretary-clerk

   c. Processing:

      (1) Collating, accessioning, pasting, marking—JM and secretary-clerk, assisted by parents' committee

      (2) Cataloging

         (a) Analysis—professional staff

         (b) Typing—secretary-clerk

      (3) Filing — parents' committee supervised by professional staff

Administrative work

1. Planning and policy-making — professional staff assisted by principal

2. Exhibits—professional staff

3. Library squad—supervised by staff

4. Circulation

   a. Borrowing—patrons check out own materials

   b. Filing, statistics, overdues—staff and parents' committee

   c. Housekeeping (carding, shelving, shelf reading) — parents' committee, library squad, staff.

5. Audio-visual materials—check-out self-service

6. Mending — HK, secretary-clerk, some parent committee members

7. Binding

   a. Selection—staff

   b. Preparation—secretary-clerk

CASIS LIBRARY SCHEDULE, MONDAY, FEBRUARY 27, 1967

KEY
(a) Organizational Work
(b) Library Instruction
(c) Reading Guidance
(d) Special Activities
(e) Working with Teachers

TIME	ALICE B. McGUIRE	JUDY MOLTZ	HELEN KEEL	SALLY LACY
7:45-8:15	Floor work (helping individuals) (a, b) Checking readers' cards for Texas Readers Club (c, d, e)	Carding and sorting books; floor work (a, b, e)	Floor work—helping children; suggesting books (a, b, c, e)	In charge of mathematics and science materials center (a)
8:15-9:00	Supervising library squad (a, e)	3 small groups of able 2nd graders learning about card catalog— 8:15, 8:30, 8:45 (b, d)	3 small groups of able 2nd graders— lesson on card catalog (b, d)	Processing books (a)
9:00-9:30	Staff meeting (a)	Staff meeting (a)	Staff meeting (a)	Staff meeting (a)
9:30-10:00	At request of teacher, went to classroom for a discussion of homonyms (d, e)	Checking readers' cards. Suggesting books (c)	Checking in a book order (a)	Preparing orders for printed catalog cards (a)
10:00-10:30	5th grade, literary appreciation, Norse myths (c)	Special—lecture to 4th grade for social studies unit—literature of Middle Ages (c, d, e)	Planning with teacher for literary appreciation on unit on Mexico (e)	Work on vertical file and picture collection (a)
10:30-11:00	Answering mail, many professional requests (a)	Floor Work (b, c, e)	Helping children with reference on Mexico (b)	Typing catalog cards (a)
11:00-11:30	Selecting books from *Booklist* (a) Helping teacher find a book to read to class (e)	Special lesson with 5th grade on poetry index (d, e)	Cataloging books (a)	Typing shelf list cards (a)
11:30-12:00	Seminar I—Reluctant readers (girls) (c, d)	Lunch	Non-graded I (3) shared biographies— *Prince Henry the Navigator* and *James Cook* to enrich unit on map skills (c, e)	Typing correspondence (a)
12:00-12:30	Lunch	Floor work (b, c, d)	Lunch	Floor work (b, c)
12:30-1:00	Helping 2 boys to tape their lectures on "Great Images" (d)	Literary appreciation; non-graded II (4)— shared Buff's *The Big Tree* to enrich unit on forests (c, e)	Working with 4th grade group who need more skill in reading (c, d)	Lunch
1:00-1:30	Cataloging books (a)	Floor work—helping with reference (b, c)	Gathering books for a teacher for a new unit (e)	Helping prepare books for unit (e)
1:30-2:00	Checking books for binding, weeding, re-ordering (a)	Processing books (a)	Non-graded II (2) unit; Mexico; shared new book, *One Luminaria for Antonio* to enrich classroom unit on Mexico (c, e)	Typing—stencil for *Gods and Goddesses;* reserve book form (a)

CASIS LIBRARY SCHEDULE, MONDAY, FEBRUARY 27, 1967 (Continued)

KEY
(a) Organizational Work
(b) Library Instruction
(c) Reading Guidance
(d) Special Activities
(e) Working with Teachers

TIME	ALICE B. McGUIRE	JUDY MOLTZ	HELEN KEEL	SALLY LACY
2:00-2:30	Working with special 6th grade groups on reading dialogues (d)	Cataloging books (a)	Desk work; helping children select books on Texas independence (a, c)	Duplicating instructional material (a)
2:30-3:15	Helping a 5th grade group with special research assignment on poetry (b, c, d)	Helping a 5th grade group with special research assignment on poetry (b, c, d)	Supervising library squad (a)	Floor work (b, c)
3:15-4:30	Arranging new exhibit; planning next day's classes; helping teachers and student teachers; book selection (a, b, c, e)	New exhibits; planning for next day's classes; helping teachers and student teachers (a, b, c, e)	New exhibits; planning for next day's work; helping teachers and student teachers (a, b, c, e)	Desk work—carding, shelving, statistics; typing correspondence, orders (a)

keen because Knapp School Libraries Project funds had made it possible to increase the extent of the facility over what had been originally planned. Project funds amounting to approximately $28,000 would provide for one classroom-size area, a listening center, and colorful and informal furniture in addition to what was already on the drawing board. There were, however, delays in beginning construction, and it was not until the second week of November, 1964, that ground was broken for the new library.

The fourth grade class taught by Mrs. Donna Carstarphen, whose classroom was nearest to the construction area, made it their project to keep a log of the building development. As is often the case, delays and frustrations were encountered in the construction of this new wing. During the unusually wet months of January and February there were many days when no work was done. March saw the brick walls go up, only to be torn down and rebuilt because the bricks had been incorrectly laid. This and all other construction developments—satisfying ones as well as frustrating ones—were observed with avid interest by the entire school. Periodically classes went together to survey the building process, and individual children undoubtedly made their own personal surveys as they arrived and left the school. Dr. Bowden often included comments on the developments in the *Daily Bulletin* which was sent to teachers. The comment might consist of a notice that a certain aspect of the construction was completed or might explain a delay.

Such enthusiastic interest on the part of the whole school indicates the importance of the library to children and teachers alike. This was not just construction to be observed, but it was "our new library" going up, and such a point of view could only be based on deep feelings about what the library meant to the children and teachers of Casis. By the time the new library was successfully completed, the 1964-65 school year had come and gone, but the library doors would be "open for business" at the beginning of the school term in the fall of 1965. Thus the library program observed by those visitors who came during 1964-65 possessed many of the qualities of an ideal library program, but

it was taking place in rather cramped quarters.

Program development during that first year was necessarily exploratory in nature. Attempts were made in various ways to find the best means of utilizing the increased staff as well as the many added resources which had been purchased with Knapp Project funds. Both the literary appreciation and library instruction aspects of the program were expanded considerably over what had been possible in years past. For example, the increased staff made it possible to offer literary appreciation to every class each week instead of every other week, which had been the case before.

Responsibility for teaching the relatively formal classes of library instruction was shared by the three staff members. The impact of this was felt most keenly by Dr. McGuire, because it allowed her so much more time for other activities than she had had in the past, when she had taught all of the library instruction. In spite of the gains made possible by this change, the library instruction classes had to be scheduled to contribute to "off-periods" for teachers. It was felt that this lack of flexibility seriously restricted the program of library service. Moreover, because these particular periods had to remain constant and run continuously throughout the year, the distressing result was that some children were completing their library instruction at about the time school was closing for the summer. Thus school was out before these children had a chance to put their learning to full use. This problem concerned the librarians deeply, and they made various attempts to find a satisfactory solution. When none was found that first year, the staff resolved to find some way around the problem in the coming year. In 1966-67, schedules were adjusted among librarians, classroom teachers, and art and music teachers so that these "off-periods" were no longer covered by the library.

Another and important kind of expansion was made possible because of the changes just described. This was the tremendous increase in time that could now be devoted to giving special attention to individual children or small groups. Thus the library program expanded in depth immediately.

This fifth grader finds much from which to choose in the Casis vertical file.

While the library program was undergoing an expansion process, plans were under way for the visitation aspect of the Project. Dr. Freeland sent letters of invitation to department chairmen and individual professors at The University of Texas as well as invitations to personnel of other institutions of higher learning. In addition, she made a careful survey of professional meetings which would be taking place in Austin and communicated with those responsible for the programs of these meetings to see whether a visit to the Project at Casis could be included in some way as a program offering. The visitations which came as a result of these contacts are interesting to study from a developmental point of view.

The first visitors tended to be classes of students from The University of Texas. These students were enrolled in classes in the College of Education, as well as in the School of Library Science. In January, 1965, the first group of students from another college—Mary Hardin-Baylor College—came to visit the Project. Along about this time the first visitors from public school districts were arriving, tending to come in groups of approximately two or three people. In February the first group coming from a professional meeting came to observe the Project. This

was a group of 26 people who were attending the Texas Association for the Improvement of Reading conference in Austin. In March a second group from another university arrived, this time from St. Edward's University, a group numbering 20 students. This group was the first to spend the better part of a day visiting the program. This provided an opportunity to try out an all-day visitation program which would include observation of various facets of the program. During this month, too, a group of 31 students from Southwestern University viewed the Project library. In April and May most of the visitors represented public schools, although one group of 15 students did come from Texas Lutheran College.

The Project at Casis had served as a demonstration center during that first year, and much had been learned from the experience of having had these visitors that would contribute to the effectiveness of the visitation program to come.

On April 30, 1965, a readiness committee came to observe the Project in action and to suggest ways of increasing the effectiveness of the demonstration of program to future visitors. This committee was composed of the following individuals:

Miss Virginia McJenkin, President, American Association of School Librarians; Supervisor, School Libraries, Fulton County, Atlanta, Georgia

Miss Freddy Schader, Elementary School Library Consultant, Arkansas Library Commission, Little Rock, Arkansas

Mr. Fred W. Hunter, President, Texas Association of School Administrators; Superintendent of Schools, Beaumont Independent School District, Beaumont, Texas

Miss Elenora Alexander, Director of Instructional Services, Houston Independent School District, Houston, Texas

Mr. Tom Anderson, Teacher, Sinclair School, Houston Independent School District, Houston, Texas

Mr. Glenn W. Kidd, President, Texas Elementary Principals and Supervisors Association; Principal, Andy Woods School, Tyler Independent School District, Tyler, Texas

The committee's visitation was scheduled to include an orientation session, with presentations by Dr. Bowden, Dr. Freeland, and Dr. McGuire regarding the philosophy of the school, the Knapp School Libraries Project, and the Casis library program. Observations of various facets of the library program followed. Activities selected for observation included work by small groups of children in the library, a literature appreciation lesson taught by a librarian in the large group learning center (cafetorium) which was correlated with an on-going social studies unit, library-based lessons conducted in classrooms by teachers, and library instruction and literary appreciation classes conducted in the library.

Since the readiness committee was to meet with the library staff and school faculty at the end of the day to share reactions, members of the local advisory committee were invited to come to school at that time in order that they, too, could be informed of the suggestions made.

At this meeting the members of the readiness committee expressed their feeling that the day was well planned. They had been given the opportunity to see a cross-section and a good sampling of the Casis program; the duplicated material with which they had been provided helped to give a picture of the Casis program. The readiness committee was pleased to see evidence of various aspects of the library program such as cooperative and correlated planning between the classroom teachers and the library staff. Moreover, it was clear that the influence of the library program permeated the school as reference materials were used freely, extensive individual reading was taking place, and library materials were flowing into classrooms. Real depth and breadth in the library program, as a result of adequate staff, materials, facilities, and excellent leadership, were reflected in provisions for many and varied library experiences throughout the grades, and for effective guidance of children's reading. In addition, the committee expressed pleasure with the effective use of regular school facilities for extending the library activities—such as using the cafetorium for library instruction classes.

The committee made a number of very helpful recommendations for ensuring a more effective library program—for the school and for observation by guests. Two prime recommendations concerned the library program itself. One suggestion was to expand the collection of audio-visual materials, at the same time stimulating independent student use of these materials and equipment. The second suggestion was to be sure to demonstrate the involvement of all members of the library staff in planning and evaluating the program.

Several recommendations were made which would improve the orientation of visitors. For example, it was suggested that information be provided to visitors, prior to their arrival, about the school, the library program, the library facility, background material relating to classroom activities in progress and leading up to those to be observed, etc. If it seemed impossible to send this information in advance, then it should be provided upon visitors' arrival, with time allowed for reading it before the Project staff's orientation-presentations. With respect to the latter presentation, the committee recommended greater use of visual aids.

It was suggested that the balance between observation of activities in the library and visits to classrooms should be maintained in the schedules made for future guests. However, classroom visits should allow the guests to see children involved in actual experiences or lessons that are related to library materials, as opposed to hearing children's reports or discussions about experiences that correlated classroom and library activities. Visitors might hear from teachers about the ways in which the fullness of the library program supports and extends what is taught in classrooms.

The readiness committee also stressed the importance of having visitation teams consist of people who represent a variety of positions in a school system. Furthermore, the committee felt that the Casis staff should prepare specifically for questions which were likely to be raised by a team thus composed. In addition, the staff should keep in mind the real and practical problems that are faced by their guests, such as lack of staff, limited budget and

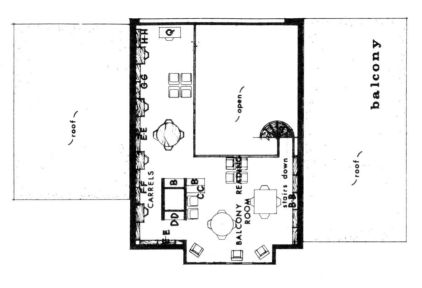

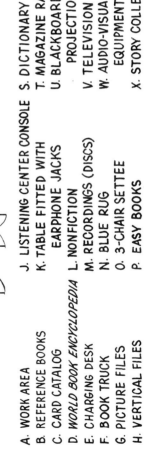

roof

FF CARRELS

balcony

roof

open

stairs down

BALCONY READING ROOM

MECH.

CLASSROOM - READING ROOM

AUDIO - SEMINAR ROOM

READING ROOM

stairs up

STOR.

WORK AREA

COURTYARD

A. WORK AREA
B. REFERENCE BOOKS
C. CARD CATALOG
D. *WORLD BOOK ENCYCLOPEDIA*
E. CHARGING DESK
F. BOOK TRUCK
G. PICTURE FILES
H. VERTICAL FILES
I. TAPE RECORDINGS

J. LISTENING CENTER CONSOLE
K. TABLE FITTED WITH
     EARPHONE JACKS
L. NONFICTION
M. RECORDINGS (DISCS)
N. BLUE RUG
O. 3-CHAIR SETTEE
P. EASY BOOKS
Q. LIBRARIAN'S DESK
R. WORK TABLE

S. DICTIONARY
T. MAGAZINE RACK
U. BLACKBOARD AND
     PROJECTION SCREEN
V. TELEVISION SET
W. AUDIO-VISUAL MEDIA &
     EQUIPMENT STORAGE
X. STORY COLLECTIONS
Y. FICTION
Z. FAIRY TALES

AA. "GREAT BOOKS" OF THE
       SOCIAL STUDIES
B-B. BIOGRAPHY
C-C. *READER'S DIGEST INDEX*
D-D. *NATIONAL GEOGRAPHIC*
E-E. MULTIPLE TEXTS
F-F. PROFESSIONAL COLLECTION
G-G. FOREIGN LANGUAGE BOOKS
H-H. AUTOGRAPHED BOOKS

so on. A final suggestion by the committee was, in effect, that the Casis staff be realistic in the visitation program it would strive for; the staff was cautioned to avoid an overload of visitors.

The reactions of the committee proved to be very helpful in the further planning that was carried on in preparation for the large visitation program which took place the following year.

The opening of the school year in September, 1965, was one of the most exciting times this school had ever known, for the new library quarters, so long awaited, were now ready for use. The facility consists of an entire new wing in the center of the school plant and directly opposite the administrative offices. Classrooms contained in the original building are on one side of the library wing, and another classroom wing, which was built at the same time as the new library, is on the other side.

The move to the new library quarters effected a much more efficient organization of materials and activities. The added staff, space, and special areas for particular phases of the program allowed the services to become even more flexible and extensive. If the occasion arose, it was possible to have three lessons taught simultaneously in the library, small groups engaged in study at the same time, as well as various individual activities which might go on such as browsing, reading, and studying. Program development now occurred at an accelerated pace with expansion in many directions, the program evolving to include five major facets.

One facet consisted of the organizational work necessary to a comprehensive program. This in-

DATA ON LIBRARY QUARTERS

Total area—3,250 sq. ft.

Total seating capacity—108

Organization of quarters

1. Main reading area: 1,512 sq. ft., seats 24
   3 square tables
   2 round tables
   20 straight chairs

2. Balcony: 716 sq. ft., seats 30
   3 round tables
   14 upholstered chairs
   20 straight chairs
   4 study carrels

3. Library classroom area: 600 sq. ft., seats 30
   3 round tables
   3 rectangular tables
   30 straight chairs, 1 stool, 1 desk and chair, blackboard, overhead projector, screen, and TV

4. Informal reading and storytelling area: 325 sq. ft., seats 12; class may be seated on carpet for storytelling
   4 upholstered chairs
   1 modern settee with 3 detachable seats

5. Area for listening, small-group discussion, and conferences: 160 sq. ft.

Console transmits to all or parts of library or to separate large-group learning area
   1 rectangular table equipped with 12 listening jacks, 12 straight chairs
   Earphones
   Storage shelves for tapes

6. Librarian's office and work room: 144 sq. ft., seats 6
   Vinyl-topped counters, storage cupboards, and closets

7. Storage room: 422 sq. ft., stores audio-visual materials and equipment

Library furniture: type and style

   15 tables—plastic covered, tangerine, middy blue, aqua, lemon, and heather
   80 straight chairs—black with white plastic seats and backs
   18 upholstered chairs—black, mustard, middy blue, tangerine
   1 settee—3 detachable seats, tangerine, blue, lemon
   Charging desk—wood, tangerine plastic top
   Catalog cases—wood, tangerine plastic top
   11 vertical files—metal, 2 drawers each
   4 study carrels—built-in
   Storage cabinets for recordings
   Wall shelves and stacks
   Special shelving—on wheels

cluded book selection, ordering, processing and cataloging, mending, statistical work, and floor work. While all four members of the library staff had responsibilities connected with this facet, the clerical duties were performed by Mrs. Lacy, the secretary. This part of the program focused on making the library attractive and inviting through educational exhibits, judicious purchase, accessibility, dispersal, retrieval and care of materials, and general assistance to all who used the library.

A second facet of the total program was the library instruction service. It will be recalled that during the first year of the Project, the librarians were not completely satisfied with what had been achieved in this part of the program, due to factors of inflexibility. During this second year two important changes were made which led to a much more satisfactory result. In the first place it was no longer necessary to schedule library instruction classes to provide "off-periods" for teachers. This was a major breakthrough. In the second place, library instruction was given this year to large groups of children in the cafetorium. Lessons were taught to all children of one grade level at the same time. An overhead projector was used during these lessons to emphasize points to the children. Since all teachers attended the lessons with their classes, follow-up in the classroom was possible. Learning was further reinforced by the librarians' giving special attention as needed to individuals or small groups of children in the library at times following the large group instruction. Because of these changes the series of ten library instruction lessons focusing on library citizenship and location and effective use of materials was completed for each grade before the first of the year. The librarians then had time to present lessons to classes on request. These lessons consisted of reinterpretation of library resources in terms of on-going social studies or science units, or of consideration of particular reference tools. In addition, the librarians could devote much more time to assisting children with their reference work in the library or to giving them individual guidance in their reading.

A third facet of the total program which became quite comprehensive was reading guidance. In literary appreciation lessons which were provided once each week for every class, various types of literature were introduced to children. Very often the topics of these lessons were related to units of study being carried on in the children's classrooms. In addition, special activities met the needs of certain groups of children. Special seminars were conducted for the very able readers during which they developed the ability to make qualitative critiques. Other activities were designed for reluctant readers in order to promote a love of reading. Reading guidance included helping children select books, listening and reacting to their comments about what they had read, and working at times with "reading groups" from the classrooms.

A fourth facet of the program might be called "special activities." This included individual and small group activities conducted by the librarians at the teachers' request. Study of folk literature, listening to taped lectures, viewing films or filmstrips, and carrying on book discussions are examples of these types of activities. A storytelling workshop was also held where university students told stories to classes of children. Next, the children studied storytelling techniques and told stories to other children. Ultimately a number of children were selected to go to the university campus and tell stories to the college class. This facet of the total program included, in addition, the librarians' availability to serve as resource people in the areas of instructional materials, study skills, and literature. The librarians were invited to give lectures in the classrooms on literary figures who were included in the "Great Images" aspect of the social studies program; they discussed the literature of historical periods, or topics such as the writing of papers based on reference work.

The fifth facet of the total program consisted of consultation with teachers. This included the librarians' participation in grade-level meetings where planning for future units of study took place. With this awareness of topics of study which would soon come to the fore in classrooms,

Dr. Alice Brooks McGuire, librarian, and Dr. Alma Freeland, field worker (at far end of table), talk with students from The University of Texas.

the librarians could provide extensive materials for each unit and prepare special displays in the library. They could also make bibliographies of resources in the library pertinent to the topics and could inform teachers of newly acquired material which would be of use. Furthermore, through constant contact with teachers, the librarians were alerted to projects that children might be carrying on in the library as well as to the type of supervision they might need. Teacher-librarian contacts also included conferences concerning the needs of individual children, cooperative selection of books appropriate for reading aloud in class by the teacher, and directing each other's attention to professional materials of interest. Together, they also evaluated the library's effectiveness.

It was this comprehensive program of library service in the new quarters, along with its impact on classroom activity, that was observed by the many guests who came to visit the Project during this second year, 1965-66.

As had been the case during 1964-65, students and faculty from The University of Texas and from other colleges and universities began to arrive early in the year and constituted a major category of visitors to the Project. Again, college classes in education, dealing with curriculum and instruction, educational psychology, and educational administration, were represented as well as classes in library science and speech.

While most of the groups made just one visit to the Project, observing in the library and hearing a talk by Dr. McGuire, a few classes made two visits—the first one following the schedule above, and the second one, a month or so later, consisting of observations in classrooms to see manifestations of the library's impact there. A number of groups viewed the Knapp Project film, . . . *And Something More.*

From many of the college and university classes visiting Casis during 1964-65 and 1965-66, Dr. Freeland obtained appraisals of the film and of their visits in order to determine what the students were learning from these experiences and whether changes in visitation procedures were needed.

Appraisals of visits to the library were secured by having a number of classes complete a reactionnaire which was also given to non-student visitors.

The students' responses clearly indicated their realization that the purpose of the visit was to observe what could be achieved in the way of an ideal elementary school library program, conducted in a model facility by master school librarians who were relatively free from routine and clerical duties. In the opinion of the students, the purpose was achieved. One reaction was stated thus: ''I feel that Casis School houses one of the most amazing and exciting projects in educational development and advancement that I have ever witnessed. My purpose was more than achieved.'' When students identified the most helpful aspect of the visit, their responses showed a good deal of variation. Some pointed to their observation of librarians interacting with children as most helpful, while others cited Dr. McGuire's explanation of components of the total library program and the philosophy underlying it as most helpful to them. Still others cited the practical hints and interesting ways of developing a library program that had been suggested by Dr. McGuire. Those who had the opportunity to visit in classrooms often mentioned that experience as having been extremely worthwhile.

The students recommended that none of the activities provided for them should be eliminated. They did, however, suggest a number of additions that they thought would make the visits even more valuable. For example, some felt that the experience of sitting in on a literary appreciation class would be more meaningful if advance information were given about the children's general ability and background in literature, as well as about classroom activities that were carried on relating to the lesson topic. Other students wanted the visit to include observations of children engaged in directed activity in the listening center, and several suggested visiting sessions conducted by the librarians for reluctant readers and for children in special education. It was also felt by some that an explanation of the organizational work of the library would be a useful addition. Students who had not observed in classrooms often mentioned that provision should be made for seeing the impact of the library there. In general, the comments implied a wish to observe a larger sample of the library program and to increase the time spent visiting the Project. Taken as a whole, students' responses in the reactionnaire strongly indicated their great interest and enthusiasm.

While the college and university classes began to arrive in September, the first large group of Project-sponsored visitors was received in November. These people participated in a work conference which was held in Austin on November 11 and 12, 1965. Conducted for principals and librarians, the theme of the conference was *Impact: School Libraries on Teaching/Learning.* It was sponsored by the Knapp School Libraries Project, Austin Public Schools and the College of Education, The University of Texas.

The conference was planned by Dr. M. G. Bowden, principal of Casis Elementary School, Dr. Alice Brooks McGuire, the Project librarian, and Dr. Alma Freeland, University of Texas liaison, assisted by the personnel at the main office of the Austin Independent School District and Peggy Sullivan, Director of the Knapp Project. Professor Arthur Jackson, principal, Edith Bowen School, Utah State University, and the Edith Bowen School librarian, Mrs. Anne Smith, served as consultants.

Invitations were sent to the principals and librarians of all of Austin's elementary schools and to persons in similar positions in towns and cities within a radius of 100 miles of Austin. One hundred ninety-two persons registered and can be identified in these categories:

Superintendents 3
Elementary principals 52
Librarians 85
Supervisors 24
Students 19
Teachers (in addition to members of
　　Casis faculty) 5
Miscellaneous (housewife, etc.) 4
Total 192

From Austin 125
From out of town 67
Total 192

The Thursday sessions at the Terrace Motel were devoted to a consideration of the curriculum needs for library services, the elements constituting good services, and how to obtain them. The opening meeting presented a perspective on the philosophy of the school library from four viewpoints. Dr. Wayne Holtzman, dean of the College of Education, The University of Texas, outlined his philosophy; Mr. E. W. Cabe, Jr., Austin assistant superintendent of schools, gave the administrator's viewpoint; and Professors Jackson and Smith discussed their concept of the elementary library.

The second morning session centered on a good library program. Professor Jackson asked questions that arise in the mind of any good principal, which were ably answered by Mrs. Smith. Miss Sullivan then discussed the Knapp School Libraries Project as a demonstration of quality programs in action.

In the afternoon the audience was divided into two sessions to consider the topic: "How to get the library your school needs." For those persons from schools without libraries and/or librarians, Mrs. Mary Boyvey told of the state's program of using and distributing the federal funds now being made available in developing elementary libraries. Mrs. William Patman, wife of a Texas state senator, then described how she as a parent had enlisted the aid of her community in securing a fine library, complete with librarian, for the Ganado, Texas, elementary school.

The second session was composed of personnel from schools with libraries. Miss Ruth Junkin, library supervisor of the Austin Public Schools, divided the section into small buzz sessions which compiled pertinent questions to be posed to a panel consisting of Miss Sullivan, Professor Jackson, and Mrs. Smith. The day's program closed with a showing of the Knapp Project film, . . . *And Something More.*

The Friday session was held at Casis School. In the morning, Dr. Bowden, principal, briefly presented the philosophy of the school. Dr. McGuire discussed the role of the library in the program. Dr. Freeland described the school's relationship with The University of Texas. This was followed by a tour of the new library wing, the new wing of eight classrooms, and of the special wing of the building devoted to exceptional children.

The late-morning session was a panel in which a librarian and two teachers from Casis gave a detailed picture of how good library services contribute to good teaching. In summarizing, Mr. M. K. Hage, Jr., principal of the Highland Park School, envisioned the elementary library of the near future as being the

core and "textbook" for a good educational program.

In the afternoon two demonstrations of the library in action were presented. One was an integrated library lesson on research resources for a unit on explorers to a fifth grade class. The other was a discussion of poetry by ten sixth graders.

Following a critique by the resource people, the work conference concluded with a consideration of the question, "How can we be sure?" from the viewpoints of Miss Sullivan, Mrs. Smith, and Mr. Jackson.

Project-sponsored teams of visitors began coming on December 1, 1965, and groups were received almost every Wednesday and Friday thereafter, with the last Project-sponsored teams visiting on April 22, 1966. By the end of that day, 153 individuals composing 31 teams had come to the Project at Casis at Project expense. Teams usually consisted of four to six people, representing a cross-section of school personnel (e.g., school board member, administrator, teacher, and librarian).

A great deal of thought and effort went into preparations for the team visits. Dr. Freeland, Dr. Bowden, and Dr. McGuire, with the cooperation of the rest of the library staff and classroom teachers, collected materials and planned a visitation schedule which they felt would ensure a profitable visit for each team. Suggestions offered the previous spring by the readiness committee guided the planning and were incorporated insofar as they were feasible.

Prior to their coming, teams were sent information about the city of Austin, hotel and motel facilities, and routes to Casis School. An advance information sheet (see page 188) was also sent, asking for the date and time of the team's expected arrival and any special requests relating to the visit. This form was to be completed and returned to Dr. Freeland as soon as possible so that specific plans could be made to accommodate the particular needs and desires of the visitors.

On this form visitors could express, in order of preference, those portions of the program which they most desired to observe. It was thought that this would allow those persons

ADVANCE INFORMATION SHEET

The Casis School Library as a demonstration center of the Knapp
Libraries Project aims to show all aspects of the elementary program:
how teachers and children use the library, the range of instructional
materials, and how these materials are used most effectively.

In order that we may make your visit more profitable, we ask you
to fill out the following information sheet and return it to Dr. Alma
Freeland, 2710 Exposition Boulevard, Austin, Texas. To benefit most
from your visit it is suggested that you spend at least one full day
at Casis.

I. General Information

    A.   Date and time of arrival_____

    B.   Date and time of departure_____

    C.   Austin address_____

    D.   Are you here at Knapp School Libraries Project
         expense? Yes_____ No_____

    E.   Personnel of your group (give number in each category)
         1. Teachers_____ 3. Librarians_____
         2. Administrators_____ 4. Other interested people
                                   (enumerate)_____

II. Areas of Interest (please check)

    A.   Tour of the school
    _____1. General school plant
    _____2. Special education wing

    B.   The library as a materials center
    _____1. A survey of instructional materials
    _____2. Organization, administration of non-book materials

    C.   The library as study laboratory
    _____1. Library instruction classes
    _____2. Individual and/or group reference or research
    _____3. Listening center

    D.   The library as a reading center
    _____1. Library appreciation classes (state grade level)____
    _____2. Story-telling program
    _____3. Reading guidance activities

    E.   The Library's impact on the classroom
    _____1. Librarians' role in team teaching
    _____2. Observation in the classroom (state grade level)
    _____3. Bibliographic services

    F.   Administrative aspects
    _____1. Staff responsibilities
    _____2. Parent's role (volunteer help, etc.)
    _____3. Children's role (squads, etc.)
    _____4. Book selection policies
    _____5. Processing

    G.   Other activities (use reverse side of page if necessary)
         1._____
         2._____

familiar with this type of program to skip some parts and thereby devote more time to study in greater depth features new to them. On the other hand, visitors from schools that were just beginning to establish central libraries might be alerted to the many facets of such a program.

Also it was felt that the best way to demonstrate the importance and value of a central library would be to provide the opportunity for guests to observe not only the program carried on in the library, but also to see the impact of this program on every facet of the school's curriculum. With the idea of such a demonstration program always before them, those responsible for the planning worked out a general daily schedule for visitors which could be tailored to fit their specific needs and desires, but which would encompass a variety of activities to demonstrate the richness and the influence of the library program on all school life. Every attempt was made *not* to disrupt the usual school life. No special "performances" were planned for visitors because it was felt that this would destroy the validity of the demonstration.

In general, the schedule for visitors followed the one outlined in the Project handbook which is included in this publication on page 10. The special interest of visitors in some aspects of the library program led to the provision of more materials for the visitors to take with them. One example of these is the following statement describing the assignments of library student volunteers:

Casis library squad

The library squad is a service group made up of boys and girls from the 4th and 5th grades. Ten children are chosen in the fall from each of the five fifth grade classes. Many of them have already been members in the spring term of the fourth grade. Every morning during the opening exercises five children come to help in the library for a half hour. A half hour before school is dismissed, another group is on duty.

These boys and girls are taught all sorts of routine activities such as carding and shelving books, shelf reading, and writing and delivering overdue notices. This experience gives them a greater understanding of the library, devel-

ops responsibility and citizenship, and creates pride in giving service. The fifth grade squad in turn helps to train the fourth graders when they begin their tour of duty.

The teachers in each class select the children who will participate in this activity. Many children are eager to be on the squad and ask their teachers to appoint them. The teachers have different ways of choosing as, for example, having children write essays on "Why I should be on the Library Squad." In all cases they are urged to select children who will benefit most from serving. This activity gives the librarian, in cooperation with the teacher, an opportunity to guide many children who may be in need of some special attention in reading, in citizenship, or in assuming responsibility.

The library squad is not to take the place of professional assistance, although as children gain competence, they are able to help with many routine tasks. They delight in this opportunity and after they have "graduated" from the library squad, they continue to offer their services to the librarian.

The library squad is recognized each spring at the annual library assembly. After the formal program, which is often a talk by some well known children's author, service awards are given to all boys and girls who have performed some special service for the library. In addition to the library squad, storytellers from the fifth and sixth grades and boys and girls who have written book reviews for the local paper are so honored.

Mrs. Helen Keel, librarian, shares story and pictures with a group in the storytelling area.

Visitation program

Although prime responsibility rested with the Director of the Knapp Project for assessing the value of the team visits, these guests were asked to complete and return to Dr. Freeland the reactionnaire mentioned above in connection with college and university visitors.

One large group of Project-financed visitors came to observe the Project at Casis School on May 3, 1966, in connection with the annual convention of the International Reading Association in Dallas, Texas. Miss Lu Ouida Vinson, school and library consultant for Field Enterprises Educational Corporation, assisted local Project personnel with the planning. Requests for transportation were honored on a "first come, first served" basis until the bus was filled to its capacity of 43 people. Although many requests had to be turned down because they were received after the bus had been filled, 20 people made their own arrangements to come on that day to Casis.

In addition to the great number of visitors who came to Casis with financial assistance from the Knapp Project, there continued to be a steady stream of guests who came at their own expense. Many schools sent groups whose composition was similar to that of the Project-sponsored teams. At times the dates of these locally financed visits coincided with those of the Knapp teams.

During the year, local Project personnel began to question the wisdom of having scheduled only one-day visits. There were two principal areas of concern. First, it seemed that in order to provide a good sampling of the library program and its impact on classroom activity, it was necessary to schedule a very full day. Second, such a day often followed an already tiring day of travel for the visitors. These problems were given much consideration but it was not possible to change the visitation plans for the Project-financed guests because the problems were not apparent until after dates for these visits had been agreed upon.

Near the end of this school year, Dr. Freeland obtained appraisals of the library and the library program from children of all grade levels. The appraisals were unstructured except for the sug-

gestion that the children tell how they felt about the library from two standpoints:

(1) What do you like *most* about your library? How has it helped you to grow as a person and as a student?

(2) What suggestions do you have for improving your library? What changes do you think we should make?

First grade children dictated their thoughts to their teachers, while all other children expressed themselves in writing.

The appraisals clearly reflected an appreciation of what the library had to offer, an understanding of how to use it as well as a love of actually using it. Changes which were suggested tended to indicate a desire for *more* of what was already being enjoyed although some "improvements" were mentioned. An example of the latter case was a fifth grader's suggestion that a period be scheduled for checking out books. Periods of this sort had deliberately not been scheduled, for it was the librarians' belief that children should have the freedom to check books out at any time.

Appraisals written by a number of children at this time could be compared to reactions which had been obtained from them the previous spring when the old library was still in use. Children who had been members of the fourth grade class which kept a log of the new library's construction expressed their feelings in April, 1965, and again in May, 1966. Additional comparisons could be made of the responses of children at the sixth grade level each year, although in this case the responses had been written by different sets of children.

In the 1965 appraisals, children showed their awareness of the need for better and more spacious library facilities, although they did not appear to be at loss for items to mention as "liked." In the 1966 appraisals, children certainly found numerous things to praise, but they had quite a large number of suggestions to make, too. This latter characteristic may well have been an unexpected result since the new library represented a vast improvement not only in space, but in the possibilities it provided for varied activities, in equipment which was available, in comfort, and in beauty. However, the result may have been indicative of a much greater awareness now on the part of the children of what a well stocked library and full library program could offer them—and they liked the idea. A survey of the most frequently mentioned suggestions for improvement revealed that in 1966, a greater number of children expressed the desire for more books, more variety in experiences, more space in the listening center, more special classes, more places to read by themselves, and more time in the library than had been the case in 1965. It seems reasonable to propose that the result might be considered a favorable commentary on the changes that had taken place.

At times during this year, meetings of the local advisory committee were called in order that they would be informed of the progress of the Project plans for the work conferences. They also viewed the film, . . . And Something More.

During the summer following this school year, the second Project-sponsored work conference was held. The theme of this meeting, conducted for superintendents, principals, supervisors, members of boards of education, parents, teachers, and librarians, was *New Dimensions for the Elementary School Library Program*. The conference took place June 13 through 15, 1966, and was sponsored by the Knapp School Libraries Project, Austin Independent School District, and the College of Education, The University of Texas. The consultants were: Mrs. Frances Kennon Johnson, School of Library Science, University of North Carolina, Greensboro, North Carolina; Miss Phyllis Hochstettler, consultant, School Libraries, State Department of Education, Salem, Oregon and chairman, Knapp School Libraries Project Advisory Committee; and Dr. Wesley Gibbs, superintendent, School District 68, Skokie, Illinois.

Most of the sessions of this conference were scheduled at the Terrace Motor Hotel, but the Casis School and the Academic Center of The University of Texas were scheduled in tours, and children, teachers, and librarians from Casis participated in simulated classroom and library activities to give conference participants an idea of the specifics and scope of the library program. In planning the conference, it had been decided

to open attendance to a larger group of persons by scheduling it at a time when school was not in session, although this meant it was not possible for participants to observe classroom instruction or to see actual library use.

The 160 persons attending this conference came from forty-eight cities in fifteen states, and represented the following positions:

Superintendent	3
Assistant superintendent	1
Principals	23
Supervisors: curriculum	16
Classroom teachers	6
Library coordinators, consultants, etc..	7
School librarians	34
School board members	4
Library science professors	1
Library clerks, parents	6
Non-registered guests, students, etc....	59
Total	160

Reactions to the conference were generally quite favorable. The suggestions most commonly given were that time in the Casis library should be increased and that opportunities should be provided for observation of children using the library, as well as engaging in classroom activity.

Before the June work conference took place, two events occurred which necessitated changes in the Project personnel for the third and final year. Dr. Alma Freeland asked that she be relieved of her position as field worker, due to research commitments which had been made, and Dr. M. G. Bowden accepted a position as Associate Professor of Education at Trinity University in San Antonio, Texas. The contributions made by both Dr. Freeland and Dr. Bowden to the Knapp School Libraries Project at Casis would long be remembered with respect, and their achievements would stand as excellent examples for those who would take their places.

During that summer, Mr. John Glenn of the Brazosport Schools in Texas was named principal of Casis and he also assumed responsibility for liaison with the Project office. Dr. Janet R. Nymann, Assistant Professor of Curriculum and Instruction, The University of Texas, was appointed to the position of field worker.

In spite of these personnel changes, continuity was particularly facilitated by the facts that (1) the program of library service was already well established by Dr. McGuire and her staff; (2) Mrs. Helen Brown, a person well acquainted with the Project and with Casis School, was appointed to assist the field worker; (3) most of the materials for distribution to visitors and correspondents had already been prepared; and (4) Mr. Glenn and Dr. Nymann were completely committed to the purposes of the Project.

The program of library service continued to expand in depth during 1966 and 1967. The teaching of library instruction lessons to large groups of middle and upper grade children in the cafetorium had been initiated the previous year, and improvements had been made as the year went along. The result of this sort of experimentation was that now the librarians had appropriate materials at hand and the series of lessons could progress smoothly to completion early in the school year. This allowed even more time than before for follow-up work with small groups.

Upon completion of all the library instruction lessons, evaluation of their effectiveness was undertaken cooperatively by the library staff and the teachers. It was concluded that the series had been successful and that the large-group approach was quite effective for children in grades four through six, but not for children in grade three. Since the teachers and librarians felt that these children needed the closeness that was characteristic of small-group instruction, provision for this was made for the 1967-68 school year.

An innovation in 1966-67 was the presentation of a few formal lessons on the use of the card catalog to a selected group of second graders. This instruction had previously been initiated at the third grade level, but these younger children had become interested in using the card catalog because one of the librarians often used their library appreciation periods to share books from each category of the informational books. The books chosen as examples could be read by the children, and they had been shown the location of the books in the library. The second grade teachers were convinced that

Membership in the Texas Readers Club concerns Miss Moltz and this student.

now was the time to stimulate this interest and that the most able students would profit from such instruction. A short series of lessons was designed by the librarians to fit the children's capabilities.

The first lesson was devoted to explaining subject cards to a group of about twenty children. On the day following the lesson, a few children came again to the library and the whole staff worked with them as they were given an opportunity to apply in a practical exercise what had been covered in the lesson. Several more children were given the same experience on the next day, and so on through the week until all members of the original group had had this practical experience. Title cards were then taken up in the same way and after that, author cards.

The literary appreciation program continued as it had in 1965-66. The kindergarten children made occasional visits to the library, and in their own classrooms the teachers introduced examples of literature from an ever changing collection chosen from the library. First graders enjoyed hearing stories told or read to them in the library each week. Children in the three second grades also had literary appreciation lessons which included listening to stories which were read or told, and participating in activities which were designed to integrate appreciation of literature with building readiness for formal library instruction. (Although these second grade library lessons were taught to individual classes, they were scheduled simultaneously so that the classroom teachers could be free at that time for team planning.)

Literary appreciation lessons for the older children tended to relate to specific topics such as the haiku form of poetry, and were often complementary to units of classroom study. For example, the librarians shared portions of *The Little House* . . . books by Laura Ingalls Wilder with fourth grade classes during their study of grasslands.

Special library activities were requested most often by teachers as they saw the possibilities which existed due to the size of the library staff. Furthermore, materials were more rapidly and readily available than ever before and the teachers were alerted to many effective ways of using them.

Dr. Nymann suggested that it would be worthwhile to keep a log of activities taking place in the library, and to show it to visitors so that it would be abundantly clear that lessons they observed represented only a very small sample of the total program. The log was made in chart form to specify lesson topics and special activities provided each month for children of every grade level. Color-coding was used to identify the aspect of the total program to which each activity was related and to indicate cases of close relationship to classroom study. The log was intended to reveal how carefully the librarians planned the sequence of offerings in the various aspects of the program, how closely they worked with teachers, and how creatively they provided for the special needs of children.

The log was developed as planned and the end result was a rather complete account of the year's library activity. Information presented in the log was obtained by interviewing the librarians at the end of each week throughout the year. The log served to emphasize the fact that the library program was much larger than the lessons which were observed might indicate.

Quite a number of guests commented that the log would be a valuable instrument for helping teachers and librarians to see tangible ways in which a full library program could contribute to the educational offerings of a school, on quite a grand scale.

Since all of the Knapp-sponsored visitations to Casis took place during the 1965-66 school year, those who came in 1966-67 consisted of college students and groups and individuals from various cities who traveled at their own expense or received financial assistance from governmental agencies.

Letters were sent at the beginning of each semester to all The University of Texas supervisors of elementary student teachers, as well as to instructors of various classes, inviting them to plan a visit. Typical procedures for handling the student groups included an orientation and guided tour of the library, observation of a class taught in the library, and a talk by Dr. McGuire in which she stressed the need for school libraries and comprehensive programs of library service, as well as ways in which teachers can make most effective use of the resources offered by such programs. Most of the student groups consisted of classes in the College of Education or the Graduate School of Library Science, but one class came from the School of Architecture for the purpose of studying the Casis library facility as a part of their study of school design.

In addition to groups from The University of Texas, students from other institutions, including Trinity University, Texas Lutheran College, and Baylor University came to visit Casis.

Most of the other visitors in this last year of Project participation were public school personnel, and a number of people represented special interests or affiliations. For example, a member of the Texas Governor's Committee on Public School Education came to observe at Casis, as well as members of the Committee for Evaluation of Libraries in San Antonio, Texas.

Casis was also visited by teams of people from school districts which had received or were applying for projects under Title III of the Elementary and Secondary Education Act. Four people who were working with the Panhandle Educational Services Organization on a Title III project came to collect information and ideas which ultimately would be disseminated to 110 schools. In addition, two larger groups came to Casis under the sponsorship of the Texas Education Agency. These groups consisted of participants in workshops conducted by the agency for teachers who had been selected by their schools to receive retraining in order that they could serve as librarians now that the schools were receiving federal aid for upgrading their libraries.

On several days during April, a total of 55 people came to the Project during the meeting of the Texas Elementary Principals and Supervisors Association which was held in Austin. This was one of several professional groups scheduling visits to the library, and its members were among the most enthusiastic observers.

Casis continued to serve actively as a demonstration center during 1966-67. The visitation program followed a more informal pattern than had been the case previously because the groups tended to be smaller, activities planned for them were not as tightly scheduled, and for the most part, no particular days were consistently set aside for visitors. Questions were answered as they came up during the visit, rather than having to be saved for later discussion. Visitors could take a second, perhaps longer look at particular objects or areas of particular interest to them, and short, quiet conversations could take place between the visitors and the librarians as activity in the library was observed. This relaxed atmosphere seemed to be appreciated greatly by those who came to Casis.

At the beginning of the year, consideration had been given to the possibilities of conducting a third Project-sponsored workshop, organizing a bus trip in connection with the Association for Supervision and Curriculum Development convention in Dallas, in 1967, and arranging for Project personnel to be on the programs of regional meetings of school board members. These additions to the visitation program were not carried out for a variety of reasons.

Reactions to the visitation program

Casis children are so accustomed to having visitors at school that, for them, no visitors would be more unusual than having a great many. From the time a child enters Casis, never a week passes that one or more strangers do not come quietly into the classroom and sit down to observe.

The teachers for this school are chosen with the idea that this demonstration function is expected of them. They reacted most favorably to the Knapp Project visitors, for they found them to be more appreciative and eager to learn about the program at Casis than the usual observer. Therefore, they felt that these visits were stimulating to both teachers and pupils. Many of the teachers remarked that they would like to have had more time to talk with the guests. They would like to have been able to explain why they were doing certain things and how a particular lesson fitted into a total unit of study. The teachers felt that they would have profited greatly from the exchange of ideas that could have come from such a discussion. Several stated quite assuredly that the Knapp Project experience had given them a new vision of their responsibility in and to the improvement of the total educational structure of the country.

The library staff was equally enthusiastic about the Knapp Project visitors and spoke often of how valuable was the exchange of ideas, suggestions, and different points of view. They felt it was a privilege to talk with such a cross-section of school people.

The message of the Project was shared in a number of other ways. For example, Project personnel acted as consultants or speakers for various workshops and conventions, as well as for in-service meetings. Some of the presentations were given for the explicit purpose of describing the Project at Casis while others were given for different purposes which were related, nevertheless, to library programs. Examples of these activities were Dr. McGuire's statement before the Subcommittee on Education of the U. S. Senate Committee on Labor and Public Welfare in February, 1965, in support of the Elementary and Secondary Education Act of 1965, and her article, "The Librarian's Role in the Literature Program" in the May, 1967, issue of *Elementary English*. This was based on a talk she had given in November, 1966, at the annual conference of the National Council of Teachers of English in Houston, Texas. As a team, Dr. McGuire and Dr. Bowden gave six talks at the Louisiana State University National Defense Education Act Institute for School Librarians in June, 1965. Dr. Bowden's several articles during this period included "Library: Instructional Materials Center for an Elementary School" in *The Leader*, the official publication of the Utah Elementary Principals Association, in the Winter, 1966, issue. Dr. Nymann, Mrs. Keel, and Miss Moltz also gave talks and demonstrations relating to the Casis School library program.

The message of the Project at Casis was also shared far and wide through articles appearing in two issues of *School Briefs*, published by Scott, Foresman and Company:

"Demonstration in Texas—What Libraries Can

Do for Learning," *School Briefs*, 31 (2) (November-December, 1966), 1.

" 'Great Books' Reading Activity for Grades 1-6 Enriches Social Studies in Austin's Casis School," *School Briefs*, 31 (3) (January-February, 1967), 3.

At a meeting of the local advisory committee which was held in February, 1967, Dr. McGuire presented a review of the Project at Casis. Discussion took place concerning the degree to which the existing library program might be continued when Knapp Project funds cease. It was recognized that the future of the Casis library program would be determined in large measure by decisions reached by the Board of Trustees of the Austin Independent School District together with administrative officers of the district, and note was taken of the fact that a report of the Project at Casis would be given at the April meeting of the board. While The University of Texas would continue to use the Casis Elementary School as a research and demonstration center for various projects, details of the association were in the process of change. The result of this discussion was that all present agreed to devote thought and energy to the search for ways to insure the program's continuation.

Preparations were begun immediately for the presentation of a quite complete report about the library program at Casis to be given at the Board of Trustees meeting. Because time for this presentation was limited, it was decided that the most effective way to bring this information to the board's attention would be to prepare a booklet for them which could be distributed in advance of the meeting and referred to during the presentation. Some of the materials already prepared for visitors seemed appropriate for inclusion, and additional materials were developed specifically in keeping with the purpose of the report.

The result, *A Summary Report of the Knapp School Libraries Project at Casis*, contained as a first section general information on the Casis library as a Knapp Project demonstration center. The second section consisted of an outline of material gains made possible by Project funds. In the third section there were several pages describing the effects of the Project on library service at Casis. The Job Analysis and Staff Assignments (page 176) were included as well as a chart showing staff members' activities during one day. The chart was presented as a means of demontrating the high quality of service that can be offered when libraries are staffed according to American Library Association standards. It was pointed out to the board that the chart showed what actually took place on a day selected at random during which the field worker simply recorded events.

This section also contained assessments of the effects of the Project on the library service program as viewed by teachers and by the library staff. These appraisals appear on pages 213-14. The fourth, fifth, and sixth sections of the booklet offered evidence of the contributions and impact of the Project at Casis on the city-wide elementary library program, The University of Texas, and the country at large.

Miss Ruth Junkin, supervisor of libraries, Austin Public Schools, reported in this booklet on how the Knapp program at Casis had contributed to the elementary school library program in Austin:

Of course, only Casis has received the extra books and materials, expanded quarters, and additional staff; but all the schools in Austin have better libraries because of this program.

1. Our pride in our growing and expanding elementary library program is justified. We knew that elementary libraries were needed, and the administration and all concerned support them. It is gratifying to have a national focus on Austin elementary libraries. Casis was chosen for this honor from 115 others with almost equally as good library programs. We are proud for the Knapp program to tell schools in the United States that there should be more libraries like those in Austin!

2. We have been enriched and inspired by hundreds of visitors from all parts of the country who have come to observe and learn but have also contributed.

3. As Casis grew and expanded rapidly with the grant from the Knapp Project, all Austin principals, librarians, and many teachers had the opportunity, in a two-

day workshop in the fall of 1965, to visit Casis, observe, discuss, and gain new ideas for improved programs. Other visits and contacts with the Casis personnel have inspired many schools to improve their total program. Not only the librarians but also the principals, teachers, parents, and children are working as teams for the enrichment of their schools through library services.

4. With Casis taking the lead, other libraries are trying out new ideas and materials, encouraging better use of what they have, planning for more flexible and effective programs, and expanding the libraries to become true materials centers that contribute to every facet of the school program.

Mrs. Dorothy Smith, librarian, Highland Park School, Austin, offered an elementary school librarian's assessment of the influence of the Casis program on the elementary library program in the Austin area:

The practice librarian in a library is similar to the practice teacher in the classroom. Each brings to his new situation content, background, and preparation. Each has theories for the job. But each must be given an opportunity to find himself in practical application.

During the summer of 1965, I was assigned as practice library worker at Casis School. There I learned the routines and operation of an efficient library system. An opportunity to work with teachers in planning library enrichment activities and teaching of library skills, both in formal class presentations as well as informal teaching of individual children, was mine. It was exciting to work with new media available today to the library patron. . . . This added vitality and individualization in learning to the library environment.

While Casis has served as a model for other schools in the southwest, library service to children in our area has improved. Mrs. McGuire and her staff encourage local librarians as well as University of Texas library students.

The concept of the library and its role in our curriculum design is not learned by observation but through participation in its operation. The tempo of work in the Casis library gives a feel of the learning environment. Enthusiasm for learning is a quiet, delicate contagion.

The following contributions of the library program to The University of Texas were identified in this booklet:

Number of University students who have observed the program in action 1,001
Number of University students who have heard presentation by Project personnel 1,507
                Total 2,508

Opportunities were provided for a great number of students to see a strong library program in action and to consult with the head librarian concerning details and philosophy of the program. Particular types of contributions are outlined below.

I. College of Education
   A. Student teachers assigned to Casis obtained first-hand knowledge of the benefits of cooperative planning between teachers and librarians.
   B. All other student teachers were given the opportunity to see this library program in action and to consult with the head librarian concerning details and philosophy of the program.
   C. Opportunities for visitation and consultation were also provided for classes in curriculum and instruction, educational psychology, and educational administration.

II. Graduate School of Library Science
   A. Presentations concerning the library program were made by Project personnel to classes in children's literature.
   B. Opportunities for visitation were provided for classes emphasizing elementary school library programs.
   C. Students doing their practice work in the Casis library during these years were able to see the program possible when services and facility meet the standards of excellence recommended by the American Library Association. Several of these people are now librarians in the Austin Independent School District.

III. School of Communications
   Students enrolled in Speech 314K participated in Storytelling Workshops, thus gaining practical experience in guiding children's growth in literary appreciation through this technique.

IV. School of Architecture
   A number of students were shown the library facility as an example of the changing concepts of the physical requirements for good library service. Members of the library staff met with these students to discuss desirable aspects and practical problems relating to the design of school libraries.

V. Visiting foreign educators
   The University has played a vigorous role in promoting world-wide understanding of our U. S. system of public education, and as such has been host to many groups of foreign educators. On numerous occasions these visitors have been brought to the Knapp School Libraries Project at Casis in order that they might see an exemplary school library program in operation.

At the meeting of the Board of Trustees, April 10, 1967, information contained in the booklet was highlighted by Project personnel, and there followed a question and answer period during which the Board's interest in and acquaintance with the contents of the report were evident. Although the Board did not take any immediate action relating to continuation of the Project, a generally positive reaction seemed to underlie the passage by unanimous vote of a motion to commend the Project personnel for the manner in which Knapp Project funds had been used. Later in the spring Miss Junkin, supervisor of libraries, submitted a report with recommendations as to "first steps." Her report to Superintendent Carruth on the subject of library personnel in Austin schools follows:

We have long been proud of the fact that the Austin Schools have trained librarians and, in the secondary schools, some clerical help; however, we also realize that the number of librarians and clerks is often inadequate. As the schools grow and library services increase, librarians are forced into almost full-time clerical roles and are frustrated because of lack of time or personnel to take care of the professional library needs adequately.

The Knapp Project, which has brought Casis up to American Library Association standards, has helped demonstrate what school libraries can do when standards are met. The Title I program which has given clerical help to some schools and extra librarians has also shown us the advantage of more personnel.

Dr. McGuire talks to a large class in the cafetorium, illustrating her points with maps, books, and pictures.

It is suggested that the Austin school library standards be raised and that our schools gradually work toward the American Library Association standards. It is suggested that the Austin schools start with the following:

1. That librarians be assigned to elementary schools by enrollment rather than to help give teachers off periods. This would give the elementary school flexible library programs instead of the rather tightly scheduled library programs now in effect in some elementary schools.* The librarian could then do more constructive work with all teachers and students.

2. That library clerks, either half time or full time, be hired for each elementary school.

3. That all librarians and clerks be hired to work one week before teachers report each fall and one week after school closes in the spring.

*About one-third of the elementary libraries have flexible library programs under the present Austin personnel allotment. About one-third have moved into flexible programs with extra personnel from Title I. About one-third of the librarians in elementary schools help give off-periods to teachers in a rather tightly scheduled program.

Another statement was included in a letter to the Board of Trustees from Mrs. William Patman of Ganado, Texas. She wrote:

In the summer of 1956, the Ganado Elementary School faculty, the principal, and a school board member visited Casis with the express idea of looking into the library program to see if they thought such a program would be worthwhile and feasible for our little school.

They came, they saw (and heard), and they were totally conquered. All of us resolved together to do something. The Casis faculty, particularly Dr. Bowden and Dr. McGuire, offered their full cooperation and help.

Under the leadership of the elementary faculty and Ganado P.T.A., a citizen campaign was launched which eventually became so broad and intense in its scope that it caught up almost the entire community of

The table opposite shows: (a) the standards outlined by the American Library Association, (b) proposed beginning standards for the Austin Schools, and (c) present library personnel policies in Austin:

Standards in Relation to Enrollment

Pupils	200-499	500-999	1,000-1,999	2,000 or More
a. American Library Association	1 librarian for 300 Ortega* Rosewood* Winn*	2 librarians for 600 3 for 900 1 clerk for 600 Anderson* Allan* Kealing* Univ. Jr.* Casis—K	4 librarians for 1,300 5 for 1,700 2 clerks for 1,200	6 librarians for 2,100 3 clerks for 1,800
b. Proposed for Austin, 1st Step	1 librarian for 400 ½ clerk for 400	1 librarian for 500-999 1 clerk Allison* Becker* Blackshear* Brooke* Campbell* Govalle* Mathews* Metz* Oak Springs* Palm* Sims* Zavala*	2 librarians 1 clerk for 1,000-1599 2 librarians 2 clerks for 1,600-1,800 Johnston*	3 librarians for 1,800 4 librarians for 3,000 2 clerks
c. Present Austin Policy	½ librarian for 150-400 Barton Hills Blanton—P Bryker Woods Cunningham Dill Lee Pease Pecan Springs—P Ridgetop St. John Summitt	1 librarian ½ clerk (in see below) for 500-999 Baker Burnet Pearce Andrews Brentwood Brown Dawson Gullett Harris Highland Pk. Joslin Maplewood Pleasant Hill Reed Reilly Rosewood St. Elmo Travis Hgts. Walnut Creek Wooten Zilker	1 librarian 1 clerk for 1,000-1,200 2 librarians 1 clerk for 1,200-2,000 Austin High Lanier McCallum Reagan Travis High Fulmore Lamar O. Henry Porter	3 librarians 1 clerk for 2,000 up

*Personnel added through Title I; K—Personnel added through Knapp Project; P—Approved for full-time librarian for 1967-68.

1,600 in a blazing zeal to have an elementary school library. There was, in the end, almost no civic or church group, no leader or school child who did not participate actively in some way to get the library Casis had convinced us we needed.

While the progress made by Ganado, Texas, was certainly an indication that one of the major aims of the Project was achieved, evaluation procedures were carried out to determine the extent to which certain other aims were attained. One aspect of the evaluation dealt with the relative success of the visitation program. Guests were asked to complete the reactionnaire form and their responses were tabulated.

Another aspect had to do with what children had gained from the expanded library program made possible by the Knapp Project. Methods of study were developed and carried out under the direction and supervision of Dr. Nymann by Miss Mary Rentz, a graduate student at The University of Texas. The procedures used in the study are briefly outlined below.

1. Analysis of compositions written about the library by Casis children in grades 2 through 6.
2. Observation and analysis of the behavior of children (selected at random) in the library.
3. Comparative analysis of what children wrote about the library and behavior exhibited there.
4. Analysis of responses made by seventh grade children (former Casis students) to a questionnaire concerning how the library had helped them.

Teachers' opinions of how the library program

had assisted them constituted still another aspect of the evaluation. They were asked to discuss the offerings of the library during one of their grade-level meetings and each grade-level chairman was to put into writing a summary of the ideas that had been expressed.

The results of all portions of the evaluation program were generally quite favorable. That is, visitors felt they were gaining good ideas of what a library can be; children were learning much from instruction given by the librarians, and were making good use of the library; teachers felt that the library contributed enrichment and extension to the opportunities they provided for children in the classroom.

There were many kinds of evidence that the Project had been successful and as the period of participation drew to a close it was fitting that a ceremony should be held to recognize what had been accomplished.

Library Appreciation Night was held May 16, 1967, with approximately 250 patrons of the Casis School and others attending. Nearly all of the people who had worked at Casis closely with the Project were able to come.

The first major part of the program was a showing of the filmstrip which had been made at Casis featuring the reading guidance aspect of the library program.

Presentation of the bronze plaque sent to the school by the Knapp Project was made by Superintendent Carruth, who gave an account of the Knapp Project at Casis.

A framed scroll which was presented to Dr. McGuire on this occasion was inscribed as indicated on the opposite page.

REPORT OF EVALUATION

The original Knapp Project proposal contained the following paragraph:

> Evaluation of methods and outcomes constitutes an important aspect of the Project. Provisions for evaluation should be incorporated in the planning for each phase of the Project, and measures to be used in collecting evidences of outcomes should be identified. It is recognized that many of the results and

> outcomes of the Project can only be measured in subjective terms, and that some can not be measured during the life of the Project; however, it should be possible to trace some identifiable outcomes for each area of Project activity. The final report for each phase of the Project should incorporate evaluation of results.

The handbook for Project personnel also stated that, ''It is important that record-keep-

ALICE BROOKS McGUIRE

Who first opened the doors of the Casis Library and then the minds and hearts of thousands of Casis children to the world of good books.

An innovator in the field of elementary libraries, Dr. McGuire has created an atmosphere of activity and creativity in the search for knowledge, information and pure enjoyment.

The library through the leadership of Dr. McGuire has become the heart of Casis — a new world opened up behind library doors — a world of books and visiting authors — a living library of activity rather than silence — a doorway to the world.

To the many national honors received by Alice McGuire, the

PARENTS AND CHILDREN OF CASIS

add their grateful and affectionate recognition.

9 May 1967

ing within the demonstration libraries not be emphasized to the point of minimizing the *demonstration* aspects of the Project as compared to the *research* aspects."

Throughout the Project at Casis, the demonstration was given priority. Evaluation procedures were designed not to interrupt or interfere with the activities carried on normally by the library staff, classroom teachers, and children.

The techniques employed in evaluating the Project at Casis were quite subjective indeed. This was, perhaps, justifiable to a point since many of the desired outcomes could be measured only in this manner. On the other hand, it is the opinion of Dr. Nymann that, from a research point of view, the lack of a carefully pre-planned program of evaluation, including provision for control of variables, constituted a serious flaw in the design of the Project at Casis.

The report of evaluation which follows is the result of the work of Dr. Nymann and Miss Rentz, the graduate student working with her.

The program of evaluation this year was designed to assess the achievements of the Project in terms of the following:

1. What visitors during 1966-67 felt they had gained from coming to the Project.

2. How children of Casis felt about the library and how they actually used the library.

3. What teachers felt they had gained during the entirety of the Project.

The procedures, results, and conclusions pertinent to each aspect of the evaluation are presented below.

Visitors: procedures

When non-student visitors came to the Project, they were given packets of material including a reactionnaire to be completed and returned.

The extent of the return of reactionnaires was disappointing; only 16 were received. However, 19 letters were received from individuals or groups who had come to the Project. The tenor of the letters was such that one might conclude that those who wrote them wished to express their feelings in a manner less structured than that permitted by the form.

Although students were not asked to complete reactionnaires this year, many comments were heard in which these young people and their instructors expressed the feeling that the visit to Casis was one of the most valuable experiences they had had.

Visitors: conclusions

It was apparent from the visitors' comments that they felt they had gained ideas of what a full program of library service could provide for children and teachers, in terms of resources and activities which were correlated with the total school curriculum. In addition they felt they had learned methods of operating such a library. Visitors also stressed that the provisions which had been made to help them learn about the program, including opportunities for observation, discussion with Project personnel, and study of printed material, had been valuable. The major suggestion they offered regarding the visitation program was to increase the duration of visits in order to allow more extensive observations of the library program.

Children: procedures

Assessment of children's learning during the Project was carried out jointly by Dr. Nymann and Miss Rentz, whose master's thesis is based on the research described in this particular section.

Four questions constituted the basis for study:

1. What attitudes and knowledge do Casis children in grades 2 through 6 have about the library?

2. How do Casis children in grades 2 through 6 behave in the library?

3. To what extent does their behavior reflect that which is expressed in writing, that is, their compositions?

4. To what extent is the Casis library program beneficial to pupils after they leave the elementary grades and move to junior high school?

The research design provided for obtaining and analyzing compositions written about the library by children in grades 2 through 6 in Casis School and also by students in grade 7 in O. Henry Junior High School who had attended Casis during one or both of the first two years of the Project. In addition, the design included plans for securing and analyzing detailed records of children's behavior in the Casis library, as well as for comparing the results of this analysis with findings relative to the attitudes and knowledge which children presently in Casis exhibited in writing.

The final procedure for determining children's attitudes and knowledge grew out of a pilot study which was conducted in January. This study included perusal of compositions about the library which had been written by children in a second grade class as the culminating activity of a unit on libraries, and a checklist was developed for use in crediting and tabulating indications of attitudes and knowledge which appeared in the compositions. Miss Rentz and Dr. Nymann tested the usefulness of the checklist by independently evaluating the compositions and then comparing results. The checklist proved to be quite useful, although it was evident that decisions were necessary as to what would or would not constitute credit in certain categories in order to increase the reliability of rating. In light of this finding, the checklist was revised to include guides for crediting and additional categories which were likely to be needed for full evaluation of older children's compositions.

It was decided at this time that children below second grade would not be included in the study because of the fact that most of their library instruction took place in their individual classrooms. In addition, it was decided that the study would not include children in special education.

Miss Rentz then sent a letter to all teachers of grades 2 through 6 requesting their cooperation and describing what she planned to do as well as what she expected of them. Every teacher agreed to participate.

It is important to note what was specified in the letter:

> For those who wish to participate, the procedure will be as follows:
>
> 1. I will come to each room and pose the questions, providing about a five to ten minute motivation, and then I will leave while the children write.
> 2. Please give the children as much time as they need to write their responses.
> 3. Since we want to keep their responses entirely free of any outside influence, I would ask you not to make any suggestions with regard to what they write.
> 4. Please do not have the children do any rewriting. If they need help spelling words please go ahead and help them, but their spelling and handwriting are not of critical importance. The ideas expressed are of most importance.
> 5. I will come to your room to collect the papers later in the day.

During the week of February 27, Miss Rentz went to each classroom and presented the motivation for writing as follows:

> Good morning, boys and girls. My name is Miss Rentz. I am interested in your school library and have watched many activities that happen in the library. I have seen some classes in the library, but I did not see every one when they came. I would like you to help me find out what the library does for you. I thought it might help me if you would write it down for me.
>
> We will start by getting out some paper and a pencil or pen. Would you please put your name in the upper right corner of the paper and under it your room number. Then look up at me so I will know you are finished. (Wait for the children to do this.)
>
> I am going to give you some questions about the library which I want you to think about. Then I want you to write to tell me what you think about the library, what it means to you, and how you use it.
>
> There isn't any right or wrong answer to the questions. It is up to you. Try to write in your nicest writing, but don't worry too much about writing or spelling. If you have questions about spelling, you may ask your teacher, but it's all right to spell the best you can by yourself. I am more interested in what you say in your paper. You will have as much time as you need to finish your paper. Don't worry about recopying it.
>
> Here are some questions that might help you decide what you want to write. I will read over them with you and then let you begin.
>
> 1. What is the library?
> 2. How does the library help you?
> 3. What things do you do in the library?
>
> Do you understand what you are to do? I'll be looking forward to getting your papers.

Children who were absent when the motivations were presented were not asked to produce compositions for the study. However, compositions were submitted by 542 of the 589 children enrolled in grades 2 through 6, or 92 percent of that population.

Two graduate students had agreed to assist Miss Rentz with evaluating the compositions. They met with her for a training period in order to ensure their understanding of the checklist and to increase their own reliability in rating. The training process consisted of their using the checklist to rate sample papers cooperatively as well as independently, always comparing and discussing the reasons for crediting or not crediting each category. Upon completion of the training period, Miss Rentz and her assistants began their work of evaluating the compositions. Then when the papers were returned to her, Miss Rentz performed a spot-check of the ratings which had been given to 30 compositions, three having been selected at random from each classroom folder.

In the longer study, *A Study of Children's Attitudes and Knowledge About the Casis Elementary School Library*, Miss Rentz has reported on sample compositions (two from each grade level) and on ratings by classroom groups. Following are the ratings compiled according to grade level:

TABLE 1

Tabulations by Grade Level

(F—Favorable; N—Negative)

Grade	2 F	2 N	3 F	3 N	4 F	4 N	5 F	5 N	6 F	6 N	Total F	Total N
Number of compositions	63		85		120		139		135		542	
I. ATTITUDES OF THE CHILDREN												
A. Toward the library												
1. Total impression (relaxed atmosphere—browse, like the library, or like something going on in the library)	24		42		82		101		105	1	354	1
2. Library citizenship (personal involvement — pride, indication of wanting to cooperate)	7		16		21		25	1	18	1	87	2
3. Librarians	11		10		46		42	2	28	3	137	5
4. Toward reading (evidence of sticking with book to finish or rereading, favorable adjectives applied to books, reading many books)	25		53		78		94		71	1	321	1
B. Toward the library program												
1. Literary appreciation (storytelling, great books, award books, etc.)	8		6		7		29		12		62	
2. Library instruction	10		1		4		10		6		31	
3. Integrated lessons	11		21		47		55		43		177	
4. Seminars	1						15		3		19	
5. Learn new words	2								1		3	
6. Get information, study	24		51		69		69		57		270	
7. Read better	9		7		4		4		3		27	
8. Texas Readers Club					1		10		2		13	
9. Library squad					1		13				14	
10. Class group getting to read at leisure							5		1	1	6	1
11. Visitors								1		1		2
II. KNOWLEDGE OF LIBRARY RESOURCES												
A. Quantity (number of "lots")	3		6	2	13	1	26		32	2	80	5
B. Diversity			3		13	3	11		25	2	52	5
1. Of areas (mention of kind of book not specified below, e.g., western, space, Davy Crockett)	22		8	2	10	2	13	1	14		67	5
2. Specific mention of books—if know what the category is							3		1		4	
a. Fiction	4		3		18	1	11	1	16	1	52	3

TABLE 1 (Continued)

Grade	2		3		4		5		6		Total	
Number of compositions	63		85		120		139		135		542	
	F	N	F	N	F	N	F	N	F	N	F	N
b. Nonfiction			1		5		5		7	1	18	1
c. Story collection	2		3		5		2		3		15	
d. Easy	2		1		4		2		2		11	
e. Biography	5		4		16		7		12		44	
f. Great books			1		2						3	
3. Mention of recordings and tapes			1		11		12		35		59	
4. Mention of filmstrips			2		13		15		33	1	63	1
5. Mention of vertical file					23		19		13	2	55	2
6. Mention of picture file			6		23		21		16	2	66	2
7. Mention of reference books	2		6		35		49	1	58	1	150	2
8. Mention of magazines					8		8		15	2	31	2
9. Mention of realia					1				2		3	
10. Mention of display and bulletin board					1		1		1		3	
11. Mention of globe					1						1	
12. Mention of transparencies							1		2		3	
C. Location of resources 1. General (awareness that there are sections of the library)	1		1		11		11		21		45	
2. Specific a. Fiction			1		8		4		2		15	
b. Nonfiction					5		1				6	
c. Story collection					1						1	
d. Easy					4		1		1		6	
e. Biography			2		8		4		1		15	
f. Listening center					2				2		4	
g. Great books					1						1	
h. Special book displays					1						1	
i. Reference							1		2		3	
j. Magazines							1				1	
III. KNOWLEDGE THAT THERE ARE MECHANICS (mere mention that he must check out a book before he takes it, or mere mention of the card catalog)	37		51		58	2	58		50	1	254	3
A. How to check out books (detailing)	4		6		7		5		3		25	
B. Use of the card catalog	2				6		10		5		23	
C. Knowledge of symbols	3		1		4		6		4	2	18	2

To indicate, on a grade level basis, the percentage of the compositions which commented favorably on specific aspects of the library program, Miss Rentz has prepared this table:

TABLE 2

Categories Mentioned Favorably with Greatest Frequency
(In Percent)

	2	3	4	5	6
Grade	2	3	4	5	6
Number of compositions	63	85	120	139	135
I A 1. Total impression (relaxed atmosphere — browse, like the library, or like something going on in the library)	38.1	49.4	68.3	72.7	77.8
I A 3. Librarians			38.3	30.2	
I A 4. Toward reading (evidence of sticking with book to finish or rereading, favorable adjectives applied to books, reading many books)	39.7	62.4	65.0	67.6	52.6
I B 3. Integrated lessons			39.2	39.6	31.9
I B 6. Getting information, study	38.1	60.0	57.5	49.6	42.2
II B 1. Diversity of areas (mention of kind of book not specified below, e.g., western, space, Davey Crockett)	34.9				
II B 3. Mention of recordings and tapes					25.9
II B 7. Mention of reference books			29.2	35.3	43.0
III. Knowledge that there are mechanics (mere mention that he must check out a book before he takes it, or mere mention of the card catalog)	58.7	60.0	48.3	41.7	37.0

Although children might make statements which could be interpreted as evidence of attitudes held or knowledge possessed, it was felt by the researchers that the real test of their learning about the library was the manner in which they used the library, particularly when they came to use it on their own rather than with a class for a lesson in the library. Thus a random sample of children was observed in the library in order not only to check their use of it, but also to check their actual behavior against behavior which could be inferred from what children had stated in their compositions.

Miss Rentz spent a part of each school day during the period from April 17 through April 28, 1967, observing children in the library. She observed and recorded details of the behavior of 104 children, a sample which represented 17.7 percent of the school population of children in grades 2 through 6. Because Miss Rentz did not wish to call attention to the fact that she was observing the children, she did not ask each one his name, nor did she make any obvious effort to find it out. It was also impos-

sible to determine the exact grade level of each child and to know whether he had submitted a composition.

The method of observation and recording of behavior was that the observer sat at a table in the library which was not in the way of activity, yet which was located where most areas of the library could be seen. Miss Rentz had note cards on which to record information, but she arranged a number of books and a notebook on the table so that attention would not be drawn to the recording process. The process began as a child entered the library, and the time of his entrance was noted, as well as his sex and an estimate of his grade level. Then his moves were recorded, such as looking up an item in the card catalog, going to the biography section, checking a book out, and leaving. At that time, his departure time was recorded so that calculations could be made which would ultimately provide an idea of how long children needed to stay in the library, and whether there was variation enough in the duration of children's library visits to warrant the efforts that had been made to keep the scheduling of the library to a minimum. Subjects for the study were selected simply according to the time they entered the library. That is, the first child to enter the library when Miss Rentz was observing was selected, and his moves were followed until his departure, at which time the next child to enter was selected. The only exceptions to this pattern occurred when the child being observed continued for some time to engage in an activity such as studying and/or taking notes from a reference book. Then if another child entered and moved about actively, he was observed simultaneously but not to the detriment of the accuracy of the behavior record for the first child. At no time were more than two children observed simultaneously.

Miss Rentz believed she maintained the unobtrusiveness that she desired during the observations. The librarians knew she was observing the behavior of children and not that of the library staff, but teachers did not know that she was conducting a part of her study through this method, and it seemed quite clear that children were not aware that they were being observed.

The information collected concerning children's behavior in the library was tabulated on a chart of activities which grew out of the activities which appeared on the notes from observation. That is, when an activity was mentioned on a card for the first time, the activity was added to the list and a tally was recorded. This made it unnecessary to try to determine just how to credit certain activities in categories and avoided any "masking" of information by the grouping-of-information process.

The observed activities were grouped and identified as shown in Table 3, page 208.

It will be recalled that a purpose of the study was to determine to what extent children's behavior reflected that which they stated in writing about the library. The results of the composition evaluations and of the behavioral records have been studied somewhat informally to arrive at some conclusions which can be stated at this time. Those results and conclusions are given on pages 210-11.

The time individual children spent in library was also recorded by Miss Rentz. See Table 4, page 209.

Another question which provided a basis for the study was concerned with the learning and attitudes of seventh grade students, who were former Casis students. In order to reach these children, permission was obtained from the principal of O. Henry Junior High School (which most Casis children attend after completion of sixth grade) to meet groups of these students for approximately 15 minutes on each of two consecutive days during the week of April 10, 1967, until essentially all of the former Casis students had been contacted. At these times, a prepared questionnaire was given to each student with instructions for completing it and returning it immediately. In addition to questions pertaining to the library program, the form provided a method by which students could indicate whether they had attended Casis during one or both years of the Project; so that students would not be confused about the exact years of the Project, the form simply provided them with a place where they would mark the grades during which they attended Casis.

Of the 155 children enrolled in the sixth grade during 1965-66, 118 were in attendance at O. Henry Junior High School and completed the questionnaire. This represented 76.1 percent of the "graduated" sixth grade class.

The following responses, in order of frequency, were made to the first question, dealing with what children reported they had learned

TABLE 3

Activities of Children Observed in the Library

Estimated Grade Level.....	2	2 or 3	3	3 or 4	4	4 or 5	5	5 or 6	6	Total
Number of children	3	3	14	8	24	16	13	9	14	104
1. Checked something in		1	2	1	2	2	2	1	2	13
2. Checked something out	1	3	11	3	7	5	4	4	8	46
3. Used card catalog		1	1	1	5	3	1		2	14
4. Used materials a. Books				1						1
b. Magazines				1		1	2			4
c. Listening center							1	2		3
d. Vertical file					1		1			2
e. Picture file				1	2					3
f. Encyclopedias				4	6	1	6	1		18
g. Dictionary					2					2
5. Received help from librarians a. Answers to questions	1	1	3	2	8	5	4	2	5	31
b. Card catalog									1	1
c. Locating			1	1	1		3		1	7
d. Check out procedure			1		1					2
1. Books								1		1
2. Magazines			1							1
3. Picture file				1						1
d. Reserving a book						1				1
6. Browsed	2	2	9	7	8	9	7	7	6	57
7. Read (quietly)				1	4	2	5	3	2	17
8. Read (and chatted at times)	1				1			1	1	4
9. Studied			1		2		1		1	5
10. Took notes			2		5	3	3	1		14
11. Disciplined			2		1	1	1	1		6
12. Wasted time (non-purposeful activity)			2	2	4	1	1		2	12
13. Wandered—looking for book					4	2				6
14. Talked to friends			3	5	10	3	4	8	6	39
15. Looked at display or bulletin board			1		1		1	2		5
16. Helped librarian								1		1
17. Filled out Texas Readers card				1		1	1		1	4
18. Disturbed by other children								1		1
19. Looked in book-due file for his class		1				1		1		3

TABLE 4
Time Spent in the Library by Children Observed

Estimated grade level	2		2 or 3		3		3 or 4		4		4 or 5		5		5 or 6		6		Total	
Number of children	3		3		14		8		24		16		13		9		14		104	
Sex	B	G	B	G	B	G	B	G	B	G	B	G	B	G	B	G	B	G	B-53	G-51
1-5 minutes	1				5	3		2	3	4	4	5	2	2	2	1	4	3	21	20
6-10 minutes		1	1	1	1	1		1	3	1	2	1			3				10	6
11-15 minutes			1		2		1	2		1		1	2	1				1	6	6
16-20 minutes		1				1			3	2				2	1		1	1	5	7
21-25 minutes						1		1											0	2
26-30 minutes							1		2		2	1		1					5	2
31-35 minutes														2					0	2
36-40 minutes									1				1		1			1	3	1
41-45 minutes										1								1	0	2
46-50 minutes										2								1	0	3
51-55 minutes									1						1		1		3	0

at the Casis library that helped them use their junior high library:

Use of card catalog 90
Dewey Decimal System 63
Use of reference materials 29
Use of vertical file 19
Use of *Readers' Guide* 12
How to locate books and materials....... 11
How to look up books and materials...... 8
How to check out books 7
Meanings of signs and symbols 7
Use of picture file 5
Knowledge of divisions or sections
of books 5
Use of magazines 4
How to use the library 4
Where to find books 4
How to card and shelve books.......... 3
How to take notes 2
Use of index and index cards........... 2
Use of *National Geographic Index*....... 2
Library manners 2
Use of the library as a good place
to learn and study 2

Responses to the second question, "What did you need to know about using a library that you didn't know when you started junior high school?" are shown here:

Nothing 79
Check-out procedures 11
Where things are located 8
How to use reference books 3
How to use the card catalog............ 3
How to read better 3

How to use maps and tapes............. 2
How to locate magazines and newspapers. 2
Use of index to periodical literature...... 2
How to use the picture catalog.......... 2
Dewey Decimal System 1
How to find other information
besides in books 1
How to work more closely with librarians. 1
Hours in the library in which he
could study 1

In response to Question Three, "Are there things you learned from your library experiences at Casis which help you now in English and Social Studies?" the 118 seventh graders named the following:

Acquaintance with finding and using
reference material 78
(Children mentioned finding information through use of Dewey Decimal System, encyclopedia, almanacs, magazines, *Readers' Guide*, indexes, *National Geographic Index*, books, using cross references, tapes, vertical file, picture file, etc.)
Knowledge of how to use library material
for taking notes and preparing oral and
written reports or compositions........ 24
Nothing 18
Everything 12
Knowledge of books good for reports in
social studies 8
Knowledge of particular kinds of books
(nonfiction, biography, mythology, history, etc.) 8
Knowledge about the card catalog........ 6
Study habits 6

Children: results

Attitudes and knowledge indicated in children's compositions. Tabulations of the ratings of attitudes and knowledge about the library which were evidenced in all the children's compositions were made for each classroom and were compiled for each grade. In addition, those categories of the checklist which were credited in the ratings of at least 25 percent of the compositions at any grade level were identified.

Table 1 shows the ratings of compositions as they were compiled for each grade level and Table 2 shows those categories which were most frequently credited at particular grade levels. In particular, it is interesting to note from Table 1 the increasing variety of items mentioned by children as they grow older and have had more and more experiences in the library. It can also be seen from that table that those aspects of the library program which are important enough for second grade children to mention in writing tend to remain important to children through sixth grade. Certain differences do exist from grade to grade but the difference is typically in degree of importance and this tends to be of an increasing nature. In instances where the degree of importance appears to diminish, for example, in categories such as attitudes toward "Librarians," "Integrated lessons," "Get information, study," and (very slightly) "Knowledge of mechanics," —all of these noted especially between fifth and sixth grades—the diminishing characteristic may be a function of *increasing* independence and maturity in using the library and even a taking for granted of the fact that the librarians do assist children, lessons are provided to help children make full use of the library for classroom study, there is a procedure for finding and checking out materials, and so forth. In fact, the less frequent mention in sixth grade of general use of the library for study is accompanied by more frequent mention of particular kinds of references.

Table 2 shows those categories which were mentioned in at least 25 percent of the compositions at any one grade level. It can be seen that a favorable attitude toward the library was evident to that extent in all grades and the percentage of children indicating this attitude in their compositions increased steadily through the grades. Also evident in all grades was a favorable attitude toward reading, which was mentioned by 39.7 percent of the second grade children, and was mentioned by 62.4, 65, and 67.6 percent of children in grades three, four, and five, respectively. In grade six, mention of this attitude dropped to 52.6 percent, which would seem not to be a drastic change since children at the end of the sixth grade are typically discovering many different interests.

Still another category which received a high degree of mention at all grade levels was the use of the library for "Getting information and study." While many children in second grade evidenced awareness of this, the awareness appeared to be heightened in the minds of third grade children. The fact that mention of this use of the library was considerably more frequent among third graders and then tapered

Fifth grade reference work may benefit from Mrs. Keel's interest and help.

off somewhat among older children might have been expected since it is often at the third grade level that much independent study is encouraged and, while it continues to be encouraged at the upper levels, it loses some of its novelty and becomes an expected pattern for those children. All grade levels exhibited a strong awareness of the fact that use of the library involves knowledge of certain procedures which are to be followed.

It should be noted that while "Diversity of areas" was indicated as receiving credit by at least 25 percent of the second grade children, older children tended to mention specific areas of the library or particular types of references rather than mentioning diversity in general terms. Thus diversity was apparent to them, but it was spoken of in a variety of specific ways and no one kind of mention occurred in 25 percent or more of the compositions at any given grade level.

Behavior of children in the library. Tabulations were made of the activities in which children engaged during their independent use of the library, and the information was compiled according to estimates of the children's grade levels. In addition, amounts of time spent in the library were tabulated and compiled in similar fashion.

From Table 3, which shows children's activities, it can be seen that younger children tended to check materials in or out, browse, and engage in relatively non-purposeful activity. Older children also exhibited some of the same behaviors, but tended to make much greater use of the card catalog, various kinds of resources, and of the library generally as a place for reading and study. Numerically at least, they all tended to use the library for the following activities most frequently:

Checking materials in or out
Browsing
Talking to friends
Receiving help from the librarians
Using references for study
Reading

In spite of the fact that the activities above represent those engaged in most frequently, it should be noted that quite a variety of resources was used by the 104 children who were observed.

The most striking kind of information which can be seen in Table 4 concerning amounts of time spent in the library may be, first, the tendency for time spent there to increase with the increase in age of children. Second, it is important to note the great variety in amount of time spent there by all children. A sizable number of children needed only to spend about five or ten minutes to accomplish their "business," while other children needed anywhere from about 15 minutes to an hour to complete what they had to do. An important result here is the finding that there seems to be no *common* amount of time that children need in the library. This is of special interest as more and more elementary school libraries move away from schedules which stipulate exactly when and how long children shall be in the library.

Comparison of attitudes and knowledge about the library with behavior in the library. Study of children's compositions resulted in the findings that children liked the library with its relaxed atmosphere and its offerings. They appreciated the help given them by the librarians, both informally and formally, such as in the provision for lessons which were correlated—or integrated—with classroom study. Children viewed the library as a place to obtain information for study from reference books and other resources, and the children realized that there were procedures to be followed in locating and checking out (and in) materials. Moreover, the children liked to read!

The findings presented above, which came from study of the children's written statements about the library, were very much in keeping with the behavior that was observed. It will be recalled that children whose behavior was observed used the library for taking materials out or returning them, browsing, reading, using references for study, obtaining help from the librarians, and talking to friends. It seems entirely possible that one important reason for children's favorable attitude toward the library is the freedom they have to say a few words to friends.

Indicative of the children's enthusiasm for the library is the following letter:

```
                                                Casis School
                                                May 24, 1966
    Dear Library,

         I love the library just the way it is.  But I think it would
    be nice if the library was a bit bigger.  I think that all the
    librarians are very nice.  You may not notice it but some of the
    chairs are a little too small.

         I love all the books you have but when you get a new book
    all the other books by the same author suddenly get very popular and
    you can't find a book and I think if you could order some of the same
    books it would be nice.

         I love to read books whenever I can (even if I do it when
    I shouldn't).  When I'm in the library I feel like I'm in another
    world.  Libraries are wonderful!

                                                Yours truly,

                                                Nancy K. Netherton

    P.S.    I Love Books.

    P.P.S.  Have a wonderful summer.
```

Attitudes and knowledge of seventh grade students. The responses made by the seventh grade students who had been at Casis to each of the three questions on the form are presented on page 209.

While a great number of items were mentioned in response to Question One, those which were included in the responses of at least 10 percent of the 118 students were: use of the card catalog, the Dewey Decimal System, use of reference materials, use of the vertical file, and use of the *Readers' Guide to Periodical Literature.*

The most common answer to Question Two was "Nothing," a response which was given by 79 of the 118 students—or 67 percent. The only other answers which might be noted were the answers, "Check out procedures," given by 11

students, and "Where things are located," mentioned by 8 students. It was probably inevitable that these answers would be given by some students, since the check-out procedure and location of materials could very well be different in the two libraries.

Question Three was "Are there things you learned from your library experiences at Casis which help you now in English and social studies?" It will be noted that 78 students made mention of one or more means of finding and using reference material. In addition, 24 students indicated as helpful their knowledge of library material for taking notes and preparing oral and written reports or compositions. A group of 18 students reported that "Nothing" had helped them in English and social studies, but another group of 12 students expressed the opposite opinion when they reported that "Everything" had helped them.

Children: conclusions

The conclusions which were reached in this study will be presented in terms of the four questions which were the basis for the research.

1. *What attitudes and knowledge do Casis children in grades 2 through 6 have about the library?* It was quite apparent from the results that the children like the library and the librarians. In addition, they like to read, and this fact seems to be very closely related to their attitude toward the library itself. They view the library as a place which offers them much to read, much material from which to learn. Children know how to check materials in and out; they know how to use the card catalog and how to find the resources they need. Moreover, they use the resources of the library to support and extend classroom studies. These children are aware of the fact that they are learning about the library and its offerings, and that the librarians are there to help them.

2. *How do Casis children in grades 2 through 6 behave in the library?* When the children come independently to use the library, they come to borrow materials from the library. In addition, they sometimes stay to browse, to read, or to use references for study. If they need help, they ask for it. While some seemingly non-purposful activity takes place, it tends to decrease as children grow older and know more about the library. Children talk quietly with others at times, but discipline is seldom necessary. The time that children need to spend in the library varies with the purpose for which they have come. When children come simply to check materials in or out, they may stay for only a few minutes; when they come to do reference work, they may need to stay for as much as an hour. This conclusion regarding amount of time spent in the library lends strong support for the very flexible scheduling that has been maintained during the Project.

3. *To what extent does their behavior reflect that which is expressed in writing?* The content of the compositions indicated what children felt about the library and what they

thought they knew about it; observations of children's behavior indicated that what they stated was, in fact, borne out in practice.

4. *To what extent is the Casis library program beneficial to pupils after they leave the elementary grades and move to junior high school?* Most former Casis students who are now in seventh grade feel that the library program they had as elementary school pupils was, indeed, beneficial to them. In particular, they are finding it useful to know about the card catalog, the Dewey Decimal System, and varieties of resource material. Moreover, they believe that learning how to use references for study and for reports was of benefit.

Teachers: procedures

In February, 1967, permission was obtained from Mr. Glenn to ask the Casis teachers to assess what they believed they had gained by having had the benefits of the Knapp School Libraries Project. A notice was sent to the teachers suggesting that they set aside part of a grade-level meeting to formulate a statement of belief. In some cases, the statements were formulated verbatim during the grade-level meeting; in other cases, discussion took place during the meeting and the grade-level chairman composed the statement.

Teachers: reactions

It can be seen from the statements received that teachers felt that the additional staff members in the library provided them with materials they needed for classroom units of study—to a degree greater than had been possible before Knapp Project participation. In addition, teachers appreciated the increased stock of resources the library had to offer. Teachers especially valued the closer relationship that was possible between librarians and children because of the enlarged staff.

Three reports from the grade level meetings held Wednesday, February 15, 1967, give the tenor of teachers' reactions:

From second grade teachers:

At second grade-level we have greatly benefited from library instruction through Knapp Project participation. The high achievers were able for the first time to learn to utilize the card catalog and solve many research problems of their own. All children were able to have assistance with location of material to answer their questions as they arose. The children were aided in selection of appropriate reading level in areas of individual interest. It enabled us to have a regular listening and story time. Children were informed of all new library materials and shown how to utilize them.

From third and fourth grade teachers:

Benefits of the Knapp Library Project:
1. More individual help for children from the librarians.
2. More individual help for the teachers from the librarians.
3. Sessions for classes to help with initiation of social studies units (reference procedures).
4. Series of special library instruction periods for every grade level.
5. More materials available.
6. Extension of the classroom in the reading and social studies programs.
7. Weekly literary appreciation periods for every class.
8. Librarians have sufficient time to act as valuable resource people in the classrooms.

From special education teachers:

The Knapp Project has helped to provide a wide selection of new and exciting books as well as sufficient library staff to give sympathetic individual guidance to each child. A visit to the library can be a futile and frustrating experience for the brain-injured child unless he is given adequate support. If a child needs help in locating the proper materials or evaluating the materials he has found, one of the librarians is available to give him guidance.

Our weekly library period, made possible by an increased staff, is an informative, enriching, and inspiring experience giving these children a great feeling for books.

SUMMARY STATEMENTS

The following statement, condensed slightly, was prepared by Superintendent Carruth:

. . . [Since 1964], approximately $75,000 has been given by the Knapp School Libraries Project and used for the following improvements: facilities, quarters, materials, and increased staff.

. . . The Casis School has worked in cooperation with The University of Texas. . . .

Each visit [by teams of administrators, teachers, and citizens] has been planned and supervised so that the contributions of good library service to the total school program may be assessed. . . .

More than 3,000 visitors from all parts of the world have had the opportunity annually to observe the effective role of this library in the school program and have been impressed by it. Since the establishment of this school, the faculty has relied greatly on the library in every facet of the program. The children have used the library widely all during these years at Casis. The library staff has cooperated with the teachers in an effective team relationship within the instructional program, which has been considered a model for such a program. Since 1935, the Austin schools have had libraries and a librarian in all of the elementary schools. The system as a whole has had a high regard for the role of libraries. Even today, only one-third of the elementary schools in the nation have established school libraries with librarians. This shows the leadership that the Austin schools have given in this field.

The Knapp Project Advisory Committee felt that the growth potential of the Casis library was great and that with the financial

This area of the library was planned for small-group listening.

help of Project funds, this could be more quickly realized. The mothers in the Casis school district have rendered invaluable aid by offering volunteer service to assist the librarian.

Four phases of library services are emphasized at Casis. First, it is the materials center of the school, containing every possible type of material and tool to enrich teaching and learning. Second, its service program is a vital force throughout the school, participating in all types of educational and reading activities. Third, there is a study laboratory where the child can use independently all types of learning materials and where he can learn to work independently and search out material for himself. Again, each child receives the broadest reading experiences possible. He learns to know all types of books and appreciate the best in literary heritage.

Fourth, the librarian, working in cooperation with the classroom teacher, can make a real contribution to child development. A wide collection of books provides guidance in their personal problems and interest. In a very real way, the library may be considered an index to the character and quality of the educational program of the school. It is a cultural center which can enrich a child's whole future. It was because of these reasons and, again, the dynamic leadership of Dr. McGuire in cooperation with the principal, teachers and patrons that the Casis School was chosen as one of the demonstration schools of the Knapp Project.

Our $75,000 Project grant enabled us to enlarge the library room which we had planned to build and has added many books and other source materials to the physical facilities. Additional personnel have made it possible to carry on the project and to meet with thousands of visitors who have come our way to see the operation of a library that could serve as a model, setting high standards for the operation of this nerve center of learning in a school if money and interest are available on the part of each local community.

. . . We can say that it has helped the Casis library and all the libraries of the city of Austin, as well as hundreds of other school districts in Texas and throughout the United States. Representatives from 25 different countries and 35 states and 2,500 college students have had the opportunity to observe the work being done here. Also, seminars of superintendents, principals, teachers, and others have been held to give to as many

as possible an opportunity to know of the program at the Casis school library and the effectiveness of its operation.

The lady who was primarily instrumental in getting this grant and in carrying out the program itself is Dr. Alice Brooks McGuire. Her vision of what a good library should be and how it should function as the educational center of any school, her boundless energy, and her great devotion to this ideal have helped her from the beginning to establish a most outstanding library for children and teachers. Her philosophy is that a library should be a vital instrument in promoting better classroom teaching and in making readers of children and creating a love for reading and learning. This has made the Casis library an outstanding project since its beginning.

In a letter to Dr. Nymann on May 31, 1967, Superintendent Carruth stated:

We plan to continue with but a slight decrease in personnel and with the program which is now in operation at Casis School. The high standards set by the Knapp Foundation will be continued, and in addition we plan to upgrade all other libraries of our city as rapidly as possible to meet the standards of Casis Elementary School.

Some indication of The University of Texas's continuing interest and support for the library program at Casis is given in Dean Wayne H. Holtzman's letter of June 8, 1967, to Dr. Nymann. He wrote, in part:

As you know from the conferences and negotiations of the past few months, The University of Texas will be working closely with Casis Elementary School over the coming years in three areas of special significance: (1) special education demonstration projects, (2) kindergarten education, and (3) extensions of the Knapp School Libraries Project. It is to the last of these three that I am addressing my other comments in this letter.

One of the truly significant achievements of the past several years has been the integration of the library demonstration program at Casis into our Teacher Education Program at The University of Texas. Both our graduate and undergraduate programs in elementary education now provide for direct experiences in the Casis Library Program to give future teachers a deeper understanding of how important an adequate library program is at the elementary level.

This activity will continue in the years to come as a cooperative activity between Casis School and the College of Education at the University.

In addition to providing these special experiences for our student teachers, the Casis Library also provides a facility for the training of elementary school librarians at the professional level. Dr. Douglass, director of the Graduate School of Library Science, has been working closely with the College of Education in the development of such programs and the Casis Library provides a cornerstone upon which this graduate program is being built.

The interest of the Graduate School of Library Science was expressed in a letter from its director, Dr. Robert R. Douglass, to Dr. Nymann on June 15, 1967. Dr. Douglass wrote:

I am pleased to have this opportunity to express the School's appreciation for the unique opportunity the Knapp School Libraries Project at Casis has afforded students in the Library School for observation and laboratory experience in a situation approaching the ideal. As you doubtless will appreciate, one of the major difficulties in the education of elementary (as well as secondary) school librarians is having access to a laboratory environment to serve as a model; this, Casis has most certainly been. It is almost an exercise in futility to talk about what good school library service is if students are unable to see it demonstrated.

Actually, under Dr. McGuire's direction the Casis Library for years has provided us with a splendid model and students have vied with one another for an opportunity to be assigned to it for their observation and prac-

tice experience. The Project, however, made it possible to bring the Library up to standards in resources, physical facilities, and staff, and to exceed the standards in the quality of its services. We are especially grateful that the influence of Casis is being extended to many sections of the state and region by our ex-students and graduates.

We look forward with satisfaction to a continuation of this fine collaboration in the years to come, a relationship that has been intensified and extended by the Knapp Project.

Report from

ROOSEVELT HIGH SCHOOL
and
PORTLAND STATE COLLEGE

FACT SHEET—ROOSEVELT HIGH SCHOOL

The Roosevelt High School in Portland, Oregon, is one of thirteen secondary schools in a district known for outstanding achievement in curriculum development. Superintendent Melvin W. Barnes supports a dynamic school library program. The ·district maintains a growing instructional materials department which provides centralized purchasing, cataloging, and processing for all school libraries.

The Roosevelt head librarian, Mrs. Lois Sayles, is a leader of unusual enthusiasm and exceptional competence. At Roosevelt she has fostered an awareness among the staff and students of the many services and opportunities to be found in a library. Many teachers have voluntarily attended in-service programs exploring instructional improvements through use of the library. The district has published a descriptive outline of the Roosevelt program as a guide for other schools. A Roosevelt Knapp Project brochure, *How Big Is an Idea?* may be purchased for $1.00 from the Curriculum Publications Department of the Portland Public Schools, 631 N.E. Clackamas Street, Portland, Oregon 97208.

Portland State College has designated Dr. John P. Picco as the field worker for this Project. He has coordinated a program whereby students in secondary teacher education from all of the colleges in the greater Portland area will participate in the Knapp Project at Roosevelt. Portland State has stimulated special interest at Roosevelt concerning the services of counselors and librarians in providing occupational information. Portland State subject matter specialists are available to Roosevelt teachers. Dr. Picco planned a library workshop held at Portland State and Roosevelt in March, 1967. The Project is one of several cooperative efforts between the college and the Portland Public Schools.

Recent developments at Roosevelt include extending hours of library service four evenings a week, recruiting and training of a large staff of student librarians, and developing auxiliary resource materials centers.

The Knapp School Libraries Project has supplied funds to increase the materials collection, double the library staff, assist in equipping the resource centers, and provide air temperature control in the library. Four librarians, assisted by two resource center aides, five library assistants, and two artist-technicians comprise the school library staff. Other qualified teachers are associated with the evening library program. This staff, which fully meets the standards for a school of eighteen hundred, has demonstrated the library's impact on the school's instructional program. Mr. Don W. James, Principal of Roosevelt High School, is the liaison person for the Project at Roosevelt.

STATISTICS

From its Project application, November, 1964
Enrollment: 1,804 students, grades nine through twelve.
Materials collection: 9,727 books, 157 periodicals, 131 filmstrips, 39 disc recordings, 39 tape recordings, 54 microfilms.
Library personnel: One full-time librarian, one full-time library assistant, one audio-visual coordinator, one full-time clerk, one half-time clerk, one full-time artist-technician, four teachers each working five hours a week in the evenings, and four teachers assisting in the library one period each day.

As of June, 1967
Enrollment: 1,770 students, grades nine through twelve.
Materials collection: 30,782 books, 185 periodicals, 523 filmstrips, 547 disc recordings, 100 tape recordings, 24 microfilm titles, 6,386 pamphlets, 1,435 slides, 4,665 transparencies, 6 newspapers, 5,110 pictures, prints, and maps. The school has access to a district collection of 9,775 filmstrips, 8,641 films, 875 disc recordings, and 487 tape recordings. The district also maintains a professional library of 10,000 books and 200 periodicals.
Library personnel: Four full-time librarians, two full-time resource center aides four full-time library assistants, one half-time library assistant, one full-time artist-technician, one assistant to artist-technician, four teachers each working five hours a week in the evenings, and seven assisting in the library one period a day.

PERSONNEL MOST DIRECTLY CONCERNED WITH THE PROJECT

From Roosevelt High School

Mr. Don W. James, Principal
Mrs. Lois Sayles, Head Librarian
Mrs. Geneva Kershner, Librarian
Miss Caroline Koster, Librarian
Miss Sharon Mozeski, Librarian
Mrs. Janice Chapman, Resource Center Aide
Miss Barbara Stayton, Resource Center Aide
Mrs. Alice Abbott, Library Assistant
Mrs. Donna Croker, Library Assistant
Mrs. Evelyn Melcher, Library Assistant
Mrs. Beverly Purvis, Library Assistant
Mrs. Selma Case, Artist-Technician
Miss Francine Casey, Artist-Technician's Assistant

From the Portland Public Schools

Dr. Melvin W. Barnes, Superintendent
Dr. Norman K. Hamilton, Assistant Superintendent
Dr. William A. Oliver, Assistant Superintendent
Dr. Laurence E. Winter, Assistant Superintendent
Mr. A. Kingsley Trenholme, Director of Instructional Materials
Mrs. Irene McHale, Supervisor of Libraries

From Portland State College

Dr. David E. Willis, Dean, School of Education
Dr. John P. Picco, Associate Profesor of Education and field worker, Knapp School Libraries Project

STEPS IN SELECTION AND AFTER

On April 1, 1965, it was announced by the various news media in Portland, Oregon, that Roosevelt High School in cooperation with Portland State College was one of the three secondary schools in the nation selected by the Knapp School Libraries Project to serve as a library demonstration center. The following statement appeared in the *Oregon Journal,* April 1, 1965:

> Roosevelt High School will receive $72,500 during the next two years to improve its library program, it was announced by the American Association of School Librarians. [Total grant to Roosevelt was later raised to $108,180 as a result of additional budget requests.]
>
> The Portland school is one of two high schools in the nation selected to participate in the Knapp School Libraries Project, financed by the AASL.
>
> Schools with "active, dynamic and creative library programs" are given funds through the Project to bring their facilities up to the standards of the AASL, reported Peggy Sullivan, Director of the program.
>
> She said Roosevelt was chosen because of its already excellent program established under the leadership of the school librarian, Mrs. Lois Sayles.
>
> During each of the next two years, the Roosevelt library will receive $11,000 for purchase of books, $3,000 for purchase of audio-visual materials, and $22,250 for staff salaries.
>
> An additional grant of $9,702 for each of the next two years will be given to Portland State College to help pay the salary and expenses of a field worker, who will be a consultant for the library.
>
> Beginning in the spring of 1966, the Roosevelt library will serve as a demonstration center and will be host to hundreds of visitors.

Portions of this section are taken from a dissertation for the doctoral degree by Mr. Don W. James, principal of Roosevelt High School. The title of the dissertation is *An Analysis of The Impact Upon Visitors To The Knapp School Libraries Demonstration.*

Following this announcement, letters of congratulation began to pour in from professional colleagues and friends of Roosevelt scattered far and wide. It was particularly gratifying to the Roosevelt staff and student body to receive recognition from numerous state officials. The governor, the secretary of state, both U.S. senators from Oregon, the mayor, and state representatives were numbered among those who expressed pride in Roosevelt's selection.

The Roosevelt staff accepted responsibility for implementing the objectives of the Project, which was funded to demonstrate school library excellence. The guide for quality was provided by *Standards For School Library Programs* prepared by the American Association of School Librarians and nineteen other national educational organizations. These standards, published in 1960, describe effective school libraries in terms of funds, facilities, staff, materials collection and program of services:

> The *Standards* recommends a staff ratio of one librarian for each 300 students, and one clerk for each 600 students; a collection of 6,000 to 10,000 books, or 10 books per pupil in schools over 1,000 enrollment, and a variety of audio-visual materials adequate in number to meet curriculum needs; from $4.00 to $6.00 per pupil annually for books— enough to purchase one book per pupil; and facilities both attractive and functional in design and spacious enough to accommodate a variety of activities.

Funds from the Knapp Project and the school district assisted Roosevelt High School in the achievement of these standards. Three additional certificated librarians were employed and the staff of paraprofessionals was increased from three to eight. Additional study centers more than doubled the seating capacity. The materials collection was built to exceed standards in most categories. Audio-visual equipment and non-print materials were substantially increased.

During its two school years of Project participation, the Roosevelt library program was financed as follows:

This is the view of the Roosevelt library seen by visiting administrator Mr. Arthur Lind.

PERSONNEL

Head librarian	Previous district commitment
3 Assistant librarians	½ librarian — New district funds 2½ librarians—Knapp Project funds
1 Artist-technician	Previous district commitment assumed at termination of Ford Foundation instructional media project.
1 Artist-technician's assistant	Title I ESEA funds
2 Resource center aides	New district funds
4½ Library assistants	2—Previous district commitment 1—New district funds 1½—Knapp Project funds
4 Teachers, each working five hours a week in the evenings and seven assisting in the library one period each day	Previous district commitment
Summer personnel	Knapp Project funds

QUARTERS

Main library	Constructed by district, 1961; air conditioning provided by Knapp Project funds
English resource center	Constructed by district, 1965
Independent study center	Renovated and furnished by district, assisted by over $12,000 provided by Knapp Project

MATERIALS

$17,700 each year	Knapp Project funds
$10,000 (approx.) each year	Continuing district commitment

The detailed budget of Knapp Project funds for Roosevelt is as follows:

	1965-66	1966-67
1. Materials		
a. Books	$11,000.00	$11,000.00
b. Audio-visual materials	3,000.00	3,000.00
c. Processing	2,200.00	2,200.00
d. Professional materials	1,500.00	1,500.00
2. Personnel		
a. Professional and clerical, school year	24,150.00	24,150.00
b. Summer	2,000.00	2,000.00
3. Quarters		
a. Air conditioning	15,480.00	—
b. Renovation and furnishing resource centers	5,000.00	—
	$64,330.00	$43,850.00

Recruitment of personnel

The first task undertaken by the Roosevelt administrative staff was that of defining job descriptions and recruiting new personnel. An agreement was reached with the district personnel office that Roosevelt administrators would have the final decision regarding the employment of all qualified personnel. Interviews were conducted by the principal, curriculum vice-principal, and the librarian, who was designated head librarian after additional certificated library staff members were employed.

Although the selection of librarians was the first order of business, paraprofessionals were requisitioned just one week following the announcement of Roosevelt's selection. The following job descriptions indicate the factors considered by the school's librarian and administrators.

Library aide—English resource center

This aide, who will work under the immediate supervision of the librarian coordinator of resource centers, should have a background in English.

The following is a brief outline of responsibilities:
1. Coordinate requests from English department chairman and teachers with librarians.
2. Oversee the daily operation of resource centers. This involves:
    Circulation routines
    Organization of materials
    Shelving and shelf reading
    Mechanical preparation of materials
    Filing magazines, pamphlets, cards, etc.
    Supervision of student assistants
    Maintaining order
3. Preparation of orders for books and other materials.
4. Typing bibliographies, lists, orders, etc.
5. Help students and teachers assemble materials. Locate simple bibliographical information—simple reference.
6. Inventory all instructional materials and supplies.
7. General housekeeping.
8. General and physical upkeep of collection.
9. Maintain all appropriate files.

Library aide—independent study center

This aide, who will work under the immediate supervision of the librarian coordinator of resource centers, should have a background in social studies. The outline of responsibilities for this position is the same as that for the library aide—English resource center, except that she coordinates requests from social studies department chairman and teachers instead of English department chairman and teachers.

Library assistant—responsibilities

1. Shelving services:
    Shelving and filing printed materials
    Caring for the order and appearance of shelves and files
    Reading shelves and files
    Shifting books, etc.
2. Circulation:
    Assisting at the charge desk
    Maintaining reserve shelf for teachers and students
    Computing circulation statistics
    Keeping record of fines
3. Attendance:
    Assigning and reserving use of small group room and attendance from study hall
    Scheduling classes for teachers
    Determining use of special rooms
4. Physical upkeep of collection.
5. Inventory of books.
6. Other duties as need arises, such as typing, etc.

Library assistant (half-time)—responsibilities

1. General care and upkeep of serial publications:
    Magazines
    Newspapers
    Continuations
2. Inventory:
    Serials publications
    Supplies
3. Typing:
    Bibliographies, lists, etc.
    Assist with order work
    Other typing as needed
4. General work with pamphlets and other non-book printed materials.
5. Ordering and general upkeep of supplies.
6. Assistance to students and teachers:
    Assembling materials to be sent to classroom
    Locating simple bibliographical information, etc.
7. Processing new books under supervision.

General skills and qualifications

The following are applicable to all workers in the instructional materials center:

Technical skills—

I. Secretarial skills
   Typing
   Filing
   Operation of machines (duplicacator, mimeograph, adding machine)
   Simple bookkeeping
II. Ability to handle a variety of routines and detail with accuracy.

Personal qualifications—

I. Good health. It is important that library personnel be physically fit, because the various demands of the job require a great deal of stamina and preclude frequent absences.
II. Ability to relate well to both students and faculty and evidence a genuine liking for and interest in young people.
III. A well developed sense of personal integrity.
IV. Good judgment and common sense which can distinguish between important and trivial details.
V. Efficient use of time.
VI. Initiative.
VII. Intellectual curiosity.
VIII. Flexibility, e.g., willingness to serve in the various parts of the instructional materials center according to need.
IX. Ability to accept responsibility for the various demands of the position, e.g., (a) arriving at work on time, (b) being willing to postpone coffee breaks whenever there is an obvious need to be on the job, (c) recognizing that the work load requires working the full eight-hour day and that personal errands after school class hours must be kept to a minimum.

Level of responsibility—

I. Deal directly with students and teachers in *educational* as well as clerical capacity.
   The library assistant must be capable of guiding and helping students in the use of *Readers' Guide*, the card catalog and in relating the utilization of a wide variety of library materials with classroom assignments. The assistant must operate in many instances under the pressures and duress of a number of urgent demands which have to be handled with equanimity. The library assistant must also be able to work with teachers and assist them with their requests.
II. Assume complete responsibility for direction of library and resource center whenever professional commitments require the presence of the librarian in the classroom or at teachers' meetings and also during a portion of the lunch hour.
III. Aid in maintaining discipline.
IV. Assist in the supervision and training of student help in library routine.
   Directing the activities of student library assistants, often working throughout the day as an educational resource person for students and teachers, exercising good judgment whenever disciplinary action is required, and needing a high level of responsibility falling far outside the range of what are commonly considered as clerical skills.

Renovating and furnishing of quarters

A major part of the demonstration facilities had already been provided by the school district. A library had recently been constructed, and an English resource center had been incorporated in a new wing with the timely completion date of August, 1965. The main problem facing the Roosevelt administration was the implementation of their dream to convert the old cafeteria to facilitate the instructional materials program.

Originally no request had been made of the Knapp Project for the improvement of facilities. When it was realized that Project support for facilities was available, $5,000 was requested and approved in May, 1965. This amount was budgeted for the renovation and furnishing of resource centers. Later still, Roosevelt officials submitted a last minute request for Project funds to install air conditioning in the main library. This request not only ensured more comfort for the demonstration in the main library, but allowed greater Project support for the conversion of the old

INSTRUCTIONAL MATERIAL CENTER

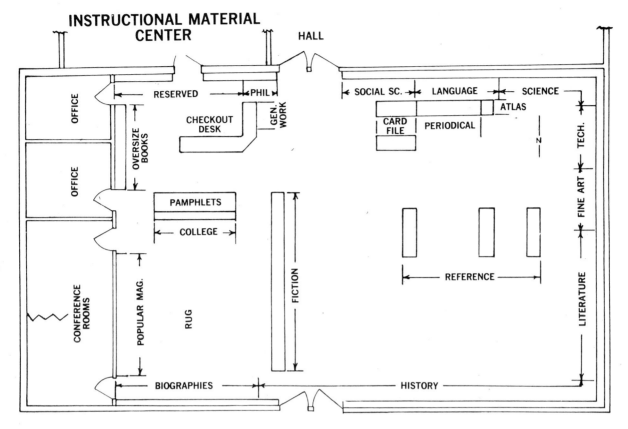

HALL

OFFICE

OFFICE

CONFERENCE ROOMS

RESERVED → ← PHIL →

CHECKOUT DESK

GEN. WORK

OVERSIZE BOOKS

PAMPHLETS

COLLEGE

POPULAR MAG.

RUG

FICTION

BIOGRAPHIES

HISTORY

SOCIAL SC. → ← LANGUAGE → ← SCIENCE

CARD FILE

PERIODICAL

ATLAS

N

FINE ART

TECH.

LITERATURE

REFERENCE

MAIN LIBRARY

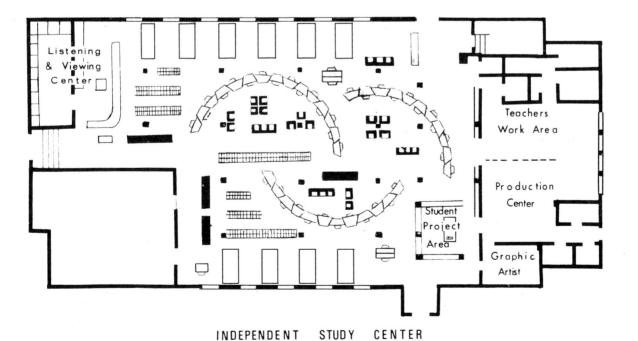

Listening & Viewing Center

Teachers Work Area

Production Center

Student Project Area

Graphic Artist

INDEPENDENT STUDY CENTER

cafeteria to what had been designated the independent study center.

The original engineer's estimate of $15,480 proved to be considerably high when the accepted contractor's bid came in at $7,780. Under the provisions of the budget agreement, it became permissible to shift the balance to the study center. Although the nearly $13,000 in Knapp funds pushed our dream toward reality, a substantial district expenditure was necessary to create the center as planned.

Acquisition of materials

At the outset, the acquisition of materials seemed to be the most simple and delightful responsibility to be discharged. It was rather exhilarating just to contemplate all the print and non-print materials to be purchased with

nearly $30,000 per year. Now students and teachers could be supplied with all materials they might desire. Although Roosevelt had already established a rather good collection, all areas could now be brought up to standards.

Duplicate copies of certain books, especially reference materials, were ordered for resource centers. Additional periodicals were purchased. Substantial increases were planned in non-print materials. For the first time, teachers could have access to a professional library right in their own building.

Exact data on holdings will be presented later in this report. In other sections dealing with problems and recommendations, it will be seen that acquiring materials was not altogether the pleasant task first imagined.

ROOSEVELT LIBRARY PROGRAM

The library program at Roosevelt High School is structured within the framework of *Standards for School Library Programs* (American Library Association, 1960). A survey taken prior to Roosevelt's participation in the Knapp Project showed that the general needs of the student body could be grouped in three broad areas: (1) adequate library skills, (2) reading guidance, and (3) strengthening of interest and appreciation for libraries, library services, and materials. To meet these needs of students, librarians and teachers must have the ability to locate instructional materials and must be able to relate them to the instructional program. The true concept of the library program means the instruction, service, and activities throughout the school rather than merely within the four walls of the library quarters.

A program of instruction in the use of the library taught through subject matter has been developed. Teachers and librarians determine student needs by administering a checklist surveying the eight basic locational skills rquired for optimum library utilization. A librarian then visits the classroom with a worksheet related to current course content and demonstrates library tools. The class visits the library to gain experience in using their new

library skills. The teacher follows up by checking comprehension through objective tests and observations. Continuity and expansion of this program of instruction in the use of the library result in cumulative growth in library, locational and research skills, and in the development of reading, listening, and viewing abilities and taste. This program is described more fully in *Curriculum Bulletin No. 39*, Portland Public Schools, Portland, Oregon.

Teachers, too, need re-education in the use of the changing and expanding library. In-service training, in which better use of instructional materials and aids was stressed, was provided at the district level in 1965-66 to approximately sixty teachers and library assistants. There was no formal in-service program offered in 1966-67, although informal training is a continuous and natural outcome of the expanded program at the building level.

Members of the faculty have been introduced to recent additions to the library through an annotated "Roosevelt Biblio News," published periodically by students from the business practice class, who use the library as one of their training stations. The large number and variety of new materials made available through the Knapp Project have brought about

Mrs. Beverly Purvis, instructional clerk, is assisted by students in organizing the English resource center.

a change in the format and distribution of this publication. Annotated bibliographies of all types of new materials, in addition to books, are now prepared for each department and sent to the department chairmen to discuss and distribute to faculty members in that subject area.

A student library staff was selected to provide a source of information to and from the classroom as well as to offer training and experience in library work. Prospective college students received basic training in library work as well as special experience in in-depth research. The library science program is now a formal elective course, open to all students, but especially recommended for sophomores who have participated in the freshman library cadet program. (A selected group of freshmen are invited, on the recommendation of their grade school teachers, to join the library as volunteer workers.) Good citizenship, an interest in libraries and in library materials, a wholesome attitude toward library work, and a desire to learn and grow are important in the selection of the student staff. The opening of the resource centers and the further integration of the audio-visual program into the library program have resulted in a broader program for the student staff, with the opportunity to specialize in an area of particular interest or aptitude.

A weekly story hour for pre-schoolers and primary grade children was begun in 1964-65. At that time, the personnel and facilities of the public library branches were limited and could not provide for this need in the community. Since then, materials and personnel have been added to our local branch libraries, and the story hour at Roosevelt has placed primary emphasis on being a training workshop for speech and home economics students studying child care. The recent addition of closed circuit television with a camera and videotape recorder has expanded the self-evaluation aspect of this program. The story-tellers can now observe themselves as well as the reactions of the children by using videotape.

Each period during the school day, one teacher is assigned to the library to give him a chance to become acquainted with materials related to his subject area, while at the same time monitoring student library activity. On the first four nights of the school week, selected teachers and library staff members work five hours to provide coverage which extends the use of the main library facilities. The opening of the resource centers at Roosevelt and of young people's rooms at the public library branches has reduced the evening use of the school library facilities in 1966-67.

Since 1962-63, Roosevelt has been a participant in the Ford Foundation-supported Oregon Program for the Improvement of Education. A direct result of this project was the addition of a full-time artist-technician to the staff. Visual aids, such as bulletin boards, overlay transparencies, and slide reproductions, are produced for instructional purposes. Materials produced by the graphic arts center are now integrated into the library and are cataloged and filed for easy reference and use by others.

Additional staff, more materials, increased space, and many other factors have brought about changes in the operation and use of the library facilities. Throughout these changes, however, our aim—to meet the standards outlined in *Standards for School Library Programs* —has remained constant.

ADVICE AND ASSISTANCE

Local advisory committee

During the summer of 1965, a local advisory committee was designated to make suggestions to the school, to assist in disseminating information about the program, and to interest citizens of the community in strengthening support for school library programs. The roster of members, plan for meetings, and example of feedback follow:

ROOSEVELT HIGH SCHOOL KNAPP
LIBRARY PROJECT ADVISORY BOARD

Dr. Melvin Barnes, Superintendent, Portland Public Schools

Mr. E. R. Barton, Chairman, Education Committee, Portland Chamber of Commerce

Rev. Joseph P. Browne, C.S.C., Head, Dept. of Library Science, University of Portland

Mr. R. W. deWeese, Board of Directors, Portland Public Schools

Dr. James Ellingson, Director of Special Consultant Services, Oregon State Department of Education

Dr. Norman K. Hamilton, Assistant Superintendent, Portland Public Schools

The Honorable Mark O. Hatfield, Governor of the State of Oregon

Mr. Don W. James, Principal, Roosevelt High School, 6941 N. Central Street, Portland, Oregon

Mrs. Jessie Mae Johnson, Supervisor, Volunteers of America Day Nursery School

Dr. Jerome E. Leavitt, Field Worker, Portland State College, 1965-66

Mrs. Carlyne McCallister, Education Librarian, Portland State College

Miss Mary E. Phillips, Librarian, Multnomah County Library

Miss Frances Postell, Head of School Service Department, Multnomah County Library

Mrs. Forrest E. Rieke, Chairman, Board of Directors, Portland Public Schools

Mrs. Lois Sayles, Librarian, Roosevelt High School

The Honorable Terry D. Schrunk, Mayor of the City of Portland

Dr. Benjamin Simmons, Director of Curriculum and Instructional Media, Oregon State Department of Education

Miss E. Diane Smith, Teacher of English, Roosevelt High School

Mrs. Betty Tice, President, Portland P.T.A.

Mr. A. Kingsley Trenholme, Director of Instructional Materials, Portland Public Schools

Dr. David E. Willis, Dean, School of Education, Portland State College

Dr. Laurence E. Winter, Assistant Superintendent, Portland Public Schools

First meeting

The committee met all day Thursday, September 30, 1965, with introductions and statements given by Mr. James, Mrs. Sayles, and Dr. Leavitt. A guided tour of the school was followed by lunch and an opportunity for committee members to comment on their own observations.

This first experience in conducting a demonstration focused our attention on demonstration techniques and gave us a measure of confidence following our somewhat successful venture. The student body in particular was impressed with the presence of the board on campus. The most important result, however, was the feedback from members. Several stayed after lunch to make helpful suggestions and lend encouragement. Notes and letters arrived the next several days.

Second meeting

Agenda for meeting 9:30 A.M., Wednesday, June 1, 1966:

1. Review of objectives—Mr. James
2. Brochure—Mr. McClure
3. Progress report on library developments—Mrs. Sayles
4. Report on visitations and evaluations—Mr. James
5. College participation—Dr. Leavitt
6. Project evaluation—Dr. Leavitt
7. Advisory board recommendations

Following is an expanded version of the "long-range goals" included in Roosevelt's application for Knapp Project participation. The local advisory board recommended that the list be reduced considerably. Although our faculty-library committee subsequently worked at consolidation, a final draft was never produced. The goals remain too numerous and too specific. However, they all are goals we have attempted to achieve.

GOALS OF THE ROOSEVELT PROJECT

1. To expand facilities, materials collection, and staff in order to provide a full program of high school library services which meet standards recommended in *Standards for School Library Programs* (American Library Association, 1960).

2. To translate into reality the concept that the library is the heart of the high school instructional program.

3. To provide library services which make possible differentiated assignments and individualized instruction.

4. To help students develop self-discipline and skills in independent study.

5. To promote teacher - librarian - student planning.

6. To promote increased student use of, and appreciation for, the entire range of instructional materials.

7. To develop cooperation among teachers and librarians for the teaching of library skills through subject matter.

8. To meet students' needs for instructional materials whether they be academic or personal.

9. To provide a library science course of study which will help students to succeed in high school, college, and the world of work by engaging them in diversified and meaningful library activities.

10. To promote faculty self-improvement through the establishment of a professional library.

11. To provide library in-service experiences for teachers.

12. To promote faculty participation in library planning through an active library committee.

13. To promote teacher use of instructional media through the expanded services of the audio-visual production center.

14. To maintain and increase the school's general enthusiasm for the library through National Library Week activities and other special events.

15. To develop through a planned program of publicity a greater public awareness of the value of good school libraries.

16. To assist the cooperating college and other teacher training institutions in the area to more adequately train prospective teachers in the use of libraries and instructional materials.

17. To demonstrate the impact of a full program of library services in such a way that visitors will be inspired to effect changes in the schools from which they come.

Meeting in December, 1966

When the advisory board met again at the high school on Wednesday, December 14, 1966, they viewed the Project filmstrip, *Three for Tomorrow,* featuring the three Phase III schools, and met Dr. John Picco, the newly designated field worker from Portland State. Progress reports on the Project at Roosevelt were presented, and plans for the conference to be held in the spring of 1967 were reviewed.

Readiness team visit

Under the provisions of the Project, a readiness team tested each demonstration school's capacity to fulfill its function. Upon the advice of Miss Sullivan, Project Director, the following team was invited to visit on one school day, December 10, 1965:

> Miss Virginia H. Mathews, Deputy Director, National Library Week Program, New York
>
> Dr. Irving Lieberman, Director, School of Librarianship, University of Washington
>
> Mrs. Anna M. Beachner, formerly Field Worker, Knapp School Libraries Project, Richland Public Schools, Richland, Washington
>
> Dr. A. C. Hearn, Professor of Education, University of Oregon, Eugene, Oregon
>
> Dr. James Ellingson, Director of Special Consultant Services, State Department of Education, Salem, Oregon
>
> Mr. Malcolm Bauer, Associate Editor, *The Oregonian,* Portland, Oregon

This excellent team, which really put us through our paces, gave us numerous suggestions during the day, and committed themselves in writing with further comments and suggestions.

VISITATION PROGRAM

The suggestions of the readiness team were presented to the full faculty and discussed in some detail. The call for greater teacher involvement was our main concern. Several teachers suggested ways to promote more staff-visitor interaction. These ranged from the suggestion that all faculty members should consistently wear name tags to personal commitments to invite visitors to classroom sessions. Several teachers decided to make a special effort to scan the list of expected visitors and, through some knowledge of persons, places, institutions, and events, find ways to make acquaintances and to stimulate conversation.

Mr. Mike Rumpakis, administrative intern on the National Association of Secondary-School Principals program, was assigned the responsibility for coordinating the classroom visitation part of the demonstration. Visiting teams were to be divided into small groups for short classroom visits scheduled between stops at the library and auxiliary centers.

A corps of student guides was also enlisted to escort small groups from place to place, and

Reports are based on many sources: books, newspapers, recordings, as these students know.

to give visitors more opportunities to quiz Roosevelt students regarding their reaction to the Project. Invariably, visitors extended compliments to the student guides at the end of the tour. Typical letters made reference to the "delightful young people who helped make our visit so pleasant."

Soon after the announcement of Roosevelt's selection in April, 1965, visitors began to arrive almost daily. They came while boxes of new books were still stacked in the corridor and new quarters were yet unfurnished. Finally, the calendar revealed March 7, 1966, the date the first Knapp Project-funded teams would be with us.

Everyone tried very hard to make the day worthwhile for visitors who had come a great distance with high expectations. In the days that followed, we waited for feedback. Most of the comments in letters were encouraging:

> We liked the atmosphere of your school, your fine orientation to the program, the assistance of your guides, and the cooperativeness exhibited by your staff. Might I simply say it was a most memorable day. I hope I can reciprocate some time.

> Our staff is now busy developing plans to put into operation some of the ideas from Roosevelt. I know we have been inspired.

> Never have we been treated more royally nor gained more from a school visit. One of our trustees, whom we brought with us, has had a negative attitude toward school libraries, but after visiting your school, talking with Mrs. Sayles and your students, he is now 100 percent behind our effort to build an outstanding library in our high school.

> Our trip to Portland to visit your outstanding school will be an experience we will long remember. We saw many interesting and worthwhile innovations and I assure you that our school program and our staff will never be quite the same again.

The Project office in Chicago also shared with us the evaluation forms requested of Project-funded teams. These were also encouraging except for the reaction to classroom visitations. The answers to the question, "Which experience would you have eliminated?" fell into two categories:

(1) None—all experiences were worthwhile.
(2) Would eliminate classroom visitations.

Examples of comments from Knapp Project-funded teams are as follows:

> The visitations to the classroom, while interesting, were not particularly critical and this would have given more time for individual investigation through longer periods in the library.

> Felt classroom visits perhaps had more value to the school (to gain teacher interest and use) than to us.

> Our group felt that even though an outstanding teaching job was done . . . we could have spent the time on some other part of the library.

After evaluating these reactions, we reduced the amount of time devoted to classroom visitations for Knapp Project-funded teams and practically eliminated them for all other groups. The only reason we maintained them at all is that we had such strong recommendations regarding the value of classroom visitations from certain members of our local advisory board and readiness team.

It is our conclusion that classroom teaching at Roosevelt looked a great deal like classroom teaching found in the schools represented by the visitors. On the other hand, the library program was far advanced. Visitors seemed to prefer to spend time in the advanced library.

Visitations by large groups

Several rather large groups visited the demonstration center throughout the two-year period. These included college education faculties, groups of student teachers, Public Library Association of Portland, city-wide P.T.A. leaders, Portland Public School's Curriculum Council, other high school faculties, district-wide administrative groups, State Department of Education personnel, Oregon School Study Council, and Pacific Northwest Library Association.

Special services

Numerous requests for special information came from persons who had visited the demonstration center. Other requests came from people who had heard of the Project but had not been able to travel. Examples follow:

> Somehow I neglected to get the brand name of the portable microfilm you are using. Would you give me this information please?

> I would appreciate having a list of the companies you obtained your equipment from.

> I am a graduate student in Library Science [in Pennsylvania] and have been asked to write a term paper and give an oral report on the Knapp School Libraries Project. Since your school participated in Phase III of this remarkable project, I would appreciate some "first hand" information from you.

> This letter is to introduce three of our students. We would greatly appreciate it if these boys could take a few pictures of your library and your old cafeteria study hall.

> It has come to my attention that you have a very successful library science or library aide's course in your high school. Would you be kind enough to share your experiences with us?

Library workshop

The two-day workshop held in cooperation with Portland State College in March, 1967, proved to be one of our most successful large group demonstration situations. The first day of the conference was held on the campus of Portland State College. A further description of the college's responsibilities and participation appears on pages 240ff. The second day, a Saturday, with Roosevelt as the meeting place, teachers and students demonstrated the impact of the library without involving the normal course of classroom events. Obviously all this had to be staged, but it revealed the progress that the Roosevelt faculty had made in rather short time.

Visitor reactions to the Roosevelt demonstrations

During the span of the Roosevelt demonstration, 1,047 of the visitors had provided their names and addresses on 3 by 5 cards. A questionnaire was developed to determine the impact of the Roosevelt demonstration and was mailed to these visitors during the third week of May, 1967. Their cooperation was most gratifying. Five hundred questionnaires were returned within one week. At the time of writing of this report, 710 questionnaires had been received.

The questionnaire which follows has compiled data inserted in the various response areas of Section I and Section II.

ROOSEVELT HIGH SCHOOL
PORTLAND, OREGON
Knapp School Libraries Demonstration Center
VISITOR QUESTIONNAIRE

A Research Project conducted
by Don W. James, Graduate
Student at the University of
Portland

N = 710

YOUR POSITION

20 ☐ School Board
    Member
226 ☐ Administrator
232 ☐ Librarian
70 ☐ Teacher
47 ☐ Student Teacher
100 ☐ Other (See next
    column)

30 College Personnel
16 Special Panel
8 Lay Persons
9 Public Librarians
28 Media Specialists
7 Graduate Students
2 Not Marked

STATE

415 ☐ Oregon
196 ☐ Washington
43 ☐ California
55 ☐ Other _____
1   Not Marked

TYPE OF SCHOOL

290 ☐ Senior
112 ☐ Junior High
67 ☐ Elementary
135 ☐ District-wide
    Responsibility

42 College
64 Not Marked

SIZE OF SCHOOL

6 ☐ Under 100
42 ☐ 100 — 299
254 ☐ 300 — 999
209 ☐ 1,000 — and over

199 Not Marked

FINANCIAL ARRANGEMENT

274 ☐ Visited at own expense
309 ☐ At District expense
94 ☐ Funded by the Knapp Project
10   State Expense
4   University Expense
19   Not Marked

SECTION I

In this section an attempt is made to elicit the effectiveness of the Roosevelt demonstration in providing a positive influence in the direction of the Knapp Project goals.

DIRECTIONS

In the boxes to the right you may indicate your judgments by placing a check mark, according to the captions at the top of the page.

You are to make ratings in answer to the question, "TO WHAT EXTENT DID THE ROOSEVELT LIBRARY DEMONSTRATION HELP VISITORS":

	Of no help	Of only slight help	Of moderate help	Of extensive help	Of very great help	Not Marked
1. Gain a better understanding of the role of the school library?	11	14	129	340	212	4
2. Judge adequacy and effectiveness of a school library program?	9	32	159	356	142	12
3. Plan for establishment and improvement of school library programs?	4	25	152	325	177	27
4. Realize the need for a higher level of support for school library service?	7	17	101	272	302	11

	Of no help	Of only slight help	Of moderate help	Of extensive help	Of very great help	Not Marked
5. Plan to promote curriculum development and innovate teaching through an improved library program?	7	40	161	316	162	24
6. Understand the contributions made by school libraries to classroom instruction?	12	27	145	303	215	8

SECTION II

This section is designed to elicit responses from visitors regarding the impact of the Roosevelt demonstration. Below are listed several features of the program. PLEASE CHECK THE TEN YOU WOULD MOST LIKE TO SEE IN SCHOOL LIBRARIES GENERALLY. Line out all items you feel you could not check because of limited knowledge of the feature in question.

353   1. Physical facilities and organization of main library.
222   2. Librarians' offices and work areas.
306   3. English resource center.
547   4. Independent study center, including carrels, lounge furniture, and display cases.
577   5. Listening and viewing center, including listening posts, projectors and microfilm reader.
434   6. Production center, including services of artist-technician.
480   7. Size and quality of professional staff of librarians.
345   8. Size and quality of library assistant staff.
453   9. Extent and quality of materials collection, print (books, periodicals).
442   10. Extent and quality of materials collection, non-print (filmstrips, recordings, etc.).
225   11. Professional library for teachers.
324   12. Special materials collection for slow learners.
104   13. Paperback book sales.
311   14. Extended hours (evening service).
181   15. Library science course (student library assistant program).
450   16. Faculty participation (teacher-librarian planning, book selection, library committee, in-service).
103   17. Special library activities (story hour, displays, National Library Week).
205   18. The teaching of locational skills through subject matter.
384   19. Independent study and independent study projects.
361   20. General philosophy and atmosphere promoted in all library centers.

SECTION III

(If you are not involved with a particular school, please check here ☐ and skip this section).
This section is designed to give you an opportunity to indicate those improvements in your school's library which have been definitely planned or already accomplished. Check below those improvements which the Roosevelt Demonstration influenced to any extent.
        ✔ one check if improvement definitely planned but not yet achieved.
        ✔✔ two checks if improvement already accomplished.

FACILITIES
_____ Improved library facilities   How? _____ New library
                                               _____ Enlarged library
                                               _____ Remodeled library
_____ Resource Centers
                          How many? _____
                          What subjects? _____
_____ Listening and Viewing Center
_____ Production Center providing services of Artist-Technician
_____ Study carrels
_____ Lounge furniture
_____ Display cases
_____ Microfilm reader
_____ A. V. equipment

PERSONNEL
_____ Professional librarian staff   _____ Librarian added to staff (None previously)
                                          _____ Librarian increased to full time
                                          _____ 2nd or 3rd librarian added
_____ Library assistants added
                          How many? _____

VISITOR QUESTIONNAIRE (Continued)

MATERIALS

_____ Book collection increased
_____ Periodicals increased
_____ Filmstrips increased
_____ Tape Recordings increased
_____ Disc Recordings increased

_____ Micro-films increased
_____ Professional library increased
_____ Special collection for slow learners
_____ Paperback book sales

PROGRAM

_____ Extended hours
_____ Library Science course
_____ General library instruction
_____ Teaching library skills through subject matter
_____ Librarian-Teacher-Pupil planning
_____ Teachers participate in book selection

_____ In-service training of teachers
_____ National Library Week activities
_____ Story Hour
_____ Faculty library committee
_____ Multi-media approach to learning
_____ Independent Study Projects

Please indicate name and address of school.

_____

Name of School   Address

This page will be removed and analyzed separately. No attempt will be made to match with other sections.

Data gathered in Section III of the questionnaire had not yet been compiled at the time of this final report. Even before all data are available, some conclusions can be drawn:

1. *The Roosevelt demonstration provided a very positive influence in the achievement of Knapp Project goals.*

Seventy-eight percent indicated that the demonstration was "of extensive help" or "very great help" in gaining a better understanding of the role of the library. Another 18 percent received "moderate help."

Seventy-one percent indicated that the demonstration was "of extensive help" or "a very great help" in judging adequacy and effectiveness of a school library program. Seventy-one percent indicated that they received "extensive" or "very great help" in planning for establishment and improvement of school library programs. Another 21 percent received "moderate help."

Sixty-seven percent received "extensive" or "very great help" in planning to promote curriculum development and innovating teaching through an improved library program. Twenty-three percent received "moderate" help.

Seventy-three percent received "extensive" or "very great help" in understanding the contributions made by school libraries to classroom instruction. Another 20 percent received "moderate" help.

When the range "moderate" to "very great" is considered, 90 percent or more of the responses fell in this area for each of the six questions.

2. *The Roosevelt independent study center and related areas made the greatest impact upon visitors.*

When visitors were asked to select the ten features of the Roosevelt demonstration they would most like to see in school libraries generally they ranked the top ten as follows: [The compilation of their rankings appears in the questionnaire form shown on page 233.]

Rank	Responses	Library Feature
1	577	Listening and viewing center, including equipment
2	547	Independent study center, including furniture
3	480	Size and quality of professional staff
4	453	Extent and quality of materials collection, print
5	450	Faculty participation
6	442	Extent and quality of materials collection, non-print
7	434	Production center and services
8	384	Independent study concept and projects
9	361	General philosophy
10	353	Main library facilities

Mr. Mike Rumpakis, intern vice-principal, confers with Miss Caroline Koster, audio-visual librarian, in planning a visit.

3. *The impact of the Roosevelt demonstration was felt in the schools from which visitors came.*

Although the data had not been fully tabulated at the time of this report, a superficial inspection reveals that over two-thirds of the 710 respondents checked items listed in Section III of the questionnaire indicating that improvements accomplished or planned could be attributed to some extent to the Roosevelt demonstration.

Public relations

A major charge to the demonstration schools by the Project was the dissemination of information and publicity. It does no good to develop a good demonstration situation if no one knows of its existence.

Several kinds of recognition were given to Roosevelt participation in the Project. These included 63,475 column inches of newspaper copy, numerous public appearances and articles by Roosevelt staff members, and articles written by other persons about the Roosevelt library program.

Problems faced during demonstration period

Personnel turnover. During the time Roosevelt participated in the Project, nine librarians were employed in four positions. Six teacher aides were employed, no more than three of them at one time. Seven library assistants have filled five positions.

The reasons for resignations are the following:

Teach overseas	1
Promotion	2
Graduate study	1
Maternity	1
Health	2
Full-time work not desired	2
Resignation requested	2

The above list seems to offer the usual explanations for turnover. However, these reasons cannot mask the fact that there was considerable difficulty in creating a fully functioning library staff. Whenever we are concerned with matters of personnel inadequacy and staff morale, we are involved with complex situations. The explanation for Roosevelt staffing difficulties can surely be found among the following:

1. Unusually demanding situation.
2. Inadequate college preparation.
3. Lack of experience of head librarian and administrators in supervising greatly expanded library staff.
4. Staff increased too rapidly.
5. Demonstration responsibilities came before library was fully organized.

Materials acquisitions. Teachers became disillusioned when materials ordered did not arrive within a reasonable time. Publishers and jobbers failed to respond to orders on countless occasions, but many materials were held up simply because new librarians lacked skills or were burdened with too many other responsibilities.

Processing. Roosevelt's budget and resulting heavy acquisitions placed a load on the district's centralized processing department that resulted in considerable delay and breakdown of service that further irritated the teaching staff. Processing at Roosevelt also moved too slowly. Teachers who saw materials in a slow-moving assembly line became increasingly critical of library services.

Demonstration responsibilities of teachers. The Roosevelt teaching staff is a good faculty.

There is, however, no pretense that it is vastly superior to other good faculties. Good classroom assignments and meaningful classroom activities will certainly rely heavily upon a sound library program, but teachers are hard put to demonstrate vividly this dependence at the "drop of a hat." The pressures of demonstration were greater than anticipated, and they created strain within the school.

Conversion of quarters. Simply stated, many anxious moments were experienced as the remodeling took place. The persistent question was, "Will the independent study center be completed in time to demonstrate?" Here, too, there were problems of timing and pressure to get ready for visitors.

Administrative load. Funds were provided for new quarters, additional materials, and new library personnel, but no provision was made to assist building administrators with all the many new responsibilities.

Recommendations

The problems listed above dictate their own recommendations, and these are shown specifically as:

1. A school needs two full years to prepare for its responsibilities in demonstration.
2. Staff should be added gradually so that those who have administrative responsibilities can provide adequate in-service orientation and clearly extend the philosophy of the unique program.
3. An administrative assistant should be provided to assume some of the new duties and some of those formerly carried by the principal, so that he is freed for his increased responsibilities.

THE FUTURE AT ROOSEVELT

The Roosevelt library program became such an accepted fact that the cost of the entire staff was included in the 1967-68 district budget. Defeat at the polls, however, affected the Roosevelt library program as it did many other facets of Portland secondary schools. Portland high school principals were informed on July 3, 1967, of the following cuts in the city-wide secondary education program:

1. School district financial support for all athletic programs
2. 50 high school teachers
3. 11 high school vice-principals
4. 42 high school secretaries, teacher aides, and library aides
5. 20 school social workers
6. 20 special and remedial reading teachers
7. All assistant supervisors
8. Approximately 1/6 of school supply funds
9. All NDEA equipment orders
10. Six-sevenths of the library materials budget

All is not lost. The Roosevelt library facilities are well developed, the materials collection exceeds standards, and many of last year's orders are not yet processed. The reduction of staff is the main curtailment. Even in this, Roosevelt faces the coming year with the kind of staff that remains a dream for most secondary schools. The 1967-68 library staff includes the head librarian and two other librarians, a resource center aide, three library assistants, and the artist-technician.

This staff is a very seasoned, experienced, and compatible group. With reduced responsibility for demonstration, they will probably serve the Roosevelt students and faculty better than during the demonstration period. Provision of this staff by the district at a time of sharply reduced budgets shows the sincerity of the district's commitment to maintain and continue to improve the library program after Project participation. In spite of certain financial setbacks, we look forward to the best years of library service in Roosevelt's history. These past two years of participation in the Knapp Project have served as an excellent learning experience.

These visitors see the range of materials, the library program in action, and classroom activity.

Circulation and use of instructional materials

The implementation of newer teaching methods and media, the expansion of facilities, the acquisition of an adequate collection, and the building of an adequate professional staff have created quite a diverse pattern of circulation and use of instructional materials. Circulation statistics based simply on the borrowing and return of materials are no longer meaningful.

A pupil now has longer and more frequent periods of independent study time. He has more time to spend in the central library and learning centers as an individual in addition to scheduled class or group visits. The pupil's assignments require research in greater depth than ever before. His interest and initiative lead him to explore and pursue all types of learning media.

The result has been more intensive use of instructional materials in the instructional materials center under the supervision of teachers assisted by the librarians. The pupil spends a great deal of time browsing, pulling out and putting together information, listening, and viewing. All sorts of learning materials are circulating and being used within the library.

For example, during the two-week period May 1st through 12th, 1966, only 970 nonfiction titles were actually borrowed from the instructional materials center. From May 15th through June 2nd, 1,173 nonfiction titles were borrowed. On the other hand, occasional sampling of nonfiction titles used by students but not checked out indicates that daily use ranges from 427 to 686. If 500 is taken as an average, then, we would have 5,000 *uses* of nonfiction during a two-week period as compared to the approximate 1,000 *loans* of nonfiction during the same period of time.

COLLECTION OF INSTRUCTIONAL MATERIALS

	1964-65	1965-66	1966-67	1967-68
Books	9,727	11,727	30,782	(approx.) 31,500
Magazines	157	160	185	185
Newspapers	5	5	6	6
Pamphlets	Four 3-drawer vertical files	Five 3-drawer vertical files	Same	Same
Films	None	None	None	None
Slides	None	1,125	1,435	N.A.
Filmstrips	131	150	523	N.A.
Recordings	39	446	547	N.A.
Microfilm	None	54 vols.	67 vols.	N.A.
Pictures, prints, etc.	None	2,400	5,110	N.A.

N.A.—Not available.

LIBRARY SERVICES TO PUPILS AND TEACHERS

1964-65	1965-66	1966-67	1967-68
Reading Guidance			
Limited work with reading program	Informally done in library by reference librarian and advanced students	Active participation in all aspects of the program: regular, accelerated, and remedial	Closer cooperation between the faculty and library staff in implementation of program; all facets of reading guidance program expected to continue
Publicity and displays in corridors and central library	General expansion of publicity	Book talks given by librarians to several classes	
Limited reference and research services	General increase in reference and research services	Provision of lists of books for general and specific interest of pupils	
		Closer observation of reading habits and a more systematic approach to relaying important information to persons who may be of help to the student	
Social Guidance			
Up-to-date materials on occupation, personality, conduct of life selected and made available to students	Opportunity to work with students in independent study projects on social behavior and adjustment	Library projects that permit students to plan and work together effectively as a group	Extension of library projects on group work, proper attitude, etc.
		Work with student groups on social points of view, proper attitude, etc.	
Guidance in Listening and Viewing			
Limited number of students served because of lack of space, equipment, and materials	A listening and viewing center organized in the independent study center; students participating in demonstrations and formal tours	The addition of a closed circuit TV facility extending the services of the I.M.C.	Active adult leadership and interest in consistent development and improvement of this service
Reference and Research Services			
Request form, "May We Help You Please" bulletin; some response from floor work	Some opportunity to work with students in independent study and research projects	Expanded services to include research in depth when needed	Continuous expansion
		In-service class in ready reference for staff	

1964-65	1965-66	1966-67	1967-68
		Instruction in the Use of Libraries and Materials	
Library orientation for grade 9	Some expansion of these services	Development of an over-all plan of integrated instruction in the use of materials for grades 9 through 12 in which the areas of knowledge and types of skills to be acquired by the student follow a developmental sequence plan	Planning and initiation of evaluation of method and need
		Test and follow-up	
		Instructional program keyed to various subject areas as well as grade level	
		Systematic inter-relations with public library established	
		Program for Student Assistants	
Limited enrollment	Too many students enrolled	A general reaffirmation of goals and concept of the program	Success hoped for in work with counselors in the selection of students for library science
	Poor selection of students for program	Provision of time for training before new lesson is begun	Librarians assuming more responsibility for teaching and evaluating the student staff
	Too much supervision, not enough teaching of skills and on the job training	A longer block of time in each center a. Preference of work b. Student participation in schedule	
	Not enough working with students	Teach, evaluate, reteach, and do remedial work	
	False assumption that a good student "knows"		
	Lack of library staff and student planning together		
	Lack of goals and general concept of the program		

PARTICIPATION OF PORTLAND STATE COLLEGE

In 1965, as Portland State College entered the Knapp Project, Dr. Jerome E. Leavitt was appointed by the college as the field worker. Early in 1963, Dr. Leavitt had expressed interest in the demonstrations of the Phase I schools and had conferred with the Project Director in Chicago. He was asked by Mr. James to assist with the writing of the Roosevelt High School application.

After selection for Phase III, the field worker initiated procedures for evaluation, invited neighboring colleges and universities to plan visitations, and was instrumental in publicizing the importance of school libraries. As an example, Dr. Leavitt edited the March, 1966, issue of *Education*. Several of the authors of the articles included were associated with the Knapp Project.

During the part of the 1965-66 school year when Dr. Leavitt was officially on leave, his responsibilities were divided among Dr. Vera

Petersen, Mr. Benson Rotstein, and Mrs. Carlyne McCallister. Each had a definite responsibility: Dr. Petersen aided in developing skills of the students conducting the story hours; Mr. Rotstein worked directly with the principal and represented the college at all visitations to the school; Mrs. McCallister served as a consultant to the principal and librarian.

In the spring of the first year, Dr. Leavitt organized a meeting of the Portland State College School of Education faculty at Roosevelt High School. At that meeting, Mr. James and Mrs. Sayles presented the program that had been organized for the visitations.

It should also be noted that students from both day and evening classes at Portland State College visited the demonstration school. Among these were reading methods classes and the student teaching seminars.

At the conclusion of the first year of Project participation, Dr. Leavitt resigned from Port-

The book room, seen in transition, becomes a working part of the library in 1965.

land State College to accept a position at the University of Arizona.

A new field worker was appointed to the Project at the beginning of the second year. Since the continuity was broken at the half-way point with a new field worker who, by background of education and experience, was a specialist in secondary education, some changes as to purpose and direction ensued. The following paragraph, taken from the application submitted by Portland State College to the Knapp Project, may serve as a point of departure for reporting participation:

> Through participation in this project we expect to have a number of long range outcomes, both for the college faculty and students. We hope that by engaging in this project, it will enable PSC to move into *specialized work for elementary and secondary teachers who will have responsibility in organizing and administering school libraries.* We hope, too, that this project will make it possible for all of *our student teachers, particularly those in secondary education, to spend time in this new model developing library.* This would enable them to observe an excellent high school library and to see the benefits to the whole school. They should then be able to encourage a district where they might secure employment to provide such a library. We think this project will be another way of uniting our faculty towards a common goal. The faculty of the Division of Education at Portland State College are committed to a number of tasks, the primary one being to work in the area of curriculum and instruction. In connection with our commitment to the curriculum and instruction, we find the school library is one of the basic necessities. Consequently, the staff supports this project wholeheartedly and hopes it can be used to improve the methods courses for teachers in training, the student teachers for teachers in training, and the college staff as well.

Teacher education programs

Personal contact was made by the field worker with the various teacher education programs in the metropolitan area of Portland with invitations to visit the demonstration library at Roosevelt High School. These schools included the University of Portland, Cascade College, Reed College, Lewis and Clark College, Willamette University, Pacific University, George Fox College, and Marylhurst College. These were institutions maintaining some form of secondary teacher education programs. A number of these schools had programs so specialized in terms of subject matter orientation that a lack of response was predicted.

During the course of the Project, visitations from the above institutions through the Portland State College contacts included twenty-nine student teachers from the University of Portland in two years and four student teachers from the secondary teacher education program at Cascade College. Known visitations from Portland State College accounted for one hundred sixty-two student teachers during the same two-year period. Groups of student teachers visited the demonstration library from the University of Oregon, Oregon State University, the University of Washington, and Washington State University. These visitors came in large organized groups and arranged their visits through the Roosevelt High School administration.

The reaction to the demonstration library by the Supervisor of Secondary Student Teaching of the University of Portland was most favorable; he expects to continue visitations by his student teachers in the future. For the most part, the reactions of the Portland State College supervisors and clinical professors were also favorable, although there was some question as to the learning value of these visitations when elementary as well as secondary student teachers were included in the groups.

The one major concern of supervisors of student teachers is that their already existing student teacher seminar schedule contains more areas of concentration than can now be covered during the regular time allotted for the field exercise of practice teaching. It should be mentioned that the visits of the student teacher seminars were most meaningful when one or more of the seminar members had their field experience at Roosevelt High School. Usually it was the responsibility of the student teacher at Roosevelt to arrange for the seminar members to meet at the demonstration school for lunch and a three-hour seminar.

Portland State field worker

The role of the field worker might be described as concentrating in the following areas during the second year of the Portland State College participation:

1. A re-cultivation of a favorable college-school relationship. In the field worker's final contact with the school teaching staff, the relationship had improved to the point where many favorable comments were directed toward the relationship.

2. Assistance in a reassessment of the roles of the staff of professional librarians in the operation of the multi-centered library. Personnel problems can be stated as the biggest drawback in the total operational picture of the demonstration library throughout the two-year period of Project participation.

3. The initiation of a working relationship between library personnel and the guidance staff at Roosevelt was attempted with some limited success. Both groups felt that a new vista had been opened to assist pupils by providing more extensive occupational information to non-college bound pupils.

The assistance of the School of Education guidance specialist proved to be of great value in motivating the Roosevelt counseling staff toward recognizing the possibilities for utilization of the school library complex for vocational guidance purposes. Hopefully, this liaison can be continued between the Portland State specialist and the two groups at Roosevelt, for it has far-reaching potential toward the finding of solutions to the high school drop-out problem.

Library conference

A two-day conference on the secondary school library in transition was held at the Viking Hall and Roosevelt High School on March 24-25, 1967. Some two hundred and fifty librarians superintendents, principals, college representatives, media specialists, architects, and teachers attended. This group of people interested in the secondary school library came from Oregon, Washington, Idaho, Montana, and California.

The conference was considered a success as a progress report of the Knapp School Libraries Project to the Pacific Northwest. Reactions in conversation and correspondence were most enthusiastic. The report of the conference had been published and copies mailed to all who attended by June 10, 1967. A limited number of copies from the first printing were available for purchase from the School of Education, Portland State College.

The conference was a joint effort on the part of the Project, Roosevelt, and Portland State, and the first day was devoted to nationally recognized speakers who are expert in the field of secondary school libraries. Mrs. Margaret Hayes Grazier of Wayne State University gave the keynote talk, "The High School Library in Transition." Discussion sessions were held on the afternoon of the first day to probe many of the questions which had been asked over the two-year period during visitations at the demonstration library at Roosevelt High School.

The activities of the second day including actual demonstrations of the operation of the library at Roosevelt High School are mentioned in another part of this report (page 231).

EVALUATION

As an introduction, a summary of the evaluative work carried on by Dr. Jerome Leavitt, the Portland State field worker during the first year of the Project at Roosevelt High School, will give some idea of the direction of evaluation at that time.

During the first year, taped recordings were made of three groups at Roosevelt High School:

the teaching staff, the administrative and library staffs, and a random sample of Roosevelt students. The first series of taped interviews of these three groups was made at the beginning of the first year of the Project, and the second series of interviews on tape was made at the end of the first year of Project participation.

The following six questions were asked each

time of the teaching staff group and the administration-library staff group:

1. Do you think the budget for the Roosevelt High School library is adequate?

2. Are the facilities, storage space for materials, study space for students, and work space for faculty adequate?

3. Does the library have the amount and variety of print and non-print material so that students are able to complete assignments given to them by their teachers?

4. What do you think of the training programs for library science students?

5. Do you think for a school of this size, that the library staff is adequately trained and adequate in size?

6. What is your philosophy for the most effective library or resource center for Roosevelt faculty and students?

The following ten questions were asked of the two random samples of Roosevelt students:

1. Were you able to complete your assignments without the help of librarians?

2. Did the librarians come to your class at all to give special instruction?

3. Did teachers or librarians help you most with library skills in the use of the library?

4. Were you able to find materials for your assignments?

5. How would you go about finding materials about manufacturing in Russia?

6. How would you find material to write a report about the life of an author of a book assigned to you by your teacher?

7. What is the name of the system for classifying books at Roosevelt?

8. What are the different kinds of cards in the card catalog?

9. What do you like best about the Roosevelt library?

10. What do you like least about the Roosevelt library?

After a comprehensive review of the taped transcriptions, the following conclusions were made by the second field worker during the early part of the second year of participation in the Project:

1. The students' reactions to the questions defied the drawing of any usable conclusions. It was then decided that other means of measuring impact of the Project on the student group would have to be made on a total student population basis.

2. Many members of the teaching faculty had left Roosevelt for other Portland high schools. It was decided that a third taped interview, using the same questions, would bring forth nothing from which valid conclusions about impact of the Project on the faculty group could be drawn in a subjective review by the field worker.

3. A number of the administrators and librarians were quite frank in their reactions to the questions and the consensus

Students check a channel before settling down to listen.

appeared to be that many of the pressing problems should "work themselves out" during the second year of operation. Again, it was decided that a third interview using the same questions would yield very little toward measuring the impact of the Project on the over-all Roosevelt staff after the second year.

Impact of Project on student groups

The field worker developed a short questionnaire which was administered to the Roosevelt seniors who had been at Roosevelt during the two years of the Project and had been enrolled two years prior to the Project. Mr. Don James, Roosevelt High School principal, administered the questionnaire in 1967 during the final weeks of the spring semester. On page 245 are the questions and the responses of the senior student group.

Analysis of the senior group questionnaire

For the most part, the results followed expectations for this group. It would seem apparent that the group of senior students does not distinguish between the professional librarians and the library assistants.

The tenth question brought forth the problem of library fines. This particular response was probably more heavily weighted since the end of the spring semester was imminent.

The questionnaire on page 246 (revised by Mr. James) was administered to a random group of underclassmen of the Roosevelt student body.

Analysis of the underclassmen questionnaire

This group of underclassmen approximated one-third of the Roosevelt student body. As with the senior student group, the responses were fairly predictable. In revising the student questionnaire for the underclassmen, Mr. James sought to ascertain preferences of materials used in the library. It would appear that little value can be drawn from comparing the materials *used* to the materials *most frequently used* at this time.

Summary of impact on two student groups

Valid or reliable assessment of the impact of the total library program on students is not possible at present. There are those students

Mrs. Lois Sayles, librarian, uses her teaching skills in orienting visitors.

who have been able to benefit by the greater availability of materials, while others have yet to realize fully what the library affords them toward academic achievement. The areas which afforded relaxation and opportunities for browsing where magazines were readily available were widely used by the younger students of Roosevelt. Many comments made to the field worker by these students indicated that these facilities and materials were not available at home and that it was a pleasure to spend school time leisurely going through colorful magazines and to talk with one's friends without great fear of chastisement. There are definite signs that the students are becoming familiar with the various types of materials, their location, and their potential in assisting toward academic achievement. Supervision of a multi-centered library will continue to be a problem until greater self-discipline on the part of students themselves is developed. This development was clearly demonstrated between the beginning and the close of the second year of the Project.

It might be tentatively concluded that a high school student needs a year and a half to become acclimated to both the privileges and responsibilities of the multi-centered library

ROOSEVELT SENIOR STUDENT GROUP QUESTIONNAIRE
(Administered to 202 seniors—Spring, 1967)

1. For what purposes do you use the library?

   Study 111   Research 140   Relaxation 38   Visiting 37   Browsing 46
   Don't use 4

2. Have you used the library differently during your junior and senior years from your first two years at Roosevelt?

   Yes 153   No 49

3. Please state why? Or how?

   More inclined to study 38   Need for research 32
   Have better library skills 31   Unclassified 46   No answer 55

4. Which facilities do you use the most?

   Main library 83   English Resource Center 48   Cafeteria 72
   Independent Study Center 76   Study hall 12

5. Why the preference?

   Materials more handy 90   More comfortable 76   Less supervision 54
   Other 41

6. Which group of people have helped you the most while working in the library centers?

   Librarians 73   Library assistants 78   Teachers 35
   Student assistants 23   None of the above 24

7. In what ways do you think the library has helped you pursue your school work?

   Broader knowledge in general 76   Chance for more self-expression 32
   Greater depth in special areas 54   None at all 47   Other 17

8. As the library has changed during the past two years, to what extent do you find you need to use the library facilities to complete your class assignments?

   Much more 68   A little more 56   About the same as before 48   Less 26
   No answer 4

9. What do you really like about the library as you compare these last two years with your first two years at Roosevelt?

   The three most frequent responses were:

   Increased quantity and variety of materials 92
   Comfort and spaciousness of facilities 66
   Help provided by the various staff members 39

10. What are the biggest drawbacks of the library program at Roosevelt at this time?

    The four most frequent responses were:

    Library fines 40   Not enough materials 37
    Library staff not helpful enough 34   Too much noise 31

11. How has the change toward student independence in the Roosevelt library program influenced you (as you are about to graduate) in the development of **greater self-direction**, greater self-reliance, and a greater willingness to accept responsibility for the person you are becoming in our society?

    Greatly 27   Considerably 59   Some 38   Slightly 27   Not at all 36
    No answer 15

Roosevelt Underclassmen Student Group Questionnaire
(Administered to 689 underclassmen—Spring, 1967)

1. Which of the following library materials have you used this year?

   Books 672   Magazines 617   Filmstrips 198   Tape recordings 162
   Disc recordings 147   Microfilms 89   8mm loop films 45   Slides 102
   Transparencies 189   Pictures 235   Purchased paperbacks 172

2. Which of the above materials have you used most frequently this year?

	Choice: 1	2	3
Books	523	91	20
Magazines	112	367	53
Filmstrips	9	30	52
Tape recordings	5	19	51
Pictures	—	15	82

3. For what purposes do you use the library?

   Study 526   Research 502   Relaxation 224   Visit 159   Browse 169

4. Which facilities do you use the most?

   Main library 396   English Resource Center 189
   Independent Study Center 242   Cafeteria 70   Study hall 61

5. Why the preference?

   More comfortable 255   Materials more handy 354   Less supervision 122
   Other 92

6. Which group of people have helped you the most while working in the library centers?

   Librarians 185   Library assistants 284   Teachers 119
   Student assistants 100   None 11

7. In what ways do you think the library has helped you pursue your school work?

   Broader knowledge in general 266   Greater depth in special areas 242
   Chance for more self-expression 96   None at all 64   Other 75

8. To what extent do you find you need to use the library to complete your class assignments?

   Often 220   Occasionally 308   Seldom 106   Not at all 13

9. What do you like best about the Roosevelt library program?

   Quantity and variety of materials 286
   Ease of locating materals in spacious facilities 119   Help provided by staff 112
   Comfort of facilities 88   Independent study facilities (carrels) 39

10. What do you like least about the Roosevelt library program?

    Supervision too strict and too much noise 136   Staff not helpful enough 80
    Not enough materials and difficult to locate 79   System for library fines 62

with its independent study feature and to learn to make adequate use of the total facility toward relating the various media and materials to his educational program.

Impact of Project as perceived by the teaching staff group

Two questionnaires were prepared to be administered to the teaching faculty of Roosevelt to ascertain immediate reactions to the Knapp Project and the library program after the two years of Project participation. The first short questionnaire was prepared by Mr. James to gain some information regarding professional and personal appraisal of the Project. The five questions and the raw scores derived from the responses follow. It is to be noted that the entire faculty was not available for the first set of reactions, and about two-thirds of the total faculty responded.

INITIAL ROOSEVELT FACULTY QUESTIONNAIRE
(Administered to 59 faculty members)

1. Has your opinion of the helpfulness of the school library changed since the inception of the Knapp Program in April, 1965?

   Yes, in a positive direction 31   Yes, in a negative direction 6
   Remained the same 11   No reaction 11

2. To what extent has the instructional program been enhanced by the expansion of Roosevelt's library program?

   To a very great extent 11   To a considerable extent 20
   To a moderate extent 15   To a limited extent 4   No change 3
   To less extent 1

3. How often do you plan class activities and assignments around library materials?

   Frequently 13   Some 15   Infrequently 12   Never 1
   Not applicable 18

4. What phases of library service have been most helpful to you?

	Choice: 1	2	3
Expanded book collection	13	8	9
Expanded periodical collection	2	4	2
Services of library staff	5	8	4
Expanded audio-visual material collection	13	7	5
Expanded facilities	12	6	12
Independent study	6	4	3

5. Now that we have come to the end of the period during which we received financial support through the Knapp Project, do you feel the district should maintain our:

	Yes	No
Increased materials budget	48	6
Staff of professional librarians	39	14
Staff of library assistants	38	12
Production department including services of artist-technician	54	3

Mrs. Ruthanne Jensen and Miss Scholastica Njoku, teacher aides, start students on a volunteer typing project.

Analysis of the Initial Roosevelt Faculty Questionnaire

It was noted that the teacher group responded much as had been expected. The one outstanding item is the fact that the majority of the teaching faculty of Roosevelt are well aware of the production department which includes the services of the artist-technician. While this element of the total library program had been started before the Knapp Project, this service provided one facility to which nearly all of the faculty members turned when making use of the enlarged library facilities.

The second teacher group questionnaire was designed to probe deeper toward ascertaining impact of the Project on the teacher in the classroom. The five general areas were chosen to evaluate the impact of the Project as seen by the teachers in terms of (1) changes in students, (2) changes in the teachers themselves, (3) the library program at the end of the two-year participation in the Project, (4) a look to the future possibilities of the library program, and (5) some reaction to the Knapp Project itself as related to their school.

Each of these five categories was subdivided into several related questions or statements to which the teacher group was to judge on either a three-point "Yes" scale, or on a three-point "No" scale. A weak "Yes" was to receive a weight of 1 to a strong "Yes" of 3; likewise for the negative responses. No provision was made for a "Not applicable" entry of judgment.

The majority of the faculty responded to the second questionnaire. Signatures were optional. The librarians and the various library assistants were not included in this group.

As a last item for Part I of the Expanded Teacher Group Questionnaire, an open-end statement asking for evidence of negative behavior on the part of the students to the new concept of independent study as a result of the demonstration library brought forth the responses shown below. The list is in order based on frequency of teacher response: (The lowest rated frequency response was five.)

1. Wasted time on the part of non-academically oriented students and too much socializing.
2. Students do not accept personal responsibility for the independent study concept.
3. Excessive truancy on the part of non-academically oriented students.
4. Need for greater teacher supervision of students.
5. General increase of student discipline problems.
6. Loss of library materials.

There were two responses by teachers of a positive observation of student behavior:

1. Students are developing self-initiative in study habits.
2. Freshman students showed improvement during the second year of the program.

Numerous teachers noted that while there was some negative observation concerning student reaction to the independent study concept, it would take time for both students and teachers to become "used to the new climate."

As a last item for Part II of the Expanded Teacher Group Questionnaire, an open-end statement asking for responses of how the library program affected teaching methodology brought forth the following information. The replies were both positive and negative and are listed in order of frequency. (The lowest frequency was five.)

Expanded Teacher Group Questionnaire
(73 faculty members responding)

PART I—CHANGES IN STUDENTS

In general, after these two years of the library program, have you observed:

(a) Any measure of increased self-reliance, self-direction, or independence on the part of students toward their own learning?

	Yes	No	No Answer
Percent	78	18	4
Weighted score	85	26	—

(b) Greater self-initiative toward scholastic achievement?

	Yes	No	No Answer
Percent	64	31	5
Weighted score	78	39	—

(c) More complete fulfillment of your class assignments with the added resource materials?

	Yes	No	No Answer
Percent	73	16	11
Weighted score	99	21	—

(d) Scholastic interest beyond your minimum class requirements because of the added resource materials?

	Yes	No	No Answer
Percent	56	30	14
Weighted score	73	40	—

(e) A school climate that makes it easier for you to teach your subject area(s)?

	Yes	No	No Answer
Percent	60	30	10
Weighted score	82	48	—

(f) That your students regard you more as a resource person than a dispenser of knowledge?

	Yes	No	No Answer
Percent	36	50	14
Weighted score	46	70	—

(g) That your students are aware of a different atmosphere toward learning than they had been used to before?

	Yes	No	No Answer
Percent	70	26	4
Weighted score	92	31	—

PART II—CHANGES IN YOUR OWN APPROACH TO TEACHING

In general, after two years of teaching with this type of auxiliary program to aid instruction, do you consider:

(a) You have made basic changes in your approach to the instruction of your subject area(s)?

	Yes	No	No Answer
Percent	56	37	7
Weighted score	66	40	—

(b) The library program has helped to implement new approaches to your teaching methodology?

	Yes	No	No Answer
Percent	65	28	7
Weighted score	84	33	—

(c) After these two years of trial and error, there is merit to continue the library program as an auxiliary aid to your teaching methodology?

	Yes	No	No Answer
Percent	71	15	14
Weighted score	100	15	—

(d) You have received assistance from this program directly toward improving your teaching techniques?

	Yes	No	No Answer
Percent	68	29	3
Weighted score	105	37	—

(e) There is a more favorable relationship between you and your students toward achievement in your subject area(s)?

	Yes	No	No Answer
Percent	56	29	15
Weighted score	71	35	—

(f) You have more confidence in your teaching ability with the library program support?

	Yes	No	No Answer
Percent	54	39	7
Weighted score	69	50	—

(g) You have become aware of shortcomings in your teaching methodology as the resource materials have become more available through the library program?

	Yes	No	No Answer
Percent	49	48	3
Weighted score	59	66	—

PART III—THE LIBRARY PROGRAM ITSELF

In general, after these two years' experience with the library program, do you consider:

(a) The program has accomplished an optimal level of general operation to justify its continuance as an over-all part of the instructional program?

	Yes	No	No Answer
Percent	81	13	6
Weighted score	105	20	—

(b) The program has now fulfilled its role of assistance to your subject area(s) at the end of this second year?

	Yes	No	No Answer
Percent	41	41	18
Weighted score	47	60	—

(c) That you, as a faculty member, have received adequate professional assistance from the program?

	Yes	No	No Answer
Percent	64	33	3
Weighted score	85	47	—

(d) You have a better working relationship with the library program including library staff members?

	Yes	No	No Answer
Percent	72	18	10
Weighted score	105	25	—

(e) You have increased the scope of your professional competence as a result of the program directly or through the students of library science?

	Yes	No	No Answer
Percent	51	38	11
Weighted score	65	49	—

(f) You have given your professional assistance to the program as best you might as it pertained to your subject area(s)?

	Yes	No	No Answer
Percent	67	22	11
Weighted score	100	24	—

PART IV—THE LIBRARY PROGRAM FOR THE FUTURE AT ROOSEVELT

With the termination of the Knapp Project assistance, the direction of library should:

(a) Retain a status quo to allow for consolidation with the total instructional program.

	Yes	No	No Answer
Percent	72	16	12
Weighted score	110	28	—

(b) Be de-emphasized and some of the resources re-channeled for more teachers and less library staff.

	Yes	No	No Answer
Percent	37	55	8
Weighted score	52	81	—

(c) Be expanded to include further innovations related to teaching methodology (team teaching, additional centers, TV, etc.).

	Yes	No	No Answer
Percent	62	27	11
Weighted score	91	34	—

(d) Include more teacher participation in terms of student supervision, materials acquisition, center jurisdiction—as pertains to subject matter orientation, etc.

	Yes	No	No Answer
Percent	63	21	16
Weighted score	98	22	—

(e) Now be directed toward initial steps for implementing flexible scheduling at Roosevelt. (If the auxiliary support is available, the instructional program changes would be more easily developed.)

	Yes	No	No Answer
Percent	49	39	12
Weighted score	68	57	—

(f) Be directed toward full implementation of the TV facility within Roosevelt.

	Yes	No	No Answer
Percent	62	28	10
Weighted score	84	40	—

PART V—ROOSEVELT'S PARTICIPATION IN THE KNAPP PROJECT

After two years of being in the national limelight with the Knapp Project, do you consider:

(a) That you as a professional educator have benefited from this experience?

	Yes	No	No Answer
Percent	78	18	4
Weighted score	112	23	—

(b) That Roosevelt High School has become a better school in which to teach?

	Yes	No	No Answer
Percent	76	15	9
Weighted score	114	16	—

(c) That the over-all professional gains outweigh any losses from participating in this Project?

	Yes	No	No Answer
Percent	76	13	11
Weighted score	120	15	—

(d) That the over-all professional losses outweigh the gains from participating in the Project?

	Yes	No	No Answer
Percent	8	71	21
Weighted score	9	111	—

(e) That outside assistance should be sought over and above the school district's effort (Knapp, or some other foundation) for the full development of the library concept as you now know it to be?

	Yes	No	No Answer
Percent	60	23	17
Weighted score	81	34	—

(f) That with the termination of the Project you can now return to a normal satisfying teaching experience?

	Yes	No	No Answer
Percent	31	48	21
Weighted score	46	71	—

POSITIVE

1. Found I was relying on the textbook too much.
2. Learned to use library facilities.
3. Learned the extent of materials available in my teaching areas.
4. The lecture method of teaching is not the best when materials and aids are available.
5. Just the idea that the library facilities were available for classroom use is a help.

NEGATIVE

1. The new materials were too slow in arriving to be of help after lesson plans had been developed based on new materials and aids.
2. Slow processing of materials and slow ordering of new materials was discouraging.
3. Lack of new materials in specific teaching areas was a handicap.

There were numerous comments that the library was unable to provide materials in many of the high school subject areas beyond materials already available to teachers.

Several teachers commented that volunteer student aides were ineffective.

As a last item for Part III for the Expanded Teacher Group Questionnaire, an open-end request was made for responses about areas in which the library had not fulfilled the total potential of the library program. These responses are listed in order of frequency with a frequency of five for the lowest rank:

1. Need for greater teacher "say" in acquisitions.
2. Lack in library staff cohesiveness.
3. Need for further expansion to include a math and science resource center.
4. Need to involve more students in the library program—not just those in library science.
5. Need to develop closed circuit TV as part of the total library facility (comment made while the TV facility was being installed).
6. Need to return the professional library to the teachers' lounge.
7. Lack of adequate communication between library staff and teaching staff.
8. Materials still lacking in depth in most teaching areas—stress on specialty subject fields—non-academic.
9. Need for more machines—stress on reading machines.
10. Need for wider range of periodicals—stress on specialty subject fields—non-academic.

As a last item for Part IV of the Expanded Teacher Group Questionnaire, an open-end statement requested responses as to future library emphasis. This brought forth the following ranked observations with five the frequency for the lowest rank.

1. Demand for more competent library staff.
2. Greater attention to occupational information specifically for non-college bound students.
3. Demand for emphasis on greater student self-discipline—library facilities are to be considered a privilege.
4. More individual study carrels and less upholstered furniture.
5. Student library science program must be upgraded to be effective and productive.
6. With the end of the Knapp Project, de-emphasize "show" aspect of the library.
7. Emphasize expanded library concept toward general school program of flexible scheduling.

As the last item of Part V of the Expanded Teacher Group Questionnaire, an open-end statement regarding the participation of Roosevelt High School in the Knapp Project brought forth the following top ranked observations:

POSITIVE

1. General appreciation for new facilities, equipment, and materials.
2. Two years have merely "scratched the surface" of this new concept of resource centers and independent study.
3. Too much is now invested to drop the concept; definite need to continue even without outside assistance.

NEGATIVE

1. Entirely too much "fanfare" and "big noise" for benefits derived.
2. The Project took too much emphasis away from traditional school programs and activities at Roosevelt.
3. In such a Project, it is too much to ask teachers to motivate high school students in this type of involvement in a less than average socio-economic attendance area as Roosevelt.

Analysis of the Expanded Teacher Group Questionnaire

One factor in compiling the data from the second teacher questionnaire was that no provision was made for a teacher respondent to judge a question or statement with a "Not applicable" rating. This rating was intentionally not used to prevent the group from being noncommittal. It was successful only to a limited extent. The result was that there was a higher-than-expected "No answer" percentage in the tabulation of the responses.

The use of the three-point scale for both the "Yes" responses and the "No" responses brought forth a much clearer picture of the total response to each of the items through the use of the weighting factor in reporting a weighted score for each item.

Summary and conclusions—impact of the Project on the teaching staff

The teacher group during the second year of participation in the Project has begun to accept the new concept much more than during the first year. There have been many comments made to the field worker that, if there had not been so much tension and the feeling of "being on parade" with the several visitations, the program would receive greater acceptance from the faculty.

It has been most apparent that the teacher group views the library program on a very personal, professional basis. The various criticisms reflect individual involvement with the library program as it pertains to the specific teaching assignment of the teacher.

It must be recognized that there are segments of the faculty in the specialized departmentalized high school instructional program who have not yet found ways and means of utilizing the expanded library facilities. More efficient communication must be established if all members of the faculty are to become involved in some way with the new concept of the library as the instructional materials center.

In terms of the Project's actual impact on the teaching staff, it is most apparent that the teachers believe themselves more ready now to receive visitors and are in a better position to exchange ideas on means they have developed for using the expanded facilities, materials, and media. They comment that only now, after the second year of participation, they have de-

Mrs. Margaret Hayes Grazier talks to a small group at the March, 1967, conference.

veloped through trial and error the necessary understandings in using some of the newer and less widely accepted ways of instruction making use of the multi-media approach.

Almost half of the teacher group are still most apprehensive of the independent study feature of the library for high school students. It has been stated that the wasted time and the need for more strict supervision of students offset much of the beneficial aspect of the overall program. While the group makes such a statement, they add that more time is needed not only for themselves to become more comfortable with the total program, but also for high school students to learn to take a greater responsibility for their own learning through the independent study concept.

While the teacher group is well aware of library personnel problems and the need for greater cohesiveness within the professional librarian staff, the large majority are most complimentary toward Mrs. Sayles, the head librarian.

There is an almost even distribution within the teacher group as to the merits of the library science program for high school students. There are those who question the necessary time and effort which go into this particular program for such a small proportion of the total enrollment. They also question the use of less capable students as student assistants. There are those, however, who feel that student participation in the staffing of the library has been beneficial in relating this activity toward greater interest and understanding of the high school program for many students. This appears to be most evident for those students who apparently come from homes where print and non-print materials are not well known and understood.

After two years of further development of the library program at Roosevelt, one conclusion is most apparent. When and where a teacher has found, or has been shown, how the library with its expanded facilities has assisted him toward making the learning process easier or more efficient, regardless of teaching assignment, that teacher is most open in his support of the continuation of the program. At the end of the second year, this attitude is more clearly noted in the academic fields of the high school educational program. If future emphasis of the library program includes the total secondary program, the concept of the instructional materials center will be assured at Roosevelt High School with full support from the teaching faculty.

Report from
FARRER JUNIOR HIGH SCHOOL
and
BRIGHAM YOUNG UNIVERSITY

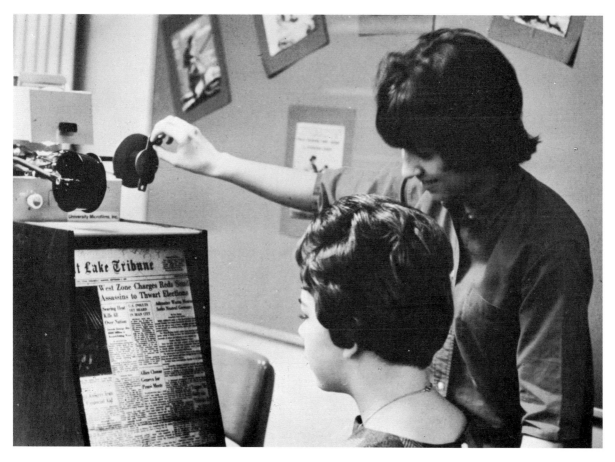

FACT SHEET—FARRER JUNIOR HIGH SCHOOL

The Farrer Junior High School is one of three secondary schools in the university town of Provo, Utah, which is located in the heart of the industrial-agricultural Utah Valley. Farrer is a relatively small school with an enrollment of approximately 800. Dr. Sherman W. Wing, superintendent, is dedicated to continuing a policy which has provided all the schools (nine elementary and three secondary) in the Provo City School District with centralized libraries and full-time librarians.

The Knapp School Libraries Project has provided funds to the Farrer Junior High School for the alteration of facilities, the salary of another full-time librarian, the salary of an instructional assistant, and the acquisition of additional materials. These additions to the library provide more extensive services for students and teachers. Mrs. Jane N. Vance, the head librarian, has been a leader in school librarianship in the state of Utah. Under the direction of Mrs. Vance and Mr. G. Gardner Snow, principal and liaison worker for the

Project, a library program has been developed and expanded so that it is used extensively by Farrer teachers in all curriculum areas. A workshop for Farrer faculty members in the summer of 1965, under the sponsorship of the Knapp Project and with the cooperation of Brigham Young University, encouraged the further utilization of instructional materials by teachers in the school.

The Brigham Young University has selected Dr. W. Dwayne Belt, Associate Professor of Secondary Education and former principal of the University's Laboratory School, as the field worker. The Provo City School District and the Brigham Young University, one of the largest teacher education institutions in the United States, have cooperated in many projects. The Provo schools have also served as training centers for many of the University's student teachers. This pattern of cooperation will enhance the contributions of the Knapp School Libraries Project.

STATISTICS

From its Project application, November, 1964

Enrollment: 785 students, grades seven through nine.

Materials collection: 6,700 books, 50 periodicals, 40 filmstrips, 91 disc recordings, 37 tape recordings, 21 drawers of vertical file materials, 55 professional books for faculty, 13 professional periodicals.

Library personnel: One full-time librarian.

As of June, 1967

Enrollment: 786 students, grades seven through nine.

Materials collection: 8,734 books, 83 periodicals, 875 filmstrips, 400 disc recordings, 40 tape recordings, 60 sets of transparencies, 18 loop films (8mm), 590 pictures, 208 subject headings in pamphlet file plus 84 subject headings in Utah pamphlet file.

Library personnel: Two full-time librarians, one full-time instructional clerk.

PERSONNEL MOST DIRECTLY CONCERNED WITH THE PROJECT

From Farrer Junior High School

 Mr. G. Gardner Snow, Principal

 Mrs. Mary S. Hales, Librarian

 Mrs. Jane N. Vance, Librarian

 Mrs. Louise Wakefield, Instructional Clerk

From Provo City School District

 Dr. Sherman W. Wing, Superintendent

 Mr. Ross B. Denham, Assistant Superintendent for Instruction

 Mr. Ray D. Warner, Curriculum Director

From Brigham Young University

 Dr. Stephen L. Alley, Chairman, Department of Teacher Education

 Dr. W. Dwayne Belt, Associate Professor of Secondary Education and field worker, Knapp School Libraries Project

INTRODUCTION

As outlined in the handbook for Project schools, the objectives of the Knapp School Libraries Project are:

1. To demonstrate the educational value of school library programs, services, and resources which fully meet the national standards for school libraries.

2. To promote improved understanding and use of library resources on the part of teachers and administrators, by relating the demonstration situations to teacher education programs in nearby colleges.

3. To guide and encourage educators and citizens from as many communities as possible, in the development of their own library programs through planned activities enabling them to study the demonstration situations.

4. To increase interest and support for school library development, among educators and citizens generally, by disseminating information about the demonstration programs and evaluating their effectiveness in reaching the stated goals.

In all phases of the Project, we have attempted to meet the requirements of each of the four objectives separately and collectively, our belief being that the objectives themselves are not isolated, and the Project is to be treated as an integrated whole. However, for the purposes of this report, certain designations will be made and areas will be spelled out with particular reference to each of the four objectives.

The status of Farrer Junior High School at the time of the original application should be noted. Information permitting comparison of the collection, personnel, and program is included in the fact sheet on page 257.

In the fall of 1963, students and teachers moved into a 43,000-square-foot addition to the Farrer building which included a central library facility. A floor plan for this addition and also the changes in the physical plant as a result of participation in the Knapp School Libraries Project are shown on page 262.

Personnel

For the 1965-66 school year, Mrs. Mary S. Hales was hired as an instructional clerk and Mrs. Cleone Boshard was transferred to the Farrer Junior High School from Dixon Junior High School. For the 1966-67 school year, Mrs. Boshard was transferred from Farrer Junior High School to Provo High School. Mrs. Hales had obtained proper certification and was employed as the assistant librarian at Farrer. Mrs. Evelyn Barton was employed as instructional clerk. In November of 1967, Mrs. Louise Wakefield was employed as an instructional clerk. Also in November, Mrs. Barton was placed on a part-time status and was released in February, 1967.

PROGRAM AND EVALUATION

Following acquisition of Project funds in June, 1965, physical changes within the school plant and the ordering of materials were begun. A two-week workshop was scheduled in August, 1965, to permit members of the instructional staff to learn more about materials available to the library. The workshop was conducted for fifteen teachers of the Farrer Junior High school faculty for a two-week period, eight hours per day, five days a week. The objective of the workshop was to help to identify the materials and resources available for the use of the various academic departments within the school.

Also emphasized were techniques for the utilization of these resources. Mrs. Hattie M. Knight, chairman of the Department of Library Science, and Dr. W. Dwayne Belt, Knapp Project field worker, arranged and directed this workshop as representatives of the Brigham Young University faculty.

The increase in the amount of instructional material available for students and teachers is indicated in the figures included in the fact sheet for the spring of 1967.

Two studies were planned and carried out by graduate students at Brigham Young Uni-

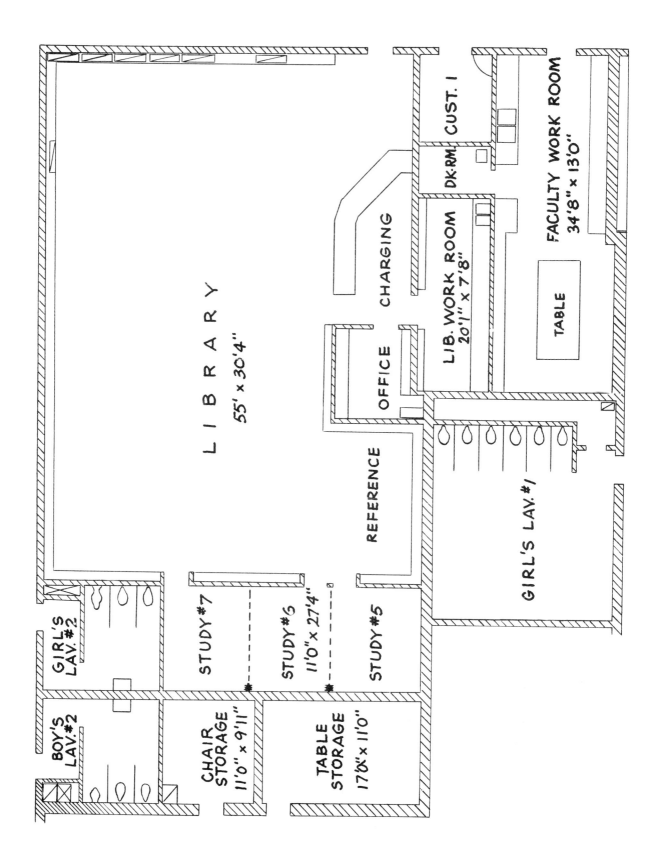

LIBRARY
55' x 30'4"

CHARGING

OFFICE

REFERENCE

LIB. WORK ROOM
20'1" x 7'8"

DK·RM. CUST. I

FACULTY WORK ROOM
34'8" x 13'0"

TABLE

GIRL'S LAV. #1

GIRL'S LAV. #2

BOY'S LAV. #2

STUDY #7

STUDY #6
11'0" x 27'4"

STUDY #5

CHAIR STORAGE
11'0" x 9'11"

TABLE STORAGE
17'0" x 11'0"

versity with reference to Farrer Junior High School's participation in the Knapp Project. One, by Mr. Stephen R. Myers, was *The Influence of Library Usage upon the Academic Achievement of Selected Eighth Grade Students at Farrer Junior High School in the Provo School District*. This was a field project submitted to the Graduate Department of Education at BYU in partial fulfillment of the requirements of the degree of Master of Education. Over a period of twenty-one weeks, 45 eighth grade students in two home rooms selected at random at Farrer were asked to record and hand in to their home room teachers a tally of their use of the school library and to note the kinds of activities in which they engaged while in the library. Mr. Myers's hypothesis was that the influence of library usage on the academic achievements of selected eighth grade students would not be statistically significant. His purpose was to obtain answers to these questions:

1. Do the students who utilize the library extensively receive high academic achievement scores?
2. Do the students who do not utilize the library extensively receive lower academic achievement scores?
3. How much time do the students spend in selected activities while in the library?
4. Which classes of students are the most frequent users of the library?

The measure of academic achievement was the standardized Iowa Test of Basic Skills, Form Three. This test was administered following a delay of three months of summer vacation at the conclusion of the twenty-one weeks of tallying of activities. Although no correlation between achievement scores and total library time was statistically significant, there was a higher correlation between arithmetic achievement and the total library time than between any of the other achievement areas and the total library time.

Fifteen students who accumulated the most time in the library were compared as a group with fifteen students who accumulated the least time in the library. The mean library time in minutes over the twenty-one-week period for these "high users" was 1,978; for

Mrs. Cleone Boshard, librarian, works with Mrs. Evelyn Barton, instructional clerk, organizing the filmstrip collection.

the "low users," it was 885. Although the high users had accumulated more than twice as much library time as the low users, the difference (5.133) in the mean achievement score of the high users (56.333) and the low users (51.200) was not significant.

The following two tables show the amount of time spent in the library by all forty-five students in the selected sample of eighth graders at Farrer Junior High School as a result of teacher assignment and the amount of time spent in the library as a result of free choice.

TIME SPENT IN THE LIBRARY
(Teacher Assignment)

Activity	Library Time in Minutes	Percentage of Total Time
Browsing	1,970	4.0
Book selection	2,480	5.0
Searching for reference	9,970	20.4
Recreational reading	1,515	3.1
Library instruction	27,550	56.4
Writing reports	4,565	9.3
Viewing films and filmstrips	780	1.5
Listening to records and tapes	0	0
Totals	48,830	99.7*

*Does not equal 100 percent because of rounding off.

TIME SPENT IN THE LIBRARY

(Free Choice)

Activity	Library Time in Minutes	Percentage of Total Time
Browsing	5,165	35.5
Book selection	1,800	12.3
Searching for reference....	1,685	11.5
Recreational reading	1,870	12.8
Library instruction	1,585	10.9
Writing reports	2,310	15.8
Viewing films and filmstrips	120	.8
Listening to records and tapes	0	0
Totals	14,535	99.6*

*Does not equal 100 percent because of rounding off.

As might have been predicted, English classes in which these students were enrolled made the largest number of visits to the library, with U.S. History classes making the second largest number of visits. Again predictably, typing classes made the least number of visits (only one), but the next lowest number of visits (3) was made by remedial reading classes.

Mr. Myers concluded his project with this statement:

The findings. Statistical analysis of the compiled data resulted in the following findings:

1. The influence of library usage on the academic achievement of selected eighth grade students at the Farrer Junior High School was not statistically significant.
2. Of the eight selected library activities recorded in this study, library instruction correlated higher with the composite achievement scores of the selected samples than did any other activity. The coefficient of correlation was .23. Had this coefficient of correlation been .29, it would have been statistically significant at the .05 level of confidence.
3. There was not a significant difference between the mean achievement score of those fifteen students who accumulated the greatest amount of library time and the mean achievement score of those fifteen students who accumulated the least amount of library time.
4. While in the library under teacher assignment, the selected sample spent 56.4 percent of the total library time in library instruction. This was the highest percentage recorded. The second highest percentage listed was in the category of searching for references with 20.4 percent. The least-used categories were listening to records and tapes with no time recorded and viewing films and filmstrips with 1.5 percent of the total time recorded. A complete percentage listing of all categories may be found in Chapter III of this study. [Reference is to Mr. Myers's field project.]
5. The selected sample, utilizing the library on its own time, spent 35.5 percent of its time browsing and 15.8 percent writing reports. The least-used categories were listening to records and tapes with no time recorded, and viewing films and filmstrips with .8 percent of the total time recorded.
6. The English classes included in this study proved to be the most frequent users of the library services. These accounted for 79.3 percent of the total recorded visits by all classes included in the study. The next highest percentage was recorded by the U.S. History classes with 10.1. It was found that the typing classes accounted for only .1 percent and the remedial reading classes listed only .4 percent of the total recorded visits.

Mrs. Jane Vance, librarian, helps an English teacher select a filmstrip.

Conclusions

The findings of this study have resulted in the following conclusions:

1. Although not statistically signficant, it may be concluded that library activities had some influence on the academic achievement of the forty-five selected eighth grade students who were studied at the Farrer Junior High School.

2. The teaching of library skills may be a valuable tool in contributing to academic achievement.

3. Students seem to engage in more worthwhile activities when using the library services under teacher assignment than when using the library services by free choice.

4. The teachers of the English and U.S. History classes included in this study seem to place more emphasis on library use than do the teachers of the other classes.

Recommendations

As a result of this study, the following recommendations were made:

1. Future research may profitably be done in the area of the influence of library usage on academic achievement under more rigid research conditions. A study wherein the students in the experimental sample are homogeneously grouped [according] to their IQ, age, sex, teacher grades, etc., and are compared to a control group of equal characteristics may reveal some important data.

2. A future study involving the recording of the amount of time spent at home using library materials, as well as the amount of time spent at school using library materials, would perhaps give additional information on the actual influence of library services on academic achievement.

3. Since library instruction had some effect on the academic achievement of the students in this study, it is recommended that the teachers of Farrer Junior High School place more emphasis on the teaching of library skills.

4. Research might be conducted at the Farrer Junior High School concerning the reasons why certain classes—such as Spanish, remedial reading, and others—do not utilize the library services to a greater extent.

5. A more complete picture concerning the effects of library usage on academic achievement might be obtained through a similar study involving a larger sample and a longer period of time.

A copy of Mr. Myers's study has been placed in the Headquarters Library of the American Library Association where it is available for loan.

Study of reading comprehension

The second study conducted at Brigham Young University and related to the Knapp Project is one by Mrs. Lucile M. Thorne in a dissertation submitted to the Graduate Department of Education in August, 1967, in partial fulfillment of the requirements for the degree, Doctor of Education. The title of this dissertation is *The Influence of the Knapp School Libraries Project on the Reading Comprehension and on the Knowledge of Library Skills of the Pupils at the Farrer Junior High School, Provo, Utah.* Chapter V of that dissertation, entitled "Summary, Conclusions, and Recommendations," is included here. This dissertation is also available from the Headquarters Library of the American Library Association.

I. SUMMARY

Librarians and educators have assumed that an active school library contributes to the academic achievements of the pupils it serves; however, few statistical studies have examined this relationship. Farrer Junior High School, Provo, Utah, was selected as a demonstration center for the Knapp School Libraries Project which provided an opportunity to test the influence of augmented school library services on pupil achievement. Through the funds from the Project, the Farrer Junior High School library was augmented to meet the standards set by the American Association of School Librarians in their book, *Standards for School Library Programs.* Dixon Junior High School, Provo, Utah, took part in the study as the control school.

Problem

The major purpose of the study was threefold: (1) to determine the influence of augmented school library services as they related to the reading comprehension of the pupils; (2) to determine the influence of augmented library services on the acquisition of the knowledge of library skills of the pupils; (3) to determine if there was any significant difference between the boys and the girls as related to the growth of reading comprehension and to the acquisition of knowledge of library skills.

Relative to the stated purposes of the study, an attempt was made to test the following hypotheses:

1. That there was no significant difference in the growth of reading comprehension of the pupils at the experimental school with augmented library services and the pupils at the control school.

2. That there was no significant difference in the acquisition of knowledge of library skills of the pupils at the experimental school and those at the control school.

3. That there was no significant difference in the boys and in the girls in the growth of reading comprehension or in the acquisition of knowledge of library skills.

Procedures

A total of six hundred and forty pupils of the seventh and eighth grades at both schools during the school year 1965-66 were included in this two-year longitudinal study. The statistical analysis required equal size groups, and random sampling was used to gain this number.

The pupils of the school district were given the Iowa Tests of Basic Skills at the end of the sixth grade and again at the beginning of the eighth grade. The scores for the reading comprehension subtest and the IQ scores of the pupils taken from the Otis Quick-Scoring Mental Ability Test given all pupils in the district in seventh grade were obtained from the school records for use in

Mrs. Hattie Knight, center, brought many materials for teachers to examine during the 1965 summer workshop.

the study. The Iowa Tests of Basic Skills, reading comprehension subtest, Form 3, was used as a post-test for the ninth-grade pupils in the spring of 1967 to complete the data. The Peabody Library Information Test was given to half of the participating pupils and the Gaver Library Skills Test to the other half. Both were repeated a year later. These raw scores, with those from the reading comprehension tests and with the IQ scores of the pupils, were used as the basis for the statistical analysis of achievement. All were data processed for use in the computer. Analysis of covariance was used as the statistical procedure for analyzing the post-test scores, and the covariates of IQ and pre-test scores were run singly and simultaneously. F ratio was used to determine significant differences.

Findings

Statistical analysis of the compiled data disclosed the following findings:

1. The differences in the growth of reading comprehension for the junior high school pupils of this study, as measured by the Iowa Tests of Basic Skills, were significant at the .005 and at the .01 levels in favor of the experimental school.

3. In the growth of reading comprehension, there were differences between the boys and the girls significant at the .0005 and at the .01 levels in favor of the boys. In the acquisition of knowledge of library skills, there were differences significant at the .0005, at the .005, and at the .01 levels, all in favor of the girls.

Using several media with third graders, Mrs. Carol Jaynes, visiting elementary teacher, demonstrates the teaching of mathematics at the 1967 conference.

II. CONCLUSION

In view of the basic findings of this study, the conclusion is made that augmented library services were influential in promoting the growth of reading comprehension and in the acquisition of knowledge of library skills.

III. RECOMMENDATIONS

In consideration of the findings and the conclusions of this study, the following recommendations for further research are made.

1. Further research might be done on the same groups from the experimental school to find if the gains indicated in this study carried over into high school.

2. Further research on the influence of knowledge and use of library skills in relation to the academic achievement of pupils would be valuable.

3. A study might be made concerning the influence of the Knapp School Libraries Project on the attitude of the teachers toward the use of the library.

4. Standardized tests of high validity and reliability need to be developed for measuring the pupils' knowledge of library skills on the junior high school level.

In consideration of the findings and conclusions of this study, the following recommendations are made for the improvement of library services in the schools.

1. It is recommended that efforts be made by school administrators to improve their school library services to meet the standards set by the American Association of School Librarians in the handbook, *Standards for School Library Programs*.

2. Since the knowledge of library skills had a positive effect on the academic achievement of the pupils in the study, greater emphasis should be placed on instruction in the use of the library.

3. It is recommended that the instruction in the use of the library be integrated with classroom assignments in the various subject fields in order that the library skills developed will be retained by the pupils.

With reference to Farrer Junior High School and its effect on school library development throughout the surrounding area, this statement, prepared by Mr. G. Gardner Snow as principal of the school, summarizes his view of progress:

In terms of our long-range goals, I should like to report the following items: The last two sessions of the Utah State Legislature have made significant appropriations that were earmarked for school library use. In the 1965 session, $750,000 was appropriated and in the 1967 session $500,000 was appropriated. These appropriations have made it possible to add a full-time library specialist to the staff of the Utah Department of Public Instruction, Miss Elsie Dee Adams. Each school library in the State has been given money, through the use of the equalization formula, to increase collections, to provide for some staffing, and to permit school districts to operate school libraries. Inasmuch as the bulk of visitors came from throughout the State of Utah, we may assume, I suppose, that we have had some effect upon what has been done. It is interesting to note that when the state formed a committee to help to develop the new standards for cataloging the "non-book" materials, it consisted of all Provo librarians. Within the Provo School District, we have had some effect. At the present time, there are ten elementary schools, two junior high schools, and one high school in the Provo School District. We have had full-time librarians in all of the schools for some time, but we have added at least one half-time person in each of these schools. These people have had some library science training and some practical experience in library services. Both teachers and students are library conscious and are asking for increasing service from the school libraries. For the first time, this past summer, some of the elementary libraries were open to students on a regular basis. For a number of months, the school libraries have been scheduling an evening or two a week when both parents and children can come to the library to study or browse. Collections have been bolstered through the wise use of Elementary and Secondary Education Act Title II monies as well as appropriations from the special funds noted above from the state legislature. It also has been our opportunity to host the total administra-

tive group from a number of Utah school districts. In all cases, we have received comment that the things that we were trying to do would work for them and that they would be implemented in their own districts. I would not be in a position to indicate just how much of this has been done, but we do still hear very positive comments. It would only be fair to indicate that much of this is the result of the excellent field work that was done in all areas of the state by Miss Adams and Dr. Lindeman of the staff of the Utah Department of Public Instruction.

TEACHER EDUCATION AND DEMONSTRATION

The Teacher Education Department of Brigham Young University submitted the part of the application which related to the co-applying institution. The approximately 1,200 certified teachers graduated from Brigham Young University each year could serve as a rich source for the dissemination of information about library programs. Dr. W. Dwayne Belt, field worker for the Knapp School Libraries Project, has made presentations relative to the Project to fifteen classes of prospective teachers, administrators, and librarians at the University during the past two years.

Three hundred twenty-six prospective teachers have visited the Farrer Junior High School Library since February of 1966. These students came from Brigham Young University, The University of Utah, Utah State University, and Weber State College, all in the state of Utah. During this same period, twenty-five students have been assigned to do their student teaching at the Farrer Junior High School. These student teachers have received orientation to the library facilities and its resources. In addition to the pre-service program for teachers, the First Intermountain Conference on Young Adult Literature, held at The University of Utah during the summer of 1966, and teachers from Elko County, Nevada, in the Elementary and Secondary Education Act Workshop spent some time at the Farrer Junior High School and discussed library resources and their utilization. During the week of June 10, 1966, the Utah Department of Public Instruction, Division of Instructional Media, sponsored a

special workshop at Brigham Young University dealing with instructional materials. As part of the workshop activity, this group visited the Farrer library.

Visits

During the sixteen month period from February, 1966, to June, 1967, there have been 1,389 visitors to the Farrer Junior High School. Teams from thirteen states were granted Knapp Project funds to pay expenses to visit the school. Other teams paid their own expenses to visit Farrer.

A typical visitor's day at Farrer Junior High School consisted of an orientation to the Knapp School Libraries Project and the Farrer Junior High School through the use of a slide-

Displays welcome the Provo representatives to Oak Park in May, 1965. Left to right: Mrs. Jane Vance, librarian, Mr. G. Gardner Snow, principal, and Dr. W. Dwayne Belt, field worker.

This home economics teacher demonstrates with fabrics and books during the 1967 multi-media conference.

sound story. This was followed by a tour of the physical facilities in the library area. An opportunity was given to visitors to meet the library staff and to ask questions. Following the conducted tour, visitors were welcome either to stay in the library or to go to classrooms to see teaching situations related to library usage. Visitors were asked to stay at Farrer for lunch in order that they might talk with members of the instructional staff to get their reactions about the improved program in library service. Following the lunch period, visitors were given a brief period of free time and then were scheduled to meet with members of the library staff, usually Mrs. Jane Vance, head librarian, in a question and answer period for approximately one hour. All visits were conducted by Dr. W. Dwayne Belt. Where special requests were made, arrangements were made with a number of feeder elementary schools and Provo High School to permit those people particularly interested in a district library operation to see an elementary school and, in some instances, a high school program in library service. In addition to this,

visits were also made to the campus of Brigham Young University, particularly to the J. Reuben Clark Library. Groups of visitors were directed to a district media center located in the Nebo School District in Salem, immediately south of Provo, when interest was expressed in this operation.

The visitors were given reaction slips, to get their reactions to the visit and to help us plan subsequent demonstrations. The generally favorable reactions received by the school frequently pointed up the part of the visit considered most helpful in statements like the following:

> It was good to see librarians so active with boys and girls; that they had sufficient time for such activities serving as librarians instead of clerks.

> The most helpful part of the visit was getting a broader vision of how the library can serve as a sort of "extra classroom" in helping students with educational experience.

> The most helpful part was seeing the librarians scheduling their library and the flexible plan they were using, the method they had of cataloging the filmstrips, and the ideas of correlating subject material.

Conferences

On January 27-28, 1967, a special regional conference dealing with "A Multi-Media Approach to Learning" was held on the campus

There was time for conversation as well as demonstrations during the multi-media conference.

of Brigham Young University in cooperative sponsorship with the Knapp Project and the Provo City Schools. Some 300 teachers, librarians, administrators, university personnel, state department of education personnel, and interested citizens attended this conference from the states of Arizona, California, Colorado, Idaho, Utah, New Mexico, Nevada, and Wyoming. National leaders in the fields of library service and instructional materials spoke during the conference. Demonstrations were presented by teachers and by librarians who were effectively using instructional materials in their classrooms in the Alpine, the Nebo, and the Provo School Districts. A complete report of the planning of this conference may be found in the Summer, 1967, issue of *School Libraries.* The proceedings have been distributed by the Knapp Project in a brochure entitled "A Multi-Media Approach to Learning." Included are shortened versions of the talks prepared by Dr. W. Dwayne Belt, Miss Carolyn Whitenack of Purdue University and member of the Project Advisory Committee, Dr. Carolyn Guss of Indiana University, and Dr. James W. Brown of San Jose State College.

Public relations

In attempting to meet the specifications for the fourth objective of the Knapp School Libraries Project — increasing interest and support for school library development — the Farrer Junior High School and the Teacher Education Department at Brigham Young University have engaged in many activities.

During the sixteen-month period the Farrer Junior High School has participated in the Knapp School Libraries Project, a number of articles have appeared in the three newspapers that serve the Provo area. The *Provo Daily Herald, The Deseret News,* and the *Salt Lake Tribune* have all given fine coverage to the progress of the Project at Farrer Junior High School.

In addition to the newspaper coverage, we have had good coverage on local television and radio stations. In the spring of 1966, Dr. W. Dwayne Belt, Mrs. Jane N. Vance, and Mr. G. Gardner Snow had an opportunity to appear on the one-hour program entitled "Perspec-

This visitor gets close to work being done by students in the library.

tive" on the local radio station KEYY. In addition to this, opportunities have been given to members of the library and the administrative staffs of the Farrer Junior High School to appear on television stations KCPX and KBYU. We have had a number of news items also on all of the television channels which serve Utah and the surrounding area.

Another activity which has been used to acquaint local community leaders with the participation of Farrer Junior High School in the Knapp School Libraries Project has been the Business-Industry-Education Day sponsored by the Provo City Chamber of Commerce. This activity has permitted us to invite many local community leaders to spend time at the school to see what a full program of library service does to help provide students with a stronger educational experience. In addition to this activity, local civic and social clubs have invited members of the library staff at Farrer Junior High School and members of the faculty from Brigham Young University to make presentations about the Project. Also, we have had a number of social clubs that have had an opportunity to see the Project-sponsored filmstrip, *Three For Tomorrow,* and the motion picture, . . . *And Something More.* Many of these contacts were made possible through members of our local Knapp Project advisory committee.

In March of 1967, at the annual Utah Administrators Conference, Farrer Junior High School and the Provo School District were given significant recognition for the work that they had been doing in the implementation of the instructional materials concept, and the provision for a full program of library services for youngsters attending local schools. This presentation consisted of a slide-sound story, and also a 16mm sound film, giving a very comprehensive review of much of the work done.

While it has been part of our ongoing program to acquaint students at the school with the facilities available to them through the regular academic program, we have felt the need to supplement this with a number of special assemblies for the total student body. These assemblies were held to acquaint students with the Knapp Project and the potential offered to the school for improving service through the Project and to give them an opportunity to know national and community leaders' feelings about our participation in the Project.

In the Mountain Plains Area, we have had opportunities to make additional presentations. Members of the library administrative staff from Farrer reported to the 1967 spring convention of the Utah Library Association. Mrs. Jane Vance attended the library section of the Colorado Education Association convention in Grand Junction, Colorado, in October, 1966, and made a very complete report of the Project here and the benefits we could receive as a result of our involvement.

REACTIONS

To get other perspectives on the effect of the demonstration program at Farrer, we have invited comments from the curriculum director of the Provo City Schools and from the library specialist of the Utah State Board of Education. The first, Mr. Ray D. Warner, wrote:

> Because of the exceptional program displayed by librarian and faculty cooperation in your project, we learned that the important part of a good library is the program and not necessarily the materials by themselves. It takes both. Because of this we in Provo elected to bring, as soon as possible, all our centers up to the standard of the Knapp Project library. This is a big order because it involves changing from a traditional schedule to one of a more flexible design in the elementary school's library program; remodeling and repairing facilities and supplying additional professional and clerical help. Much of this has been accomplished as of this date. [May, 1967.]
>
> It also means changing the philosophy to some extent within each of the libraries. The librarian is now becoming a teacher in the true sense of the word. She is generally becoming the curriculum expert within the school.
>
> Processing and cataloging procedures have been changed to include the color banded cards within the card catalog bringing together all media under one subject. Cross-media teaching and learning are becoming a reality where all media are being used in an effort to reach every child.
>
> The book-oriented library has changed to an instructional materials center. Audio-visual materials and their production are becoming routine.

Mr. Jay L. Nielsen, Provo High School industrial arts teacher, demonstrates a rear screen projection unit constructed in his shop.

A student consults with his teacher, Mr. Lyman, during a research unit in the library.

I appreciate the Knapp Project and the Knapp conference we held last January. We tried to show, and I think successfully, that the cross-media approach was a tremendous way to reach individual children. If participants did not get the message from those making presentations at the conference, then they will not get the message any other way.

Perhaps in summary, let me say that the Knapp Project has supplied the motivation and the technical assistance we needed to move the entire district toward a modern instructional materials center concept. In the next year or so, we will come closer to realizing our own goals.

Library specialist Miss Elsie Dee Adams wrote:

The Knapp School Libraries Project has been most helpful to us as a state educational agency because we are attempting to help educators see the importance of using a multi-media approach to learning. We believe that more attention must be given the individual child so he can progress according to his own abilities.

Persons who cannot see the vista of the library as an instructional media center have been pleased to realize that the center can become a reality. Having the Farrer Junior High School available to visit has given many educators a better understanding of what it means to use many resources while working with students, both individually and in groups. One professional person said after making a visit to Farrer Junior High, "I have seen such materials many times, but the great thing about the Knapp School is that the professional staff uses these materials wisely and skillfully. Teachers and

students may have access to all resources in the center all of the time!"

We congratulate you on providing an excellent example of an instructional media center within our state. Because of our state personnel being able to easily visit this facility, the media field has moved forward at a much greater rate than would have otherwise been possible.

A look to the future

In the initial application made to the Knapp School Libraries Project, the Provo School District made a commitment to maintain the Farrer Junior High School at the level of operation achieved during participation in the Project, insofar as the limitations of local budget and available personnel would permit. In accordance with this commitment, the decision has been made by the administrative staff and the board of education of the Provo School District that the school will continue to operate with the present library staff complement. This means that Mrs. Jane N. Vance, head librarian; Mrs. Mary S. Hales, assistant librarian; and Mrs. Louise Wakefield, instructional clerk, will continue their work at the Farrer Junior High School through the 1967-68 school term. In addition, the materials collection will continue to expand to meet the needs of an increasingly complex educational structure. Funds from the district budget, from the Utah Library-Extended Program, and the provisions of Title II of the Elementary and Secondary Education Act will be used for this purpose.

Invitation has been extended to the Department of Teacher Education and the Depart-

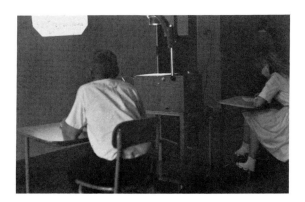

ment of Library Science at Brigham Young University to continue to work with the Farrer Junior High School on a cooperative program. This program will operate much as it has under the provisions of the Knapp School Libraries Project, though more informally. It is intended that prospective teachers, school administrators, librarians, and lay persons will continue to visit the Farrer and the other schools in Provo as they have done during the formal participation in the Knapp Project.

Every effort will be made, as has been done during the last thirty-five years, to continue to improve the program and expand the scope of library service for all of the students who attend school in the Provo School District.

Report from

OAK PARK AND
RIVER FOREST HIGH SCHOOL
and
UNIVERSITY OF ILLINOIS

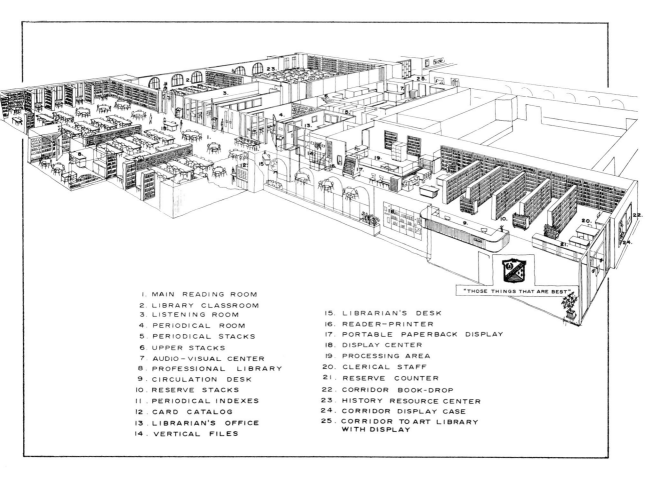

"THOSE THINGS THAT ARE BEST"

1. MAIN READING ROOM
2. LIBRARY CLASSROOM
3. LISTENING ROOM
4. PERIODICAL ROOM
5. PERIODICAL STACKS
6. UPPER STACKS
7. AUDIO-VISUAL CENTER
8. PROFESSIONAL LIBRARY
9. CIRCULATION DESK
10. RESERVE STACKS
11. PERIODICAL INDEXES
12. CARD CATALOG
13. LIBRARIAN'S OFFICE
14. VERTICAL FILES
15. LIBRARIAN'S DESK
16. READER-PRINTER
17. PORTABLE PAPERBACK DISPLAY
18. DISPLAY CENTER
19. PROCESSING AREA
20. CLERICAL STAFF
21. RESERVE COUNTER
22. CORRIDOR BOOK-DROP
23. HISTORY RESOURCE CENTER
24. CORRIDOR DISPLAY CASE
25. CORRIDOR TO ART LIBRARY
    WITH DISPLAY

FACT SHEET—OAK PARK AND RIVER FOREST HIGH SCHOOL

The Oak Park and River Forest High School, a nine-twelve comprehensive high school with an enrollment of 3,498 students, serves the residential suburbs of Oak Park and River Forest, Illinois, with a combined population of approximately 70,000. This school has maintained a special interest in the development of its school library program by reaching out into other areas of the school, and by providing departmental resource centers.

With the support from the Knapp School Libraries Project, two new resource centers were opened in the fall of 1965, the mathematics and science resource center and the foreign language resource center; the American History center received additional equipment and materials. Each of these three centers is under the supervision of a librarian trained in the discipline of the resource center. Funds from the Project have doubled the professional staff making it possible to delegate a librarian to work with each of the major curriculum areas of the school. The addition of a secretary and six half-time library aides has made the expanded program possible.

In addition to the three new professional librarians whose salaries come from Knapp Project funds, the library staff includes an audio-visual director, a bibliographer, an assistant librarian, and the head librarian, Miss Lura Crawford. Dr. Gene L. Schwilck, superintendent and principal of this one-school district, has acted as the liaison worker for the Project.

The University of Illinois, as the co-applicant, has appointed Dr. Jerry Walker, Assistant Professor of Education and Supervisor of Student Teachers, as field worker for the Project. Dr. Walker has assisted with the in-service training workshop on the library for the school's new teachers. He also works to encourage the more than forty student teachers in the school to make better use of the library and its facilities.

The Knapp School Libraries Project has enabled the library to make needed additions in equipment and materials. The problem of a noisy reading room floor was solved with acoustical floor covering. The film collection has been enlarged. More multi-media materials are available for the gifted program, for team teaching and independent study groups, and the new humanities courses.

Participation in the Knapp School Libraries Project has released new energies for developing a more significant program for a school library and has given the impetus for making still greater strides for the learning center of tomorrow.

In 1966, the school received a $1,300,000 grant under Title III of the Elementary and Secondary Education Act for development of a library-located instructional resource center capable of electronically storing vast amounts of information instantly retrievable for individual or small-group instruction.

STATISTICS

From its Project application, November, 1964

Enrollment: 3,255 students, grades nine through twelve.

Materials collection: 37,732 books, 151 periodicals, 650 filmstrips, 277 films (16mm), 227 disc recordings, 50 tape recordings, 300 transparencies, 20 microfilms.

Library personnel: Three full-time librarians (one with responsibility for audio-visual program); one part-time bibliographer; two full-time secretaries, two half-time secretaries.

As of June, 1967

Enrollment: 3,498 students, grades nine through twelve.

Materials collection: 44,692 books, 260 periodicals, 1,000 filmstrips, 399 films (16mm), 47 films (8mm), 541 disc recordings, 381 tape recordings, 722 transparencies, 2,940 slides, 536 microfilms.

Library personnel: Six full-time librarians (one with responsibility for audio-visual program); one part-time bibliographer; two full-time secretaries; one part-time secretary; six half-time library aides; two half-time secretaries.

PERSONNEL MOST DIRECTLY CONCERNED WITH THE PROJECT

From the Oak Park and River Forest High School

Dr. Gene L. Schwilck, Principal and Superintendent

Miss Lura Crawford, Head of Library Services

Mrs. Nancy Blemaster, Assistant Librarian

Mrs. Katherine Heimann, Mathematics and Science Librarian

Mr. David Boyd, Audio-visual Director

Miss Margarette Seibel, History Librarian

Mr. Henry Wieman, Foreign Language Librarian

Miss Lola Bane, Bibliographer

Mrs. Mary Lee Brown, Library Aide (half-time)

Mrs. Helen Gombiner, Library Aide (half-time)

Mrs. Elizabeth Rhodes, Library Aide (half-time)

Mrs. Ann Swanson, Library Aide (half-time)

Mrs. Margaret Tucker, Library Aide (half-time)

Mrs. Lisbeth Weiser, Library Aide (half-time)

Mrs. Eleanor Brierley, Clerical Secretary, (half-time)

Mrs. Carol Hajic, Clerical Secretary (half-time)

Mrs. Mildred Harman, Clerical Secretary

Mrs. Nadine Lewis, Clerical Secretary (part-time)

Mrs. Lovey Shaughnessy, Clerical Secretary

Mrs. Elizabeth Stuart, Clerical Secretary (half-time)

From the University of Illinois

Dr. Rupert Evans, Dean, College of Education

Dr. Charles M. Allen, Associate Dean, College of Education

Dr. Jerry Walker, Assistant Professor, College of Education; Supervisor of Student Teachers in English; and field worker, Knapp School Libraries Project

THE SUPERINTENDENT'S REPORT

The faculty of the Oak Park and River Forest High School has always considered the library an integral part of the school curricular program. In 1957, its services were enhanced when the library was moved into larger and newly remodeled quarters. It became an instructional materials center which daily attracted over one thousand students who used its resources.

In 1963, the school was chosen by the Illinois State Department of Public Instruction as one of three high schools in the state to serve as demonstration schools. During the four years since then, many teachers and administrators within the state and the nation visited the school. These visits stimulated the faculty to a continuous program of curriculum revision in relation to the library services and served as a motivating factor in the decision to apply for participation in the Knapp School Libraries Project. With the funds received from the Project, the number of staff members in the library was expanded, additional materials were purchased, and a significant number of visiting lecturers and consultants were brought to the school. Within six months, the faculty and the board of education pledged continued financial support for the increased library program. In the fall of 1967, the staff numbered twenty-three (the equivalent of eighteen full-time people, seven of whom are professional librarians). The support of the board of education, the enthusiasm of the faculty, and the response of students have confirmed the value of the Knapp Project to this community.

Several experiences during the Knapp Project demonstration years were important in extending the thinking of the faculty and the school administrators concerning the role of a school library:

1. The increased number of library personnel encouraged faculty and students to use the library resources more extensively. Teachers were able to give more creative assignments to students and to rely less upon adopted textbooks. The improvement in curriculum content seemed noticeable to many department chairmen. This was the predominant evaluation of the faculty at the conclusion of the demonstration.

2. The many visitors who were guests in the school brought suggestions and inspiration to our faculty and library staff. We were impressed to hear of the many outstanding school library programs throughout the country, and we were often able to adopt an idea presented by one of the guests. During the Knapp demonstration, many of our faculty members were able to travel and visit in secondary schools and junior colleges. The inspiration and vision gained through these visits provided the impetus in applying for a Title III Elementary and Secondary Education Act grant. The program also served to stimulate many members of the community to more awareness of the need for greater library services for students. Members of the local Knapp advisory committee were of assistance in interpreting the program to citizens of the community.

3. Students of the school profited from the increased materials and expanded staff, and attained a greater pride in their library program as they observed hundreds of guests who came to visit the library.

4. The three resource centers, partially financed by the grant, replaced three traditional study halls. These centers—staffed with a librarian, a teacher, and paraprofessionals—demonstrated to faculty and students the significance of independent study. As a result of these "trials," the faculty is anticipating the establishment of additional and larger resource centers. The twelve-million-dollar addition to the building will make possible an expansion of the library facilities to an area twice the present size.

5. As principal of the school, I have had the opportunity of visiting with other administrators, school librarians, and members of boards of education. Through this program, I have become more aware of the importance of the standards of the American Library Association, and have been able to play a modest role in interpreting these standards to my colleagues. The administrators of this school

are convinced that one responsibility of a Knapp Project school is to share the enthusiasm of the faculty and administrators with other schools in order that they may be assured of the importance of extended library services in the school curricular program.

Miss Lura Crawford, Director of Library Services, has been the key person in the development of our library. It is through her insight and planning that the library continues to expand in services. She personally received vast numbers of Knapp visitors. Her staff, who have responded with enthusiasm to the leadership of Miss Crawford in the Knapp School Libraries Project, shared in her pride over the recognition given to her when she became the 1967 recipient of the Grolier Award.

Music, new equipment, an energetic staff, a dead language—each has its place in the production area with Mr. Joseph Schefter, audio-visual librarian, in charge.

THE LIBRARIANS' REPORT

This section has been prepared by Miss Lura Crawford, head librarian, with Mrs. Katherine Heimann, Miss Margarette Seibel, and Mr. Henry Wieman reporting on the resource centers for which they are respectively responsible — mathematics and science, American history, and foreign language.

What happens when a school library elects "to demonstrate the educational value of a full program of library services" for two years? Does the school achieve the outcomes hopefully listed in the original application? Were the objectives of the Project—for meeting the American Library Association standards, for providing in-service education through cooperation with a nearby teacher education institution, and for serving as a demonstration center —realized? Some of the answers may be found in the following reports from the administration, the library staff, the field worker, the faculty, the students, and the visitors who came by the hundreds to observe.

Of consistent help in establishing objectives and estimating the extent to which they were achieved were members of the local advisory committee. They were:

Dr. Gene L. Schwilck, Chairman, Super-

intendent, Oak Park and River Forest High School

Mr. James Boula, Instructional Materials Consultant, Office of the Superintendent of Public Instruction

Miss Lura E. Crawford, Librarian, Oak Park and River Forest High School

Mrs. Frank J. Krivanek, Board of Education

Miss Kathryn McDaniel, Community Representative

Sister Peter Claver, Director, Department of Library Science, Rosary College

Dr. Victor E. Ricks, Director, Division of Education, Chicago Circle Campus, University of Illinois

Mr. Lester Stoffel, Librarian, Oak Park Public Library, Scoville Institute

Miss Elinor Yungmeyer, Consultant in Library Services, Oak Park Elementary Schools

The physical changes made early in the Project proved to be assets in the development of the library's program. The acoustical floor covering which corrected the problem of a noisy reading room met with unanimous approval. The transformation of traditional study halls into resource centers complete with furniture, equipment, and multi-media materials offered the opportunity for students, librarians, and teachers to work together. The same areas also provided space for the student to work independently at his own rate with varied materials to stimulate his interest. Our experience based on observation of use, attendance statistics, and evaluative comments from faculty and students has convinced us that this is the direction our future resource centers will take whether located in or out of the central library complex. Our current plan for the future is to locate the mathematics and science resource center in the first floor of the library, to enlarge the art library adjacent to the art department rooms, and to develop a business education center in the midst of the business education area.

Most important to the development of the library's total program has been the increase in staff made possible by the Project. The addition of three professional librarians, each with a strong subject background, a secretary, and four half-time library aides made it possible to carry on the activities that characterize a good, modern, secondary school library program in greater depth and with more systematic development than was possible before. In spite of the added interesting but time-consuming obligations of demonstration and constant visitation, the library has provided more individual service to both teachers and students than was possible with the former staff. In 1965, the staff consisted of three and a half professionals, two full-time clerical secretaries, and two half-time circulation assistants. Since the library is an instructional center with a full audio-visual program, a staff of three and a half librarians in a school of over three thousand was inadequate and far below the national standards for school library programs.

Since the turn of the century, the school has been fortunate in having able, well-trained, dedicated librarians on its staff and an outstanding faculty who demanded teaching materials of high quality and made extensive use of the library. These demands on the library have increased with the explosion of knowledge and new patterns of teaching.

In 1959, the board of education and the community had given support to the building of extensive new library quarters. With attractive new quarters, adequate budget, and the nucleus of a good staff, the library still sorely needed more adequate staffing to reach the level of excellence. The Knapp School Libraries Project provided the opportunity.

The administration and the librarian, in their concern for assisting a larger number of students to gain greater skills in independent study and self-direction, felt this was the time to experiment with additional resource centers, maintained and staffed by library personnel. To find the right personnel to develop these learning materials centers, subject background was stressed in the letters sent out to the library schools over the country asking for candidates. The administrator responsible for recruiting personnel asked for librarians with competencies in one of the following fields: foreign languages, history and social sciences, and mathematics and science, since these were the curriculum areas for resource center development.

The scouting letter indicated that participation in the Knapp School Libraries Project should provide some exciting and stimulating opportunities for the librarians working in the demonstration program. The library schools were cooperative and expressed interest in the program, but few had candidates to suggest for the positions. Some had excellent candidates who preferred their present situations or opportunities elsewhere.

We finally recruited three librarians with special competence in the subject areas we needed, plus many other desirable attributes for successful work. In addition to sound academic backgrounds where they won honors, the three had masters' degrees in library science from Rosary College where courses including audio-visual materials and automation had prepared them well for modern school librarianship.

Two of the librarians had had successful experience as teachers and librarians; the third was a promising beginner who had gained experience in summer work in her high school, college, and community library. One of the librarians had also served as a children's librarian in a public library for a year.

All three candidates expressed enthusiasm and interest in working with students and faculty. The administrators and the head librarian in all interviews try to stress the importance of giving service to the school, to all students and teachers, remembering always that techniques and organization are only means to this end.

The three new librarians all had personal characteristics important for school librarians. They are pleasant, personable, industrious, intelligent, interested in cultural and world affairs, and can work well with an outstanding teaching staff and student body. They are well poised and they enjoyed meeting the school's many visitors, an important part of our demonstration program.

In September, 1965, each of these new librarians was assigned the responsibility of developing a resource center and working with the faculty of one of the large curriculum areas of the school. The librarians attended department meetings, worked on curriculum committees, helped select materials, prepared bibliographies, gave instruction to teachers and students in the use of the centers, and set up simple circulation procedures.

In the months following the appointment of the three new librarians, the reaction was strong and favorable from department chairmen and individual faculty members. Better service can be given when one librarian concentrates his energies on one department instead of spreading himself thin over many areas.

The librarians responsible for the resource centers were assigned central library duties, too. Each librarian spent three periods in the main reading room where he was available for reference and reading guidance. The challenging experience of working with the more than one thousand students a day who come to the library should sharpen and broaden a librarian's skills. Two library aides, one in the morning and one in the afternoon, were as-

signed to the reading room each period to help with the supervision of the students. Library aides were also hired to record attendance and facilitate student supervision in the resource centers. The school has been fortunate in finding people of high caliber for this work, mostly mature, educated women of the community with an interest in working with young people. They also promote good public relations with the community.

Indeed, the whole library staff, before and after the Project, show high quality in their work. They are committed to the library's program. The library is fortunate to have knowledgeable, gracious, willing personnel in the key areas where good rapport with students, faculty, and visitors is essential.

In the past and present, the library's clerical and paraprofessional staff has served as a recruiting ground for the profession. The new library secretary, hired the first year of participation in the Project, went on to library school the second year where she said her experience in the Knapp program proved valuable. The morning aide in the mathematics and science resource center is currently working for her master's degree in library science, and a second aide in the foreign language resource center started her work in 1967. One of the half-day circulation assistants who has been working on her library degree was given an appointment by the school as a half-day cataloger in the fall of 1967.

With the clerical staff increased by Knapp Project funds, the secretarial assistant who had divided her time between the main library and the audio-visual division became a full-time secretarial assistant in the audio-visual quarters. By the end of the Project, a second clerical assistant had been hired for six hours of the school day and also a part-time materials designer assistant, a student at the Illinois Institute of Technology.

The addition of a secretary made it possible for the secretarial assistant in charge of book preparation and library records to transfer some of the general typing and to take over the posting of the library's bills.

The chief responsibilities held by the original

professional staff were widened and deepened by the Project's addition of personnel. The librarian who had been charged with the responsibility of the audio-visual division prior to the Project had been scheduled to spend three periods in the reading room, a schedule that had become increasingly difficult to keep with the fast-growing demands of audio-visual services. With the advent of the Project, the audio-visual director spent full time in the dual role of making equipment and materials available to the faculty and students and producing and assisting in the production of materials and programs.

The audio-visual director, who left after the first year of the Project to take a fellowship for advanced study, received his master's degree in library science with additional work in the audio-visual field. The second director has his degree in media with additional work in library science. Both backgrounds are compatible with the library's program. Both men have taught college audio-visual courses and have done considerable visiting of industrial and educational installations of new technology.

All of the library's professional staff have been involved since the fall of 1965 in the

Volunteers learn various responsibilities from Mrs. Nancy Blemaster, librarian.

planning of a random-access instructional materials retrieval system. The Knapp Project sparked our application and the approval for both a planning grant and an operational grant under Title III of the Elementary and Secondary Education Act for a "library-located instructional resource center utilizing an electronically stored information process which can provide information instantly to individuals or for small-group instructions." This installation will be discussed later by the director of our Title III project.

Besides sharing in the excitement of finding new electronic means to improve learning, both the head librarian and the assistant librarian found their daily activities changing. The assistant librarian in charge of technical processing of materials and supervisor of the main library's staff of forty student assistants spent one less period in the reading room. Although the considerable addition of materials made possible from the joint funds of the Knapp Project, the school district, and Title II of the Elementary and Secondary Education Act necessitated more cataloging, this librarian kept the work steadily flowing by using clerical and paid student help during the school year and the summer session. For the first time, the library had an adequate summer staff to take care of the current needs of a six-and-a-half-week enrollment of 1,900 students plus the ordering and processing of books for the coming regular session.

The assistant librarian continued to share cheerfully with the head librarian all the activities in a busy library program. A typical day could find her giving a freshman library orientation lesson, building a school alumni author file, compiling a bibliography for the art department, assembling a book truck of materials for a home management class, classifying some paperbacks needed immediately for a team teaching class, and perhaps ending the day showing an adult patron sent over from the public library how to use the microform reader-printer.

The role of the part-time librarian-English teacher who compiles bibliographies, assists with the library instruction program, and acts

Portable videotaperecorder makes it possible for swimmers to observe themselves later.

as liaison between the library and the English department was enlarged to include being hostess to many of the visitors, particularly those interested in the English curriculum or the cooperative team teaching class in history and literature. During the first year of Project participation, this library bibliographer edited a brochure describing the Knapp Project at Oak Park and River Forest High School. The brochure and her many bibliographies have gone all over the world. Even with the librarians on the staff compiling bibliographies and reading lists in various subject areas, the chief bibliographer has a file of waiting requests.

With everyone else working, what does the head of library services do? Keeping track of eighteen people on the staff requires time and planning. The head librarian has discovered that her role also has to have changes in emphasis. She needs to work more with heads of departments, committees, and faculty than with individual students. She regrets this. Working with students has always been her first interest. However, she knows the students have not been short-changed because the additional staff has offered greater opportunities for individual help. In fact, she suspects there is less of "I hate to bother you" apology from the student when he wants guidance from a

librarian scheduled to help him than there was in the past, when over-scheduled personnel in desperation tried to get their work done while supervising the reading room.

At the beginning of Project participation, the head librarian scheduled herself for periods in the reading room, but as the new staff demonstrated their effective rapport with the students and as the schedule of visitations grew heavier, she found herself spending most of her time with visitors and attending conferences with faculty committees ranging from planning for a humanities conference to selecting fabrics for chair coverings. Participating in the various titles of the Elementary and Secondary Education Act has also taken considerable time the past two years, but the school is that much richer in materials.

Although the librarian has had to assume new administrative duties, she has been able to relinquish other tasks better done by her secretarial staff. No longer does she post the bills or write the requisitions for materials required through the year. She still authorizes all of them, but many of the materials ordered will have been selected by the other librarians knowledgeable in their subject fields. The head librarian is free occasionally to observe a tele-lecture or to accept the invitation of a team teaching class using library materials. She can confer with the president of a boys' conference about a bibliography and display. She can talk to a new teacher about the materials available for a class unit. She can meet with the English teacher working on a research paper tape for the retrieval system. She can attend an 8:00 A.M. meeting of department heads without worrying about the activities in the library. She can spend time with a Canadian library school student who has asked to do her practice work in a Knapp Project school. She can consult with the carpenters about the new paperback book truck they have built, and let the practice librarian initiate it with a book talk. The head librarian herself may give fewer book talks, but she knows that because of the library's involvement with the total school program, more books and materials are being brought to the students than ever before. She also realizes that the potential sources for building an environment to nurture the "will to learn" have scarcely been touched, but the Knapp Project has laid the groundwork.

The goal originally stated in the school's Knapp Project application of bringing the library closer to the 1960 ALA school library standards has been fulfilled. The staff has been doubled with an additional position budgeted for the 1967-68 school year.

The book collection in June, 1967, includes 44,692 volumes compared with 37,732 at the time of the Project application in November, 1964. During this period, 11,331 volumes were added and 4,371 were discarded. The addition of more staff has made systematic weeding possible, which is important in keeping the collection current. The periodical titles have increased from 151 in 1964 to 250 in 1967. The addition of the resource centers, the closer work with the teachers, and new emphases in some of the course offerings have been contributing factors. The microfilm collection of periodicals has grown from 20 reels to 536. The addition of *The New York Times* with the indexes should be a valuable reference tool for years to come.

The school library and the Oak Park Public Library exchange their holdings. The school library offers the services of its reader-printer to the patrons occasionally sent by the public library.

The microfilmed materials are used both for reference and browsing. Students taking the course in Asian Studies use the *Journal of Asian Studies* intensively. Students in the mathematics and science resource centers read the microfilmed science titles sometimes for assignments and sometimes for general interest and curiosity.

With the support of Knapp Project and federal funds, the library has more than doubled its holdings in films, filmstrips, disc recordings, tapes, and transparencies. Slides numbering 2,940 have been added to the library's resources, including the Carnegie collection of *Arts of the United States.* All these materials were carefully selected, often with screening by the teachers as well as the librarians. All are fully cataloged in the main library union catalog and are listed in the resource centers. The type of material is stamped on the catalog card: film, filmstrip, disc, tape. In the summer

French art prints add to the atmosphere of the foreign language resource center.

of 1967, a special catalog of the art library's slide collection was completed.

The faculty and students were quick to voice their approval of the additions of material to the library. In the final evaluations secured from the faculty, these were typical comments volunteered in answer to the question of what were the benefits of the school's participation in the Project:

> The *Arts of the United States* slides are very valuable in the American History course. In view of the lack of treatment given by textbooks of American culture, these slides are most welcome.—U.S. history teacher.

> My whole Project of Independent Study in Asian History could never have been the success that it was without the expert library assistance and materials. (This class made heavy use of the Sandak slide collection, "The Arts of Japan," and borrowed, bought, and developed many tapes of their own.)—Asian Studies teacher.

> Making source materials for projects available, extra manpower help, and visual and listening aids.—Humanities and music teacher.

> Because of additional staff members, my students have received more assistance in their research projects. Both my students and I have benefited greatly from the additional books, records, and films made available by the Project.—English teacher

> Ownership of films that were previously rented has been a help since we teach different courses of biology and need them at different times.—Chairman, Biological Sciences.

> Opportunity to encourage students to use the current science materials as a supplement to their text, and individual instruction through tapes, films, etc. . . .—Science teacher.

> My students have made considerable use of library and resource center materials for required outside reading, for Advanced Placement reading, and for browsing and listening.—Language teacher.

> Through the science and math resource center I have employed two or three new teaching techniques this year, the most significant being "tutorial teaching" through tape lessons.—Biology teacher.

The above sampling of quotations shows that, given increased resources and personnel, the library program will expand, more services will be demanded, and the climate for learning will improve. We have come nearer to the *Standards for School Library Programs*, and we are nearer to the accomplishments hoped for in our original Project application. We feel that our well stocked and well staffed resource areas have provided more opportunity for students, librarians, and teachers to work together and have given impetus to independent study programs involving both the gifted and the slower learner.

Although there is constant need for improvement, our book collection, which was good at the beginning of the Project, is close to excellent at the end. We have built and strengthened curriculum collections like that for the Asian Studies (which the instructor rates as one of the best high school collections), an outstanding foreign language collection, and improved literature holdings with more materials by modern writers and critics. As background for a new course in World Civilization with a humanities approach, we have purchased scores of titles in the fields of music and the arts. In addition to meeting the academic demands, including such significant purchases as a set of one hundred of Frank Lloyd Wright's building plans, the library increased its stock of books for the general reading interests of the students. In the two-year period, we added 2,000 volumes in fiction and biography. In addition, Knapp Project funds provided for a paperback browsing collection with all reading levels represented. The school carpenters built a well constructed display truck for this collection which can be wheeled to a class for a book talk or kept as a circulating display in the library.

At the end of the Project, we felt we were well on our way to reaching our stated goal of the "coordination of all quality instructional materials readily available to teacher and student." The audio-visual division was revising its catalog of holdings to triple the size of the one issued in 1965. Quarters adjoining the circulation room were being prepared for the arrival of the 25 electronically equipped carrels, the first stage of the retrieval system that will make instantly available to each student the material he wants when he needs it. Many of the audio materials developed and purchased during the Knapp Project will be transferred to high-speed tapes for the retrieval system. All associated with our exciting Title III Project feel that the Knapp Project was our springboard, and we will continue to talk about it to the visitors for years to come.

Demonstration of the library's program to visitors has been a major concern of the library staff since Oak Park and River Forest began to participate in Phase III of the Project. The administration and members of the board of education had affirmed their belief that the school was qualified to serve as a demonstration center based on past experience. At the end of the Project, all concerned with the local administration of the demonstration program felt it was successful.

"Visitors today!" came to be the daily greeting of the library's personnel. The hosting of 2,500 visitors from nearly all the states of the Union and 26 foreign countries was an exciting and challenging experience. (The details of the handling of the visits are given later in this report.)

Apparently our procedure of demonstrating the library's function in our school was satisfactory on the whole, since the majority of the visitors sent gracious and often enthusiastic reports and letters expressing their satisfaction with the day spent with us. In fact, the greatest complaint was that they would like a second day. It is hoped that many of them will make return visits, but two-day visits would have been impossible with the volume of people coming during the two years of Project participation.

The value and appeal of demonstration as a means of promoting educational ferment was shown by the large numbers of people who wanted to come. No doubt the Project office could have tripled its number of teams if it had been feasible. The Knapp Project-financed teams that came to Oak Park and River Forest numbered 295 people and they came from 24 states. Although the largest number of people came from the Midwest, the state of New York

Miss Lura Crawford, head librarian, at end of table, and on her left, Dr. Jerry L. Walker, field worker, and Dr. Gene L. Schwilck, superintendent-principal, meet with members of the readiness team.

tied with Wisconsin in sending 33 people. Iowa, Illinois, and Ohio were close behind. Several states on the Eastern seaboard were represented as well as Arkansas, New Mexico, and Texas in the Southwest.

Following the guidelines laid down by the Project, the make-up of the teams included 89 administrators from 21 states and 84 librarians from 22 states. Teachers and curriculum people were next with 35 from 16 states. It was gratifying that 21 school board members were in the groups. They especially enjoyed exchanging views with Mrs. Krivanek, the Oak Park and River Forest board member who served on our local advisory committee and so faithfully supported the Project's whole program. Her article on her association with the Knapp program at Oak Park appeared in *School Boards,* March 15, 1966. We agreed with the visitors who said we were lucky to have so fine a board member. We also agreed with the librarians and administrators who commented on the wisdom of the Project planners for including members of the local school boards in the visiting teams.

Four school board members from three different states were represented in the groups who visited at their own expense. Usually they came with the local administrator and architect to get ideas for their new instructional materials centers. Personal contact with these many planners point to many exciting school plants on the drawing boards. One school board member from Connecticut came to the school between flights at O'Hare Airport to take ideas back with him.

In the groups of visitors who came without support by Project funds, there were 85 superintendents and principals from 15 states, 45 teachers and curriculum personnel, and 164 librarians. Eighty librarians came from Illinois, including many from neighboring schools, new and well established ones. Both the Project-supported teams and the non-supported teams drew from 20 of the same states. The non-supported teams included the "additional" states of Alabama, Arizona, California, Colorado, Kentucky, Maine, Oregon, Rhode Island, Ten-

nessee, West Virginia, and the District of Columbia.

The large geographic spread and variety of positions among visiting teams included a wide variety of schools and centers, private and public, large and small school systems. Many of the groups were in the midst of planning new materials centers; others were searching for new ideas for their remodeling.

The whole school as well as the library staff was intrigued with the 40 visitors from 26 foreign countries. Besides giving them our usual tour and explanation, we tried to establish any other contact in the school that would please them. At lunch time we paired the South Americans with our Spanish teachers who had studied or traveled in their countries. Our German teachers made good hosts for the three different groups of educators from Germany. One of these groups went off to see the Frank Lloyd Wright buildings. Another asked especially for the issue of our student literary magazine commemorating Ernest Hemingway's graduation from the high school in 1917.

We found a student who spoke the language and had visited the country for the guest from Yugoslavia. The schoolmistress of one of our exchange students stopped during her trip to the States. Another delightful educator from Australia, who wrote that his visit with us was "one of the highlights of his trip," sent us a generous supply of material on Australia for our collection. The benefits from our foreign visitors were certainly two-fold. We learned from them as we hope they did from us. As the Project was ending, we were pleased to have other requests from overseas visitors for the following year. We were glad to know our small part in international relations would continue.

The greatest number of visitors—over 1,400—came in large groups. There were five groups from National Defense Education Act institutes, including the first group of NDEA institute leaders who came on September 2, 1965, at the beginning of our time in the Project. In the summer of 1966, four NDEA institutes came. One was from Western Michigan University, one from the University of Wisconsin, and two from Indiana University—an institute for school librarians and one for media specialists. In the summer of 1967, after Project participation, three more NDEA institutes scheduled visits.

A group of 25 Experienced Teacher Fellowship students and five faculty members came from Wayne State University in April, 1967. Purdue University sent groups of educational media and library science classes in May, 1966, and again in 1967. The University of Illinois Graduate Library School, the Graduate Library School of the University of Chicago, and Rosary College—three library schools accustomed to sending classes to Oak Park in the past—continued to send them during the two years of the Project. The library staff and the faculty also gave interviews and filled out numerous questionnaires for library schools and graduate students making special studies of school libraries.

Several school library associations of the surrounding area visited Oak Park: two groups came from Milwaukee; others included the school librarians of Rockford, the Southwest Suburban area, school librarians from Hammond, Indiana, and the High School Librarians of Chicagoland. This last group of 165 school librarians came for a full Saturday meeting with exhibits, tours, luncheon, and program. Miss Sullivan, the Director of the Project, gave a talk and showed slides which later became the filmstrip, *Three for Tomorrow*.

Miss Sullivan was the featured speaker at the library section of the Cook County Teachers' Institute held at the school October 25, 1965. The film, . . . *And Something More,* was shown to this audience which included many elementary school librarians. After attending this meeting, Dr. Charles R. Keller, Director of the John Hay Fellows Program, wrote back: "I was particularly excited by the Library Project, and I say Hurrah for librarians who are really on the move!"

The library was visited by a group of 50 library leaders from the American Library Association Midwinter Conference, January 26 and 27, 1966. These librarians not only showed keen interest at the time of their visits but later sent for additional information and bibliographies. They ranged from elementary school library supervisors to a university librarian who was serving on his local high school planning board. It was also interesting to have representatives from various departments of the headquarters staff of the American Library Association for a visit on December 8, 1966.

The conference that probably brought the greatest feedback was the group estimated at 140 from the meeting of the North Central Association of Colleges and Secondary Schools in Chicago on March 28, 1966. Many of the visiting administrators sent their librarians and other school personnel back to observe later in the year.

The Conference on the Humanities financed with Knapp Project funds, and further described in the field worker's report, also brought considerable follow-up requests for materials that had been displayed or mentioned at the meeting. Displays of the varied kinds of materials being used in the school's humanities program were set up in the library and art corridor areas adjacent to the coffee and rolls table. Simultaneously, tapes of early music prepared by the music humanities teacher could be heard; colored slides, made by the World Civilization teachers in the audio-visual center, were shown from an automatic slide projector; and hundreds of books, prints, and filmstrips were exhibited on the tables. Members of the humanities committee including the library staff were on hand to answer questions and get acquainted. This beginning display and coffee mixer gave a festive start to a most stimulating conference. As proof of the sustained interest, the discussion groups lingered overtime on a beautiful fall Saturday. Many expressed a desire to hold an annual humanities conference in the area.

The attendance figures of all the Knapp Project-supported conferences and programs held at Oak Park and River Forest High School came to a total of 6,600 students and adults. One hundred and ten registered for the humanities conference, including teachers, librarians, and students from the Chicago metropolitan area, and a bus load from Ohio. Eight hundred and fifty was the estimated figure for the four

Hemingway commemorative lectures which drew people from the community as well as students and faculty. The thirteen "Careers in Art Series" and history lectures and telectures planned primarily for the students, both during and after school hours, reached an estimated total of 5,640 students.

The library was part of the published tour and visitation plan for the 309 visitors who came to see the State Demonstration Center for the Gifted in which the high school was also participating. These visitors included 71 teams who came from 66 cities in Illinois. There were also three teams from Indiana, one from Nebraska, and one from Iowa. Their make-up was similar to the Knapp Project-financed teams with administrators and teachers, but with more guidance workers and fewer librarians. All came with the same dedicated purpose of finding means for helping boys and girls.

At the end of the Project, we had had registered visitors from 47 states. We hope in the future we will have people from Alaska, Idaho, and Wyoming. We know there were countless guests who did not get registered.

We liked these thousands of visitors with a purpose and they liked us. We, too, often wished their stay could have been longer. Mr. Arthur Pelz, the chairman of our art department, where many of the guests wanted to linger, summed up his feeling: "The visitations of educators could be expanded to a two or three day discussion, demonstration, and dialogue. The Knapp program brought some fascinating people of the world and yet their stay was almost always too short."

Demonstration must be worth doing to justify the energy and time consumed by both the visitors and the visited. That it is worth doing is perhaps best told in the words of those who came from different posts in education but all with the same purpose—to find better tools for learning:

I was afraid I might be subjected to dry details of the Dewey decimal system or the like. It was a pleasant surprise to catch a glimpse of the many fascinating possibilities of the future in making "resource material centers" more attractive, useful and accessible.—Board of education member, Adrian, Michigan.

We came away feeling that we had gained much more than we have from many conferences—Librarian, Decatur, Illinois.

We are impressed with your physical facilities—how you remodeled in an old building and have an arrangement superior to many libraries in new buildings.—Coordinator of Library Services, Brookville, Pennsylvania.

I believe I will be a better teacher as a result of your generous sharing of your ideas and materials.—Lecturer, Department of Librarianship, Emporia, Kansas.

We believe the insights we gained will help us to become better school librarians. —Students, Chicago State College.

The size, quality, and character of your library, in toto, was a revelation to me as I have not seen a large secondary school library in many years.—University Learning Materials Center Librarian, Whitewater, Wisconsin.

From the many comments which I heard during our tour, I know these audio-visual specialists received many ideas which they will be testing out in their own systems next fall.—Professor of Education, Audio-Visual Center, Indiana University.

Many of the visitors commented on the help and inspiration they had received from the superintendent of the school, Dr. Gene L. Schwilck, who gave generously of his time to address the visiting teams and groups.

In the Project application in 1964, the head librarian had written:

An essential strength of our program is the enthusiastic support of the school's superintendent-principal. He wholeheartedly believes that a library program of high quality is a necessary means to quality education, and he has made that clear to the faculty, administration, and parents.

Among the many comments of visitors about Dr. Schwilck's abilities and interests, there is this one which sums up their reaction:

Finally, the leadership of your superintendent, I'm certain, allowed this kind of school library development to become a reality. His philosophy of education, his respect and admiration for the entire faculty were obvious from the beginning of our visit. In talking with members of the library staff and faculty, we knew that this feeling was returned. What a healthy atmosphere in which to teach!—Department Head for School Libraries, Trumbull, Connecticut.

In our original application, we had said our program's chief strengths were cooperation with the faculty and accessibility to the students:

Intensive use by all instructional departments in an excellent school is one of the major strengths of our school library program. An excellent spirit of cooperation exists between the library staff and the faculty. The librarians try to keep the confidence of the teaching staff by maintaining a willing spirit of service and by taking the initiative in offering the library's services in various activities to tie-up with curricular and extracurricular projects.

Our library is used. Students are welcome: the reluctant readers, the average and the gifted. . . . A librarian is always ready to offer help and instruction in finding materials or to suggest a good book to read. . . . The staff strives to keep a focus on the individual student.

One member of our readiness committee observed:

By comparison with my previous teaching experience, I have been most impressed with the fact that the library is so readily available to the students. Too often, the most able students have no opportunity to utilize library facilities.

By the end of the Project term, we had found ways to reach more students and to better serve the faculty. We were glad our findings proved stimulating to the many other educators who came with plans of exciting instructional materials centers of their own.

At the closing plaque-presentation ceremony, the head librarian listed all the departments in the school that had contributed to the Project's success—the administration, the faculty, guidance counselors, business office, secretarial staffs, the food department, and the engineering and maintenance staff. The support of members of the board of education, and the assistance and counsel of the Project Director were especially noted.

Acknowledgment was made of the fine cooperation afforded the Project by the University of Illinois College of Education, whose field worker, Dr. Jerry Walker, came to be accepted as a welcome part of the library staff. His reports on his work with the student teachers have been in demand over the country.

A final word of deep gratitude should be expressed to the Advisory Committee of The Knapp School Libraries Project, the leaders of the American Association of School Librarians, whose vision and work made the Project possible. Lastly, we give thanks to the Knapp Foundation that cared enough for the improvement of school libraries in our country to fund the Project.

Mathematics and science resource center

The mathematics and science resource center was established to bring together a variety of materials in related subjects; the students are not limited to the printed word. Part of the book collection in mathematics and science is now located in the center, and other media have been introduced. The center is administered by the library with cooperation from the mathematics, physical sciences, and biological sciences departments.

Included with this report (page 292) is a summary of the materials in the center.

MATHEMATICS AND SCIENCE RESOURCE CENTER
(May, 1967)

Materials available:

850 books

Reference books

Card catalog with main entry card

Periodicals (current issues only) 18 titles

Readers' Guide, 1948—

Biological Abstracts, 1966—

Pamphlet file—3 file drawers

In eight study carrels:
    Filmstrips and viewer
    8mm cartridge films and projector
    Microfilm reader and *Scientific American,* 1949—, *Science Digest,* 1959—, *Science News Letter,* 1959—, *Popular Science,* 1960—
    2 calculators
    IBM keypunch
    Typewriter
    Tape recorders for taped tutorials in biology and mathematics

2 Teletypewriters for transmitting programs to the Illinois Institute of Technology for processing on IBM System/360 Computer

Discussion tables for 18, total seating for 30

Program:
    Study hall for three science classes each period
    Other students come on special slips, just as to library

Teacher to assist students when possible, either in small groups or individually

Library aide to take attendance and supervise individual study area

Student assistant to circulate materials

Librarian to supervise program, select materials with faculty assistance, give reading guidance and instruction in use of the materials and machines to faculty and students

Open before and after school, from 8 A.M. to 4 P.M.

Because of crowded conditions in the school, the center is located in the back of a large study hall which has been divided by a glass partition. In a carpeted alcove are eight carrels. Seating in the rest of the center is at trapezoid tables, which were chosen to allow the students a place for discussion.

Of the more than 800 books, there are duplicates of titles in the main library only when use demands more than one copy. An effort was made to maintain a balanced collection in both collections. There were differing opinions on a divided book collection, but it has been a smaller problem than anticipated. The students are usually interested in particular information rather than a specific title. Included in the center are classroom sets of programmed learning texts which are being used for introducing a unit, review, and individual enrichment. The collection in the center is permanent and is supplemented throughout the year by material relevant to a current project. Circulation is handled in the center in the same manner as in the library. With 34 percent of the titles and 23 percent of the volumes in the school's pure science holdings, the center was responsible for 53.6 percent of the circulation in pure science during the year 1966-67.

Much of the material in the room is curriculum-oriented, although the room is also used for exploration and recreation. During the year, books are put on reserve and special reading lists are prepared. These have included a continuous but changing collection of materials for advanced placement chemistry, a collection on rational numbers, a group of books on marine botany, and a reading list and collection on biological clocks. Since the material is available, teachers have made more supplementary reading assignments. *Scientific American* has been used in paper copy, on microfilm, and in classroom sets of offprints. As one teacher commented, "[We are] . . . making the attempt to have students use the current material as a supplement to their text."

The keypunch and teletypewriters are used by the mathematics students taking a semester course in computer programming. Since the school does not have a computer, time is rented on the machine at the Illinois Institute of Technology. The school is part of an experimental program with IIT and several other suburban high schools to demonstrate that, by involving many schools, it is possible for a high school to afford time on a remote computer. In addition to the computer programming class of 20 students each semester, 13 classes in advanced and intermediate algebra have a ten-lesson unit in computer programming and actual experience with the computer. Students from the computer programming class spent their study periods in the center instructing the more than 300 algebra students in the use of the equipment.

Teachers have begun to experiment with other ways to use the facilities. New equipment which the school is considering, such as a

teaching machine, can be placed in the center for student trial. Borrowing from the ideas of Dr. Samuel Postlethwait at Purdue University, one of the biology teachers has prepared three units for tutorial taped sessions; one carrel is set up with a tape recorder and all the necessary apparatus to learn the principles of weight and measurement, statistics, or significance in measurement. The students are given a two-week period in which to listen to the tape and then are expected to be ready for discussion. A similar approach has been used by a mathematics teacher in reviewing simplification of radicals, solving determinants, and in teaching approaches to geometric proof.

Simply having the materials available is not enough; adequate staffing of a resource center has been an important part of the program. A librarian, library aide, student library assistant, and mathematics or science teacher assist the student in the center.

The librarian, besides doing general reference work in the main library, is responsible for building and maintaining the center's collection and materials, implementing the program, and serving as a liaison person between the library and three academic departments. By having a closer contact with a part of the faculty, she can be more aware of their projects. She tries to participate in departmental activities to alert personnel to new materials and to receive their suggestions. The additional library staff has also made it possible to organize and incorporate much departmental material for improved use.

The library aides are paraprofessionals who work a half day in supervising the study hall. One of these aides also plans and prepares the bulletin boards for the center.

Each period, one student assistant is responsible for delivering library slips to study halls and charging out books. He also shelves books and types overdue notices.

A mathematics teacher is assigned to the resource center each period and, because he is relieved of study hall duties, he is available to help the students. Having teachers in the center has been an effective way to bring the faculty into contact with library materials.

The library instruction program in the resource center is carried on in addition to the general library instruction. Since the majority of the students using the center were from the adjacent science study hall, the first few days of the semester were spent acquainting them with what is available; students were instructed in groups of 20 and about one-third of the student body was reached this way. The students often brought friends in to show them what they had discovered and how to use it. Instruction of the faculty was more limited; the librarian spoke to the mathematics department on institute day, to the new teachers at an in-service workshop, and to the cooperating departments at the beginning of the year. Most often, instruction of both students and faculty was done individually when specific materials were needed.

Created from a traditional study hall, the center has become the site of varied activity. Students come in to finish typing a report, prepare a computer program, use a calculator to find the average of their biology data, or review the filmstrip on the common solution to linear equations. Hopefully, the resource center has made their studying more effective.

John K. Van Dyke, head of the mathematics department, agrees with this evaluation of the Project in the following comment:

> I think it has encouraged members in my department to try innovations in their teaching that otherwise would not have been feasible.
>
> To a surprising degree I believe many students have become aware for the first time that a truly fine library and its program contribute substantially to the learning process.

American history resource center

What is the American history resource center? It is a physical entity but, more important, it is service and the communication of ideas. It is the promise of excellent school library service being realized; the dream of an expanded, vital school library program becoming reality. Most significantly, it is the opportunity to bring together faculty, students, librarians, and instructional media and to do so with the active, informed support of an intelligent school administration.

The resource center became a physical reality in September, 1965, when the Knapp School Libraries Project made it possible to transform 1,435 square feet of study hall space into an attractive 81-seat extension of the library. Space within the school is and will be limited until an addition to the building is completed. It was not possible, therefore, to assemble the desired quantity of students, materials, and equipment within the strict physical boundaries of the room. It *was* possible to locate the center across a corridor from the audio-visual center, where non-book history materials are kept. The room is immediately adjacent to a listening-viewing area and to the library classroom, which houses the collection of history books on other countries, and where an entire history class or small groups of history students may work together. The center is only a few feet from the main library.

Biography, historical fiction, economics, and political science, as well as history, are found among the center's collection of print materials, e.g., periodicals, reprints, pamphlets, and books, and of non-print materials, e.g., filmstrips, slides, tapes, discs, films, transparencies, and microfilm. Student use of these materials is facilitated by two factors: first, the available and capable assistance of a history teacher and two student assistants during each of the school day's nine 40-minute periods, and of a history librarian who is in the center during five periods and is as close as the main library during three other periods; and second, the implementation of a flexible circulation policy which attempts to meet the demands of a variety of situations while basically maintaining a two-week loan of materials from the general collection and an overnight loan of materials on reserve. Also, use of a charging machine, of the student identification card as a library card, and of a print-out as a registration file has increased the speed with which related procedures may be performed and has eliminated the need for deciphering student hieroglyphics and struggling with faculty memories.

A speech class meets in the library classroom.

Although it is impossible to accommodate more than United States history students and materials within the center until completion of our construction and remodeling program, the interests identified with the center encompass other areas of the social sciences, e.g., Russian, Latin American, Asian and world histories, economics, government, and sociology, and include the following services: (1) preparation of bibliographies and collections of materials related to particular units and topics; (2) introductions to and suggestions for maximum use of available resources, i.e., subject-integrated instruction on the use of an instructional materials center; (3) preparation and delivery of "book talks"; (4) selection and some cataloging and classification of history materials (faculty participation in the former, i.e., selection, is invited, is welcomed, and is received); (5) provision of reference and readers advisory assistance, of a general nature in the main library and of a more specific nature in the resource center to students and faculty; and (6) participation in academic depart-mental meetings, in meetings with small groups of teachers and/or students, and in conferences with individual teachers or students.

As services were provided to meet existing needs, a spiral phenomenon became obvious: increased services produced increased demands which made an increase in service desirable. A partial explanation may be found in the fact that the quality and quantity of available library resources and services stimulated (and rendered more possible) multi-media, innovative approaches in the classroom. A second partial explanation is found in the impact made upon the library by increasing faculty involvement with curriculum experimentation and especially with the preparation of software for use, beginning September, 1967, in a random-access retrieval system.

Brief discussions of two recent additions to course offerings—specifically Asian Studies and World Civilization—well illustrate library-curricular interaction and the deep involvement of the history resource center in the history program.

Asian Studies,* a one-semester elective initially funded by the Illinois Plan for Program Development for Gifted Children and begun in February, 1966, offers college-bound seniors an independent study program having Asian history as the core and providing an opportunity to use a wide variety of resources in pursuing their general course work and their individual research.

A basic, college-level collection of approximately 500 book titles, as well as appropriate domestic and foreign periodicals, were acquired. Also procured were a slide collection presenting the history of Japan as told in that nation's arts and a complete collection of the *Journal of Asian Studies* in microfilm.

An illustrated bibliography, which like so many of its kind needed a supplement almost before it was completed, was prepared to provide faculty and students with an annotated listing of appropriate Asian-related library materials available when the course began.

A number of scholars were invited to present addresses in person, such as Wisconsin's Dr. Michael Petrovich, or via telelecture, such as Harvard's Dr. John K. Fairbank. Each guest who came to our campus not only gave four different lectures, one each to the three sections of Asian Studies and one to a large group assembly, but also occasionally had conferences with small groups of students whose research projects were related to the speaker's sphere of activity. With rare exceptions, both the live lecturers and the telelecturers agreed to the taping of their presentations and consequently made a substantial contribution to our tape library.

Because the Asian Studies course broke away from many traditional high school patterns and, in fact, more nearly resembled a college course, it was necessary first for the students involved to have frequent and prolonged use of the library, and second, to have access to more specialized and greater quantities of material than it was possible to provide within

*See Thomas N. Tegge, "Oak Park-River Forest, Illinois: Independent Work in Asian Studies," *The Bulletin of the National Association of Secondary-School Principals*, January, 1967, pp. 43-47.

our own institution. The first was a local matter and easily solved; the second also was readily dispatched as a result of the generous cooperation of public and university libraries which, when informed about our program and problem, made their resources available to our students.

One continuing objective for the Asian Studies program is to improve the quality of instruction in Asian history and culture and to offer our students a significant educational experience. A second is to investigate the feasibility of, need for, and interest in the development of a set of materials, including, for example, a course of study, copies of tapes, and bibliographies, which could be shared with other secondary schools.

The second course receiving special emphasis is World Civilization, beginning in September, 1966. This four-semester program represents a humanities-oriented, team teaching approach to world history. It is offered at the freshman-sophomore level and interprets its title quite literally, i.e., the subject is "World," not "Western," civilization.

Expertise and guidance for the four classes of freshmen, who pioneered the course this year and will complete it during their sophomore year for history and humanities credit, were provided by two history teachers, who served as "anchor men," by members of the music, art, and English departments, and by persons from the communities of Oak Park and River Forest, who are among our invaluable human resources.

The very nature of the course content in World Civilization and of the teaching techniques employed provide an obvious indication of the quantities of diverse media dealing with many subjects which are appropriate for and indispensable to such a humanities program. The library assistance provided for World Civilization was not unlike that for Asian Studies with two major exceptions: Student use of extra-mural library facilities was not arranged; nor was an exhaustive bibliography of pertinent, related materials prepared.

Quite naturally, we suffer from professional impatience concerning the actualization of our remodeled resource center. There is great potential for service and the beneficial impact upon the library program, which undoubtedly will accompany the increase in physical size to accommodate not only desirable quantities of students, materials, and equipment, but also a variety of activities involving individuals, small groups, or entire classes, and the expansion of facilities to include both wet and dry carrels and connection with the retrieval system.

We have not created a utopia, nor do we pretend to have solved all the problems relating to school libraries. We do have a sense of accomplishment, of challenge, and of exhilaration emanating from the realization that we have precipitated an increasing demand for many types of good library service and materials.

Foreign language resource center

The foreign language resource center was developed by the library and the foreign language department, which includes courses in French, German, Latin, Russian, and Spanish. The center is designed to give the language student individual experience for growth and depth beyond his regular classroom activities. While this enrichment program is culturally oriented, the center's main object is language training.

The center is adjacent to the foreign language laboratory and a study hall seating 65 language students. The foreign language de-

FOREIGN LANGUAGE RESOURCE CENTER
(June 7, 1967)

RESOURCES		
Books	Titles	Volumes
French	241	374
German	76	115
Latin	30	40
Russian	137	208
Spanish	196	332
TOTAL	680	1,069
Classroom supplementary sets of foreign language books (stored in main library)	111	4,071
Recordings		
Spoken	94	104
Musical	39	39
Tapes	29	30
Filmstrips/Sets of slides	75	78
Periodicals	28	—
Art prints	40	—

PHYSICAL FACILITIES
  7 octagonal tables, 24 chairs
  2 listening carrels, 2 phonographs
  2 viewing carrels, 2 slide/filmstrip projectors
  Book shelving sections, magazine display rack
  3 filing/storage cabinets
  Librarian's desk

partment administers the language laboratory with its 30 full record carrels. A librarian with language background and a library aide administer the foreign language resource center. The center itself seats 24 students and provides two listening carrels and two viewing carrels for student use. All beginning language students are assigned to the resource center study hall on a regular basis; other language students come to the center from regular study halls.

The center's collection includes books, periodicals, recordings, tapes, filmstrips, slides, and art prints. In addition to outside reading materials, the book collection includes background information on the culture of the various languages taught. Selection of materials is done with the language department to ensure that these materials fit the curriculum. For example, the center's book collection includes titles from the advanced placement reading lists; recordings include musical settings of German poems studied; certain art prints are selected because of their appropriateness to materials studied in class. The periodicals collection includes at least one pictorial-type and one general cultural periodical for each language. Weekly newspapers in French, Spanish, and Russian are received. Because the student receives materials for drill in his classroom and in the laboratory, the tapes and recordings are literary and musical. Foreign language texts are available to accompany most of the audio-visual materials.

Circulation and attendance figures have increased steadily, as has the enthusiasm of both students and teachers. The opportunity to link the library program directly to the curriculum and the centralizing of foreign language materials are significant factors in providing better library services.

The following description of the use made of the library by the language department was given at a faculty institute program by one of the foreign language teachers:

> Only upon . . . the establishment of the resource center did the foreign language department *begin* to have sufficient funds for adequate outside reading books, twenty-six current magazines and newspapers, film-

strips, slides and phonograph records. Advanced students go to the resource center on an individual basis to supplement class work and to do special projects. There are dictionaries and other reference works, essays, biographies, novels, plays, collections of short stories, and poetry.

A student who is reading a seventeenth-century play by Moliere goes to the resource center in order to listen to excerpts of that play recorded by artists of the Comedie Francaise; he chooses another play of the period as outside reading; he studies a filmstrip of Louis XIV and the court at Versailles. A French student with special interest in history listens to recorded speeches and writings of the French Revolution or of World War II. A German student with particular interest in music prepares a written theme or an oral report on Goethe and compares various versions of *Faust*. A Spanish student who is interested in art goes to the resource center to view a filmstrip of the paintings of Velazquez; he finds reproductions available for study, and as outside reading chooses *Las Meninas*, a book by a contemporary dramatist dealing with Velazquez's most famous painting. A Latin student who is also enrolled in World Civilization or in Humanities listens to a recording of Virgil's *Aeneid* and chooses a book describing our classical heritage. The student of Russian also makes excellent use of the resource center to avail himself of books, magazines, and recordings.

. . . The library offers invaluable service in providing films to be shown at the proper point in the teaching of a given unit. For example, the previously mentioned study of the period of Louis XIV and his court is made increasingly vivid by showing films based on his life, on Moliere and the Comedie Francaise, and a feature film of one play

studied, *Le Misanthrope*. The third-year Spanish classes study a cultural reader of Spain and have a program of colored films made in Spain. These films present a variety of subjects from scenery and industry, monuments, bullfighting, painting, and dancing, to short plays by Cervantes. Because these films have French or Spanish sound tracks, the foreign language continues to be the vehicle of communication. Apart from regional differences in pronunciation or dialect, language is not being studied in itself; rather, the purpose is to communicate information on the subject which has been filmed.

FIELD WORKER'S REPORT

The teacher education goals of the Knapp Project at Oak Park and River Forest High School were pursued on the local school level, the state level, the national level, and even to some extent on the international level. On the local level, programs were devised to encourage both beginning teachers and experienced teachers to make wide use of library resources and to instruct them in effective use of the library, including materials and staff. On the state level, persistent attempts were made to convince teacher education institutions of the need to prepare student teachers with both the desire and the skill to use library resources effectively. On the national level, an attempt was made to disseminate research information that would demonstrate the value of and need for teacher education programs which would prepare teachers experienced in the ways of multi-media instruction. That same information was sent on request to librarians and teacher education personnel in Thailand, Australia, Japan, and Chile.

During the course of the two years of Project participation, a total of 56 student teachers representing the entire range of subject fields were trained at Oak Park and River Forest High School. At the beginning of each student teaching period, a library orientation session was conducted not only to acquaint the student teachers with the library and its personnel, but also to discover how much knowledge about the library they had and how those of us involved in the Project could be of the most use to them.

During the 1965-66 school year, the approach we took was to acquaint the student teachers with the library and its resources and to urge them, but not force them, to come to the library regularly to become further acquainted with the resources and to seek our help with their teaching projects. Though the field worker made frequent visits to the student teachers' classrooms to inquire how they were doing and to offer library services, very few of the student teachers, except those the field worker was actually supervising for the University of Illinois, returned to the library for materials or help. The problem was created in part by the lack of support from cooperating teachers and university supervisors who regarded what happened in the classroom as the only important part of student teaching. Some textbook-oriented cooperating teachers refused to require that their student teachers use audio-visual materials or supplementary reading materials. Many university supervisors, unschooled in the location and use of library materials themselves, could hardly make a strong argument for something they saw fit not to use. The field worker received no response at all from a letter sent to the heads of student teaching in surrounding colleges and universities inviting them to visit the library facilities and to bring groups of student teachers at the expense of the Project. The field worker, bringing groups from his own university, was the only one to bring student teachers to the school during the first year.

The field worker and librarians decided that it would be necessary to show statistically the state of student teachers' ignorance of the availability and use of library materials to demonstrate the need for support of our efforts by school and university personnel. To that end, a questionnaire containing 13 items dealing with the availability and use of library resources was administered to student teachers currently practicing at Oak Park and River Forest High School and those at Roosevelt High School, another Knapp Project school in Portland, Oregon. The results of the study, which clearly demonstrated how little those student teachers knew about resources essential to the effective teaching of their subjects, were distributed along with recommendations for action to cooperating teachers and teacher education institutions throughout Illinois. This study was conducted in May, 1966. The questionnaires were distributed to student teachers in the high school library and were also completed and collected there. A copy of the questionnaire appears on page 301.

The results of that study were cast into article form and published under the title, "Student Teachers' Knowledge of Library Resources and Services," in a 1966 National Council of Teachers of English publication, *New Trends in English Education*. In addition, the field worker and the librarian attended the NCTE Conference on English Education held at the Carnegie Institute of Technology in April, 1966, to discuss the results of the study and to seek national support for teacher education programs to remedy the situation.

A shortened version of that same article was printed in *School Libraries* (Winter, 1967) under the title, "What Do Student Teachers Know about Libraries?" The field worker stated in the article that copies of the questionnaire used to gather the data and the complete write-up of the study were available on request. A total of 250 requests was received from librarians and teacher education personnel scattered throughout this country and foreign countries. Many of the people who requested the information indicated that they intended to disseminate the information locally to those who had not seen it, or that they intended to use the information to modify the design of their local teacher education programs. The overwhelming response to the article resulted in the longer article's being reprinted and made available through the Knapp Project office. Within a few weeks, approximately 7,500 copies had been distributed by that office.

Miss Margarette Seibel, librarian, confers with a history teacher in the history resource center.

With the need demonstrated, support for the field worker's and librarians' efforts to involve the student teachers in more extensive library training was easier to obtain. Many cooperating teachers accompanied their student teachers to the library in search of new ideas and new materials. Student teachers were told to be sure to spend at least one hour a week in the library, and a record of their visits was kept as a way of making it seem more imperative. When they came to the library, they were usually given individual attention in locating and using materials to enrich and sometimes change their usual teaching strategies. More than once, the field worker heard a student teacher exclaim, "I didn't even know that existed!"

Also, during the second year, many of the personnel in charge of teacher education in colleges and universities throughout the state came to the Oak Park and River Forest High School library to see for themselves what a good library looked like and what it could do for a teacher. In addition, groups of student teachers from the University of Illinois and Purdue University visited the school as a part of their teacher education preparation.

Simultaneously with the drive to acquaint student teachers with the advantages of library knowledge, a concerted effort was made to provide in-service motivation and education. Efforts to encourage experienced teachers to make wider use of library resources were greatly aided by the funds made available through the field worker's Project budget to bring into the school outside speakers and con-

LIBRARY QUESTIONNAIRE

Teaching area_____ College major_____

1. You can locate a book through the card catalog by looking up its_____
    _____, _____, or_____.

2. If a student wanted to see if any magazine articles had been written on
    a topic you had given him to explore, what reference work would you
    direct him to?_____

3. Name two reference works you might direct a student to if he wanted to
    get some information about a famous living writer._____
    _____

4. The number classification system used in most libraries is called_____
    _____

5. If you wanted to find out the approximate reading level of a work of
    fiction what references might you consult?_____
    _____

6. If a student wanted to find out the titles of books written by a
    particular author, what source would you direct him to?_____
    _____

7. What source could a student consult to find out who said some famous
    line?_____

8. The main difference between an opaque projector and an overhead
    projector is that _____

9. If you wanted to see if there were any filmstrips available on a given
    topic, what reference would you consult?_____
    _____

10. What materials are usually kept in a library's vertical files?_____
    _____

11. If a student wanted to do some research on the Cuban missile crisis,
    what sources would you direct him to?_____
    _____
    _____

12. How can the library be of service to you in your teaching?_____
    _____
    _____

13. How can the librarian be of greatest service to you in your teaching?
    _____
    _____

sultants. The belief that new ideas in the school would result in wider use of related materials proved to be well founded. Teachers were forced to turn to the library for supplementary materials for themselves and their students.

More obviously related to in-service training, an audio-visual fair was conducted with Knapp Project funds. The school's audio-visual specialist planned the program and arranged with producers of audio-visual equipment to set up displays of hardware and software to capture the teachers' interest. The materials were on display throughout the day; many teachers returned to inquire about them and test them several times. As part of the same program, an audio-visual specialist from the University of Illinois presented a lecture-demonstration on the theory and practice behind effective use of audio-visual materials. This fair must be considered one of the most effective in-service activities conducted during the two years of Project participation.

The success of these activities points to the fact that all in-service training programs need not be called library-centered activities. A large part of the job of getting teachers to use more library resources and to use them better is simply getting them into the library. Presenting them with stimulating ideas through workshops and speakers awakens new interests and needs that many teachers will go to the library to satisfy. Following are some of the comments teachers made in the final evaluation questionnaire:

> The day devoted to audio-visual materials and the speaker who demonstrated the over-head—both were very helpful.

> The guest lecturers have been outstanding. The impact on the class has been much better than expected and the students in my class want to hear more of the same.

> The students have gained from exposure to well known historians. Personal contact with authors of books they read has quickened their curiosity.

> The Hemingway series, while not directly concerned with languages, could not but stimulate great interest among humanities-oriented students.

It is important to note that the teaching staff at Oak Park and River Forest High School had favorable attitudes toward the library and its staff even at the start of the Knapp Project. A study of their attitudes, and those of the staff at Roosevelt High School in Portland, Oregon, was made at the beginning of the Project to determine where they stood and what needed to be done. The study showed that the teachers and librarians in these two schools were actually in very close agreement about what the roles of the library and the librarian should be in the total school program. That study was reported in the September, 1967, issue of the *ALA Bulletin* under the title, ''Changing Attitudes toward the Library and Librarian.'' The questionnaire used in this study in May, 1966, begins on page 303. Teachers received the questionnaires in their mailboxes and were asked to return them to the library.

The addition of personnel and materials made possible by participation in the Knapp Project did make teachers more enthusiastic about the use of the library and more aware of the benefits to be gained from the use of its resources. In a final evaluation questionnaire, teachers were asked about the benefits they thought they had gained from participation in the Project and whether the additions to the library staff, materials, and facilities had had any appreciable effect on their teaching. A sample of their responses follows:

> Yes, the resource center is a necessary function of the classroom work in my teaching.

> The ability to call upon a librarian who is knowledgeable in my teaching subject is a tremendous assistance—both as a time-saver and a source of new ideas.

> In general, the upgrading and improvement of materials and services have enabled us to serve the students' needs more adequately than ever before.

> The options open to the teacher from the additional materials, both book and non-book, and the time saved by having bibliographies furnished have made planning by the teacher an easier task, carried out more efficiently.

LIBRARY QUESTIONNAIRE

1. Subject(s) you teach_____

2. College major(s)_____

3. College attended_____

4. Number of years you have taught_____

5. Did your college work include instructions in library skills?_____

   If yes, check the context in which it was
   given: ____Orientation period

                                                   ____Special library class

                                                   ____Part of other classes

                                                   ____Other (name)_____

6. Did your college work include instruction in how to use the library and
   its facilities effectively in your teaching?_____

   If yes, check the context: ____Special library class

                                                   ____Part of methods class

                                                   ____Other (name)_____

(Complete the statements begun in items 7 and 8 with as many words as
you wish.)

7. The librarian should be

8. The library should be

Check items 9-34 in columns to the right:	Strongly agree	Mildly agree	Agree	Disagree	Mildly disagree	Strongly disagree
9. School librarians should be considered part of the school's instructional staff.						
10. High school students should be given instruction in library skills.						
11. Librarians should help to direct student's leisure reading.						
12. Audio-visual equipment and supplies should be centered in the library.						
13. All of the library's resources should be centered in one location.						
14. Librarians should help students select research topics.						
15. Classroom teachers should be required to spend time on a regular basis in the library working with students.						
16. Librarians should help students locate information required by teachers.						
17. The librarian ought to establish separate resource centers equipped with pertinent equipment and supplies for every academic area.						

	Strongly agree	Mildly agree	Agree	Disagree	Mildly disagree	Strongly disagree
18. The library and its resources are more essential to English and social studies than to other areas.						
19. Library work offers an effective means to individualize instruction.						
20. Librarians should visit classes and give book talks.						
21 Librarians should keep teachers informed of new materials available for their use.						
22. The librarian should help students with reading and writing assignments they do in the library.						
23. The librarian should maintain an extensive teachers' reference collection.						
24. Regularly scheduled previews of new books and audio-visual materials should be held.						
25. The librarian should distribute sets of reference materials to individual classrooms when requested.						
26. Librarians should consult teachers before purchasing new books and audio-visual materials.						

	Strongly agree	Mildly agree	Agree	Disagree	Mildly disagree	Strongly disagree
27. Librarians should be certified teachers.						
28. Room libraries are more effective than resource centers or a central library.						
29. Many teachers don't use the library and its facilities effectively.						
30. The library should be open either in the evenings or on Saturdays, or both.						
31. Instruction in effective use of the library should be given as part of a teacher's in-service training.						
32. The library staff should include someone to help teachers prepare audio-visual aids.						
33. The librarian's main job is to store and locate information.						
34. Teachers would use the library more effectively if they knew more about what resources are available and how to locate them.						
35. Librarians should be required to teach some classes.						

36. (Complete the sentence.) The school librarian can help me most by_____

_____

_____

I feel the benefit has been to our students first—and second to the faculty for the enrichment of materials and professional assistance the project has afforded us.

The materials have also been of immense value to me in class preparation because of their immediate availability.

Of particular interest in a final evaluation of the Project is the number of references teachers made in their comments to benefits gained by the students as a result of the school's participation in the Knapp Project. Students, naturally, are sometimes not aware of direct benefits gained from a particular activity in which they or their teachers take part because they are not always aware of changes in school programs, teaching methods, or educational objectives. Nevertheless, they did reap benefits from the increased interest in and use of library resources on the part of their teachers.

As part of the final evaluation of the Project, a sampling was taken of student opinions regarding the school's participation in the Project and the library services that were the most use to them. On the first issue, the students were generally proud of their school's

Mr. Arthur Pelz, head of the art department, consults a book in the art resource center next door to his classroom.

being chosen as a demonstration center. That feeling is evident in many of their statements:

It [having visitors] didn't disturb me because I realized that we have an excellent library and consequently we should use it to demonstrate to other schools how it is run.

I was proud when I saw visitors coming to visit our school library.

I'm flattered that our marvelous library is the center of such attention.

Most of the students in the sample considered the library good if they could find the information they needed for projects assigned in their classes. Some made specific comments about the value of the telelectures and the humanities conference, but for the most part they commented on the reference materials available in the main reading room and in the resource centers. This is a typical statement:

I have used the math-science resource center very consistently. I have also used the reference materials, magazines, and others often in the last few years. Also, the history room has proved beneficial.

Many students simply made gross statements of their over-all evaluation of their school library:

For all my assignments that use library, everything needed is easily found.

I never had trouble trying to find a particular book.

I think that in comparison to other school libraries ours is the best.

A library functions, of course, to serve teachers and students, and, as a demonstration center, the library is showing visitors one way those services can be effectively performed. The handling of visitors so that they can see not only just how the library operates, but how it operates in the total school context to serve the community, staff, and student body is crucial. A program must be planned to give visitors an overview of the school, then a specific examination of its parts, and then an opportunity to ask questions about what they

Knapp Project Evaluation

Although it is difficult to separate the effects of one school project from the others, we are required to submit evidence of the effects of the Knapp Project in our final report. We ask, therefore, that you answer the following questions in order to give us your perceptions of possible benefits of the Project.

Dr. Jerry Walker
University of Illinois Field Worker
for the Project

Attached to this questionnaire* is a list of some of the materials and activities which Knapp funds have made possible.

Please return your answers to my mailbox.

Thank you for your help.

Lura E. Crawford

May 17, 1967

*A copy of this questionnaire was distributed by school mail to each faculty member.

The back of this sheet or a separate sheet may be used, if needed, for your answers to the following.

1. What do you think is the greatest benefit of the school's participation in the Knapp School Libraries Project?

2. Have the additions to the library staff, materials, and facilities had any appreciable effect on your teaching? Please explain.

3. Have the conferences and speakers which have been financed with Knapp funds been useful to you? Please explain.

4. Have you noticed during the last two years any changes in the students' attitudes toward the library or in the kind and quality of work they undertake in the library?

5. In order to assist other schools involved in establishing and/or serving as demonstration centers, do you have any suggestions regarding the policies or procedures of such centers so that they enhance and do not interfere with the effective operation of the school?

KNAPP PROJECT
STUDENT EVALUATION

1. What uses have you made of the library in the past two years?

2. Has the reference collection been adequate for your reference assignments?

3. Do you find the school library a good source for your general reading?

4. Do you regularly read any periodicals in the library? If so, which ones?

5. Have the conferences and speakers financed with Knapp funds been useful to you? (Examples: Humanities Conference, Hemingway Commemorative Programs, telelectures, "Careers in Art" series.)

6. Have you used the resource centers? If so, what type of materials were used?

7. Have you been aware that our school library was participating as a demonstration library? Did the presence of visitors disturb your studying?

These evaluation sheets were distributed to approximately 350 students from May 29 through June 9, by random distribution from the circulation desk in the library and by distribution to one basic English class, one regular team teaching class in American literature and history, and one honor study group.

saw or how they could implement what they saw.

The reactions of a readiness committee who visited the school early in 1966 were most helpful. Members of that committee were:

Dr. Charles M. Allen, Associate Dean of Instruction, College of Education, University of Illinois, Urbana, Illinois

Mr. David Diedrich, Director, Department of Social Studies, Glenbard East High School, Lombard, Illinois

Miss Leila Doyle, Library Consultant, Gary Public Schools, Gary, Indiana

Mrs. Frank Krivanek, Member, Board of Education, Oak Park and River Forest High School, Oak Park, Illinois

Dr. Karl R. Plath, Superintendent, Highland Park High School, Highland Park, Illinois

Dr. Miriam E. Peterson, Director, Division of Libraries, Chicago Board of Education, Chicago, Illinois

Planning such a program for visiting teams made up of people with different backgrounds and interests is a difficult task, and during the Project, several program changes were made to accommodate the diverse needs and interests of the visitors.

Initially the visitors were kept together for a tightly scheduled program which lasted nearly the whole day. The program began with a quick tour of the main reading room led by Miss Crawford or one of her staff. The field worker also took part in this phase of the program. Following the tour of the main facility, visitors convened in the library classroom for a brief welcome from Miss Crawford and an introduction to the school and community by Dr. Schwilck or, in his absence, by Mr. Fuog. This meeting provided an opportunity for administrators in the group to hear from another administrator how a very good library program could and must be maintained in the interests of the students, whatever the costs. The meeting also gave the librarians in the group an opportunity to hear an administrator sing the praises of a good librarian.

That meeting was usually followed by visits to the foreign language, mathematics and sci-

Students work together on key punch equipment in the mathematics and science resource center.

ence, and art resource centers. The subject-matter librarians in the foreign language and mathematics and science resource centers met the group and introduced them to the operation of the centers. A little of the history of the centers was given along with a description of the current operation, including assignment of staff and students and acquisition and use of materials. Bibliographies were always available for visitors who were interested in various aspects of the collections. Visitors were given a chance to browse in resource centers and to ask whatever question they had regarding their operation. Visits to the resource centers were usually limited to 20 or 25 minutes. Since there is no art librarian, Mr. Arthur Pelz, the department head, was usually available to help Miss Crawford explain the operation of the art center. The same opportunity to browse and ask questions was provided there.

Following visits to the resource centers, visitors were usually taken to the audio-visual department to meet the people in charge of that operation and to get a complete description of the holdings, operation, and staffing of the department. Because the room housing the audio-visual department at Oak Park and River Forest High School is small, this meeting sometimes tended to be less than satisfactory because it was crowded when a group of more than ten was visiting. In spite of the discomfort, having the meeting right in the facility added to the presentation, because it made the point that space and convenience are not necessarily essential for effective audio-visual operation. Visitors seemed to be especially interested in the school's audio-visual program. "How many projectors does the school have?" "Do the teachers make their own transparencies?" "How much do the students do?" Questions like those clearly reflected areas of great concern and doubt in the visitors' minds, and the audio-viual specialists answered in great detail, giving specific details and up-to-date figures.

Following the audio-visual visit, the group was taken to lunch in the teachers' cafeteria. The lunch period usually lasted for an hour. Those who finished lunch early and wished to go back to something they had seen earlier were encouraged to do so. Many visitors took this opportunity to visit the faculty lounge and get acquainted with some of the staff. Here, visitors could sense the high morale of the staff, and here much good was done to promote the total school program.

After lunch the visitors returned to the library classroom to hear from Miss Seibel, the history librarian, about the operation of the American history resource center and about the various experimental programs taking place in the social studies department. The librarian stressed the good working relationships she had developed with the teachers, and she enumerated the things she and Miss Crawford had done to develop those relationships. Services to the students were discussed, too. Again, bibliographies were available.

Following this, the visitors usually heard from the field worker about what had been done in the school to educate both teachers and student teachers in the effective use of the library and its resources. Since many of the visitors were not clear about the University of Illinois's responsibility in the project, that topic was also discussed. Librarians and administrators, as well as the teacher education representatives in the group, were extremely receptive to ideas they could try out in their own schools.

The conclusion of the day's program included the filling out of information cards (name, school, position), the passing out of Knapp Project materials, and having tea with as many members of the library staff as were available on a given day.

Although this was essentially the schedule maintained for visitors throughout the Project, several changes were made. The feedback received from the first visitors indicated that they wished to have more time to follow up by themselves those aspects of the program in which they were most interested. Administrators felt they would like to spend more time looking at the whole school program, while librarians wanted more time to investigate specific library techniques. With those purposes in mind, Miss Crawford and the field worker decided to relax the schedule to provide for more individual investigation, which meant allowing a little more unscheduled time. Tea was dispensed with in the afternoon, also, so that visitors could use that time to explore their interests in more depth. While the same over-all schedule was generally maintained, opportunity was provided for visitors to sample the day's program according to their individual interests in the scheduled activity.

Another change in procedure was to provide more personal attention to each visitor by dividing visitors into smaller groups. During the last year of the Project, the initial tour of the main reading room was nearly always done in groups ranging from four to six visitors. Miss Crawford, Dr. Walker, and the librarians escorted groups around. Groups of 20 or more visitors were nearly always divided into two groups to visit the mathematics and science and foreign language resource centers. These smaller groups allowed each visitor to ask more questions and to get to know different members of the staff better.

During the last year of the Project, a more concerted effort was made to meet the visitors before they reached the library and to point out some of the more interesting features of the building. This helped to give the visitors a better sense of the school's character.

We believe the original visiting program was sound, but the changes helped to make it better. By the end of the Project, letters received from people who had visited the school were positive in nearly every case. Statements like these were common:

The visit was all and more than we imagined it could be. From the moment that we arrived until we left, every minute was filled with inspiration and stimulation.

The librarian and her assistants did all that was humanly possible to make the visit a rewarding experience for all of us.

I think that the staff at Oak Park and River Forest did an outstanding job of guiding us through the several areas and explaining their materials and method of operation.

The visit to Oak Park and River Forest High School library was one of the most outstanding educational experiences I have had.

We were given the theory, but, more important, we were able to observe the practice.

The activity was handled efficiently so that we not only were briefed on background, purposes, and program, but we also had a good opportunity to see for ourselves what was going on.

Of course, it was desirable to have the visitors react favorably to the program, but it was much more important to have them leave with specific ideas in mind to try out when they returned to their own schools. The following quotations taken from follow-up letters and questionnaires indicate that the program was successful in that regard, too:

The division of the library into resource centers seems a very practical solution . . . and with all the efforts made to have it staffed properly, it seems to have worked well.

. . . [Our social studies department] would be interested in a combined study hall social studies library as an adjunct to the general library. Until this can be done, we may equip a book truck with material for special use within the social studies classes.

. . . [A faculty member], who is a consistent user of the library for enrichment of science students, was interested in the science and mathematics library. The concentration of materials in this area would be very useful in one of our third floor study halls, where the science classes are located. If this could not be done, perhaps we'll try to establish a science study section in the library.

Use of subject-specialist librarians; use of library aides to handle routine matters, thus freeing the librarians to work with students and materials.

Hope to establish better communication between administration, library personnel, and faculty. More emphasis on planning and pre-planning with total staff involved, particularly for building of library collection.

PROSPECTUS

In January, 1966, under the sponsorship of an Elementary and Secondary Education Title III study grant, several members of the high school faculty began a special study of current problems in the use and storage of instructional materials and the possibilities of truly individualized instruction. By the time this study got under way, the resource centers made possible by Knapp Project funds were already well established. In operation, these resource centers were demonstrating the validity of several key facts. By putting students and teachers in a physical situation which makes possible a more effective utilization of the books, machines, films, records, periodicals, and staff of the library, these centers were demonstrating that: (1) students can profit from opportunities for independent and individualized study; (2) improvements in the availability and use of instructional materials can be achieved when physical facilities themselves are flexible and accessible; (3) class-

room instruction can be enriched by the teachers and the library staff; (4) students and teachers can wisely employ a greater diversity of instructional materials than current library equipment can make available; (5) flexibility in student schedules can be achieved within the "lock-step" of a traditional nine-period day if the necessary diversity in study quarters is provided.

The relationship between the Knapp and Title III Projects soon became obvious. Supported by the lessons of the Knapp Project

demonstrations, the study committee proposed the creation of a library-located random access instructional materials retrieval system. By tapping the full potential of modern electronic technology, such a system should be able to provide enriching instruction on an individual basis. True random access to stored materials would make possible a highly sophisticated advancement of the work begun in the resource centers. Clearly, the Knapp Project experience made a significant contribution to the development of the proposal for the retrieval system.

ARTICLES ABOUT THE
KNAPP SCHOOL LIBRARIES PROJECT

Adams, Hazel. "The Changing Role of the Elementary School Library," *The Reading Teacher*, 18 (7) (April, 1965), 563-66.

Reading specialist at Central Park Road and other schools cites implications and values that a good school library has for the reading program.

"Advisory Committee Outlines Phases of Knapp School Libraries Project," *School Libraries*, 12 (3) (March, 1963), 17-19.

Statement announcing the Project, also published as separate brochure. (See page 000.)

Barnes, Donald L. "Allisonville Shapes Up," *School Library Journal*, 12 (6) (February, 1965), 28-30; *Library Journal*, 90 (4) (February 15, 1965), 942-44.

Recounts the planning and action undertaken as the Allisonville School readied itself for Project participation.

————. "Make Me Another Dream," *School Libraries*, 16 (3) (Spring, 1967), 59-61.

Dr. Barnes, who coordinated two summer workshops for teachers and librarians at the Allisonville School, outlines the necessary planning and tentatively evaluates the workshops.

Belt, W. Dwayne, and Snow, G. Gardner. "Knapp Project Sponsors Media Conference," *School Libraries*, 16 (4) (Summer, 1967), 51-54.

The field worker and junior high school principal in Provo, Utah, outline the teamwork that made the January, 1967, conference on "A Multi-Media Approach to Learning" a success.

Bowden, M. G. "Casis School: Three Way Stretch," *School Libraries*, 14 (3) (March, 1965), 37-41.

Background information on the elementary school shortly after its selection for Project participation, provided by Dr. Bowden, who was principal from the time the school began until 1966.

Bradbury, John. "The Standards Are Minimum: Conclusions Based on the Knapp Project Applications," *School Libraries*, 13 (2) (January, 1964), 34-36.

Survey of strengths and weaknesses of applications presented for Phase I.

Chisholm, Robert L. "How to Evaluate a Good Library and Program," *American School Board Journal*, 151 (5) (November, 1965), 24-41.

In outlining means and results of evaluation of library programs, the Richland superintendent of schools cites some of the methods and findings of evaluation at Marcus Whitman.

————, and Savitt, Robert F. "Caught Knapping," *School Library Journal*, 10 (1) (September, 1963), 36-37; *Library Journal*, 88 (16) (September 15, 1963), 3272-73.

Comments of Superintendents Savitt and Chisholm, of Plainview and Richland respectively, at the time the Phase I schools were selected. These statements are from the June, 1963, press conference.

Chun, May C. "Hawaii Goes to Knapp: Knapp Centers Challenge Hawaiian Visitors," *School Libraries*, 16 (1) (Fall, 1966), 25-28.

An unusual Project grant made it possible for Hawaiian visitors to observe in all of the Phase III schools, and Mrs. Chun reports their reactions and follow-up activities.

Crawford, Lura E. "Resource Centers: Oak Park and River Forest High School," in "*Scholastic Teacher* Reports: Knapp School Libraries Project, Phase III," *Scholastic Teacher*, 88 (14) (May 13, 1966), 9-10.

The head librarian of the largest school in the Project describes the concepts and procedures involved in establishing and maintaining subject area resource centers.

————. "Functional Staffing for the High School Library," *School Libraries*, 15 (3) (March, 1966), 27-33.

Miss Crawford, in outlining the steps taken at Oak Park and River Forest High School in recruiting and deploying staff, provides guidelines for other school libraries where the library staffs are growing.

DuBose, Dorothy. "A Library is for Learning and for Fun," *Scholastic Teacher*, 24 (10) (April 10, 1964), 9T-11T.

A staff writer reports on her own observations of children using the library of the Central Park Road School.

Elementary Librarian's Committee of the Northern Ohio Unit, Catholic Library Association. "The Knapp School Libraries Project," *Catholic Library World*, 36 (2) (October, 1964), 94-95.

Team report of Project-sponsored visit to Central Park Road School and outline of the group's plan for program development.

Fast, Betty. "The Knapp Project Film—Something More than a Movie," *School Libraries*, 15 (1) (October, 1965), 53-57.

Report of audience response to . . . *And Something More*, and suggestions for school librarians who introduce or schedule it for programs.

Fenwick, Sara I. "Knapp Foundation Awards AASL Million Dollar Grant," *School Libraries*, 12 (2) (January, 1963), 11-12.

One of the first announcements of the Project and its goals by a past president of the American Association of School Librarians.

"Films to Make Reading Instruction More Fun," *Educational Screen and Audiovisual Guide*, 46 (8/471) (August, 1967), 18-58.

In a retrospective review of several films, comments on . . . *And Something More*, the Project-sponsored documentary.

Gaver, Mary V. "Dream Come True," *School Library Journal*, 9 (4) (December, 1962), 2; *Library Journal*, 87 (22) (December 15, 1962), 4578.

Chairman of the Project Advisory Committee provides background on how the Project was initiated. First announcement of the Project in the library press.

———. "Give Them Libraries," *The Rotarian*, 108 (3) (March, 1966), 44-61.

The leadership of Project schools is highlighted in terms of the need for further development of school libraries throughout the United States.

———. "The Knapp School Libraries Project," *American Library Association Bulletin*, 59 (9) (October, 1965), 806-9.

As retiring chairman of the Project Advisory Committee, Miss Gaver gave this report at the July, 1965, meeting of the Council of the American Library Association.

Goodwin, Georgie. "The Knapp Project at Allisonville," *School Libraries*, 15 (4) (May, 1966), 38-39.

As supervisor of school libraries for the state of Indiana, Miss Goodwin puts the Allisonville School in perspective and notes its impact as a demonstration center throughout the state.

Houck, Pauline. "When Losers Are Winners," *School Libraries*, 14 (2) (January, 1965), 45-49.

Mrs. Houck, librarian in a suburban Indianapolis school, reviews the efforts and benefits of applying, although unsuccessfully, to be a Knapp Project school.

Hurley, Richard J. "Talking Shop," *Catholic Library World*, 37 (5) (January, 1966), 326-27.

Supervisor of School Libraries in Fairfax, Virginia, decribes visit as leader of Knapp-sponsored team to the Central Park Road School.

Jackson, Clara, and others. "Living School Libraries," *School Library Journal*, 12 (12) (October, 1965), 166; *Library Journal*, 90 (18) (October 15, 1965), 4552.

A group of Ohio educators evaluate the first Project-sponsored sound filmstrip (out of print since 1966) and consider it a disappointment.

James, Don W. "The Teacher and the Library," *Education*, 86 (9) (May, 1966), 546-49.

Principal of Roosevelt High School tells how his school staff, motivated by Knapp grant, improved and extended the use of library materials and services in the instructional program.

Keeler, Donald S., and Hull, Radia. "Many Happy Returns," *School Libraries,* 14 (4) (May, 1965), 26-58.

The Elmira, New York, superintendent of schools and a Pocatello, Idaho, school librarian present reports on their team visits to Central Park Road and Marcus Whitman respectively.

Krivanek, Mrs. Frank J. "The New School Library," *School Boards,* 9 (5) (May, 1966), 14-15.

Member of Oak Park and River Forest High School board describes how an excellent library program has enabled the school to keep abreast of the vast expansion of knowledge.

Lindenmeyer, Ruth. "Knapp School Libraries Project Selects Phase III Sites," *School Libraries,* 14 (4) (May, 1965), 45-63.

As administrative assistant in the Project office, Mrs. Lindenmeyer provides an introduction to the secondary schools selected to participate in the Project.

———. "That Knapp Film Catches On," *School Library Journal,* 12 (7) (March, 1965), 106-7; *Library Journal,* 90 (6) (March 15, 1965), 1470-71.

A report on the kinds and number of showings of . . . *And Something More* in the first few months after its premiere.

Mary Esther, R.S.M., Sister. "Making Education Live!" *Catholic School Journal,* 67 (5) (May, 1967), 56-57.

Librarian of a Catholic girls high school in Rochester, New York, reports on a team visit to the Mount Royal School and notes some new insights and approaches for her own school library program.

McGuire, Alice Brooks. "A Modern Fairy Tale: the Knapp School Libraries Project," *Scholastic Teacher,* all elementary editions (February 4, 1966), 20-21.

Librarian at the Casis School describes the greater flexibility in the school's library program and the impact she believes the Project has had on education in general.

———. "New Wing at Casis," *School Library Journal,* 12 (4) (December, 1965), 22-24; *Library Journal,* 90 (22) (December 15, 1965), 5460-62.

Describes new library at Casis and the improved services it provides. Includes complete data on sizes, furniture, etc.

Moulton, Priscilla L. "Impact: the School Library and the Instructional Program," *The Horn Book Magazine,* 43 (4) (August, 1967), 492.

One of the first reviews of the Project's first book-length report.

Murray, Marguerite. "Impact: the School Library and the Instructional Program," *School Library Journal,* 15 (1) (September, 1967), 59-60; *Library Journal,* 92 (16) (September 15, 1967), 3127-28.

A critical evaluation by an elementary school librarian of the published report on Phase I.

Paxman, Shirley B. "Board Motivates Local Library Program," *American School Board Journal,* 151 (5) (November, 1965), 38-40.

Member of Provo, Utah, Board of Education describes commitment to the library as an essential part of school program, outlines present status and plans to overcome weaknesses.

Pitts, Elsie, and Beachner, Anna M. "Knapp Project Progress Report," *School Libraries,* 13 (4) (May, 1964), 51-53.

The Project librarian and the field worker at Marcus Whitman give background and outline progress a year after Project selection.

Salinger, Lucy. "Oak Park's Title III Project," *School Library Journal,* 14 (5) (January, 1967), 41-42; *Library Journal,* 92 (2) (January 15, 1967), 309-10.

A staff-written account of the plans for the million-dollar project in information retrieval at the Oak Park and River Forest High School.

Sarvello, Ruth. "The Knapp Project Field Workers," *School Libraries,* 15 (2) (January, 1966), 35-38.

The administrative assistant in the Project office provides thumbnail sketches of the eight faculty members named as Project field workers, and describes their roles and responsibilities.

Sayles, Lois. "Faculty Library Committee: Roosevelt High School," in "*Scholastic Teacher* Reports: Knapp School Libraries Project, Phase III," *Scholastic Teacher*, 88 (14) (May 13, 1966), 9-10.

The head librarian at Roosevelt High School outlines the purposes and functions of the committee of teachers which serves the library in an advisory capacity.

———. "Teaching Library Skills Through Subject Matter," *Education*, 86 (7) (March, 1966), 412-16.

Librarian of Roosevelt High School shows how library instruction, integrated with classwork and taught as needed, can be meaningful and absorbing experience for high school students.

Schwilck, Gene L. "How Oak Park Revitalized its Library Resources," *Nation's Schools*, 77 (3) (March, 1966), 94-98.

Principal of Oak Park and River Forest High School reports on the establishment of resource centers, placing great emphasis on faculty involvement and staffing of library. Describes projected electronic retrieval system of information for individualizing instruction.

———. "The Library Needs the Principal," *The Bulletin of the National Association of Secondary-School Principals*, 50 (306) (January, 1966), 6-9.

The role of a principal in an excellent school library program is described by the super-intendent-principal of Oak Park and River Forest High School.

———. "Million Dollar Carrels," *School Library Journal*, 14 (5) (January, 1967), 38-40; *Library Journal*, 92 (2) (January 15, 1967), 306-8.

Description of the high school's plan for a system of information retrieval and relationship of the plan for the future to the present library program.

Sullivan, Peggy. "Dawn After Dream," *School Libraries*, 12 (4) (May, 1963), 31-32.

Project Director's first statement on the Project's goals and expectations.

———. "In Full Swing," *School Library Journal*, 12 (9) (May, 1965), 24-26; *Library Journal*, 90 (10) (May 15, 1965), 2328-30.

Overview of the Project's second year.

———. "The Knapp High Schools and the ALA Standards," *School Library Journal*, 13 (9) (May, 1966), 69-71; *Library Journal*, 91 (10) (May 15, 1966), 2609-11.

The Project Director assesses the strengths and weaknesses in terms of ALA standards of the schools selected for Phase III. Corrections of errors made in editing appear in the September issue, which should be used in reading the article in the May issue. For corrections see *School Library Journal*, 14 (1) (September, 1966), 91; *Library Journal*, 91 (16) (September 15, 1966), 4243.

———. "The Knapp Project in Motion: Search, Decision, Action," *School Libraries*, 13 (3) (March, 1964), 27-29.

Description of how the producer, site, and content of . . . *And Something More* were selected.

———. "The Knapp School Libraries Project," *The Reading Teacher*, 17 (3) (December, 1963), 172-77.

Article on the Project in general prepared for an issue featuring school libraries.

———. "The Knapp School Libraries Project: A Survey of Applicants," *The Bulletin of the National Association of Secondary-School Principals*, 50 (306) (January, 1966), 82-88.

Such factors as size of library staff, materials selection policies and procedures, and indications of library program development in the sixty-two Phase III applicants are assessed by the Project Director.

———. "The Knapp School Libraries Project—Up to Date," *Film News*, 22 (6) (December, 1965), 13-16.

Illustrated article recounts progress in all phases of the Project with some emphasis on audio-visual aspects of Project schools' services and Project reports.

———. "A Knapp-sack of Progress," *Wilson Library Bulletin*, 39 (5) (January, 1965), 392-96.

Based on reports received from visitors to the two Phase I schools, the article points up their varied reactions and notes the composition of typical Project-supported teams.

————. "A Librarian's Dream Come True," *National Education Association Journal*, 53 (6) (September, 1964), 46-47.

Description of library program at Marcus Whitman School highlighting innovations stimulated by the Project.

————. "Materials: Problems for Teachers of the Culturally Disadvantaged," *Educational Screen and Audiovisual Guide*, 44 (3/443) (October, 1965), 24-26.

Citing experiences with Mount Royal School, author points out the need for materials for pupils in the "poverty spiral."

————. "Recent Library Demonstrations and Research," *Education*, 86 (7) (March, 1966), 387-91.

A brief survey of several school library projects and related research, including the Knapp Project.

————. "The School Library as a Demonstration Center," *School Libraries*, 13 (1) (October, 1963), 19-22.

Special problems foreseen as affecting Project schools are described, and the value of demonstration as a means of effecting change is stressed.

————. "This is the Way It Ends . . . ?" *School Libraries*, 17 (1) (Fall, 1967), 37-40.

Tells to what extent Phase II and Phase III demonstration centers attained or surpassed the long-range goals stated in their original applications, paying special attention to the continued employment of library staff following removal of Project financial support.

————. "Underway: the Knapp Project's First Year," *School Library Journal*, 10 (9) (May, 1964), 17-19; *Library Journal*, 89 (10) (May 15, 1964), 2143-45.

A report on selection of the Phase I schools and other events of the Project's first year.

————, Rees, Louise, and Fuller, Muriel. ". . . *And Something More* Premieres and Two Authorities Comment," *School Libraries*, 14 (1) (October, 1964), 59-62.

The Project-sponsored film, first shown at the American Library Association conference in St. Louis, in June, 1964, is reviewed by two librarians.

Tozier, Virginia. "The Child and the Library Center," *Educational Leadership*, 21 (4) (January, 1964), 223-61.

The librarian of the Central Park Road School states her philosophy of good school library service.

Trenholme, A. Kingsley. "Knapp Library Tour Inspires Questions from Visitors," *Audiovisual Instruction*, 9 (7) (September, 1964), 488-89.

Instructional materials director comments critically on a Department of Audiovisual Instruction tour of Central Park Road School.

Vance, Jane. "Audio-Visual Workshop: Farrer Junior High School," in "*Scholastic Teacher* Reports: Knapp School Libraries Project, Prase III," *Scholastic Teacher*, 88 (14) (May 13, 1966), 9-10.

The librarian at Farrer Junior High School reports on the Project-sponsored workshop for teachers which was conducted during the summer of 1965.

Walker, H. T., and Graham, Mae. "Introducing Knapp Project Director," *School Libraries*, 12 (3) (March, 1963), 21-22.

Biographical sketch of the Project Director by two of her former colleagues.

Walker, Jerry L. "Changing Attitudes toward the Library and the Librarian," *American Library Association Bulletin*, 61 (8) (September, 1967), 977-81.

Dr. Walker, field worker at Oak Park and River Forest High School, reports and interprets results of questionnaire administered to teachers and librarians there and at Roosevelt High School regarding the role of the librarian and characteristics of a good library program.

————. "What Do Student Teachers Know About Libraries?" *School Libraries*, 16 (2) (Winter, 1967), 17-23.

As part of the research effort at the high schools in the Project, the University of Illinois field worker assesses the extent of student teachers' knowledge of library tools and practices.

White, Ruth. "Focus on Three," *Film News*, 24 (4) (September, 1967), 29-30.

A library educator reviews the 1967 set of sound filmstrips about the Phase II schools.

————. "Three for Tomorrow," *Film News*, 23 (4) (September, 1966), 26-27.

A review of the Project-sponsored sound filmstrip on the library programs of the Phase III schools.

Wiese, M. Bernice, and Rusk, Alice. "Mount Royal Elementary: Remodeling in an Inner-City School," *School Library Journal*, 12 (4) (December, 1965), 19-21; *Library Journal*, 90 (22) (December 15, 1965), 5457-59.

The director of library services and library specialist in Baltimore outline the steps in planning and completing the enlargement of the library at this Project school.

Williamson, Walter W. "Developing an Instructional Materials Center in the Mount Royal School," *Educational Leadership*, 25 (2) (November, 1967), 167-73.

Towson State College field worker notes progress at the Mount Royal School and affirms: "A multi-media approach does make learning an exciting adventure and stimulates thinking by opening many new avenues to obtain information."

————. "Project Tape Library Promotes Increased Interest," *Educational Screen and Audiovisual Guide*, 46 (1/465) (January, 1967), 26-27.

Field worker from Towson State College describes advantages of prerecorded tape library in improving learning of inner-city school children at the Mount Royal School.

Ziskind, Sylvia. "School Libraries up to Standard," *The Catholic Educator*, 35 (1) (September, 1964), 66-68.

Relationship of the Knapp Project to American Library Association standards and a statement of anticipated outcomes.

APPENDIX

CONTENTS

GUIDELINES
from the KNAPP
SCHOOL LIBRARIES
PROJECT

THE KNAPP SCHOOL LIBRARIES PROJECT, a five-year demonstration project, was funded by the Knapp Foundation, Inc., and administered by the American Association of School Librarians, a division of the American Library Association and a department of the National Education Association. The grant of $1,130,000.00 provided for the selection and further development of eight demonstration school libraries in New York, Washington, Indiana, Maryland, Texas, Oregon, Utah, and Illinois in cooperation with neighboring teacher education institutions, and for travel grants to teams of visitors planning to observe these school library programs. The Project has also sponsored production of the film, . . . *And Something More,* and several other publications.

As the Project concluded its third year, ten school library leaders who were serving or had served as members of the Project's Advisory Committee met in Chicago with the Project Director and the Deputy Executive Director of the American Library Association who acted as moderator. They discussed some of the most relevant concerns of the Project's part in development of school libraries, and offered guidelines which have frequently been sought by the Project's demonstration schools, by visitors attempting to assess needs and chart plans for the future, and by others who have seen the Project schools as models.

Not all of these recommendations are in practice in Project schools, but some of them were developed in these schools. The experience the Advisory Committee has had with the Project schools and with other areas of school library program development gives import to these statements.

THE LIBRARY IS THE RESOURCE CENTER OF THE SCHOOL. It contains all types of instructional materials* used in intellectual pursuits by teachers and students and the equipment

*"Instructional materials include books — the literature of children, young people, and adults — other printed materials, films, recordings, and newer media developed to aid learning." This definition from *Standards for School Library Programs* (American Library Association, 1960) is the one used throughout this statement.

Brochure, guidelines from Project Advisory Committee.

necessary for their use. These materials are organized for easy access; they are provided in sufficient quantity and depth to allow groups of materials to be sent to classrooms or to special resource centers for as long a time as they are needed. The necessary equipment is housed where it is accessible for teachers and students for group and individual use.

We reaffirm the principle that a strong central library serving as an instructional materials center is the keystone of quality education in each school, regardless of size or organization of the school. From this central library many points of access to instructional resources can be provided through mobility of library staff and of library materials.

An important objective of the instructional program is to help students become proficient in independent study. Independent study centers differ from traditional study halls, in that they surround the student with enlarged and diversified resources for learning and individual study. Students using these centers have been inspired and taught to use these resources to best advantage. Areas designed for independent study are needed within each school's central library. Where auxiliary resource centers exist, sections of them may also be reserved and equipped for independent study.

Factors such as size of school, staffing, architecture, and patterns of organization determine whether additional points of access, such as auxiliary resource centers, are needed. Philosophically and administratively, such additional points of access are branches of the central library service with respect to staffing, collection (selection, bibliographic control, and utilization), and services.

To accommodate expanding library services, it may become necessary either to add to the central library facility areas specializing either in certain subjects or in type and format of materials or to have auxiliary resource centers strategically placed throughout the school and administered by the library staff. These auxiliary resource centers would have some materials placed there permanently, some assigned there

BEFORE DECIDING to establish auxiliary resource centers, the school administration should carefully consider these advantages and disadvantages:

ADVANTAGES

Quick and easy access to materials from the teaching areas and study centers is possible.

The professional librarian responsible for the auxiliary resource center serves a smaller number of teachers and students, and has the opportunity to know them and their needs better.

The professional librarian may more easily visit classrooms and become identified with the faculty of the subject or grade level that is his special responsibility.

It is sometimes more feasible to add auxiliary resource centers than to expand existing library facilities.

Auxiliary resource centers may become independent study centers or the major part of such centers.

The provision of additional spaces throughout the school encourages independent study and use of materials.

Professional librarians can be assigned according to their competency in specific subjects or special areas of work.

Auxiliary resource centers provide the flexibility of access needed to meet the demands of team teaching, ungraded groups, and large schools' enrollments and physical facilities.

DISADVANTAGES

Increased budget for duplication of materials is necessary since most materials in the auxiliary resource centers should also be provided in the central library, and possibly in more than one auxiliary resource center.

Additional professional and clerical library personnel will be needed to staff each center.

Problems in cataloging materials exist, since the user should be helped to find which materials are in the auxiliary resource center, which are in other resource centers, and which are in the central library only. Each auxiliary resource center must have a catalog, and the central library's catalog must indicate locations of all materials.

Dispersal of materials tends to fragment knowledge and to limit the user of an auxiliary resource center in his search for information.

Breadth of opportunity for browsing may be curtailed for the user who visits only one resource center.

temporarily, and the necessary equipment for listening and viewing.

As the instructional materials center for the school, the library administers sets of textbooks, which are organized and shelved separately from the library collection. Textbooks are made available to individual students and teachers. This responsibility requires special financial support and adequate clerical staff.

All equipment related to the use of instructional materials is under the supervision of the library staff.

In addition to each individual school library, a resource center serving the entire school district should house and make available materials that are extraordinarily expensive, infrequently used, and/or which require special inspection and maintenance.

The school library staff will arrange for students to use other, more specialized libraries, when the local school and public libraries cannot provide the materials needed.

The school library staff has the responsibility for securing interlibrary loans for students and teachers when necessary. Students are encouraged to use the resources of their school and public libraries before requesting loans or service from nearby college or specialized libraries.

THE PROGRAM OF THE SCHOOL LIBRARY...

may be defined as the sum total of all its activities designed to fulfill the objectives of the school. These include:

Selecting, organizing, and distributing materials to meet the needs of the curriculum

Planning service to students and teachers

Providing reference and bibliographic services

Teaching library and study skills

Providing guidance in listening, reading, and viewing

Engaging in inservice education with teachers

In short, any contribution the school library can make to the learning of students and to the improvement of teaching can be considered part of the school library program.

Guidelines (continued).

As affirmed in *Standards for School Library Programs* (American Library Association, 1960), "The most important part of the library program is the work with students and teachers, those activities and services that make the library an educational force in the school."

The development of the school library program stems from the school's unique characteristics and goals. The entire faculty plans and implements the school library program, which is established and maintained to undergird the curriculum.

FULL AND EFFECTIVE USE OF LIBRARY RESOURCES . . . requires informed, competent teachers. Opportunities for inservice growth in teacher expectations, knowledge, and utilization of the library come through involvement of teachers in planning the library program. The foundation for effective use of instructional materials by students and teachers should be acquired in the preservice education of teachers. Inservice education should provide further opportunity for their participation.

Innovations in school organization and instruction intensify needs for library resources and require librarians to increase considerably the time and effort spent in enabling teachers to use appropriately a wider variety of instructional materials.

Teachers, strongly supported by the library staff, can assume major responsibility for:

1. Library skills instruction integrated with study skills and subject disciplines.

2. Optimum utilization of library resources in large group, small group, and individual learning.

3. Development of students' competence in reference and research skills.

We believe that librarians should continue to allot time to maintain their direct, unique generalist/specialist relationship with students, especially in individual guidance in reading, listening, viewing, and reference skills.

Characteristics of a sound program of library service are:

1. Broad involvement of the principal, every teacher, librarian, and other specialist in planning and implementing the program.

2. Definitions of individual and shared responsibilities of teachers and librarians.

3. Provisions for inservice growth of teachers in the use of various instructional materials and methods.

4. Facilitating, through maximum flexibility of access, continuous cooperative planning, and effective organization, the development of sound instructional practices, including diagnosis of learning needs, flexible grouping, and individualization of instruction.

Initiation of planning for the library program is a leadership function of the principal, the librarian, and the school library supervisor. Participation is the responsibility of every faculty member.

Steps include:

1. Organizing the faculty for setting the objectives of the library program and planning ways to achieve them.

2. Analyzing the curriculum of the school in order to identify:

   a. Types of teaching, guidance, and adadvisory services needed by pupils and teachers.

   b. Opportunities for services, e.g., areas of the curriculum for which the library has unique responsibilities and to which it can make specific contributions.

3. Assessing students' particular needs, abilities, and objectives.

4. Appraising ways and means for implementing the program, including:

   a. Staff: the relationships and responsibilities of the teachers and the librarians with recognition of the knowledge and skills each needs and can share with others.

   b. Resources: the adequacy of materials, equipment, and facilities to support the desired program.

Guidelines (continued).

c. Organization for learning: the practices affecting grouping and scheduling.

5. Formulating over-all plans for the program.

6. Identifying means for evaluating the effectiveness of the program.

WE STRONGLY REAFFIRM . . . the desirability of flexibile scheduling of library use as opposed to rigid scheduling of library visits that do not necessarily spring from the students' own needs. Effective flexible scheduling practice makes the library available, at the point of need, for class visits and for individual and small group use. It permits a teacher to send an individual or a group or to arrange for an entire class to visit the library wherever he thinks it is desirable.

Flexibility in scheduling requires that teachers plan and initiate with the librarians the assignments and projects that require frequent, possibly daily, use of library resources by individuals and by small and large groups of students. New techniques in the administration and control of student schedules can assure every student of access to library resources.

Preparation for effective scheduling includes thorough understanding by the principal, faculty, and library staff that this kind of scheduling represents a basic and important improvement, and that time and effort will be required to achieve it. This preparation will provide for step-by-step progress from more rigid scheduling of class use of the library through a program of partial scheduling to the achievement of maximum use of library resources in an unscheduled program.

Steps toward flexible use of library facilities and resources include:

1. Provision of blocks of time in the daily library schedule for flexible scheduling of groups.

2. Encouragement of individual and small group use of the school library throughout the day.

Readiness for more flexibility is assured when (1) a clearly defined program of library serv-ices has been developed by the staff and (2) teachers understand and accept their responsibility for utilization of library resources and services.

Appraisal of the effectiveness of flexible scheduling should take into account not only the quantity of library attendance and circulation of materials, but also the quality and effect of group and individual use of library resources.

IN ANY LIBRARY . . . there are professional library functions and responsibilities and non-professional library functions and responsibilities. The school library should have the services of professional, technical, and clerical personnel. Each position requires definition by job description to differentiate the range of tasks and skills.

Selection and assignment of the school librarian requires the same care as selection and assignment of a master teacher, with consideration of the specialized preparation and background as well as the unique personal qualifications essential for effective teaching. In addition to competencies in the selection and organization of all forms of material, the librarian should possess skill in human relationships, in the development and planning of curriculum, in individual and group guidance, and in administration and management.

A fully qualified librarian has at least a fifth year of library education and state certification as a school librarian.

A supervisor of school library service is a fully qualified librarian who has additional professional education in administration and/or supervision and successful experience.

A person who has state certification as a teacher and minimum certification requirements as a school librarian may serve as a school librarian, but should work only under the direction and supervision of a fully qualified librarian. This fully qualified librarian may be the librarian of the individual school or the librarian responsible for the program at the area or system level, depending on the size and complexity of the system and its organization.

Guidelines (continued).

Where excellent supervision is available, some schools may have only a librarian with minimum qualifications.

In schools where two or more librarians are assigned, one should be appointed head librarian with the rank of department head.

In determining the number of professional and non-professional staff positions assigned to a school library, major considerations should be (1) the instructional program of the school, (2) the characteristics of the physical plant, and (3) the size and nature of enrollment.

Non-professional tasks in the school library program are assigned to clerical and technical aids who have at least a high school education including clerical and technical education and/or experience. The financial compensation for their employment should be determined by the depth and kind of their skills, training, and job responsibilities and by the pay scale for other clerks and technicians employed by the school or school district.

Students are not to be considered as a source for staffing unless they are paid for performing routine library tasks consonant with abilities. The purpose of groups of student assistants is educational. Their activities are a part of the extracurricular program of the school.

Adult volunteers may be useful in school libraries when, under the supervision of a librarian, their energies are channeled into appropriate activities. They are not a substitute for paid staff members. The number of volunteer assistants should be limited to avoid undue demands on the time of the professional staff responsible for their supervision.

Young men and women who are eligible for training and work experience under federal programs may serve in school libraries as library clerical assistants, pages, etc. However, the purpose of these types of programs is not to relieve schools of the responsibility of employing adequate professional library personnel and trained clerical assistants.

Library materials should be processed in the most efficient and economic way possible so that professional library staff members are free to work with students and teachers. In order to accomplish this, the school system should study carefully:

a) the possibility of establishing its own processing center; and

b) the possibility of associating with a regional processing center; and

c) the different types of commercial processing available.

Guidelines (continued).

The Knapp Foundation Grant for Demonstration of Excellent School Library Programs

What happens in a school where a dynamic school library program is put into operation? How do excellent school library services contribute to the total school program? A concerted national effort to help educators find answers to these questions begins in the Fall of 1963 when the Knapp School Libraries Project gets under way. The Knapp Foundation of New York has made a grant of $1,130,000 to the American Library Association to support a 5-year project of the American Association of School Librarians "to demonstrate the educational value of a full program of school library services."

The need for this project arises from inadequacies reported by the U. S. Office of Education. Two-thirds of public elementary schools lack libraries. Only a small percentage of secondary school libraries are staffed and equipped to support instructional programs effectively. Yet good school library programs are essential for the quality education every school strives to provide.

The Knapp School Libraries Project is designed to demonstrate a very good school library program in action. In 8 different schools in different parts of the country, the school library services and facilities will be brought up to the standards of excellence recommended in *Standards for School Library Programs* (American Library Association, 1960). Each demonstration will show how a good school library operates and what it contributes to the school's total instructional program. Through the participation of a nearby teacher education institution, student teachers will be able to observe and

learn, and the teachers in the demonstration school will be helped to make effective use of the library. Administrators, teachers, school board members and civic leaders from other districts and States will be encouraged to visit the demonstration schools. Team visits of 1 or 2 days will be scheduled, with expenses paid.

The effects and findings of the Project will be given nation-wide publicity. Detailed information will be provided for observers and visiting teams. The Project Director and the staff of the demonstration schools will participate in meetings of professional and civic groups. Through such means, the Project's values will be carried far beyond the 8 demonstration schools and their immediate communities.

In what ways may your school benefit from the Knapp School Libraries Project?

(1) If your school meets certain criteria, you may apply to become one of 8 demonstration schools in one of the 3 phases of the 5-year program. Criteria for Phase I are described on page 3; applications for Phase I must be received no later than April 1, 1963.

(2) Representatives of your school system may arrange to visit the nearest demonstration schools starting in the Fall of 1963.

(3) Publications and a film about the demonstration school libraries will be available by 1964. Watch for announcements and secure these informational materials for your school system.

Brochure announcing Phase I.

The Project is planned in three phases

Phase I will establish demonstration libraries in 2 elementary schools in which the school system has already made a substantial investment in the library program. Only in such schools can services and physical provisions be brought up to the national standards and to maximum effectiveness in a short time so that visits and observations may begin without delay. These schools will be selected by May, 1963 and will be ready for the demonstration in September.

Phase II will also involve elementary schools. In 1964, 3 more elementary schools will be added to the first 2. They will represent different geographical areas and will include situations where less adequate provision (but nevertheless a beginning) has been made, and where school authorities are ready to make both an immediate contribution to the demonstration and a continuing investment. Since a longer time will be needed to bring these schools to the level required for demonstration programs, the period for the project in these schools will be 3 years. Application blanks with more detailed information will be available by the Fall of 1963, since planning by schools and teacher education institutions should begin as soon as possible.

Phase III is concerned with secondary schools. Although most high schools have libraries and librarians, their effectiveness is frequently limited by inadequacies of staff, budget, materials, or quarters. In 1964 (or early 1965), 3 secondary schools will be selected and supported on a basis comparable to the elementary schools. Schools where the librarians are working with new patterns of curriculum organization, team teaching, flexible scheduling, and the like will be considered as well as schools with more typical patterns of organization and curriculum.

Selection of schools in all 3 phases will depend upon (1) the accessibility of the school to a teacher education institution willing to cooperate in planning and assisting demonstration programs for educators and students; (2) availability of transportation and other facilities to make a demonstration program practicable and productive; and (3) commitment on the part of the administration and faculty of the school to support and develop a continuing good school library program.

Phase I brochure (continued).

Selection of Schools for Phase I

To assure prompt availability of the demonstrations, elementary schools which have made a substantial investment in their libraries and already have a good program in operation are invited to apply for Phase I.

Application forms must be submitted no later than April 1, 1963. They may be initiated either by the elementary school or by the cooperating teacher education institution, but should be jointly prepared and signed by officials of both institutions.

CAN YOUR SCHOOL QUALIFY?

For Phase I, schools will be selected on the basis of the following criteria, in addition to those stated at the foot of the opposite page:

(1) An enrollment approximating 600 students

(2) A faculty which is already oriented to library use and is interested in participating in the demonstration and observation program

(3) One full-time librarian, already employed, who has outstanding qualifications and has demonstrated leadership qualities in the school

(4) A library collection which at least closely approaches national standards with some provision of newer educational media and professional materials

(5) Accessibility to: (a) a teacher education institution which will cooperate as described below and (b) transportation facilities to make team visits possible.

WHAT IS THE TEACHER EDUCATION INSTITUTION EXPECTED TO CONTRIBUTE?

The cooperating institution of higher education is expected to make a faculty member available to coordinate the program of teacher training and citizen education and cooperate with the faculty of the demonstration school and the Project Director. As a liaison person on the college faculty, he will also be expected to stimulate observation by student teachers and related teacher training activities of benefit to the college. Criteria for selection are:

(1) Interest in improving the library background of student teachers

(2) Ability to assign at least half time of regular faculty member to serve as field worker.

WHAT WILL THE GRANT PROVIDE?

On the basis of the needs presented in the application, the Project will provide a grant sufficient to finance the following for a 2-year period:

(1) Purchase of book resources sufficient to meet the national standards (including commercial processing if necessary) for the library of the elementary school; additional funds may be made available for newer educational media and professional materials, as required

(2) Salary of additional professional and clerical personnel required to meet the standards, including funds for summer operation of the project

(3) A specified sum estimated to equal half the salary of the field worker assigned by the teacher education institution, plus sums for clerical assistance and travel

(4) Travel and hotel expenses of 12 teams of 6 observers each for each of the 2 years of the grant

(5) Consultant service by the Project Director.

If your school is selected, an agreement will be worked out specifying the contributions and responsibilities in greater detail.

Phase I brochure (continued).

KNAPP SCHOOL LIBRARIES PROJECT APPLICATION

FOR DEMONSTRATION SCHOOL LIBRARY AND

RELATED TEACHER - EDUCATION PROGRAM

Phase I

Mail one copy to: Knapp School Libraries Project
                   % American Association of School Librarians
                   50 East Huron Street
                   Chicago 11, Illinois

Deadline for Phase I application: April 10, 1963

This application is to be submitted jointly by the school system (or its equivalent) and the cooperating teacher education institution.

Do not send any exhibits or supplementary material not specifically requested on the application.

Before filling out the application please read carefully the enclosed flyer which describes in detail the conditions under which the project will operate.

Name of School District_____

Address_____

Name of School_____

Address_____

Principal_____Librarian (Head)_____

Library Supervisor (if any in district)_____

Name of Teacher Education Institution_____

Address_____

The signatures below indicate approval of the total proposal and intention to support its objectives.

Superintendent of School System   _____
                                              Signature

Head of School or Department of Education _____
                                              Signature

                                       _____
                                              Title

Application for Phase I.

2.

SECTION I PARTICIPATING SCHOOL

Grade	No. Classes	No. Students
K		
1	_____	_____
2	_____	_____
3	_____	_____
4	_____	_____
5	_____	_____
6	_____	_____
7	_____	_____
8	_____	_____
Special education class	_____	_____
Total	_____	_____

2. Number of classroom teachers
    Number of librarians full time in this school   _____
    Number of special subject teachers full time in this school _____

3. List the consultants and special services personnel provided to work with
    this school, including both system wide consultants and itinerant staff
    members shared with other schools:

Type of service:	Full time in this school	Part time in this school	On request in this school
Curriculum specialist			
Psychologist	_____	_____	_____
Health specialist	_____	_____	_____
Reading specialist	_____	_____	_____
Library coordinator	_____	_____	_____
Research or test specialist	_____	_____	_____
Other (specify)_____	_____	_____	_____

4. Is the board of education entirely responsible for the provision of the
    school library staff, funds, materials, and consultant service?
    YES____ NO____   If NO explain in detail:

5. Fill in for school system:

Type of School	No. of schools	Total enrollment
Elementary	_____	_____
Junior high	_____	_____
Senior high	_____	_____
Combined	_____	_____
Total	_____	_____

Per pupil expenditure for elementary education _____

Phase I application (continued).

3.

6. School library staff:
    Number of years library has been in operation under the direction of a full time librarian_____
    Professional qualifications of librarian (give information for additional librarians on separate sheet):

Degrees held	University	Date received
_____	_____	_____
_____	_____	_____
_____	_____	_____

Number of semester hours in:

	Undergraduate	Graduate
Library science	_____	_____
Education	_____	_____

Number of years in this school as librarian: _____

Non-professional assistants (other than student assistants):

	Employed	Volunteer
No. of persons	_____	_____
No. of cumulative hrs/wk	_____	_____

7. School library collection in school building (as of Feb. 1, 1963)

	General Collection	Professional materials for teachers
Books (volumes)	_____	_____
Periodicals	_____	_____
Filmstrips	_____	_____
Recordings	_____	_____
Other audio-visual materials (specify)_____	_____	_____
Number of drawers of pamphlets and other informational materials	_____	_____

List below areas of strengths and weaknesses in the collection in terms of subject coverage, picture books, reference books, reading levels, filmstrips, etc:
Strengths:_____
_____
Weaknesses:_____
_____

8. School board expenditure and future budget for this school:

	1961/62	1962/63	1963/64
Library books (other than encyclopedias)	_____	_____	_____
Encyclopedias	_____	_____	_____
Professional books for teachers	_____	_____	_____
Professional magazines for teachers	_____	_____	_____
Audio-visual materials (purchase) (exclude equipment)	_____	_____	_____
Audio-visual materials (rental)	_____	_____	_____
Supplies	_____	_____	_____
Binding	_____	_____	_____
Total	_____	_____	_____
Library salaries (professional)	_____	_____	_____
Library salaries (clerical)	_____	_____	_____

Phase I application (continued).

4.

9. Accessibility of materials:

Can all library books (other than reference books) be withdrawn for home use by all students? Yes____ No____
If NO, explain in detail any restrictions which are imposed and what grades are affected:

Can individual students use filmstrips in the school library? Yes____ No____.

Can individual students use recordings in school library? Yes____ No____.

Is it a general practice to send collections of materials from the library to the classrooms for short term loan? Yes____ No____.

Are audio-visual materials listed in the school library card catalog? Yes____ No____.

If school-owned audio-visual materials are separately housed or serviced outside the school library but in the school building, how are they administered (person in charge, location, services provided)?

10. Library quarters and equipment:
Describe location of the library within the school, in terms of accessibility, relation to classrooms, etc.:

Give size for following areas:	Total Sq. Ft.	Seating Capacity
Main library	_____	_____
Office	_____	_____
Work storage	_____	_____
Audio-visual	_____	_____
Production of materials	_____	_____
Professional materials for teachers	_____	_____
Others (specify) _____	_____	_____
_____	_____	_____

Furniture and equipment in library:

Tables	Number		Chairs	Number
25"	_____		14"	_____
26"	_____		15"	_____
27"	_____		16"	_____
28"	_____		17"	_____
Total	_____		Total	_____
Card catalog drawers	_____			
Vertical file drawers	_____		Shelving sections	_____
Charging desk	_____			

Phase I application (continued).

5.

Audio-visual equipment:

	Number in library	Number available in other parts of school
16 mm projectors		
Filmstrip-slide projectors		
Individual filmstrip viewers		
Overhead projectors		
Opaque projectors		
Record players		
Tape recorders		
Others (specify)_____		

11. Estimate what the school needs to meet the national quantitative standards for school libraries (See STANDARDS FOR SCHOOL LIBRARY PROGRAMS p.24-25):

Professional staff_____

Clerical staff   _____

Materials   _____
                  _____
                  _____

Equipment   _____

Quarters   _____

<u>The following information should be reported on separate sheets:</u>

12. Characteristics of the school: Identify (1) any particular characteristics of the student body or community; (2) any special programs or studies completed or in progress in areas of curriculum, organization, etc.; or (3) other special features of the school.

13. Describe the testing program of the school, giving names and forms of tests used, grade levels where administered, and frequency of administration. Describe also other statistical data, cumulative records, etc. available in the school.

14. Describe briefly the nature of the summer program, if any, carried out for students and for faculty of this school (e.g. enrichment, library services, workshops for teachers, and the like).

15. Describe in some detail any system wide library services provided for the school system by the school board (e.g. centralized processing or cataloging, professional library for teachers, instructional materials center, supervising of consultant services, audio-visual center, and the like).

16. What qualifications does the school possess which would provide for a successful demonstration? Consider factors such as readiness and qualifications of principal, teachers and librarian(s) to participate, ability of the school to accommodate and provide for the proposed visits, probable stability of the school situation during the project, and the like.

17. What plans have already been made by the school administration for development of school libraries in the school system during the next two to five years?

18. If your proposal should be approved, please state frankly what the possibilities are for your being able to continue the support of the school library at the level provided by the foundation.

6.

The following questions should be considered jointly by principal, librarians, representative teachers, and consultant staff:

19. Assess as objectively as you can the strong and weak points of your current library program (See STANDARDS FOR SCHOOL LIBRARY PROGRAMS, Chapter 3)

20. How would you extend and/or improve your present school library program if you receive the grant? Is there any one type of service or activity which you would like to emphasize?

21. What long range outcomes does the school hope to achieve through participation in this project? (Identify desired effects or goals for pupils, teachers, other schools in the system, etc.)

Please put below dates when your school will have spring vacation this year.

_____

Phase I application (continued).

7.

SECTION II COOPERATING TEACHER

EDUCATION INSTITUTION

22. By what agencies is this institution accredited?_____
_____

23. Total enrollment in college or university_____
    Number of students in the school or department of education:
        Undergraduate_____Per cent in elementary education_____
        Graduate   _____Per cent in elementary education_____

24. Number of faculty members in school or department of education:
                            Full time   _____
                            Part time   _____

25. Describe what laboratory school facilities are available for your prospec-
    tive teachers and indicate whether these are used for observation only or also
    for practice teaching:

26. Library resources for the teacher education program:
        (In giving the following information make as reliable estimates as possible.
        Do not include any materials provided in laboratory or demonstration school
        library. Use separate sheets if necessary).

        Number of volumes in field of education   _____
        Number of periodicals in field of education_____
        Briefly describe the size and scope of curriculum related materials, such
        as textbooks, courses of study, instructional units, tests, etc.; indicate
        hours when collection is open for use and library staff available.

        Briefly describe the size and scope of the juvenile literature
        collection(s); indicate hours when collection(s) is open for use;
        library staff available, and annual budget:

Phase I application (continued).

8.

Describe briefly any materials available that deal with school library services and materials:

What provisions are made for access to audio-visual and programmed instruction aids? Are these serviced as a part of the library or as a separate unit? Describe briefly the extent of the collections and the staff.

The following questions should be reported on separate sheets:

27. Describe and evaluate the instructional program provided for prospective teachers and administrators in relation to school library services and materials. (See STANDARDS FOR SCHOOL LIBRARY PROGRAMS, p. 67-70)

28. If your institution cooperates in this project, what qualifications would you look for in the person to be selected from your faculty (preferably in the areas of curriculum and administration) to serve as field worker? In addition to the qualifications of the candidate indicate also college title or rank, salary, and experience.

29. State briefly the long range outcomes which you hope will accrue to the college faculty and student teachers through your participation in this project.

Please put below dates when your institution will have spring vacation this year.

_____

Phase I application (continued).

CHECKLIST - VISITS TO SCHOOLS APPLYING TO PARTICIPATE
IN KNAPP SCHOOL LIBRARIES PROJECT

SCHOOL:

PERSONNEL Librarian	Inade- quate	Adequate	Good	Superior
Leadership skills				
Organization skills				
Understanding of students' needs, interests and abilities				
Awareness of the basic content of subject areas				
Awareness of educational trends and research				
Knowledge of curriculum practices				
Understanding of the community and its importance to school				
Knowledge and understanding of how to utilize local resources				
Knowledge of the administration of the instructional materials program				
Knowledge of the selection and securing of quality materials				
Knowledge of the organization of instructional materials				
Knowledge of how to teach use of the library				
Knowledge of the production of instructional materials				
Knowledge and skill in exhibit and display techniques				
Working relationships with faculty				
Certification Status				
Principal				
Leadership skills				
Organizational skills				
Knowledge of the administration of the instructional materials program				
Understanding of the community and its importance to the school				
Ability to create an atmosphere for cooperative effort by staff and students				
Ability to interpret school program to the community				
Understanding of the role of the school library				

Checklist of Director's visits to schools applying.

Faculty	Inade-quate	Adequate	Good	Superior
Awareness of the various facets of library program				
Sense of cooperative effort with librarian				
Opportunity (time, etc.) for further development of the library program (cooperative study, planning)				
QUARTERS Size, location, etc.				
Accessibility to building entrances				
Appearance				
Space available for class and visitors				
Accoustics				
Accessibility to classrooms				
Arrangement and Furnishings				
Book Shelving				
Magazine Shelving				
Displays				
Vertical files, etc.				
Card Catalogs				
Tables				
Chairs				
Open Areas				
MATERIALS COLLECTION Books				
Quantity				
Quality				
Condition				
Balance:				
Reference Books				
Fiction				
Non-Fiction				
Easy Reading, Etc.				
Availability to teachers				
Availability to students				
Projection Equipment, etc.				
Accessibility to library				
Accessibility to classrooms				
Quality				
Condition				
Relation to Curriculum				

Checklist (continued).

	Inade-quate	Adequate	Good	Superior
TEACHER-TRAINING INSTITUTION				
Head of Department or College				
Understanding of school's program				
Understanding of purposes of demonstration				
Understanding of role of field worker				
Potential Field Worker				
Understanding of school library program				
Understanding of Curriculum				
Ability to Interpret Program to Public				
Understanding of role				
Leadership ability				
Knowledge of community				
Knowledge of Institution's students				
Organizational skills				
COMMUNITY FACTORS				
Legal status of school system with respect to integration				
Current practice in this respect				
Ability of school to accept and accommodate visitors				
Proximity and quantity of suitable lodging accommodations				
Proximity and quality of restaurants, etc.				
Prospect for recruitment of an assistant librarian				

Checklist (continued).

The Knapp School Libraries Project

A $1,130,000 five-year Project, funded by the Knapp Foundation, Inc., and administered by the American Association of School Librarians, a division of the American Library Association and a department of the National Education Association,

INVITES YOU TO:

* VISIT one of two demonstration school libraries selected from 115 applicants to participate in Phase I of the Knapp School Libraries Project

* SEE the effect of the demonstration library on the instructional program of the Project school

* INFORM your community about the program you have observed as a community leader

* REPORT to the Project your views on the program you have observed and the effects of your visit on the library program of your school or school district.

DEMONSTRATION SCHOOL A:

Central Park Road Elementary School
Plainview - Old Bethpage School District
Gerhard Road
Plainview, New York

COOPERATING TEACHER-EDUCATION
INSTITUTION WITH SCHOOL A:

Teachers College
Columbia University
New York, New York

DEMONSTRATION SCHOOL B:

Marcus Whitman Elementary School
Richland School District
1805 Lee Boulevard
Richland, Washington

COOPERATING TEACHER-EDUCATION
INSTITUTION WITH SCHOOL B:

Eastern Washington State College
Cheney,
Washington

All visits must be arranged and scheduled in advance.

Visits will be scheduled after January 1, 1964.

Programs for one- or two-day workshop visits will be planned with the visiting groups' special interests in mind.

Although the Central Park Road Elementary School and the Marcus Whitman Elementary School are the first schools to participate in the Knapp School Libraries Project, three more elementary schools in other geographic areas of the United States will be added as demonstration centers for this Project in 1964 and three secondary schools will be included in the Project in 1965. Opportunities for groups to visit these schools will be announced after these additional schools are selected.

GROUPS MAY REPRESENT:

the administrative and instructional staff of a school or school district interested in improvement of its school library program

faculty and staff of teacher-education institutions interested in the education of teachers in the use of instructional materials centers

School board members and representatives of organizations interested in improved educational programs with library facilities

any combination of personnel selected from the three categories listed above

Brochure announcing Phase I visits.

AT THEIR OWN EXPENSE, groups may schedule visits by writing four weeks in advance of the date of the proposed visit.

To visit Central Park Road School, write to:

Dr. William J. Nelligan, Assistant Superintendent
Plainview-Old Bethpage Central School District #4
Plainview, New York

To visit Marcus Whitman School, write to:

Mrs. Anna M. Beachner
Richland School District
615 Snow Avenue
Richland, Washington

OR

GROUPS MAY REQUEST PROJECT FUNDS TO PROVIDE:

round-trip transportation by automobile at the rate of ten cents per mile for round trips not in excess of one thousand miles

hotel or motel accommodations, based on double occupancy, at hotels and motels selected by the Project

informative materials relating to the Project, the school library visited, and means of developing school library programs elsewhere.

Groups requesting Project funds will receive announcements of the groups selected to receive funds early in 1964.

Groups selected to receive funds will be reimbursed after submitting a record of expenses incurred on the visit.

Members of the group will be asked to respond to a brief questionnaire at the time of the visit. The leader will be responsible for preparing a report immediately after the visit, and a follow-up report on the results of the visit within a year.

IF YOU WISH TO APPLY FOR ONE OF THESE TRAVEL GRANTS, COMPLETE AND SUBMIT THE APPLICATION ATTACHED TO THIS BROCHURE. MAIL IT TO:

Miss Peggy Sullivan, Director
Knapp School Libraries Project
American Library Association
50 East Huron Street
Chicago, Illinois 60611

DEADLINE: December 31, 1963

Phase I visits brochure (continued).

POINTS OF INTEREST ABOUT THE PHASE I SCHOOLS

The two schools selected for Phase I have some similarities, since both are located in areas where tremendous growth of the population and especially of the school-age population has occurred since World War II. Richland, one of the Tri-Cities of eastern Washington, has engaged in a number of cooperative projects and workshops with other school districts, especially in the area of curriculum development. Plainview, one of the more recent communities in Nassau County, Long Island, has, in its short history as a school district (Central School District Number 4), introduced such instructional innovations as closed-circuit television at the Central Park Road School and team-teaching. The expenditure per capita for elementary education approximates the expenditure for the schools' respective states, and there has been consistent expenditure for the library program in each of these school districts.

In the 1962-1963 school year, the Central Park Road School's enrollment was 592 pupils in grades kindergarten through six, the Marcus Whitman School's enrollment was 771 pupils in grades kindergarten through six. Each school had a library administered by a librarian on a full-time assignment. Mrs. Virginia Tozier is the librarian at Central Park Road School, Mrs. Elsie Pitts at Marcus Whitman School.

The special features of the library program at the Central Park Road School are the rapport between librarian and faculty, the library's contributions to the closed-circuit television programs, creative use of the library suite which was moved and expanded to new quarters during the summer of 1963, the well-selected, curriculum-related collection of library materials, and the support of such additional facilities as a library processing center for the school district and the services of a library supervisor for the school district.

At Marcus Whitman School, major changes in the physical facility were also undertaken during the summer of 1963. The pattern of library development had been established with emphasis on development of the instructional materials center concept, well-planned program for library instruction at all grade levels, and projected plan for the librarian to serve as curriculum consultant within the school.

The Knapp Project is providing funds for the purchase of additional books, audio-visual materials and equipment for both of these schools, as well as salaries for the additional professional and clerical library assistants recommended by STANDARDS FOR SCHOOL LIBRARY PROGRAMS. Columbia University and Eastern Washington State College receive funds for the half-time salary and other expenses of field workers to be assigned to work with the Project schools. Additional Project grants are made to underwrite workshops for faculty members of the Project schools, student teachers, and other interested personnel.

Phase I visits brochure (continued).

Demonstration of Excellent School Library Programs
The Knapp School Libraries Project

The Knapp School Libraries Project announces the opportunity for elementary schools to apply to participate in Phase II of the Project. Three elementary schools, to be selected by mid-1964, will receive Project funds to raise their present library programs to the level recommended in Standards for School Library Programs (American Library Association, 1960) and will serve as demonstration centers where visitors may observe excellent programs of elementary school library service during three school years, beginning in the summer of 1964.

As the two schools already selected to participate in Phase I, the Marcus Whitman Elementary School in Richland, Washington, and the Central Park Road Elementary School in Plainview, New York, will start the 1963-1964 school year with additional library books, additional professional and clerical assistants on the library staff, and plans for more purchases of instructional materials and for an improved program of library service for the faculty and students of the schools. Visitors who wish to plan one- or two-day workshop-visits to these schools may contact the Project Director for information about applying for funds for such visits during the 1963-1964 and 1964-1965 school years.

This progress has been made possible by a $1,130,000 grant from the Knapp Foundation of New York to the American Library Association to support a five-year Project of the American Association of School Librarians "to demonstrate the educational value of a full program of school library services."

By the third year of the Project, eight schools (five elementary, three secondary) in different parts of the United States will have been selected to participate. As in Phase I, in which 115 applications were received from which the Marcus Whitman and Central Park Road Schools were selected, Phase II and Phase III selections will be based on applications submitted by the schools. Eastern Washington State College in Cheney, Washington, and Teacher's College, Columbia University, New York, are the co-operating teacher-education institutions for the Washington and New York schools respectively.

Each demonstration will show how a good school library operates and what it contributes to the school's total instructional program. Through the participation of a nearby teacher-education institution, student teachers will observe and learn the values of a school library, and the faculty of the Knapp Project schools will be helped to make effective use of the library. A field worker, appointed on a half-time assignment from the faculty of the teacher-education institution, will plan and coordinate workshops and other teacher-related aspects of the Project and will work with the staff of the school in planning, conducting and evaluating visits to the school by teams of observers including administrators, librarians, teachers, and other personnel.

Research and evaluation will be major parts of each Phase of this Project. Articles in periodicals and reports will be prepared on various aspects of the school program as affected by participation in the Knapp School Libraries Project. The Project Director and the staff of the Project schools will participate in meetings of professional and civic groups. The effects of this Project are intended to go far beyond the eight demonstration schools and their communities.

The Knapp Foundation, Inc., has since its inception in 1929 contributed to many studies and projects for the advancement of health and welfare and education. Its founder is commemorated in the Joseph Palmer Knapp Building housing the Institute of Government at the University of North Carolina, a major benefaction of this Foundation. From the beginning, the Foundation has shown special interest in improving programs which have been initiated and supported locally.

Brochure and preliminary application for Phase II.

The time-table for the Knapp School Libraries Project is..

Phase I { Two elementary schools have been selected. Services and physical arrangements will be brought up to standard in the course of the Project. Visits and observations at these schools will be scheduled beginning in early 1964.

Phase II { Three elementary schools in different geographic areas will be selected from those applying schools where a start has been made in building a school library program.

These schools will receive Project funds and assistance for staff, materials, structural changes, and other library needs from the summer of 1964, through June, 1967.

Phase III { Three secondary schools will be selected for participation and funds and assistance will be provided by the Project for the period from the summer of 1965, through June, 1967.

IF YOU REPRESENT A SCHOOL WHICH MAY QUALIFY FOR SELECTION FOR PHASE III, you may plan now to evaluate the secondary school's present library program in terms of the STANDARDS FOR SCHOOL LIBRARY PROGRAMS, contact a teacher-preparation institution which may be interested in co-applying with the school, and request an application for Phase III when they are available some time in 1964.

Phase II brochure (continued).

If you represent an elementary school which may qualify for selection for Phase II, act now.

YOUR SCHOOL MAY APPLY IF....

(1) The administration supports a plan to improve library service
(2) The school has a central collection of library materials, administered by a qualified school librarian who spends at least half-time as librarian of this school and whose salary is paid by the school board or other school administrative agency
(3) The enrollment of the school is between 300 and 900
(4) It may be defined as an elementary school (most of the elementary grades, one through eight)
(5) There is a teacher-preparation institution which will co-apply with the school

WHAT WILL THE GRANT PROVIDE?

(1) Funds for the purchase of books and other library materials to bring the library collection up to recommended standards
(2) Salary of additional professional and clerical personnel required to meet standards, including summer employment
(3) Half-time salary for the half-time services of the field worker assigned by the teacher-preparation institution, plus funds required for clerical assistance and travel
(4) Consultant service by the Project Director
(5) Funds for structural changes in the library facility if required

HOW WILL APPLICATIONS BE JUDGED?

(1) On the present development of the school's library program
(2) The potential for demonstration and research in the school, the school district, and the teacher-preparation institution
(3) Evidence of the potential for maintaining the level of program made possible by the Knapp Project
(4) Geographic accessibility for potential teams of observers
(5) Geographic spread of schools selected for Phases I and II

AND KEEP IN MIND THAT....

Schools which applied for Phase I may apply for Phase II. All applications must be submitted on the forms which will be sent when requested on the attached preliminary application form.

Applications must be received by the deadline noted on the application form.

Only one application may be submitted from each school district. Teacher-education institutions may co-apply with more than one school.

Schools may co-apply with only one teacher-education institution. All applications will be acknowledged, and applicants will be notified when final selection is made. This correspondence will be directed to the superintendent or other authority with final responsibility for the school applying.

A preliminary application form is attached. Fill it in, detach it, and mail it to: Peggy Sullivan, Director, Knapp School Libraries Project, 50 East Huron Street, Chicago, Illinois, 60611.

Phase II brochure (continued).

MAIL THIS PRELIMINARY APPLICATION FORM
NO LATER THAN OCTOBER 10, 1963

TO: Peggy Sullivan, Director
Knapp School Libraries Project
50 East Huron Street
Chicago, Illinois 60611

Please send an application form for Phase II of the Knapp School Libraries Project. The elementary school for which we plan to apply has a central library and collection administered by a librarian on at least a half-time basis.

Please send the application to:_____

_____

_____

_____

Grades served by school _____

Enrollment of school _____

Number of volumes in library collection _____

Our library facilities consist of ☐ main library, ☐ office, ☐ work storage area, ☐ other _____

We intend to co-apply with this teacher-education institution:

_____
(NAME)

_____
(YOUR NAME)

_____   _____
(YOUR POSITION)   (YOUR ADDRESS)

_____
(NAME OF SCHOOL)

_____
(NAME OF SCHOOL DISTRICT)

Phase II brochure (continued).

KNAPP SCHOOL LIBRARIES PROJECT APPLICATION
FOR ELEMENTARY SCHOOL LIBRARY
AND
CO-APPLYING TEACHER-EDUCATION PROGRAM

Phase II

Mail one copy of this application to: Knapp School Libraries Project
50 East Huron Street
Chicago, Illinois 60611

Deadline for Phase II application: December 31, 1963

This application is to be completed by personnel of the school system (or its equivalent) and the co-applying teacher-education institution.

Do not send any exhibits or supplementary material not specifically requested on the application.

INFORMATION AND AUTHORIZATION FOR
SCHOOL DISTRICT

Name of school district_____

Address_____

Telephone_____

Name of school_____

Address_____

Superintendent of district_____

Principal of school_____

Librarian (Head)_____

Library supervisor of district (if any)_____

- -

This total proposal has been approved. If selected to participate, we intend to support its objectives.

_____
(Signature of superintendent)

INFORMATION AND AUTHORIZATION FOR
TEACHER-EDUCATION INSTITUTION

Name of Teacher-Education Institution_____

Address_____

Telephone_____

Department from which field worker will be assigned_____

Name and title of field worker_____

- -

This total proposal has been approved. If selected to participate, we intend to support its objectives.

_____
(Signature of dean or head of department of education)

Final application for Phase II.

- 2 -

SECTION I -- PARTICIPATING SCHOOL

1. Grades included in this school _____

2. Grade | No. Classes | No. Students

Grade	No. Classes	No. Students
K	_____	_____
1	_____	_____
2	_____	_____
3	_____	_____
4	_____	_____
5	_____	_____
6	_____	_____
7	_____	_____
8	_____	_____
Special education (Specify)	_____	_____
Total	_____	_____

3. Number of classroom teachers _____

4. List the consultants and special services personnel provided to work <u>with this school</u>, including system-wide consultants and itinerant staff members shared with other schools:

Type of service	Full time this school	Part time this school	On request this school
Curriculum specialist	_____	_____	_____
Psychologist	_____	_____	_____
Health specialist	_____	_____	_____
Reading specialist	_____	_____	_____
Library coordinator	_____	_____	_____
Research or test specialist	_____	_____	_____
Other	_____	_____	_____

5. Fill in for school system:

Type of school	No. of schools	Total enrollment
Elementary	_____	_____
Junior high	_____	_____
Senior high	_____	_____
Combined	_____	_____
Total	_____	_____

Per pupil expenditure for elementary education, excluding capital outlay, 1962-63

_____

6. What agencies are financially responsible for the provision of the school library staff, funds, materials, and consultant services?

☐ Board of Education   ☐ University or college
                                        (if a demonstration school)

☐ State funds   ☐ Other (Specify)

7. Number of years library has been in operation under the direction of a librarian on the faculty of the school _____

Phase II final application (continued).

- 3 -

8. Specify:
   Librarian serves this school full-time ☐
   more than half-time ☐
   half-time ☐

   If not at present full-time in this school, is the librarian available for full-time employment?

9. Educational qualifications of librarian

Degrees held	University	Date received
___	___	___
___	___	___
___	___	___

   Certification status of the librarian in this state _____

   Number of semester hours in:

	Undergraduate	Graduate
Library Science	___	___
Education	___	___

10. Number of years the present librarian has served this school
    full-time_____   half-time_____

11. Non-professional assistants (other than student assistants):

	Employed	Volunteer
No. of Persons	___	___
Total number of hours per week	___	___

12. School library collection in school building (as of September 1963)

	General collection	Prof. materials for teachers
Books (volumes)	___	___
Periodicals	___	___
Filmstrips	___	___
Recordings	___	___
Other audio-visual materials (specify)	___	___
Number of drawers of pamphlets and other informational materials	___	___

13. School board expenditure and future budget for this school:

	1962-63	1963-64	1964-65 (estimate)
Library books (other than encyclopedias)	___	___	___
Encyclopedias	___	___	___
Professional books for teachers	___	___	___
Professional magazines for teachers	___	___	___
Audio-visual materials (exclude equipment) Purchase	___	___	___
Rental	___	___	___
Supplies	___	___	___
Binding	___	___	___
TOTAL	___	___	___

Phase II final application (continued).

- 4 -

Librarian's salary (pro-rate if part-time)   _____ _____ _____
Salary for library   _____ _____ _____
 clerical assistants

14. If funds for library materials are budgeted on the basis of enrollment or
    attendance, indicate the amount budgeted per elementary student for 1962-
    63_____   for 1963-64_____

15. List below the areas of greatest strengths and weaknesses in the collection
    in terms of quantity and quality of subject coverage, reference books,
    varied reading levels, filmstrips, etc.:

    Strengths_____   Weaknesses_____
    _____   _____
    _____   _____
    _____   _____
    _____   _____

16. Accessibility of materials:

    Can all library books (other than reference books) be withdrawn for home use
    by all students?   Yes_____   No_____

    If NO, explain in detail any restrictions which are imposed and what grades
    are affected:

    Can individual students use filmstrips in the school library? Yes____ No____

    Can individual students use recordings in school library?   Yes____ No____

    Is it a general practice to send collections of materials from the library to
    the classrooms for short term loan?   Yes_____   No_____

    Are audio-visual materials listed in the school library card catalog?
    Yes_____   No_____

    If school-owned audio-visual materials are separately housed or serviced
    outside the school library but in the school building, how are they admin-
    istered (person in charge, location, services provided)?

17. Library quarters and equipment:
    Describe location of the library within the school, in terms of accessibility,
    relation to classrooms, etc.:

Phase II final application (continued).

- 5 -

Give size for following areas:

	Total Sq. Ft.	Seating Capacity
Main library	_____	_____
Office	_____	_____
Work storage	_____	_____
Audio-visual	_____	_____
Production of materials	_____	_____
Professional materials for teachers	_____	_____
Others (specify_____	_____	_____
_____	_____	_____

Furniture and equipment in library:

Tables	Number	Chairs	Number
25"	_____	14"	_____
26"	_____	15"	_____
27"	_____	16"	_____
28"	_____	17"	_____
Total	_____	Total	_____
Card catalog drawers	_____	Linear feet of shelving	_____
Vertical file drawers	_____		
Charging desk	_____	Picture book shelving	_____

Audio-visual equipment:

	Number in library	Number available in other parts of school
16 mm projectors	_____	_____
Filmstrip-slide projectors	_____	_____
Individual filmstrip viewers	_____	_____
Overhead projectors	_____	_____
Opaque projectors	_____	_____
Record players	_____	_____
Tape recorders	_____	_____
Other (specify) _____	_____	_____
_____	_____	_____

18. Estimate what the school needs to meet the national quantitative standards for school libraries (See STANDARDS FOR SCHOOL LIBRARY PROGRAMS p. 24-25):

Professional staff_____

Clerical staff   _____

Materials   _____
                    _____
                    _____

Equipment   _____

Quarters   _____

Phase II final application (continued).

- 6 -

The following information should be reported on separate sheets. Please limit answers to one per sheet:

19. Characteristics of the school: Identify (1) any particular characteristics of the student body or community: (2) any special program or studies completed or in progress in areas of curriculum, organization, etc.; and (3) other special features of the school.

20. Describe the testing program of the school, giving names and forms of tests used, grade levels where administered, and frequency of administration. Describe other statistical data, cumulative records, etc., available about the students enrolled in this school, as well as the research and testing facilities in the school district or area which might be available for the purposes of this project.

21. Describe in some detail any system-wide library services provided for the school system by the school board (e.g. centralized processing or cataloging, professional library for teachers, instructional materials center, supervising or consultant services, audio-visual center, and the like).

22. What qualifications does the school possess which would provide for a successful demonstration? Consider factors such as readiness and qualifications of principal, teachers and librarian(s) to participate, ability of the school to accommodate and provide for the proposed visits, facilities (hotels, motels, restaurants, etc.) in the area for nondiscriminatory accommodations for visitors, probable stability of the school in terms of enrollment and staff (particularly librarian and principal), and other pertinent factors.

23. What plans have already been made by the school administration for development of school libraries in the school system during the next two to five years?

24. If your proposal should be approved, please state frankly what the possibilities are for your being able to continue the support of the school library at the level provided by the foundation.

25. If a part of the grant is needed for construction, prepare on graph paper a sketch indicating present size and arrangement of the library, and proposed alterations. Indicate the estimated cost and time required for such construction.

26. Assess as objectively as you can the strong and weak points of your current library program (See STANDARDS FOR SCHOOL LIBRARY PROGRAMS, Chapter 3)

27. How would you extend and/or improve your present school library program if you receive the grant? Is there any one type of service or activity which you would like to emphasize?

28. What long-range outcomes does the school hope to achieve through participation in this project? (Identify desired effects or goals for pupils, teachers, other schools in the system, etc.)

29. Has the school or school district had any previous cooperative project with the teacher-education institution which is co-applying? If so, describe the kind of project, the dates of its initiation and termination, and the purposes of it.

Phase II final application (continued).

- 7 -

30. Comment on the potential for the library's development into a complete instructional materials center as defined in STANDARDS FOR SCHOOL LIBRARY PROGRAMS.

31. Has the school district received any grant of funds from a foundation, government agency, etc., for the instructional materials or library program of the school district? For the school applying for this Project? If so, describe in detail the plan, projected outcomes, and present status of such a grant. Are there any applications for such grants pending? If so, describe the plan and projected outcomes of such applications.

Phase II final application (continued).

- 8 -

SECTION II -- COOPERATING TEACHER-EDUCATION INSTITUTION

32. By what agencies is this institution accredited?_____
    _____
    _____

33. Total enrollment in college or university_____
    Number of students in the school or department of education:
        Undergraduate_____   % in elementary education_____
        Graduate   _____   % in elementary education_____

34. Number of faculty members in school or department of education:
                                    Full time   _____
                                    Part time   _____

35. Library resources for the teacher-education program:
    (In giving the following information make as reliable estimates as possible.
    Do not include any materials provided in laboratory or demonstration school
    library. The following information should be reported on separate sheets.
    Please limit answers to one per sheet.)

    Number of volumes in field of education   _____
    Number of periodicals in field of education   _____

    Briefly describe the size and scope of curriculum-related materials, such as
    textbooks, courses of study, instructional units, tests, etc.; indicate hours
    when collection is open for use and library staff available.

    Briefly describe the size and scope of the juvenile literature collection(s);
    indicate hours when collection(s) is open for use; library staff available,
    and annual budget.

    Describe briefly any materials available that deal with school library services
    and materials.

    What provisions are made for access to audio-visual and programmed instruction
    aids? Are these serviced as a part of the library or as a separate unit?
    Describe briefly the extent of the collections and the staff.

    The following information should be reported on separate sheets. Please limit
    answers to one per sheet.

36. Describe and evaluate the instructional program provided for prospective
    teachers and administrators in relation to school library services and materials.
    (See STANDARDS FOR SCHOOL LIBRARY PROGRAMS, p. 67-70)

Phase II final application (continued).

- 9 -

37. If your institution cooperates in this project, a member of the Education
faculty would be assigned to half-time duty as field worker. In this capacity,
he would (1) work with the faculty of the project school in making best use
of the library, (2) plan and coordinate visits by teams of observers, (3)
plan and conduct workshops for the Education students in conjunction with the
project library, (4) maintain rapport with the faculty of the Department of
Education, and (5) assist in evaluating the project. What qualifications
would you look for in the person from your faculty to serve in this capacity?
Also state the name(s) of tentatively-selected field worker(s), college title
or rank, and experience. Indicate the amount of salary the project should
provide for this half-time assignment.

38. State briefly the long-range outcomes which you hope will accrue to the
college faculty and student teachers through your participation in this
project.

Phase II final application (continued).

THE Knapp School Libraries Project
TURNS THE SPOTLIGHT TO:

1

THE ALLISONVILLE SCHOOL
Metropolitan School District of Washington Township
4900 East 79th Street
Indianapolis, Indiana
and its cooperating teacher education institution:
BALL STATE UNIVERSITY
Muncie, Indiana

2

MOUNT ROYAL SCHOOL
121 McMechen Street
Baltimore, Maryland
and its cooperating teacher education institution:
TOWSON STATE COLLEGE
Towson, Maryland

3

CASIS SCHOOL
2710 Exposition Blvd.
Austin, Texas
and its cooperating teacher education institution:
UNIVERSITY OF TEXAS
Austin, Texas

These schools and teacher education institutions are the participants in Phase II of this $1,130,000.00 five-year Project funded by the Knapp Foundation, Inc., and administered by the American Association of School Librarians, a division of the American Library Association, and a department of the National Education Association.

You Are Invited to:

Visit one of these demonstration school libraries which were selected from more than one hundred applicants throughout the United States to participate in Phase II of the Project.

See the effect of the demonstration library on the instructional program of its school.

Share with other members of the school and school district, college or university, of your community the experience of a visit to one of these schools.

Report to the Project your views on the program which you have observed and the effects of your visit on the library program of your school or school district.

The Knapp Project office invites applications from leaders of teams of four, five, or six persons who wish to visit one of these schools for a full day and to participate in the program which will be arranged with their special interests in mind.

Teams selected to receive project funds will receive:

Round trip transportation at the rate of 10c per mile (maximum total available for each team is $100.00 for transportation).

Expenses budgeted at $15.00 per day for lodging, meals, and similar expenses for each individual on the team.

Brochure announcing Phase II visits.

Informative materials concerning the Project and school library development which will be available for team members when they visit the Project school.

The deadline for mailing the attached application is October 15, 1965.

Leaders of teams which are selected to receive reimbursements will be notified by November 15, 1965 concerning their applications. At that time a date for their visit will be set and information about how reimbursement may be requested will be provided.

Applicants whose teams are not selected to receive reimbursement will also be informed so that they may plan to make other arrangements to visit the Project schools at their own or at their school district or institutional expense.

It is anticipated that the Project will be able to select for reimbursement only a limited number of applicants. Priority will be given to those which in-

clude among their team members:

The administrative and instructional staff of a school or school district interested in improvement of its school library program

Faculty and staff of teacher education institutions interested in education of teachers in the use of instructional materials centers

School board members and representatives of organizations interested in improving the educational program

Any combination of personnel selected from the above three categories

Persons who have not participated in a Project-supported team visit to either of the Knapp Project Phase I demonstration centers

Representatives from communities where the potential for further improvement of the school library program is recognized

For further information about the Knapp Project write to:

MISS PEGGY SULLIVAN, *Director*
Knapp School Libraries Project
American Library Association
50 East Huron Street
Chicago, Illinois 60611

■ *More About Phase II Schools*

■ THE ALLISONVILLE SCHOOL, of the Metropolitan School District of Washington Township, Marion County, Indiana, is in a growing suburban community adjacent to Indianapolis. The school district has established central libraries in each of the fourteen schools. Mrs. Audrey Michels, who had been assigned to the Allisonville School as music teacher half-time, and as librarian half-time, was enabled by the Knapp School Libraries Project to expand the library program by serving as full-time librarian. An additional full-time librarian and a clerical assistant have also been employed with Project funds.

Library services at the school district level include direction from two coordinators of libraries, one for elementary, and one for secondary. Centralized ordering, cataloging, and processing are provided.

Ball State University in Muncie, Indiana, has designated Dr. Donald L. Barnes, associate professor of Education, as its Field Worker for this Project with the Allisonville School. Dr. Barnes's experience as field worker for the Midwest Program of Airborne Television Instruction has included the conducting of teacher workshops, seminars, and individual consultations with school faculty members. Ball State has a record of cooperation with the Metropolitan School District of Washington Township. Ball State student teachers have been assigned to schools in

this district, and several extended academic curriculum offerings have been provided cooperatively. In June, 1965, a workshop for elementary teachers on utilizing instructional materials in the classroom was offered under the sponsorship of Ball State, the Metropolitan School District of Washington Township, and the Knapp Project.

The curriculum and educational program of the Washington Township Schools was surveyed and evaluated by a team from Ohio State University in 1962 and 1963. This and other studies and statements of goals have led to the school district's plan for continuous improvement. The Knapp Project's provision of funds for salaries, materials, equipment, and construction is intended to implement that plan, especially as it relates to the further development of an instructional materials center at the Allisonville School.

■ THE MOUNT ROYAL SCHOOL, an inner-city school in Baltimore, Maryland, opened in February, 1959. The faculty of the school includes a number of young persons who have had experience in schools in other sections of the city and who are now eager to work with young children in an inner-city neighborhood.

Mrs. Idella Nichols has served as librarian at the

Phase II visits brochure (continued).

school since September, 1959. Her full-time assignment there is one indication of the emphasis placed on serving the special needs of this school's community. During the 1964-65 school year, Project funds have provided one additional librarian and a library aide, plus additions to the physcal facility, equipment, and materials collection.

System-wide library services in the 203 Baltimore City Public Schools include supervising and consultant services, centralized processing and cataloging, professional library service, access to a sample collection of 4,000 titles recommended for purchase, and access to the services of a central instructional materials center for the school system. Mrs. Alice Rusk, School Library Specialist, has been released from some of her other responsibilities to work more closely with the Mount Royal School library program and to further its development as an instructional materials center for the school.

Towson State College has named Dr. Walter W. Williamson the Field Worker for this Project. Dr. Williamson is professor of Education at Towson State College. He has been an elementary classroom teacher and has had extended experience as an instructor in elementary education. He has worked in the Sequential Tests of Educational Progress (STEP) and School and College Ability Tests (SCAT) Testing Programs for the Educational Testing Service. He is a member of the World Tapes for Education Association and is Chairman of the Teaching Methods and Materials section of that group. The college and the school system see in the selection of the Mount Royal School as a demonstration center the opportunity for further cooperative projects and conferences.

■ **THE CASIS ELEMENTARY SCHOOL,** as one of sixty-three schools in the Austin Independent School District, Austin, Texas, has, from its beginnings more than twelve years ago, served also as an active, cooperative research and demonstration center for The University of Texas and the school district. Dr. M. G. Bowden, principal, and Dr. Alice Brooks McGuire, librarian, have served at the school since its opening, and have been leaders in the school's growth as a center for curriculum development and demonstration.

The Knapp School Libraries Project, by providing funds for additional staff for the library program, for materials to replace outworn materials in the collection and to enlarge the non-print materials collection, and for equipment and furnishings for the new library quarters, makes possible the achievement of standards in staffing in this school, and also provides for further demonstration of the present excellent program of library service at the Casis School.

Library services at the school district level for the schools of the Austin Independent School District include assistance from two library supervisors and provision for centralized purchasing of materials.

Dr. Alma M. Freeland, associate professor of Elementary Education at The University of Texas, has been named Field Worker for this Project with the Casis School. Dr. Freeland has worked in similar cooperative projects, and brings to the Knapp Project a background of success as teacher, school administrator, and curriculum specialist. Her extensive writings have included social studies and reading textbooks as well as numerous articles dealing with teaching and instructional problems.

The Casis School, as a laboratory-demonstration school, is owned and operated jointly by the Austin Public Schools and The University of Texas. The mutual interest provides an exceptionally favorable climate for the cooperative commitment of university and school district to the Knapp School Libraries Project.

Selection and arrangements for Project-supported team visits will be made by the Project office. Arrangements for visits by other teams or individuals may be made by requesting appointments at least four weeks in advance and by communicating with the person in each school who has the responsibility for such arrangements. These are:

For the Allisonville School
MR. DONALD SELLMER, *Principal*
Allisonville School
4900 East 79th Street
Indianapolis, Indiana 46250

■ *For the Mount Royal School*
DR. WALTER W. WILLIAMSON
Professor of Education
Towson State College
Towson, Maryland 21204

■ *For the Casis School*
DR. M. G. BOWDEN, *Principal*
Casis School
2710 Exposition Blvd.
Austin, Texas 78703

Many professional associations, students in teacher education and librarianship, and others with special interests will also be planning group visits to these Project schools during the 1965-1966 and 1966-1967 school years. To share in this opportunity as the guest of the Knapp School Libraries Project we invite you to complete the application form which is attached to this brochure and to mail it to the Knapp Project office no later than October 15, 1965. Select the Project school which is nearest you or which serves an area most like the one in which you and your fellow team members are interested. Indicate the three dates which are your first, second, and third choices for making this visit. Invite four or five others to join your group in this application. Present your reasons for making application.

Phase II visits brochure (continued).

THE FOLLOWING INFORMATION SHOULD BE TYPED

BUDGET REQUEST FOR THIS VISIT:

_____ Persons at $15.00 per day per person $_____

Round trip transportation at 10c per mile   _____
(Maximum of $100.00 per team)
                 TOTAL BUDGET REQUEST $_____

*   *   *   *   *   *   *

The members of this group will be:

NAME	TITLE OR POSITION	SCHOOL OR OFFICE ADDRESS
1.		
2.		
3.		
4.		
5.		
6.		

Our special interest in the elementary library program is:_____

_____

Our purpose in making this visit is_____

_____

The present status of our elementary library program is_____

_____

_____   _____
Signed   Title or Position

_____   _____   _____
Address   City   State

Please complete all answers on this sheet, completing on the reverse side. Applications must be postmarked no later than October 15, 1965, and mailed to:

MISS PEGGY SULLIVAN, *Director*
Knapp School Libraries Project
American Library Association
50 East Huron Street
Chicago, Illinois 60611

Phase II visits brochure (continued).

APPLICATION FOR FUNDS TO VISIT A
KNAPP SCHOOL LIBRARIES PROJECT DEMONSTRATION CENTER

We have read the brochure about the Knapp School Libraries Project Phase II demonstration centers. We are requesting Project funds for a visit to:

ALLISONVILLE SCHOOL, INDIANAPOLIS, INDIANA

Our preferred dates for a visit are noted as 1, 2, 3 below:

1965-66

____Friday, December 3	____Friday, April 29	____Monday, May 23
____Friday, December 10	____Monday, May 9	
____Monday, April 18	____Friday, May 20	

1966-67

____Monday, October 3	____Friday, October 28	____Monday, December 5
____Friday, October 7	____Monday, November 7	____Friday, December 9
____Monday, October 17	____Monday, November 14	____Friday, December 16

1967 dates to be determined. Teams wishing to visit Allisonville School may indicate a date in April or May, 1967, which would be convenient for them; confirmation of dates for visits will be sent later.

MOUNT ROYAL SCHOOL, BALTIMORE, MARYLAND

Our preferred dates for a visit are noted as 1, 2, 3 below:

1965-66

____Thursday, December 9	____Friday, February 18	____Friday, May 6
____Monday, December 13	____Friday, February 25	____Monday, May 9
____Wednesday, December 15	____Wednesday, March 2	____Wednesday, May 11
____Tuesday, January 4	____Friday, March 4	____Tuesday, May 17
____Wednesday, January 12	____Monday, March 14	____Tuesday, May 24
____Friday, January 14	____Wednesday, March 16	____Friday, May 27
____Tuesday, January 18	____Wednesday, March 23	____Thursday, June 2
____Thursday, January 20	____Tuesday, April 5	____Tuesday, June 7
____Monday, January 24	____Thursday, April 21	____Thursday, June 9
____Wednesday, January 26	____Tuesday, April 26	
____Wednesday, February 2	____Tuesday, May 3	

1966-67 dates to be determined. Teams wishing to visit Mount Royal School may indicate a date in the 1966-67 school year which would be convenient for them; confirmation of dates for visits will be sent later.

CASIS SCHOOL, AUSTIN, TEXAS

Our preferred dates for a visit are noted as 1, 2, 3 below:

1965-66

____Wednesday, December 1	____Friday, January 21	____Wednesday, April 20
____Friday, December 3	____Wednesday, February 9	____Friday, April 22
____Wednesday, December 8	____Friday, February 11	____Wednesday, April 27
____Friday, December 10	____Wednesday, March 2	____Friday, April 29
____Wednesday, January 12	____Wednesday, March 9	____Wednesday, May 11
____Friday, January 14	____Wednesday, March 16	____Friday, May 13
____Wednesday, January 19	____Friday, March 18	

1966-67

____Wednesday, October 5	____Friday, January 20	____Wednesday, April 12
____Friday, October 7	____Wednesday, February 1	____Friday, April 14
____Friday, October 14	____Friday, February 3	____Wednesday, April 19
____Wednesday, October 26	____Wednesday, February 8	____Friday, April 21
____Friday, October 28	____Friday, February 10	____Wednesday, April 26
____Wednesday, November 30	____Wednesday, February 15	____Friday, April 28
____Friday, December 2	____Friday, February 17	____Wednesday, May 3
____Wednesday, December 7	____Friday, February 24	____Friday, May 5
____Friday, December 9	____Wednesday, March 1	____Wednesday, May 10
____Wednesday, January 11	____Wednesday, March 8	____Friday, May 12
____Friday, January 13	____Wednesday, April 5	
____Wednesday, January 18	____Friday, April 7	

Phase II visits brochure (continued).

The K*napp school libraries project*

enters PHASE III in 1965

Will your secondary school be one of three demonstration centers to participate?

In the third phase of a $1,130,000 Project, funded by the Knapp Foundation, Inc., administered by the American Association of School Librarians, a division of the American Library Association and a department of the National Education Association, three secondary schools will be selected to participate as demonstration centers for a period extending over two school years (1965-66 and 1966-67). Their demonstration will be intended to show how school libraries serve the school and the instructional program by providing the full program of services recommended in *Standards for School Library Programs* (American Library Association, 1960, $2.50).

One aspect of the Project is the assignment of a half-time field worker from a teacher-education institution cooperating with the Project school. Qualifications of the faculty member receiving this assignment should include appropriate education and experience in curriculum development, secondary school teaching, and the education of teachers. The field worker's assignment would include work with the staff of the secondary school in making the best use of the school's library program, research and evaluation of the further development of the present program, relation of the implications of such a program to the curriculum of his institution, and planning and conduct of workshop-visits for school administrators, community leaders, faculty members, prospective teachers and administrators, and others committed to further development of school library programs.

The Project offers financial assistance to enhance and expand the present secondary school library program in staff, materials, and physical facilities and to reimburse the teacher-education institution for the half-time salary of the field worker and other expenses incurred in Project participation.

Brochure and preliminary application for Phase III.

Interest in this Phase of the Project has been so great that a number of schools, already in correspondence with the Project office, have taken these preliminary steps:

1. Evaluation of the present library program in terms of the qualitative and quantitative recommendations of *Standards for School Library Programs*

2. Determination of the amount of financial aid required to bring the present library program to the level of the standards

3. Discussion and correspondence with the state school library supervisor or other representative of the state's educational agency to alert them to the school's intention of applying for Project participation

4. Planning conferences or correspondence with representatives from the department or school of teacher-education from a neighboring college or university, concerning the institution's interest and ability to co-apply for Project participation

5. Drafting of a plan for achievement of the goals of the school library program

Other schools interested in Phase III of the Knapp School Libraries Project are encouraged now to follow the same preliminary steps noted above, and to prepare and submit a preliminary application as an indication of their interest. A preliminary application is included on a tear-off sheet with this brochure.

With recognition of the need for a firm basis for further development, the Project Advisory Committee has established the following criteria, and has stated that all of them must have been in effect at least since September, 1963:

A school enrollment including at least three of the grades, seven through twelve

A library established and functioning with a well-developed plan for library service to the curriculum and with the financial and administrative support of the school and school district, as represented by the board of education, or, in private schools, by the chief administrative agency

A qualified school librarian responsible for the library program on a full-time basis. This librarian should have the interest and ability to plan, organize, and demonstrate a library program functioning at the level of the national standards

An established pattern for the staffing, administrative and financial support, and curriculum development in the school and school district

In Phases I and II of this Project, demonstration centers were established in five elementary schools in five states. No schools from those states may apply for Phase III participation. These schools are:

Marcus Whitman Elementary School in Richland, Washington

Central Park Road Elementary School in Plainview, New York

Allisonville School in Washington Township, Indiana

Mount Royal Elementary School in Baltimore, Maryland

Casis School in Austin, Texas

Schools in the remaining forty-five states of the United States are invited to apply for Phase III participation. One factor to be considered in applications for Phase III will be the potential for locating demonstration centers in geographic areas of the country not yet represented in the Project.

The demonstration aspects of this Project require that the schools selected be located in communities where visitors will have access to restaurant and hotel or motel

Phase III brochure (continued).

accommodations on a nondiscriminatory basis; the communities should also be convenient and accessible to a large population.

Only one school in a school district may apply, but a teacher-education institution may co-apply with more than one school.

What the Knapp School Libraries Project can provide to the participating schools and teacher-education institutions:

Financial assistance for materials, staff salaries, and physical quarters to bring the school library to the level of national standards

Consultant assistance from the Project Director

Assistance from the field-worker named by the teacher-education institution

Opportunity for cooperative effort by the school and teacher-education institution in demonstrating a school library program at the level of national standards

What the Project looks for in the schools selected for participation:

A commitment to the improvement of school library programs, including at least the potential to maintain the level of financial assistance provided by the Project, after the school's two-year period of Project participation has ended.

A library program which combines achievement with potential—a good program underway, which can be brought to optimum effectiveness by the funds provided by the Project.

An instructional program which demonstrates the effective use of instructional materials and library services as a major factor in curriculum development.

A school library functioning as one part of a school district program which recognizes the need for library development at all grade levels and in all schools.

With the aim of selecting the three schools for Phase III some time in the spring of 1965, the Knapp School Libraries Project will follow this schedule:

October 1, 1964—Deadline for receipt of all preliminary applications
at the Project office

November 30, 1964—Deadline for receipt of all final applications
at the Project office

Spring, 1965—Announcement of the three schools selected for participation

Summer, 1965—Beginning of Project participation for these schools

June, 1967—Termination of Project participation for these schools

The brief preliminary application form should be completed in full and forwarded without additional materials or exhibits to:

Miss Peggy Sullivan, Director
Knapp School Libraries Project
50 East Huron Street
Chicago, Illinois 60611

All persons presenting preliminary application forms will be notified whether the schools for which they are applying are eligible to receive final application forms.

The superintendents or chief administrators of schools making final application will be notified of the schools selected for Project application.

Phase III brochure (continued).

The major strengths of the school library program at present are

_____

_____

_____

The major needs of the school library program at present are

_____

_____

_____

Name of school district
_____

Address
_____

Number of schools included in the school district:
_____

Secondary _____ Elementary _____

Number of schools with centralized libraries:
_____

Secondary _____ Elementary _____

Chief librarian or supervisor of libraries in the school district:

Name _____ Title _____

Chief administrative officer of school district:

Name _____ Title _____

Address _____
                    (Street)

_____   _____
        (City)   (State)

Name of college or university with which the school plans to co-apply:

_____

Please forward the necessary copies of the final application form to:

Name _____
                Title of Position

Address _____

City _____ State _____

Complete in full and forward to: Miss Peggy Sullivan, Director
                                    Knapp School Libraries Project
                                    50 East Huron Street
                                    Chicago, Illinois 60611

Phase·III brochure (continued).

Phase III — Knapp School Libraries Project
PRELIMINARY APPLICATION FORM

Name of school_____

Address_____
            (Street)   (City)   (State)

Grades included in the school and served by the school library_____Enrollment_____
Name of the librarian who has been assigned to the school full-time since at least September, 1963, and who
will be available to direct the library program in the school through the 1966-67 school year

_____

To attain the levels recommended in *Standards for School Library Programs*, these are the major needs of
the school library:

MATERIALS COLLECTION

Types and quantities of materials

_____

_____

_____   *Estimates of funds
                                                                  required*

_____

_____ $_____

PERSONNEL

Number and kind of positions

PROFESSIONAL   CLERICAL

_____   _____

_____   _____   *Annual salary needs*

_____   _____ $_____

_____   _____

_____   _____

PHYSICAL FACILITIES

Square footage expansion and type of areas needed

_____

_____

_____

_____

TOTAL FUNDS REQUIRED FOR A TWO-YEAR PERIOD $_____

Phase III brochure (continued).

KNAPP SCHOOL LIBRARIES PROJECT APPLICATION
FOR SECONDARY SCHOOL LIBRARY
AND
CO-APPLYING TEACHER-EDUCATION PROGRAM

Phase III

Mail one copy of this application to: Miss Peggy Sullivan, Director
Knapp School Libraries Project
50 East Huron Street
Chicago, Illinois 60611

This Phase III application must be postmarked on or before November 30, 1964

This application is to be completed by personnel of the school system (or its equivalent) and the co-applying teacher-education institution.

Do not send any exhibits or supplementary material not specifically requested on the application.

INFORMATION AND AUTHORIZATION FOR SCHOOL DISTRICT

Name of school district _____

Address _____

         Street   City   State

Telephone (School district) _____ Telephone (Applying school) _____

Name of school _____

Address _____

         Street   City   State

Superintendent of district _____

Principal of school _____

Librarian of school who would have major responsibility for this project _____

Library supervisor of district (if any) _____

This total proposal has been approved. If selected to participate, we intend to support its objectives.

_____
(Signature of superintendent)

Final application for Phase III.

- 2 -

SECTION I - PARTICIPATING SCHOOL

A. Grades of School   No. Students   B.   Faculty
                      (as of April 15, 1964)

Grade	No. Students		
7	_____	No. full-time	
8	_____	classroom teachers	_____
9	_____	No. part-time	
10	_____	classroom teachers	_____
11	_____	Total No. of faculty,	
12	_____	both full & part time	_____

C. Library Program

    1. Provide the following information for each member of the school library
       staff, including full- and part-time professional and clerical personnel,
       but excluding volunteers and student assistants: Name, title of position,
       major educational qualifications and degrees, major experience qualifica-
       tions, date of original employment in present position, and certification
       status.

    2. Cite the major strengths of the school library program.

    3. Cite the major weaknesses of the school library program.

    4. Status of collection owned and administered as part of the school
       library as of April 15, 1964:

	Number
Books (volumes)	_____
Periodicals	_____
Films	_____
Filmstrips	_____
Recordings	_____
Other audio-visual materials (specify)	_____
	_____
	_____
	_____
	_____
Vertical file materials (drawers)	_____
Professional books for faculty	_____
Professional periodicals for faculty	_____

5. Complete the following information for budget for the 1965-66 and 1966-67
    school years. In preparing this, refer to Standards for School Library
    Programs (American Library Association, 1960, $2.50) and include requests
    for Project funds as supplements to anticipated funds, to bring the lib-
    rary to the level of standards in materials, physical facilities, staff,
    etc.

    If the budgets for 1965-66 and 1966-67 can not be reliably anticipated,
    compute them by adding the budgets for the three years preceding (1962-63
    through 1964-65) and dividing by 3.

Phase III final application (continued).

- 3 -

	Actual Budget 1963-64	Anticipated Budget 1965-66	Project Supplement 1965-66	Anticipated Budget 1966-67	Project Supplement 1966-67
Books					
Periodicals					
Films					
Filmstrips					
Recordings					
Other audio-visual materials (specify)					
Processing of materials					
Professional materials for faculty					
Salaries-Library staff					
Improvement or enlargement of physical facilities					
Audio-visual equipment					
Totals					

If the budget was computed on a 3-year average, as suggested above, check here. ☐

If capital outlay or other special funds were included in any of the above budget items, check here. ☐

If so, indicate amounts, purposes, and terms of such special funds.

_____

_____

_____

_____

Indicate the sources and approximate amounts for all funds included in the above budget which come from sources other than the school or school district or other administrative agency directly responsible for the school library program.

_____

_____

_____

_____

Phase III final application (continued).

- 4 -

6. Does the school have a statement of policy on selection of library materials? If so, include it here.

7. Describe the procedures followed in selection of library materials, indicating whether faculty members participate in selection, the tools used by the library staff in selection, etc.

8. Indicate the areas of greatest strengths and weaknesses in the collection in terms of quantity and quality of various subject areas, reading levels, etc.

9. Indicate below the major forms of materials loaned for the periods listed, indicating the type of items included in each category:

   Overnight loan   _____
   Less than seven days   _____
   Seven to 13 days   _____
   14 to 28 days   _____
   28 days to one semester _____
   More than one semester _____

10. If there is a reserve or restricted area in the library, indicate the kinds of materials normally included in it and the conditions governing their loan or use.

11. Describe any collections of instructional materials housed elsewhere in the school, noting the numbers, forms, subject, and specific use of the collections, and indicating whether or not these are administered as parts of the school library collection.

12. Comment on the potential for the library's development into a complete instructional materials center as defined in STANDARDS FOR SCHOOL LIBRARY PROGRAMS.

13. Prepare and submit a sketch of the present library facility, indicating arrangement of major items of equipment (card catalog, charging desk, etc.) and location of the various parts of the materials collection (e.g., periodicals, a-v, non-fiction books, reference books, etc.) Indicate the scale to which the sketch was drawn (e.g., 1/8" = 1'0")

14. If the library facility is less adequate than recommended in Standards for School Library Programs, prepare and submit a sketch of the additional areas needed. Use the same scale as on the sketch of the present library facility. Include an estimate of the funds and time required for completion of construction and a statement of the amount which could be paid by the school district or other administrative agency.

15. Prepare and submit a sketch showing the location of the major areas of the school building - e.g., administrative offices, classrooms, laboratories, library, etc. Indicate the scale to which the sketch was drawn.

Phase III final application (continued).

- 5 -

16. Give the present seating capacity of the various parts of the library:

Reading room   _____
Work area   _____
Audio-visual screening area   _____
Audio-visual storage area   _____
Library staff office   _____
Professional materials area   _____
Library classroom   _____
Library conference room   _____
Periodical storage   _____
Listening areas   _____

17. Indicate the quantities of each of the following major kinds of audio-visual equipment:

	Housed in library	Housed elsewhere in school
16 mm projectors	_____	_____
Filmstrip projectors	_____	_____
Filmstrip previewers	_____	_____
Slide projectors	_____	_____
Overhead projectors	_____	_____
Record players	_____	_____
Tape recorders	_____	_____
Television sets	_____	_____
Radios	_____	_____
Others (Specify)	_____	_____

_____
_____
_____
_____
_____

18. What hours and what days is the library regularly open?

19. If the library is open late afternoons, evenings, weekends, or summer, indicate how these times were determined, and the date when this schedule was initiated.

20. What is the library's average daily attendance? (Specify number of faculty, number of students)

21. What is the library's average daily circulation? (Specify books, periodicals, other print materials, and non-print materials)

Phase III final application (continued).

- 6 -

D. Instructional Program

1. By what regional accrediting associations and/or state agencies is the school accredited? Include dates of most recent evaluations by both types of agencies.

2. What is the major curricular emphasis of the school? Is the school a comprehensive high school? Academic? Vocational? Junior high? Other?

3. In what ways does the library strengthen the instructional program?

4. Describe the testing program of the school, giving names and forms of all tests administered at least once a year to 20% or more of the students. Indicate grade levels where administered and frequency of administration.

5. Describe in some detail any special program or studies underway in areas of curriculum, organization, etc., in this school.

6. Characterize the major strengths of the faculty of the school, commenting on the years of education or degrees earned, tenure in this school, special areas of interest and ability, etc.

7. If student teachers were assigned to this school in 1963-64, indicate how many, what subject areas and grade levels, and which teacher-education institutions they represented.

Phase III final application (continued).

- 7 -

E. General

1. Characterize the student body and community of the school, indicating average years of education of parents, average age of homes, etc., and commenting on the geographic area served by the school, how students are transported to school, etc.

2. Are there sufficient lounge, luncheon, parking, closet facilities, etc., available within the school for teams who may visit if the school participates in the Project? Estimate the maximum number of visitors who may be scheduled for visits relating to this Project in any one day.

3. What long-range outcomes in terms of effects or goals for pupils, teachers, etc., does the school hope to achieve through participation in this Project?

4. Comment on the school's qualifications for a successful demonstration center for the 1965-66 and 1966-67 school years, noting such factors as: What qualifications does the school possess which would provide for a successful demonstration? Consider factors such as readiness and qualifications of principal, teachers and librarian(s) to participate, ability of the school to accommodate and provide for the proposed visits, facilities (hotels, motels, restaurants, etc.) in the area for nondiscriminatory accommodations for visitors, probable stability of the school in terms of enrollment and staff (particularly librarians and principal), and other pertinent factors. Include the names and addresses of at least three hotels or motels which you know provide nondiscriminatory accommodations within 25 miles of the school.

5. Has the school had any previous cooperative project with the teacher-education institution which is the co-applicant? If so, describe the kind of project, the dates of its initiation and termination, its purposes, and its results.

6. Has the school received or applied for any grant of funds from a foundation, government agency, etc.? If so describe in detail the plan, projected outcomes, and present status of such a grant. Are there any applications for such grants pending? If so, describe the plan and projected outcomes of such applications.

The information included in Section I has been prepared chiefly by

_____

Name(s)   Title(s)

Phase III final application (continued).

- 8 -

SECTION II - SCHOOL DISTRICT OR GENERAL
ADMINISTRATIVE AGENCY

Note. It is understood that some applying schools may not be part
of districts or systems. In those cases, questions number
1, 2, and 3, Section II may be omitted.

1. What factors led to the selection of the school for which this application is being made, as the one school in the district to apply?

2. Describe in some detail the consultative, supervisory, and administrative services provided by the school district to work with the
applying school's instructional program.

3. Describe in some detail any system-wide library services provided
for the school system by the school board (e.g. centralized processing or cataloging, professional library for teachers, instructional
materials center, supervising or consultant services, audio-visual
center, and the like).

4. The following questions are to be answered on this sheet:

a. Schools of the school district	No. of schools	Total enrollment
Elementary		
Junior high		
Senior high		
Other (Specify)		
Totals		

  b. Per pupil expenditure for secondary education, excluding capital
outlay, 1962-63_____

  c. Per pupil expenditure for elementary education, excluding capital
outlay, 1962-63_____

  d. If funds for library materials are budgeted on the basis of
enrollment or attendance, indicate the amount budgeted per
secondary student for 1962-63_____1963-64_____

  e. Total budget for library materials for this school
1962-63_____1963-64_____

5. What plans have already been made by the school administration for
development of school libraries in the school system during the next
two to five years?

6. If this school should be selected to participate in the Project, what
are the possibilities for the school district's being able to continue
the support of the school library at the level provided by the Project?

7. What factors led to the selection of the co-applying teacher-education
institution as the co-applicant?

8. Has the school district had any previous cooperative projects with co-
applying teacher-education institution? With the faculty member
designated as field worker? If so, describe the type of project, the
dates of its initiation and termination, its purposes, and its results.

Phase III final application (continued).

- 9 -

9. Has the school district received any grant of funds from a foundation, government agency, etc., for the instructional materials or library program? If so, describe in detail the plan, projected outcomes, and present status of such a grant. Are there any applications for such grants pending? If so, describe the plan and projected outcomes of such applications.

The information included in Section II has been prepared chiefly by

_____

Name(s)   Title(s)

Phase III final application (continued).

- 10 -

SECTION III - CO-APPLYING TEACHER-EDUCATION INSTITUTION

Note. If the teacher-education institution is co-applying with two
       or more schools for Phase III of the Knapp School Libraries
       Project, only one copy of Section III is to be forwarded to:

Peggy Sullivan, Director
Knapp School Libraries Project
50 East Huron Street
Chicago, Illinois 60611

INFORMATION AND AUTHORIZATION FOR TEACHER-EDUCATION INSTITUTION

Name of Teacher-Education Institution

_____

Address_____
                    Street   City   State

Telephone_____

Department from which field worker will be assigned_____

_____

Name and title of tentatively-selected field worker_____

_____

Name and title of dean or head of department of education_____

_____

This total proposal has been approved. If selected to participate, we intend
to support its objectives.

_____
(Signature of dean or head of department of education)

Phase III final application (continued).

- 11 -

1. List the schools with which this institution is co-applying:

    Name of School   Name of School District

    _____

    _____

    _____

    _____

    _____

    _____

2. By what agencies is this institution accredited? (Include dates of
    most recent accreditations.)

3. Supply these answers on this sheet:

    Total enrollment of the college or university for 1963-64:_____

    Number of students in school or department of education:_____

    Undergraduate_____Number in secondary education_____

    Graduate_____Number in secondary education_____

    Number of faculty members in school or department of education:

         Full-time_____

         Part-time_____

4. Briefly describe the size and scope of the curriculum library, learning
    resources center, or other collection of curriculum materials. Indicate
    types of materials included, such as textbooks, courses of study,
    instructional units, tests, etc.; indicate hours when collection is open
    for use and library staff available.

5. Briefly describe the size and scope of the collections of materials
    (books, A-V materials, etc.) for elementary and secondary students,
    other than those in the laboratory or demonstration school. Indicate
    hours when collection(s) is open for use; library staff available,
    annual budget, and the bases on which these materials are circulated.

Phase III final application (continued).

- 12 -

6. Describe briefly any materials available that deal with school library services and resources.

7. What provisions are made for access to audio-visual and programmed instruction aids? Are these serviced as a part of the library or as a separate unit? Describe briefly the extent of the collections and the staff.

8. Describe and evaluate the instructional program provided for prospective teachers and administrators in relation to school library services and materials. (See STANDARDS FOR SCHOOL LIBRARY PROGRAMS, p. 67-70)

9. State briefly the long-range outcomes which you hope will accrue to the college faculty and student teachers through your participation in this project.

10. If your institution cooperates in this project, a member of the Education faculty would be assigned to half-time duty as field worker. In this capacity, he would (1) work with the faculty of the project school in making best use of the library, (2) plan and coordinate visits by teams of observers, (3) plan and conduct workshops for the Education students in conjunction with the project library, (4) maintain rapport with the faculty of the Department of Education, and (5) assist in evaluating the project. What qualifications would you look for in the person from your faculty to serve in this capacity?

11. State the name of tentatively-selected field worker, college title or rank, and experience. Indicate the amount of salary the project should provide for this half-time assignment for the 1965-66 and 1966-67 school years. Relevant information should include degrees held, kinds and places of teaching experience, date of assignment in present faculty position, and other factors which led to the designation of this faculty member as field worker.

The information included in Section III has been prepared chiefly by

_____

        Name(s)   Title(s)

Phase III final application (continued).

THE **KNAPP SCHOOL LIBRARIES PROJECT**

turns the spotlight to:

 ROOSEVELT HIGH SCHOOL
   6941 North Central Street
   Portland, Oregon

*Portland State College is its cooperating
teacher education institution*

 FARRER JUNIOR HIGH SCHOOL
   100 North 600 East
   Provo, Utah

*Brigham Young University is its cooperating
teacher education institution*

 OAK PARK AND RIVER FOREST HIGH SCHOOL
   East Avenue and Ontario Street
   Oak Park, Illinois

*The University of Illinois, Urbana, Illinois, is its
cooperating teacher education institution*

*Plan now to visit one of the three secondary
schools participating in Phase III of the
Knapp Schools Library Project*

These schools and teacher education institutions are the participants in Phase III of this $1,130,000 five-year Project funded by the Knapp Foundation, Inc., and administered by the American Association of School Librarians, a division of the American Library Association, and a department of the National Education Association.

Brochure announcing Phase III visits.

• *In a visit to one of these schools, you can:*

SEE the impact of the demonstration library on the instructional program of the school.

SHARE with other representatives of your community (your school, school district, college, or university) the experiences of a visit planned with your special interests in mind.

REPORT to the Project office your views on the program you have observed and the effect of your visit on the library program of your school or school district.

Plans for a visit can be made directly with the liaison person representing the school you wish to visit.

OR

Application for Project funds for the travel expenses of a team of visitors can be made to the Knapp Project office.

Teams eligible for these travel expenses may include a team leader and four or five other persons representing:

The administrative and instructional staff of a school or school district interested in improvement of its school library program.

Faculty and staff of teacher education institutions interested in the education of teachers in the use of instructional materials.

School board members and other community leaders interested in improving the educational program of a community.

Any combination of personnel selected from the above three categories.

Individuals who have received Project funds for visits to schools in Phase I or II of the Knapp Project are not eligible for travel funds for Phase III.

Teams representing school districts, teacher education institutions, or other agencies which received funds for visits to schools in Phase I or II of the Knapp Project are not eligible for travel funds for Phase III.

While it is recommended that school librarians and school library supervisors, as representatives of school or school district staff, should be members of visiting teams, those teams composed exclusively or primarily of school library staff members are not encouraged to apply for Project funds.

The attached application sheet indicates the dates when Project-supported visits will be scheduled during the 1965-1966 and 1966-1967 school years. It should be completed and mailed to the Knapp Project office no later than January 7, 1966. Leaders of teams selected to receive reimbursement will be notified by February 1, 1966. At that time, a date for their team visit will be confirmed and information will be provided about how reimbursement will be arranged. Leaders of teams not selected to receive reimbursement will also be informed of the decision made on their application by February 1, 1966.

Teams selected to receive Project funds will be reimbursed for: Round trip transportation between their home community and the Project school at the rate of ten cents per mile for a team. This provision, with a customary maximum of $100.00 per team, is made to encourage teams to travel together by automobile to exchange ideas obtained during their visit.

Expenses budgeted at $15.00 per day per person for lodging, meals, and similar expenses incurred during the round trip.

In addition, informative materials concerning the Project and school library development will be available for all visitors to Project schools.

For further information about the Knapp Project write to:

Miss Peggy Sullivan, *Director*
Knapp School Libraries Project
American Library Association
50 East Huron Street
Chicago, Illinois   60611

• *Information about the Schools in Phase III of the Knapp School Libraries Project*

THE ROOSEVELT HIGH SCHOOL

in Portland, Oregon, is one of twelve secondary schools in a district known for outstanding achievement in curriculum development. Superintendent Melvin W. Barnes supports a dynamic school library program. The district maintains a growing instructional materials department which provides centralized purchasing, cataloging, and processing for all school libraries.

The Roosevelt head librarian, Mrs. Lois Sayles, is a leader of unusual enthusiasm and exceptional competence. In two years at Roosevelt, she has fostered an awareness among the staff and students of the many services and opportunities to be found in a library. Many teachers have voluntarily attended in-service programs exploring instructional improvements through use of the library. The district has published a descriptive outline of the Roosevelt program as a guide for other schools.

Phase III visits brochure (continued).

Portland State College has designated Dr. Jerome E. Leavitt, Professor of Education, as the field worker for this Project. Dr. Leavitt has been interested in the Knapp Project since its inception in 1963. He is coordinating a program whereby students in secondary teacher education from all of the Colleges in the Greater Portland Area will participate in the Knapp Project at Roosevelt. This Project is one of several cooperative efforts between the college and the Portland Public Schools.

Recent developments at Roosevelt include extending hours of library service to four evenings a week, recruiting and training of a large staff of student librarians, and the development of auxiliary resource materials centers.

The Knapp School Libraries Project has supplied funds to increase the materials collection, double the library staff, assist in equipping the resource centers, and provide air temperature control in the library. Four librarians, assisted by two resource center aides, two library assistants, two instructional clerks, and an artist-technician comprise the school library staff. Other qualified teachers are associated with the evening library program. This staff which fully meets the standards for a school of eighteen hundred is prepared to demonstrate its impact on the school's instructional program. Don W. James, Principal of Roosevelt High School, is the liaison person for the Project at Roosevelt.

THE FARRER JUNIOR HIGH SCHOOL

is one of three secondary schools in the Provo City School District. It is a relatively small school with an enrollment of approximately 800. Dr. Sherman W. Wing, Superintendent, is dedicated to continuing a policy which has provided all the schools in the district (nine elementary and three secondary schools) with centralized libraries and full-time librarians.

The Knapp School Libraries Project has provided funds to the Farrer Junior High school for the alteration of facilities, the salary of another full-time librarian, the salary of an instructional assistant, and the acquisition of additional professional and non-print materials. These additions to the library should pro-

vide more extensive services for students and teachers. Mrs. Jane N. Vance, the head librarian, has been a leader in school librarianship in the state of Utah. Under the direction of Mrs. Vance and G. Gardner Snow, Principal and liaison worker for the Project, a library program has been developed and expanded so that it is used extensively by Farrer teachers in all curriculum areas. A workshop for Farrer faculty members in the summer of 1965, under the sponsorship of the Knapp Project and with the cooperation of Brigham Young University, encouraged the further effective utilization of instructional materials by teachers in the school.

The Brigham Young University has selected Dr. W. Dwayne Belt, Associate Professor of Secondary Education and former principal of the University's Laboratory School, as the field worker. The Provo City School District and the Brigham Young University, one of the largest teacher education institutions in the United States, have cooperated in many projects. The Provo schools have also served as training centers for many of the University's student teachers. The pattern of cooperation will enhance the contributions of the Knapp School Libraries Project.

THE OAK PARK AND RIVER FOREST HIGH SCHOOL

a 9 through 12 grade high school with an enrollment of more than 3,000 students, has maintained a special interest in the development of its school library program and collection. A staff including professional librarians with skills in administration of all varieties of instructional materials, a bibliographer, and clerical assistants, is headed by Miss Lura Crawford who has participated actively in local, state and national professional library associations. This school library has reached out into other areas of the school by providing departmental resource centers, and plans to continue this development with support from the Knapp School Libraries Project. Dr. Gene L. Schwilck is the Superintendent and Principal.

University of Illinois, as the co-applicant, has appointed Dr. Jerry Walker, Assistant Professor of Education and Supervisor of Student Teachers, as field worker for the Project.

Selection of teams to receive Project funds for travel will be made by the Project office. Arrangements for visits by other teams or individuals may be made by requesting appointments at least four weeks in advance and by communicating with the person in each Project school who has the responsibility for such arrangements. These are:

For Roosevelt High School
Don W. James, *Principal*
Roosevelt High School
6941 North Central Street
Portland, Oregon

For Farrer Junior High School
Dr. W. Dwayne Belt, *Associate Professor of Secondary Education*
Brigham Young University
Provo, Utah

For Oak Park and River Forest High School
Dr. Gene Schwilck, *Superintendent-Principal*
Oak Park and River Forest High School
East Avenue and Ontario Street
Oak Park, Illinois

Phase III visits brochure (continued).

BUDGET REQUEST FOR THIS VISIT:

_____ Persons at $15.00 per day per person $_____

Round trip transportation at 10c per mile for the team $_____
(Customary maximum of $100.00 per team)

                                        TOTAL BUDGET REQUEST $_____

                          *   *   *   *   *   *   *

The leader and members of this team will be:

NAME	TITLE OR POSITION	REPRESENTING (school, school district, college, organization, etc.)
1.		
2.		
3.		
4.		
5.		
6.		

Our purpose in applying for funds for this visit is_____

_____

The present status of the school library program in our area is_____

_____

_____

Our reason for selecting the_____to visit is
                                    Name of Phase III Project School

_____

_____

_____

_____
Signature of team leader

_____
Address   City   State

All information requested on both sides of this sheet should be provided. Applications must be postmarked
no later than January 7, 1966, and mailed to:

                          MISS PEGGY SULLIVAN, *Director*
                          Knapp School Libraries Project
                          American Library Association
                          50 East Huron Street
                          Chicago, Illinois   60611

Phase III visits brochure (continued).

APPLICATION FOR FUNDS TO VISIT A
KNAPP SCHOOL LIBRARIES PROJECT DEMONSTRATION CENTER

We have read the brochure about the Knapp School Libraries Project Phase III demonstration centers. We are requesting Project funds for a visit to:

■ ROOSEVELT HIGH SCHOOL, PORTLAND, OREGON

Our preferred dates for a visit are noted as 1, 2, 3, below:

Spring, 1966

_____Monday, March 7	_____Monday, April 4	_____Tuesday, May 3
_____Wednesday, March 9	_____Friday, April 8	_____Wednesday, May 11
_____Monday, March 21	_____Monday, April 11	_____Friday, May 13
_____Wednesday, March 23	_____Tuesday, April 12	

1966-1967 School Year

_____Tuesday, October 4	_____Monday, November 21	_____Friday, March 3
_____Monday, October 10	_____Wednesday, November 30	_____Tuesday, March 7
_____Wednesday, October 19	_____Tuesday, December 6	_____Wednesday, March 29
_____Friday, October 21	_____Monday, January 9	_____Monday, April 3
_____Tuesday, October 25	_____Wednesday, February 1	_____Wednesday, April 5
_____Tuesday, November 1	_____Friday, February 10	_____Tuesday, April 11
_____Friday, November 4	_____Tuesday, February 14	

■ FARRER JUNIOR HIGH SCHOOL, PROVO, UTAH

Our preferred dates for a visit are noted as 1, 2, 3, below:

Spring, 1966

_____Wednesday, March 2	_____Tuesday, April 12	_____Thursday, May 12
_____Thursday, March 17	_____Wednesday, April 27	
_____Monday, March 21	_____Tuesday, May 3	

1966-1967 School Year

_____Monday, September 26	_____Wednesday, December 14	_____Thursday, March 30
_____Wednesday, October 12	_____Wednesday, January 18	_____Friday, April 14
_____Friday, October 28	_____Thursday, February 9	_____Tuesday, April 18
_____Tuesday, November 8	_____Friday, February 24	_____Monday, May 8
_____Friday, December 2	_____Wednesday, March 15	

■ OAK PARK AND RIVER FOREST HIGH SCHOOL, OAK PARK, ILLINOIS

Our preferred dates for a visit are noted as 1, 2, 3, below:

Spring, 1966

_____Thursday, March 3	_____Thursday, April 7	_____Thursday, May 5
_____Tuesday, March 8	_____Thursday, April 14	_____Monday, May 9
_____Friday, March 18	_____Tuesday, April 19	_____Tuesday, May 24
_____Tuesday, March 22	_____Monday, April 25	_____Thursday, June 2

1966-1967 School Year

_____Thursday, October 6	_____Tuesday, December 13	_____Tuesday, March 21
_____Friday, October 14	_____Tuesday, January 10	_____Thursday, April 6
_____Thursday, October 20	_____Monday, January 16	_____Thursday, April 13
_____Thursday, October 27	_____Thursday, February 2	_____Tuesday, April 18
_____Tuesday, November 1	_____Friday, February 10	_____Monday, April 24
_____Thursday, November 10	_____Thursday, February 16	_____Tuesday, May 2
_____Thursday, November 17	_____Thursday, February 23	_____Thursday, May 11
_____Monday, November 21	_____Thursday, March 2	_____Tuesday, May 16
_____Thursday, December 1	_____Tuesday, March 7	_____Thursday, June 1
_____Thursday, December 8	_____Monday, March 13	

Phase III visits brochure (continued).

REPORT OF VISITING TEAM   (PLEASE SUBMIT 3 COPIES)

1. Please give names and titles:

LEADER OF TEAM AND COMPILER OF THIS REPORT _____

OTHER MEMBERS OF THE TEAM 1. _____

                           2. _____

                           3. _____

                           4. _____

                           5. _____

SCHOOL DISTRICT OR AGENCY WHICH THE ABOVE PERSONS REPRESENT:

_____

_____

City_____   State _____

NAME OF THE PROJECT SCHOOL VISITED _____

2. CHIEF REASON FOR SCHEDULING THIS VISIT WAS _____

_____

3. THIS VISIT SERVED OUR PURPOSES BY PROVIDING _____

_____

4. WE INTEND TO REPORT ON OUR VISIT TO OUR COMMUNITY AND/OR STAFF IN THE
    FOLLOWING WAY: _____

_____

5. THE GREATEST NEED IN OUR ELEMENTARY SCHOOL LIBRARY PROGRAM AT THIS TIME IS

_____

6. THE MOST HELPFUL PART OF THE VISIT IN WHICH WE PARTICIPATED WAS _____

_____

7. THE LEAST HELPFUL PART OF THE VISIT IN WHICH WE PARTICIPATED WAS _____

_____

8. FURTHER COMMENTS _____
    (please use other side if necessary)

9. PLEASE ENCLOSE WITH THIS REPORT ANY WRITTEN REPORTS, ARTICLES, PHOTOGRAPHS,
    OR CLIPPINGS CONCERNING THE VISIT WHICH YOU CAN PROVIDE.

10. RETURN TO: MISS PEGGY SULLIVAN, DIRECTOR
                                  KNAPP SCHOOL LIBRARIES PROJECT
                                  50 East Huron Street
                                  Chicago, Illinois 60611

Report of visiting team (Phase I).
This report and the materials on following pages were provided to leaders of visiting teams.

BUDGET FOR TEAM VISIT TO THE CENTRAL PARK ROAD ELEMENTARY SCHOOL
THE MARCUS WHITMAN ELEMENTARY SCHOOL

TEAM LEADER: _____

Name

_____

School district or other affiliation

_____

Address - City   State

Number of team members _____

Round-trip distance as reported in application for funds _____

Transportation is budgeted on the basis of automobile transportation,

at ten cents per mile.

Housing and personal expenses are budgeted at $15.00 per person per day.

This team will be eligible for reimbursement on the following basis:

Transportation

Housing and per diem _____

$

Dates for this visit will be _____

AS TEAM LEADER, I UNDERSTAND AND AGREE TO OBSERVE THE TERMS OF THIS
TRAVEL GRANT AND THE BUDGET INDICATED ABOVE.

_____

Signature

_____

Date

Budget for team visit (Phase I).
Modified for use in Phases II and III.

REPORT OF VISITING TEAM

(Please Submit 3 Copies to Project Office)

Date _____19_____

_____
Name of Team Leader   Position

_____
Address: Street   City   State   Zip Code

_____
School Visited   Date of Visit

I.   What was the main purpose of your team visit? Did you feel that this
     purpose was achieved?

II. From your observation experience what do you regard as helping you most
     to achieve your reason for coming?

III. (a) Which experiences would you have eliminated?

     (b) Which experiences would you have added or included?

IV. When we have other guests who hold positions similar to yours, what
     do you suggest we do to make the visits profitable? (Use other side)

V.   Please note how you intend to report on this visit to your staff and/or
     community.

VI. PLEASE ENCLOSE WITH THIS REPORT ANY WRITTEN REPORTS, ARTICLES,
     PHOTOGRAPHS, OR CLIPPINGS CONCERNING THE VISIT WHICH YOU CAN PROVIDE.

Report of visiting team (Phases II and III).

REPORT OF VISITING TEAM (ONE YEAR AFTER VISIT)

1. NAME OF PROJECT SCHOOL WHICH WE VISITED _____

2. DATE OF OUR VISIT _____

3. THIS VISIT HAS HAD THE FOLLOWING LONG-RANGE EFFECTS _____

    _____

    _____

    _____

4. THE GREATEST NEED IN OUR ELEMENTARY SCHOOL LIBRARY PROGRAM AT THIS TIME IS__

    _____

5. WE HAVE REPORTED ON THIS VISIT TO OUR COMMUNITY AND/OR STAFF IN THE FOLLOWING
    WAY: _____

    _____

    _____

6. PLEASE ENCLOSE WITH THIS REPORT ANY ADDITIONAL REPORT, ARTICLES, PHOTOGRAPHS,

OR CLIPPINGS RELATING TO THIS VISIT WHICH YOU CAN PROVIDE.

SUBMITTED BY _____
             Name of leader

             _____
             SCHOOL DISTRICT OR OTHER AGENCY REPRESENTED ON THE TEAM

PLEASE RETURN THIS REPORT TO: MISS PEGGY SULLIVAN, DIRECTOR
                                    KNAPP SCHOOL LIBRARIES PROJECT
                                    50 East Huron Street
                                    Chicago, Illinois 60611

Year-later report of visiting team (Phases I and II).
Modified for use in Phase III.

Sample Press Release

NEWS ABOUT THE (Name of School System, Teacher-Education Inst., etc.)

For Further Information   For Immediate Release

Contact: (Name of Team Leader)   Exclusive To: _____
(Phone Number)   _____

(Name of School System, etc.) GROUP VISITS (City of Project School) ON GRANT

(Name of Team Leader) will lead (No. of Team Members) representatives of the
(Name of Sch. System of other Institution identifying team's make-up) on a trip
to (Location of Project School) on (Date of Visit) to observe the program and
services of a model elementary school library in action. A grant to cover
travel expenses to one of the three such "demonstration centers" was awarded this
team by the Knapp School Libraries Project, a five-year project funded with
$1,130,000 by the Knapp Foundation, Inc., and administered by the American Associ-
ation of School Librarians, a division of the American Library Association and a
department of the National Education Association.

The (Name of City/Location that would Identify Team's Representation)
team's final selection came as a result of a nationwide, open competition conducted by the Knapp School Libraries Project and testifies to the promise of
(Name of Unit represented by team: e.g., "district's...", "university's...",
"association's...", etc.) continuing effort to establish and develop excellent
school library services for the (Name of School System, etc.). Selection of the
team to receive these funds from the Project was partly based on the team's
description of its aims as well as the acumen with which they had evaluated the
present status of their own library program.

(Name of Team Leader), official leader of the team visiting (Name of Project
School), explained the impact of this opportunity to view the "model" library's
effect on the school's instructional program: (Quote from statement of team
leader which would succinctly describe the effect of this visit on future plans).
Represented on the team going to (Name of Project School) were: (List all
visitors on team besides team leader).

Sample press release (Phase II).

<u>Sample Press Release</u>

NEWS ABOUT THE (<u>Name of School System, Teacher-Education Inst., etc.</u>)

For Further Information   For Immediate Release

Contact: (<u>Name of Team Leader</u>)   Exclusive To: _____
(<u>Phone Number</u>)
                                                             _____

    (<u>Name of Team Leader</u>) will lead (<u>No. of Team Members</u>) representatives of
the (<u>Name of School System or Other Institution identifying Team's Make-Up</u>) on
a trip to (<u>Location of Project School</u>) on (<u>Date of Visit</u>) to observe the program
and services of a model secondary school library in action. A grant to cover
travel expenses was awarded this team by the Knapp School Libraries Project, a
five-year Project funded with $1,130,000 by the Knapp Foundation, Inc., and
administered by the American Association of School Librarians, a division of
the American Library Association and a department of the National Education
Association.

    The selection of the (<u>Name of City/Location that would Identify Team's
Representation</u>) team testifies to the promise of the (<u>Name of Unit Represented
By Team: e.g., "district's...", "university's...", "association's...", etc.</u>)
continuing effort to establish and develop excellent school library services.
Selection of the team to receive these funds from the Project was partly
based on the team's description of its aims as well as the acumen with which
they had evaluated the present status of their own library program.

    (<u>Name of Team Leader</u>), official leader of the team visiting (<u>Name of
Project School</u>), explained the impact of this opportunity to view the "model"
library's effect on the school's instructional program: "(<u>Quote from state-</u>
<u>ment of team leader which would succinctly describe the effect of this visit
on future plans</u>)."

    Represented on the team going to the (<u>Name of Project School</u>) are:
(<u>List all visitors besides team leader, including their titles and positions.</u>)

Sample press release (Phase III).

INDEX

Due